Bedford County, Pennsylvania Quarter Sessions

1771–1801

Gerald H. Smith, CG^{SM}

HERITAGE BOOKS
2010

HERITAGE BOOKS
AN IMPRINT OF HERITAGE BOOKS, INC.

Books, CDs, and more—Worldwide

For our listing of thousands of titles see our website at
www.HeritageBooks.com

Published 2010 by
HERITAGE BOOKS, INC.
Publishing Division
100 Railroad Ave. #104
Westminster, Maryland 21157

Copyright © 2010 Gerald H. Smith

CG and Certified Genealogist are Service Marks of the Board for Certification of Genealogists used under license after periodic evaluation by the Board

All rights reserved. No part of this book may be reproduced or transmitted in any form or by any means, electronic or mechanical, including photocopying, recording or by any information storage and retrieval system without written permission from the author, except for the inclusion of brief quotations in a review.

International Standard Book Numbers
Paperbound: 978-0-7884-5253-6
Clothbound: 978-0-7884-8485-8

Contents

Acknowledgements i
Preface iii
Introduction 1
    Abstracting Practices 3
Docket 1: 1771–1789 7
Docket 2: 1771–1801 71
Terms & Definitions 287
Index 289

Acknowledgements

This book would not have been possible without the support of Jonathan Stayer, Head, Reference Section, Pennsylvania State Archives, and the archives staff. Thanks also go to Gillian Leach and Ray Jackson at the Bedford County, Pennsylvania, Historical Society.

The proofreading of Joan Shipley, Beverly Yackel, and Carol York, all of the Monmouth County, New Jersey, Genealogical Society, improved the quality of the work tremendously. Any errors that remain are mine.

Thanks also to my wife Cathy for her tolerance for the crates of paper, and to my sons Kenny and Alan for the proofreading they did on their holiday breaks.

These Quarter Sessions abstracts are an ongoing project and Docket 3 is underway. Comments and suggestions are welcome at the email address below.

>Gerald Smith, CG^{SM}
>Ocean Township, New Jersey
>QS@penngenealogy.com
>www.penngenealogy.com

Preface

Certain types of court records have significant genealogical and historical value, yet genealogists tend to overlook them. Abstracts and microfilms make some types of court records easy to access, yet Quarter Sessions records remain less available.

When I became aware of the existence of the Bedford County Quarter Session records, a quick look at them solved several "brick wall" genealogy problems. For example, the record of an illegitimate child (naming both parents) cleared up a number of issues in one lineage.

Individuals from all social strata appear in these records: elected county officials, appointed township officials, common citizens as jurors or witnesses, and, of course, the miscreants.

The dockets offer insight into history and the times. Oaths of office at the formation of the county reflect the political and religious climate in Britain, while the oaths used after the American independence have nothing to say about claimants to the British throne or religion. While most of this work abstracts court case information, certain items of historical interest, such as these oaths, are fully transcribed.

My hope is that these abstracts will be useful to others in researching their Bedford County ancestry.

Introduction

"An Act for Erecting a Part of the County of Cumberland into a Separate County" established Bedford County on March 9, 1771. A Court of Quarter Sessions of the Peace was among the courts that the Act commissioned for the new county.[1]

Courts of Quarter Sessions derive from British common law.[2] Pennsylvania's 1715 statute to establish a Court of Quarter Sessions of the Peace, gave these courts broad jurisdiction in a variety of areas:

> there shall be a court styled the general quarter-sessions of the peace and gaol delivery, holden and kept four times in every year... And each of them shall keep and cause to be kept the peace of our Lord the King, his heirs and successors, and all acts and statutes made and to be made for the conservation of peace, and for the quiet rule and government in the respective counties where they shall be commissioned. And according as those acts do or shall direct, to chastise and punish all persons offending against the common law or the form of those acts and statutes—(excepting in cases of treason, murder and other such crimes as are or shall by the laws of this province be made felonies of death), by fines, ransoms, amercements, forfeitures or otherwise. And to commit to prison, let to bail, and discharge offenders for offences or crimes cognizable before them... And generally to administer common justice...[3]

Quarter Sessions dockets contain administrative entries, such as oaths of office; governmental entries, such as petitions for roads; petty criminal offenses such as nuisance and keeping a tipling house (unlicensed sale of alcoholic beverages); more serious criminal offenses, such as assault & battery, riot, forcible entry, house burning, and horse stealing. Illegitimate children and illicit relationships are found with charges of fornication, bastardy, and bigamy.

In Bedford County Quarter Sessions Dockets 1 and 2 one finds sentences ranging from fines of a few pence to a 1787 sentence for horse

---

[1] Act of March 9, 1771 (1 Sm.L.330 Ch629).
[2] *Law and Genealogy: A Theme Issue of the National Genealogical Quarterly*, vol. 95, No. 3 (September 2007) provides an excellent background in law and the history of American courts.
[3] Act of 1715 (3 St.L.33 Ch202).

stealing that included a whipping of forty nine lashes to the bare back, having both ears cut off and nailed to the pillory, followed by imprisonment in the pillory for one hour (as well as a fine).

The dockets also tell us about participants in historical events. In Bedford County we find charges of riot and treason against individuals who erected Liberty Poles during the Whiskey Rebellion (Docket 2 page 199L). The immediately following 124 indictments name alleged participants in that event.

Because of the wide charter granted to the Court of Quarter Sessions, the names found in the dockets cut across all social strata. Names include those who were elected or appointed to public office, including township constables, overseers of the poor, and highway supervisors. The common citizen is found on juries, as witness for the prosecution or defense, as a victim, or perhaps as the owner of a property named in a road petition. And, of course, there are those charged with committing offenses. The dockets record all cases heard, including those where the Grand Jury did not find sufficient evidence to return an indictment.

Genealogically speaking, the dockets name husbands and wives, associate individuals with their township of residence, and clarify parentage in cases of illegitimate children. They also provide insight into an ancestor's role in society.

These abstracts were taken from the original dockets now in the collection of the Pennsylvania State Archives, Record Group 47, Records of the County Governments, Bedford County, Quarter Session Dockets, Series {#47.264}.

The dockets are not in their original bindings. The present bindings include some of the original covers. The original volumes did not break at the same points as the present bindings.[4] Thus, should a reference to a Quarter Sessions Docket number and page be found elsewhere, the researcher may need to use the session date to find the docket entry.

Breaks from strict chronological order occur when an item that takes a large amount of space was written a page or so ahead so that it would appear all on one page (often seen with election results and oaths of office). Shorter case entries then continue to be recorded up to that item leaving that item out of strict chronological order. In addition to this recording practice, it seems apparent that some of the more deteriorated

---

[4] There is some material noted in Docket 2 that is more indicative of a minute book, but this appears to be due to the inclusion of loose papers in the modern binding.

pages came loose from their earlier binding and are now bound at a place other than their original location. These abstracts preserve the order seen in the present bindings.

Examination of the ink and handwriting in the original dockets makes apparent a clerical behavior that these abstracts cannot: A case may return an indictment and be continued over several terms. During the course of these continuances the clerk updated earlier entries. Thus, the earliest entry for a case may include notations dealing with events at later continuances, or even the eventual sentence. The court's sentence was sometimes recorded with the first docket entry and other times recorded with the final docket entry; the practice was not consistent. As an example, in the case of The King v. Lorentz Counts, the Grand Jury returned indictment in April 1774. The clerk amended that earliest April 1774 entry to note that the defendant plead not guilty in July, and further annotated that entry to show that the defendant was discharged on proclamation and payment of costs the following October.

Some of the terms found frequently in the Bedford Quarter Sessions are found in the **Terms and Definitions** (page 287). This glossary is not exhaustive, so a legal dictionary, (particularly an older edition of *Black's Law Dictionary*) may be a useful resource.

Abstracting Practices

Abstracting any set of records presents problems unique to that material. While, overall, these abstracts follow standard guidelines[5], several practices are worth noting:

- Since the dockets are not in their original bindings and it is apparent that pages are bound out of order (with some loose case papers also bound in the dockets) one cannot assume that pages without dates are in their original order (or are in chronological order). Some of the docket pages have a date at the top; some do not. Where a date is present at the top of a docket page, these abstracts show that date immediately after the page number. Where material on the page includes a date, or permits the date to be deduced, these abstracts show that date after the page number in square brackets. Where no date appears after a page number, care needs to be taken when asserting a date for entries on that page. Do not assume that such a

---

[5] Elizabeth Shown Mills, editor, *Professional Genealogy: A Manual for Researchers, Writers, Editors, Lecturers, and Librarians* (Baltimore, Maryland: Genealogical Publishing Company, 2001), chapter 16.

page is part of the preceding or following session. The loose case papers may establish the date of such a docket entry. Out-of-order pages are prevalent in Docket 2. The chapters for each docket begin with a table showing the known dates for the pages in that docket.

- Names appear as spelled in the dockets. Since spelling was phonetic during this time period, one must use spelling variants when researching specific individuals. The index attempts to group well known phonetic equivalents for local family surnames, but no attempt at such a convenience can be exhaustive. Also remember that phonetic equivalents may use different first letters for the surname, such as with the Urie surname, found in these records as both Urie and Oury.

- The abstracts do not include metes and bounds descriptions for roads. The dockets record only a few names in the metes and bounds. A comment in square brackets indicates the presence of metes and bounds, and that comment will include any names found in the metes & bounds.

- Use of apostrophes is not consistent in the dockets and that usage carries over to the abstracts.

- Numbering is inconsistent in the dockets and those inconsistencies carry over to the abstracts. Numbers usually enumerate indictments within a session although there are a few occasions where recognizances are numbered (such as the long list of indictments after the Liberty Pole incident during the Whiskey Rebellion).

- When perusing original dockets the researcher will encounter the abbreviation jur˜, an abbreviation indicating that oath was sworn as a juror. This abbreviation should not be confused with abbreviations for junior, often seen in the original records as j^r. To keep confusion at minimum, these abstracts do not include the abbreviations for oath sworn. They do include notations for junior. Some jury members affirmed rather than taking an oath. These abstracts note affirmations as they may indicate the juror was of Quaker faith.

- Docket 2 contains a large number of signatures as those taking an oath of office signed the docket. This was the standard practice, so these abstracts do not note every signature.

April Sessions 1775
The Grand Jury

1. Charles Cessna foreman jr.
2. Robert Culbertson Jr.
3. Hofer Read Jr.
4. John Fisher jr.
5. Obadiah Sidwell jr.
6. Benjamin Swan jr.
7. John Wenrysel affir.
8. Samuel Paxton jr.
9. Daniel Hoy jr.
10. Allan Rose jr.
11. Joseph Johnston jr.
12. James Henry jr.
13. Edward Cabins jr.
14. Henry Warford jr.
15. Michael Whitmore jr.

Bedford County, Pennsylvania, Court of Quarter Sessions and the Peace, docket 1, page 82. Pennsylvania State Archives, Record Group 47 (County Records), Series {#47.264}.

Docket 1: 1771-1789

Docket 1 includes sessions held April 1771–July 1778 and April 1789. At some time in the past, pencil numbers were added to each page. This chapter cites the penciled page numbers.

Dockets 1 and 2 both begin with events at the formation of the county. Docket 1 begins with case entries and Docket 2 begins with oaths of office and oaths of allegiance. Thus, at the formation of the county two registers were kept concurrently.

Docket 1	
Pages 1–5	April 1771 session
Pages 6–9	Undated
Page 10	October 1771 session
Page 11	Undated
Pages 12–14	October 1771 session
Pages 15–24	January, April 1772 sessions
Page 25	July 1772 session
Pages 26–29	Undated
Page 30	October 1772 session
Pages 31–36	Undated
Pages 37–38	October 1772 session
Page 39	January 1773 session
Pages 40–43	Undated
Pages 44–47	April, May 1773 sessions
Pages 48–52	July, October 1773 sessions
Pages 53–56	January 1774 session
Pages 57–58	Undated (includes October 1773 election result)
Pages 59–72	April, July, October 1774 sessions
Pages 73–95	January, April, July, October 1775 sessions
Pages 96–104	January, April 1776 sessions
Page 105–107	September, October 1777 sessions
Pages 108–125	January, April, July 1778 sessions (also see p. 168)
Pages 126–129	Blank
Pages 130–131	April 1789 session
Pages 132–167	Blank
Page 168	April 1778 session

Page 1 April 1771
At a Court of Quarter Sessions of the Peace held at Bedford for the County of Bedford the sixteenth day of April 1771 before:

    William Proctor   Robert Cluggage
    Robert Hanna   George Wilson
    William Lochery   William McDonald, Esquires.

Grand Jury:
        James Anderson, foreman

Charles Cessna	Frederick Naugle
James McCashlin	Thomas Hay
Thomas Kenton	Samuel Drennin
Allen Rose	Edward Rose
George Millikin	Samuel Skinner
John Moore	William Parker
Robert Culbertson	Christopher Miller
George Funk	Thomas Croyal
John Huff	Adam Sam
Rinard Wolfe	Jacob Fisher
Valentine Shadacer	David Rinard

The Court proceeded to divide the said county into the following townships [each with boundary description; no individuals named]: Air, Bedford, Baree, Dublin, Colerain, Brothers Valley,

Page 2 April 1771
Fairfield, Mt. Pleasant, Hempfield, Pitt, Tyrone,

Page 3 April 1771
Spring Hill, Ross Straver, Armstrong, Tullileague.

On motion Bernard Dougherty, Esq., Robert Magaw, Esq., sworn as attorney of this court. On motion Mr. Magaw, Andrew Ross, Philip Pendleton, Robert Galbreath, David Sample, and James Wil[son], Esqs., also admitted as attorneys of this court.

Page 4 April 1771
John Kirts and Thomas Croyal, yeomen, acknowledge to owe the King: John Kirts £100 and Thomas Croyal £50 upon condition of appearance of John Kirts at next session to answer.

Ordered that all persons vending liquors apply for license at next session.

Tavern Keepers recommended to the Governor: Margaret Fraser, Jean Woods, Frederick Naugle, George Funk, John Campbell.

At Bedford 21 April 1771 before Arthur St. Clair, William Proctor Jr., and George Wood. Robert Moore discharged as Colerain Township Constable on account of his service as Commissioner for running the county line. John Moore appointed in his stead.

At Bedford 31 May 1771 before John Fraser, William Procter, and George Woods, Esqrs. John Evalt and Allen Rose appointed appraisers for Township of Bedf[ord]. [Bottom of page cut off.]

Page 5 [July 1771]
At Bedford 16 July 1771. Before:
>John Fraser
>Robert Hanna
>William Lochery
>William Proctor
>George Wilson
>Robert Cluggage
>William McConnel
>George Wood, Esqs.

Grand Jury:
>Thomas Coulter, foreman
>Thomas Kenton
>Adam Sam
>Samuel Drennin
>Richard Wells, senior
>Samuel Barrett
>Abraham Keble
>Henry Rhoads, junior
>George Milligan
>Michael Sells
>Edward Rose
>Gabriel Rhoads
>George Wells
>Thomas Croil
>George Sells
>Reynarde Wolfe
>John Hight

On motion of Mr. Wilson, David Grier, David Espy, and George Brent, Esqs., admitted as attorneys of this court.

The King v. John Mallon. Felony. True Bill. Arraigned. Pleads guilty. Judgment to restore value of goods stolen, pay fine £6, 22 lashes on his bare back tomorrow, and pay costs of prosecution.

The Grand Inquest present that the Gaol of this county is insufficient.

Page 6
The King v. Joseph Kelly. Felony. True Bill. Arraigned. Pleads not guilty. Jury of John Miller, John Spurgeon, Samuel Moore, John Dodrige, Joseph Morrison, Robert Bradshaw, John Fleharty, Peter Smith, Michael Huff, Jacob Rhoads, William Parker, John Peters find defendant not guilty.

The King v. Peter Resner & others. Forcible Entry & Detainer. True Bill. Abraham Ritchey pleads not guilty. Jury of John Miller, John

Spurgeon, Samuel Moore, John Dodrige, Joseph Morrison, Robert Bradshaw, John Fleharty, Peter Smith, Michael Huff, Jacob Rhoades, William Parker, John Peter find Abraham Ritchey not guilty.

The King v. Peter Resnor & others. Forcible Entry & Detainer. True Bill. Peter Resnor and John Beans plead not guilty. Peter Resnor, Nicholas Christ, Ezekiel Hickman in £300 for the appearance of Peter Resnor. John Beans, Nicholas Christ, Peter Resner in £50 each for the appearance of John Beans. John Shearer, William Shearer and Joseph Jones each in £40 for the appearance of William Shearer to prosecute.

William Ritchey and Jacob Tucker being three times called do not appear [bottom of page cut away].

Page 7
The King v. Henry Spears & others. Forcible Entry & Detainer. True Bill. John Hosler and Jacob Keller plead not guilty. John Hosler & John Huff in £50 on appearance of John Hosler. Jacob Keller, Peter Resner, and John Beans in £50 on appearance of Jacob Keller.

Henry Spear, Henry Spear the younger, George McCoullough, Adam Young, John Williams, Isaac Williams, Basil Stoker, Henry Presser, George Corn, Solomon Corn, Ebenezer Corn, Francis Keller, Patrick McGaghon, Aaron Delong, Aaron Delong the younger, Zachariah Delong, Solomon Delong, and Francis Delong being three times called do not appear. Process awarded.

The King v. Daniel Smithson. Assault & Battery. True Bill. Defendant pleads not guilty. Daniel Smithson and William McConnell, Esq., in £50 for appearance of Daniel Smithson.

The King v. John Houser & Elisabeth Houser. Trespass. True Bill. Defendants plead not guilty. John Houser, Elisabeth Houser, Henry Rhoades the elder, and Wendal Urie in £300 for appearance of John Houser and Elisabeth Houser and they to keep the peace to Daniel Smithson and his wife in particular.

The King v. William Linn. Riot. True Bill.
William Linn, Mary Linn, Benjamin Linn, Basil Stoker, Henry Presser, Catherine Presser, George Corn, Solomon Corn, Zachariah Delong, Aaron Delong, Solomon Delong, Francis Keller, John Ash and Thomas Elvey being three times called do not appear. Process awarded.

Page 8
The King v. John Williams & others. Assault & Battery. True Bill.
John Williams, Francis Keller, Solomon Corn, Catherine Presser, Henry

Presser, George McCoullogh, Isaac Williams, Patrick McGaghon, and Basil Stoker being three times called do not appear. Process awarded.

The King v. Benjamin Linn. Assault & Battery. True Bill. The defendant being three times called does not appear. Process awarded.

The King v. John Reddock. Forcible Detainer. Ignoramus.

The King v. Samuel Skinner. Felony. Ignoramus

The King v. Mary Myers. Assault & Battery. Ignoramus.

The King v. Thomas Shores. Felony. Ignoramus.

The King v. Samuel Clem. Samuel Clem and Joseph Ross being three times called do not appear. Process awarded. Oliver Miller in £40 to appear and prosecute.

Lydia Davis and John Kirts discharged from recognizances. Michael Springer, Aaron Delong the elder, Zachariah Delong, Aaron Delong the younger, Peter Hilderbrand, William Linn, Mary Linn and Henry Spears being three times called do not appear. Process awarded.

Christian Bealer appointed Constable of Township of Ross Straver in the room of William Linn. Lawrence Irwin appointed Constable for Township of Pitt in the room of William Troop. John Moore who was appointed Constable of Colerain is continued for ensuing year.

Page 9
At request of William Lochrey, Esq., Solomon Sheppard, David Kilgore, Abraham Leaser, James Fletcher, Joseph Eaker, and Jeremiah Lochrey appointed to straighten main road through Mt. Pleasant Township.

On petition of Robert Hanna, Esq., James Pollack, and others setting forth need for road through Fairfield Township. Road to begin at plantation of John Hinkson at Squirrel Hill on Conemagh thence to Arthur St. Clair's mill, thence to Ligoner. Ordered John Hinkson, John Ward, Thomas Jameson, James Pollack, Garret Pendergrast junior and Samuel Shannon view the same and make return at next court.

Petition of James Anderson, Arthur St. Clair, Esq., and others setting forth that James Anderson opened a road separating from the Great Road leading from the town of Bedford to Fort Pitt at a small distance to the westward of Smiths Run then extending by aforesaid James Andersons and joining the Great Road about one mile to the westward of the Shawnee Cabin Creek asking this be made a public road. Ordered

Thomas Kenton, James Dunlap, George Wisecarver, William Riddel, Allen Rose, and James Dalto[n] to view and make return.

Petition of Edward Combes, Moses Read & others desiring road from Bedford to Moses Reads mill on Great Tonnalloway. Ordered Obadiah Stillwell, James Graham, Andrew Man, Christopher Miller, Michael Huff senior and Joseph Friend to view and make return.

Tavern Keepers recommended to the Court: James Anderson, Joseph Irwin, Andrew Bonjour, John Miller, Thomas Campbell, Samuel Paxton.

Page 10 [October 1771]
At Bedford. October 1771. Before:
    John Fraser
    Thomas Gist   Robert Hanna
    William Lochery   George Wilson
    William McConnel   William Proctor
    Robert Claggage   George Woods, Justices

Grand Jury: James Snider, foreman
    Thomas Kenton   Frederic Reighard
    Adam Iaam   Henry ____
    Henry Rhoads   George Keller
    Oliver Miller   George Milligan
    George Sills   Joseph Friend
    Michael Sills   John[Walker
    Rheynhart Wolf   Nathan [Young?]

The King v. Peter Reasnor. Forcible Entry and Detainer from July session 1771. Defendant pleads not guilty. Jury of Samuel Drenning, William McComb, Hugh Ferguson, George Wells, Allen Rose, Thomas Hay, James Daily, Moses Read, John Fisher, John Mallot, Jacob Money, Bernard Money finds defendant guilty of forcible entry [rest cannot be read].

The King v. Richard Wells. Riot & Assault. True Bill. Defendant pleads guilty. Fine of one shilling and pay costs [page cut off. Remainder may be "and give surety for peace & good behavior."]

Page 11
Richard Wells, Richard Brown each £40 on condition that Richard Wells keep the peace and good behavior.

The King v. James Wells et al. Joseph Wilson arraigned. Pleads guilty. Judgment that he pay fine of one shilling and costs and give surety for peace and good behavior. Joseph Wilson and Richard Brown each £40 conditioned that Joseph Wilson be of the peace and good behavior until next term.

John Casebold, William Fredrigal, and Christopher Miller each bound on £100 conditioned that John Casebold be of the peace particularly to John Cessna for the term of six months and also that the said John Cessna be of good behavior.

John Sinclair bound in £40 to appear at the next session to prosecute indictment against James Wells and others.

The King v. Daniel Smithson. True Bill found last session. Daniel Smithson, William McConnell, Esq. discharged from recognizance.

The King v. John Baltzer Myer and Mary his wife. Trespass. Having been three times called, do not appear. Process awarded.

Oliver Miller discharged from recognizances to prosecute indictment against Samuel Clem and Joseph Ross.

The King v. Samuel Shannon. Forcible Entry. True Bill. Process awarded.

The King v. James Borden. Felony. Ignoramus.

The King v. James Johnson. Felony. Ignoramus

Page 12   October 1771

Peter Riasnor three times called does not appear. Recognizance forfeit.

Nicholas Christ and Ezekiel Hickman three times called. Nicholas Christ does not appear. Recognizance forfeit.

John Beans three times called does not appear. Recognizance forfeit.

Nicholas Christ and Peter Reasnor three times called. John Beans is not brought. Recognizance forfeit.

John Hosler three times called does not appear. Recognizance forfeit.

John Huff three times called does not produce John Hosler. Recognizance forfeit. Process awarded.

Order for a road to Moses Read's mill on the Great Tonolloway Creek to continue in force until next term. John Mallot and Henry Rush appointed to view in the room of Obadiah Stillwell and John Graham.

Petition of [E?]mpson Brownfield, Philip Rogers and others for road from shallow ford on Monongehila at the mouth of Cheat River to the trading path above Conrad Wallers at the foot of the Laurel Hill to continue over the [Forks?] of the Roads. Ordered Frederic Myers, James McKay, Joseph Caldwell, Andrew Da__, Michael Cairns, and James Hughy to view the same.

In pursuance of order from July Term last to lay a road separating from the Great Road from the Town of Bedford to Fort Pitt. Thomas Kenton, James Dunlap, George Wisecarver, William Riddel, Allen Rose, and James Dalton to make return.

Page 13 October 1771
[Metes & bounds for road. Mentions post standing by James Andersons barn.] Order issued to open and clear.

In pursuance of order from July Term last to lay road from plantation of John Hinkson on Squirrel Hill on Connymach in Fairfield Township to Ligoner. John Hinkson, John Woods, Thomas Jameson, James Pollock, Garret Pendergrast make return [gives metes & bounds; mentions corner of John Hinksons fence, John Simon, James Pollock, house of John Campbel in Ligoner formerly the property of Tom G___]. Ordered opened as it is laid out.

On petition of Moses Read, William Hunt and other inhabitants of Air Township for road to begin at house of John Burd at Licking Creek [faded] to Jacob Trueaxe thence to John Conners thence to Ridge of the Connothaway.

Page 14 [consistent with October 1771; mostly cut away]
[metes and bounds for road mention George P____ and Joseph Warford.]

Ordered that James Smith, Charles Sykes, Thomas Pa__on, John Reynolds, Richard Morton, and Martin Longstrath view the same and make return. Return quashed for informality 07 January 1772.

Benjamin Burd, Samuel Sample, Robert Culbertson recommended to keep public houses.

Indenture made 01 October 1771 between Daniel Hoge, Esq., Sheriff of Bedford County of one part and William Crawford, James Anderson, Oliver Miller, John Moore, Assistant Judges, and John Pomroy, Richard Wells, William Powell, Samuel McKee, Martin Longstrath, Ezekiel Hickman, James Culbertson, James Little, Robert Bell, Thomas Kenton, William Parker, Archibald Lochrey, and George McDowell, inspectors, freeholders of said county, the following elected Commissioners: Robert Hanna, Dorset Pentecost, and John Stephenson. Elected Assessors: James Pollock, Samuel Miller, Solomon Sheppard, Joseph Bealor, James Cav__, Richard Wells junior.

Ordered that John Mallen, indentured servant to Joseph Kelly, now in the custody of the Gaoler serve six years to satisfy Joseph Kelly for the time he absented himself from his master's service.

Page 15 [January 1772]
At Bedford 14 January 1772 before:
John Fraser George Wilson
William Crawford William McConnel
Dorsey Pentecost Robert Cluggage
Robert Hanna William Proctor Jr.
William Lochry George Wood, Esqrs.

Grand Jury: James Piper, foreman.
John Moore Samuel Wells
Richard Wells Jr. Robert Culbertson
Joshua Meek David Gibson
James Myers Richard Brown
William Sherrar John Nichols
Adam Hatfield James Culbertson
William Robertson James Carnachan

The King v. Abraham Teagarden. Riot, Assault & Battery. True Bill. Process awarded.

The King v. Henry Spear. Forcible Entry found July session 1771. Defendant pleads non. cul. Jury of Thomas Coulter, John Stevenson, Joseph Ervin, James Pollock, Solomon Sheppard, James Cavel, James Kincaid, Garret Pendergrast jr, James Fletcher, Ezekiel Heckman, Thomas Campbell and Thomas Jones find defendant guilty of forcible entry. Fined £5 and costs; to stand committed until complied with. Testified for prosecution: Ignatius Jones, John Fulton, John Jones. Testified for defense: Ezekiel Hickman, Joseph Jones, Benj^m Patton.

Page 16 January 1772
The King v. William Linn. Riot. Found July session 1771. Defendant pleads guilty. Fined six pence and costs.

The King v. James Wells et al. Riot and Assault found October session. Benjamin Collins, James Wells, Thomas Ogle, Philip Bell being arraigned plead guilty. Fine one shilling each and costs.

The King v. Henry Spear & others. Forcible Entry found July session. Aaron Delong retracts plea of non. Cul. and pleads guilty. Fine one shilling and costs.

The King v. John Hosler. Forcible Entry found July session 1771. Defendant retracts plea of non. Cul. and pleads guilty. Fine six pence and costs.

Evidences bound on recognizance to prosecute James Price are discharged, the prisoner having made his escape out of gaol.

Jacob van Matire appointed Constable of Ross Straver Township in the room of Christian Bealer who is discharged.

Page 17 January 1772
Benjamin Wells appointed Constable of Tyrone Township in room of Samuel Lyon who is discharged.

Robert Morton and John Burd £40 each conditioned that Robert Morton testify against William Howard.

Clerk give notice by advertising in the most public place that those recommended for licenses to keep public houses take out licenses before next court otherwise they will be prosecuted as having Tipling Houses.

Henry Dedior and Giles Charier two run-away servants to serve two years each to satisfy Gaol fees and loss of time. £7.19.3 cash.

Matthew Haley indentured servant to Richard Brown to serve eighteen months to satisfy his said master for Gaol fees and loss of time.

Petition of Nathan Hammond, Thomas Cook, Adam Wickerham and others for road from mouth of Pigeon Creek to James Estingus's ferry on the Monongehela from thence to new cut road that leads from Tho[s] Gisly to Paul Fromans somewhere near Dorsey Penetecosts, Esq. Ordered that John Decker, Evan Williams, Daniel McGugan, William Price, Henry Hogland, and Morris Brady view and make return next session.

Petition of Dorsey Pentecost, Esq., Prior Theobold, and others for road from nine Mile run beyond Ligoner where the Fort Pitt road crosses it to the mouth of Jacobs Creek over Youghiogeny to said Pentecosts and thence to James Estungus's Ferry. Ordered that John Nichols jr, John Carnachan, Christopher Bealor, Thomas Reardon, Nathaniel Husk, and Archibald Lochry view and make return next session.

Page 18 January 1772
Petition of Fredrick Nagle, Adam Iaam and others, inhabitants of townships of Bedford and Colerain, for road from Bedford through the narrows to the mills in Colerain where the creeks will be avoided which are often impassible. Ordered Bernard Dougherty, Esq., Christian Miller, John Cessna, Robert Moore, William Rose, and Abraham Miley to view and make return next session.

Petition of Samuel Anderson and others, inhabitants of township of Barré, for road from the Standing Stone or Harts Log by the Banquets Spring up Woodcock Valley to the crossings of Yellow Creek from thence adjoin the Great Road near Bloody Run. Ordered that James Little, William Shirley, Robert Friggs, Hugh Guthrey, and Richard Long view the same and make return.

Petition of George Brent and others for road from Bedford to the little Tonolloways near John Powels. Ordered William Spurgeon, James Spurgeon, John Perrin, John Friend jr, Joseph Friend, and John Johnson view and make return at next session.

Petition of Edward Thompson, James Carnachan, and others, inhabitants of Hemp Field township, for public road now ____ ____ township. Ordered Solomon Sheppard, David Kilgore, Abraham Leazer, James Fletcher, Joseph Eacre, and

Page 19 January 1772
Samuel Miller view the road prayed for beginning where the new Road through Mt. Pleasant Township ends and running to Joseph Ervins, Esq., thence to the long bridge on the Fort Pitt road, and make return to next court.

Petition of William McConnel and others for road from township of Air to begin at Point Lookout thence to the fork of S__wells Ridge thence to continue on each side of the ridge to John Fishers and George Pecks thence to meet at Joshua Warfords thence to the Provincial Line. Ordered Edward Combs, Moses Read, John Combs, [blank for given name] Linn, William Hart, and Benjamin Truax to view and make return to next court.

Petition of Bernard Dougherty, Esq., and other inhabitants of Cumberland Township for road to begin where the Maryland Road is crossed thence by line of this Province continued the best way to the town of Bedford. Ordered that Samuel Drenning, Allen Rose, Edward Rose, Thomas Coulter, Thomas Davis, and Samuel Barrel view and make return.

Page 20 January 1772
Tavern Keepers Recommended: John Peters, Frederic Helm, John Nicholas, Michael Huff.

At Bedford 25 March 1772. Private sessions before John Fraser, Arthur St. Clair, George Wood, Esqs.

Michael Feather and John Miller appointed Overseers of the Poor for Township of Bedford for ensuing year.

Thomas Davis and Joseph Kelly appointed Overseers of the Poor for Cumberland Township.

Page 21 [April 1772]
At Bedford 14 April 1772 before William Proctor, William McConnel, George Wood, Abraham Keble.

Grand Jury sworn: John Cunningham, foreman
- Charles Quainy
- James Cunningham
- John McKinly
- Evan Jenkins
- Andrew Man
- James Gibson
- Thomas Simpson
- Thomas Paxton
- Jacob Alexander [affirmed]
- Francis Patterson
- James Smith
- John McKinney
- John McLellan
- Moses Read

The King v. Abraham Teagarden, William Teagarden, John Death, Andrew Gudgel, Michael Cox, Jacob Colemane, George Meyers, John Hupp, Henry Thomas. Riot, Assault & Battery.
Jacob Coleman pleads guilty. Judgment £1.5.0 and costs.

The King v. Ignatius Jones. Assault & Battery.
Defendant pleads guilty. Fined one shilling and costs.

Page 22 April 1772
The King v. James Wells et al. Riot. Assault & Battery on John Sinker.
Robert Eastep pleads guilty. Fined one shilling and costs.

The King v. John Baltzer Myer. Trespass. Defendant arraigned, pleads non. Cul. Jury of John Cessna, Allen Rose, Edward Rose, James Dunlap, Jacob Money, John Mallot, John Yerryhouse, Jacob Rush, Peter Smith, Reinhart Walkinghoff, John Mortimore, and Joseph Morrison find defendant guilty. Daniel Smithson testified for the prosecution.
Judgment is fine of forty shillings and costs.

The King v. George Lighterberger. Tipling House.
Defendant arraigned pleads non. Cul. Jury of John Cessna, Allen Rose, Edward Rose, James Dunlap, Jacob Money, John Mallot, John Yerryhouse, Jacob Rush, Peter Smith, Reinhart Walkinghoff, John Mortimore, and Joseph Morrison find defendant not guilty.

The King v. William Howard. Felony.
Defendant arraigned and pleads non. Cul. William Howard in £200. John Mortimer and Joseph Morrison each in £100 for appearance of William Howard at next session.

The King v. Joseph Jones. Assault & Battery.
Defendant arraigned pleads guilty. Fine one shilling and costs.

Page 23 April 1772
Robert Scott and Robert Morton in £40 each for their appearance next session to testify against William Howard.

The King v. John Burk. Assault & Battery.
Defendant arraigned pleads non. Cul. Jury of John Cessna, Allen Rose, Edward Rose, James Dunlap, Jacob Money, John Mallot, John Yerryhouse, Jacob Rush, Peter Smith, Reinhart Walkinghoff, John Mortimore, and Joseph Morrison find defendant guilty. Fine six pence and costs.

The King v. James Benford. Tipling House.
Defendant arraigned pleads guilty. Fine £5 and costs.

The King v. Thomas Campbell. Tipling House. Ignoramus.

Stephen Robenot appointed Constable for Cumberland.
Thomas Watson appointed Constable for Barree Township.

Samuel Anderson & George Jackson appointed Overseers of the Poor of Barree Township.

John Wilson & James Little appointed Supervisors of Barree Township.
Thomas Bays appointed Constable for Mt. Pleasant Township.
Henry Creighton appointed Constable of Bedford Town.
Thomas Kenton appointed Constable of Bedford Township.

Robert Culbertson and William McCombe appointed Overseers of the Poor.

William Teagarden Constable of Pitt fined 20/ and William Pawel appointed in his place.

John Friend junior appointed Constable of Colerain Township.
John McLellan appointed Constable of Air Township.

Page 24   April 1772
Andrew Hendricks appointed Constable of Brothers Valley.
Andrew Bonjoir appointed Constable of Fairfield.

Henry Slaughter & James How appointed Overseers of the Poor of Fairfield.

Daniel Lavoyer appointed Supervisor of Public Roads for Fairfield.
Joseph Jones appointed Constable of Ross Straver.
The delinquent Constables fined 20/ each.

At Bedford on 14 April 1772 in Private Session before William Proctor, William McConnel, George Wood, and Abraham Keble, Esqs., Justices.

John Burk, indentured servant belonging to Thomas Wood, to serve his master three months for runaway time and pay Gaol fees and costs over and above the time mentioned in his Indentures.

Page 25   [July 1772]
At Bedford on 14 July 1772 before John Fraser, Esq., and his associate Justices.

Grand Inquest: James Pollock, foreman
    John Nicholas   Samuel Moore
    William Parker   Samuel Drenning
    Samuel Davis   Adam Sam
    Wendal Oury   Joseph Morrison
    Abraham Miley   Absolom Little
    Robert Bradshaw   Michael Cryder
    John Huff   Christopher Miller
    Joseph Kelly   Charles Cissnay
    Giddion Ritchy

The King v. Peter Titus. Fornication. True Bill. Process awarded.

The King v. Elizabeth May Hall. Felony. Ignoramus.

The King v. Janet Karr. Fornication. True Bill.
Defendant arraigned and pleads guilty. Fine £10 and costs or 21 lashes on her bare back well laid on.

Page 26
Janet Karr in £20 and James Karr in £10 for appearance of Jennet Karr at next session to give evidence.

The King v. Margary Pain. Felony.
Arraigned, pleads not guilty. Jury of Isaac Mason, Ezekiel Hickman, Robert Culbertson, Garret Pendergrass jr, James Lyttle, William Shirly, Hance Ireland, William Deen, Renard Wolf, Henry Rhoades jr, Zebuland Moore, and Robert Smily find defendant guilty. Defendant to be taken to the public whipping post at nine tomorrow and receive 15 lashes on her bare back, make restitution of goods stolen and pay a fine equal to value of the goods stolen.

The King v. Patrick McCaughen. Forcible Entry.
Defendant arraigned pleads guilty. Fine six pence and costs.

The King v. John Marshall and Ann Coffman. Burglary. True Bill.

The King v. Peter Hantz. Tipling House. True Bill.

The King v. William Howard. Felony.
Defendant arraigned and pleads non. Cul. Jury of Isaac Mason, Ezekiel Hickman, Robert Culbertson, Garret Pendergrass jr, James Lyttle, William Shirly, Hance Ireland, William Deen, Renard Wolf, Henry Rhoads junior, Zebuland Moore, and Robert Smily find defendant not guilty.

Page 27
The King v. Margaret Hays. Assault & Battery.
Defendant arraigned and pleads guilty. Fine one shilling and costs.

The King v. William Covel. Tipling House.
Defendant arraigned and pleads guilty. Fine £5 and costs.

The King v. William Wright. Robbery. True Bill.

The King v. John Fisher and wife. Assault & Battery. True Bill.
[this entry is repeated twice in the docket.]

Alexander Peobles in £100, John Burg in £50, John Proctor in £50 for appearance of Alexander Peobles at next Court of Oyer & Terminer and Gaol Delivery.

Thomas Kinton to continue as Supervisor of Bedford Township.

The King v. Thomas Campble. Misdemeanor. True Bill.
Thomas Campble in £100 and William McKenzie in £50 for appearance of Thomas Campble at next session.

The King v. James McCausland. Assault & Battery. Ignoramus.

On motion of Mr. Wilson, Margaret Kreamer is discharged from servitude of Thomas Hays.

Page 28
On motion of Robert Magaw, Esq., Andrew Scott admitted as attorney of this court.

Constables
Air: John McLellan
Cumberland: Jonathan Bishop
Dublin: James Foley
Brothers Valley: John Hendricks
Mt. Pleasant: Thomas Bays
Pitt: William Powell
Spring Hill: John Masterson
Armstrong: Samuel Craig
Bedford Town: Henry Creighton
Bedford: Thomas Kinton
Barree: Thomas Weston
Colerain: John Friend
Fairfield: Thomas Cheany
Hempfield: Robert Vance
Tyrone: [no name]
Ross Straver: Peter Hance
Tullilague: [no name]

Petition of inhabitants of Bedford County setting forth that a bridle road leads from the foot of Sidling Hill to William McConnel, Esq., and thence to the top of Tuscarora Mountain has been much frequented. Petitioners apprehend that a public road would be of greater utility and request same. Ordered that Benjamin Jolly, James Smith, William Latta, Thomas Paxton, Nathaniel Davis, and James Martin lay out the same and report next session.

Page 29
Petition of Brothers Valley residents for road from town of Bedford to Youghiogeny River beginning at the town of Bedford then to the Glades of Yough and Stoney Creek and by Sewekely to the River. Ordered John Nickles, Hance Ireland, James Wells jr, Thomas Kiton, John Forgisson, and Richard Brown to view and make report.

Petition of inhabitants of Barree and Colerain Townships for road from the standing stone or Harts Log by Bouquests Spring and up Wood Cock Valley to the crossing of Yellow Creek and thence to join the Great Road near Bloody Run. Ordered Richard Long, Hugh Guthrey, Samuel Thompson, James Little, Samuel Anderson, and Walter Clark to view and make report next session.

John Campble recommended to the Governor for license.

Page 30 [October 1772]
At Bedford on 13 October 1772 before John Fraser, Esq., and associate Justices.

Grand Inquest: John Burd, foreman
 Richard Wells Joseph Bealor
 James Montgomery George E[i]re
 Thomas Hays John Cessnaa
 James Fletcher William Christy
 Jacob B___man John Kelly
 Robert Bradshaw John Mortimore
 James McKinze William Sparks

The King v. Peter Titus. Fornication. Defendant Arraigned. Pleads guilty. Fine £10. Pay Jannet Karr 20 shillings for lying in. Give security to the township for maintenance of the child after 29 May.

Page 31
The King v. Eneas McKay. Assault & Battery. True Bill. Defendant arraigned. Pleads Guilty. Fine 2/6 and costs. Ann Read testified.

The King v. Benjamin Tate. Assault & Battery. True Bill. Defendant arraigned. Pleads guilty. Fine 2/6 and costs. Ann Read testified.

The King v. Thomas Campble. Misdemeanor.
Jury of Charles Cessnaa, George Breton, Robert Moore, Hugh Forgeson, John Creighton, John Ramsey, James Smith, Richard Wells, Stophel Hos, John Miller, William Parker, and John Moore find defendant not guilty.

The King v. James Benford. Tipling House. Ignoramus.

Petition from inhabitants of Bedford for road from Town of Bedford to Abraham Mileys mill thence to Neals gap thence to Little Tonoloway near to Mr. Powels at the Province line.

Page 32
Appoint John Johnson, William Spurgeon, Joseph Bennett, John Spurgeon, Jacob Meeks, and Abraham Miley to view and make report next session.

Petition of inhabitants of townships of Tyrone and Springhill for road beginning near the camping place of Col. Dunbars on the road leading from the Colony of Virginia to Fort Pitt to the mouth of Big Redstone Creek. Appoint Philip Shute, Moses McClay, William Calwell, Andrew Linn, Jesse Martin, and Alexander McClean to view and make report next session.

In pursuance of order to view and layout road from township of Bedford to the Youghiogeney River John Nickles, James Wells jr, Thomas Kenton, John Ferguson, and Richard Brown have viewed and laid out the road with Hance Ireland and make report.

Pages 33, 34, 35 [metes and bounds for road; no individuals named.]

Page 36
Court order the road cut, cleared, and bridges of breadth of 33 feet.

Petition of inhabitants of Great Cove in Air Township who have for some years been reinstated in possession of their once abandoned habitations and now with something considerable to vend have no way of disposing of this overplus to advantage but by taking it to some sea port Town on the eastern side of our Continent which lays us under the necessity of crossing the North Mountain and as Daniel Reyers has almost completed a mill at the place formerly McMeans in said Cove which will be of considerable advantage we ask for a road from Reyers mill to the foot of Stoney Batter where the road from Sideling Hill to

Page 37 [October 1772]
Baltimore crosses it. Appoint Thomas Paxton, Thomas Stevens, Benjamin Stevens, William Harred, James McKinley, and Benjamin McClellan to view and report next session.

John Burd continued Supervisor for the ensuing year.

This Indenture made 01 October 1772 between John Proctor High Sheriff of Bedford of the one part and Robert Hanna, Abraham Kebble, William McConnell, Esq., and John Moore assistant Judges, and Henry Rhoads, Robert Bell, Samuel Thompson, David Vance, John Friehart, John Sampson, Allen Rose, William McGeary, Thomas Jones, William McCall, and William Gutrey Inspectors Freeholders of the said county of the other part. Witnesseth that James Piper of Colerain Township was elected Commissioner for the County of Bedford.

This Indenture made 01 October 1772 between John Proctor High Sheriff of Bedford of the one part and Robert Hanna, Abraham Kebble, William McConnell, Esq., and John Moore assistant Judges and Henry Rhoads, Robert Bell, Samuel Thompson, David Vance,

Page 38 [October 1772]
01 October 1772 John Friehart, John Sampson, Allen Rose, William McGeary, Thomas Jones, William McCall, and William Gutrey Inspectors Freeholders of the said county of the other part. Joseph

Bealor, William Parker, Richard Wells, James Smith, James Pollock, and James Ca__ were elected Assessors for the County of Bedford.

Tavern Keepers Recommended: Conrad Walter, Raloh Cherrys, Philip Gillelan.

In Private Session at Bedford 10 November 1772 before William Proctor, George Woods and Abraham Kepple, Esqs., Justices.

Duskey Death and Frederick Wimer appointed Supervisors of Highways for Brothers Valley Township.

Page 39 [January 1773]
At Bedford on 12 January 1773 before John Fraser, Esq., and associate Justices.

Inquest sworn   Samuel Sinclair, foreman
William Pettyjohn   Joseph ShoneWolf
Richard Wells   Jacob Shilling
Thomas Croyle   Andrew Steel
Absolom Little   Samuel Skinner
John Evalt   Reynard Wolf
James Milligan   George Milligan
Charles Stewart (affirmed)   Gideon Richey

The King v. John Beans.
Defendant retracts his plea; pleads guilty. Fine 6^d.

The King v. William Sparks. Ignoramus.

Petition from inhabitants on the west side of Allegany Mountain setting forth that the road from said mountain to Fort Pitt needs repair and the same not being confirmed by the Court the petitioners cannot legally repair the same and

Page 40
request confirmation and approval to repair from Andersons Road to the east side of the mountain. Appoints James Anderson, Samuel Shannon, Samuel Morehead, Archibald Lochry, James Mires, and Thomas Lyon to view and report next session.

Petition of Bedford County inhabitants for road from Dunbars Incampment to the mouth of Big Redstone Creek. Appoints James McClea, Isaac Pears, Philip Shute, Andrew Linn, Thomas Banfield to lay out and report next session.

Petition of Bedford County and Dublin Township inhabitants for road from mouth of Aughwick to the Great Road leading from Bedford to Baltimore. That some petitioners have already viewed the ground from Silvarses ford on the Juniata about one mile from the mouth of the Aughwick to Robert Clugage Esq. mill, thence until it intersect the Waggon road near the Burnt Cabbins. Appoint Benjamin Elliott, John Ramsey, John Walker, Gaven Cluggage, Lawrence Swop, and James Carmichael to view and report next session.

Page 41
Whereas petition was made last October session for road from Town of Bedford to Abraham Mileys mill thence to Neals Gap thence to little Conalloway near Mr Powells at the Province line your petitioners represent that the road if laid out to the aforesaid petition places them at great disadvantage and your petitioners beg to acquaint the court with a convenient road, easy made and repaired, that can be laid out from the Town of Bedford through Dunnings Narrows and thence through the Plantations of Bernard Dougherty Esq., William Fredrigill, and John Friend senior to Neals Gap and to the Provincial Line. Appoint John Cissna, Edward Rose, Gideon Ritchey, Robert Moore, Ezekiel Worley, and John Fleehart to lay out same and report next session.

Petition of James Piper, Commissioner, represents that on the first day of October last he was elected Commissioner. That he together with Joseph Bealor was informed by Mr. St. Clair [that he] was appointed a commissioner before the first day of October in room of John Stevenson who had declined as acting. The Board met at the house George Woods Esqr. in the Town of Bedford thirtieth day of October last and issued precepts to Township Assessors to bring in a list of taxables this side of Laurel Hill and appointed first day of December to meet at house of

Page 42   [January 1773]
George Woods Esq. to assess the taxables on this side of the said Hill and the twenty ninth day of December to take returns beyond Laurel Hill at the house of Thomas Hanna Esq. He together with James Pollock, Richard Wells, James Smith, and William Parker County Assessors met at the house of George Woods on the day aforesaid but Joseph Bealor and Dorsey Pentecost did not attend. Charles Cessna was unanimously appointed a Commissioner and John Fraser Esq. County Treasurer. He together with William Parker and Charles Cissna met at the house of Robert Hanna as aforesaid. At that meeting Joseph Bealor told James Piper that he was not a Commissioner. John Stevenson insisted on acting as Commissioner but was opposed by James Piper upon which Dorset

Pentecost Esq., Robert Hanna Esq., James Pollock, and James Carvel appointed the said John Stevenson Commissioner. By reason of which James Piper, Charles Cissna, and William Parker declined acting as they imagined what they would do in consequence of Mr Stevensons appointment would be irregular and accordingly returned home without being able to do anything for the good of the County.

14 January 1773

> Court's opinion that John Stevenson & Dorsey Pentecost be fined each £50 to Provincial Treasurer and £10 each to the County Treasurer. [There is an interlined note in different handwriting noting that in April session 1773 the Court remit the fine against Dorsey Pentecost he having given satisfactory reason for nonattendance.] John Stevenson making reasonable excuse the Court remit his fine of £50 and remit the fine of £10 to 6^d.

Bethel Township to begin at David Browns and run along the mountain to Evan Jenkinses thence along the ridge thence a straight line to Dublin Township.

Page 43
Tavern keepers recommended: William McCall, William Elliot, Jacob Sinnett, Daniel McConnell, Zachariah McConnell, Jane Hannah.

Court appoints Joseph Cox Overseer of the Poor in room of Looke Collins of Springhill Township.

Constables	
Air Township	John McLellan fined 20/
Bedford	Thomas Kinton discharged
Cumberland	Jonathan Fisher fined 20/
Barree	Thomas Weston fined 20/
Dublin	James Foley
Colerain	John Friend
Brothers Valley	John Hendricks fined 20/
Fairfield	Thomas Cheany fined 20/
Mt. Pleasant	Thomas Bays fined 20/
Hempfield	Robert Vance fined 20/
Pitt	William Powell fined 20/
Tyrone	Benjamin Wells fined 20/
Springhill	Thomas Masterson
Ross Straver	Peter Hance fined 20/
Armstrong	Samuel Craig fined 20/
Bedford Town	Henry Creighton

BEDFORD COUNTY QUARTER SESSIONS

Page 44 [April 1773]
At Bedford 13 April 1773 before John Fraser Esq. and associate Justices.

Grand Jury: William Latta, foreman
- Andrew White
- Richard Stephen
- George Has
- Thomas Johnson
- Richard Brown
- Moses Read
- Samuel Drenning
- William Sloan
- Robert John
- William Kerney
- Robert Moore
- John Freeharty
- Evan Jenkins
- Adam Young

The King v. John Burd. Assault & Battery. Ignoramus.

The King v. Thomas Burd. Assault & Battery. Ignoramus.

The King v. Degory Sparks. Assault & Battery. Ignoramus.

The King v. Thomas Hays. Assault & Battery. Ignoramus.

The King v. John McKenny. Felony. Ignoramus.

The King v. [Hans Hamilton][page cut off; the upper portions of the name remain and appear to match Hans Hamilton. Recognizances for Hans Hamilton are seen later in the docket.]. Assault & Battery. Ignoramus.

Page 45 April 1773
The King v. Charles McGill. Assault & Battery on John Burd. Defendant pleads not guilty. Andrew Allen prosecutor. Jury of Samuel Moore, Thomas Hey, Joseph Morrison, Hugh Ferguson, William McComb, Charles Sipes, John Miller, George Ensloe, Martin Longstrech, Allen Rose, Jacob Saylor, and William Parker find defendant guilty.

The King v. Degory Sparks.
Indictment for feloniously stealing two Spanish milled dollars from John Burd. Continued from July 1773. Defendant pleads not guilty. Jury of John Cessna, Martin Longstrech, George Ensly, Andrew Man, Jacob Rush senior, Jacob Rush junior, James Graham, Hugh Bigham, Daniel McConnel, Thomas Paxton, Alexander Querry, and Allen Rose find not guilty.

Petition of inhabitants of Air and Bethel Townships for road from the Great Road near the Crossings of Juniata to Moses Read's mill thence to the Provincial Line. Ordered James Graham, Obadiah Stilwell junior, Abraham Covalt, Edward Comb, William Hart and Joseph Comb to view and make return next session.

Page 46   April 1773
Petition of inhabitants of Great Cove in Air Township for road beginning at Daniel Reyer's Mill to foot of Stoney Batter where the road from Sideling Hill to Baltimore crosses it. Ordered Thomas Stephens, Benjamin McClellan, Evan Shelby, James Cunningham, David McCrorey, and John Harred to view, lay out and report next session.

<u>Constables Appointed</u>
Bedford Town	Samuel McCashlan
Bedford Township	David Reynard
Air Township	Abraham Lowrey
Barree Township	Charles Caldwell
Brothers Valley	Philip Kemble
Colerain	Robert Bradshaw
Cumberland	Evan Cessna
Dublin	John Bale

John Freeharty of the Grand Jury fined five shillings for being drunk and 10 shillings for contempt in so doing while on the duty of that office and coming into Court in that condition.

Fines set upon the Constables of Air, Brothers Valley, Cumberland, Tyrone, Mt. Pleasant & Hempfield are remitted they having shown satisfactory reasons for their non attendance.

Page 47   [May, July 1773]
11 May 1773 Gideon Ritchey and Abraham Miller appointed Overseers of the Poor for Colerain Township.

At Bedford second Tuesday of July 1773 before Bernard Dougherty Esq. and associate Justices.

Grand Jury sworn: Thomas Hay, foreman
Daniel Royer (affirmed)	Frederick Ambrozer
Samuel Davison	Ezekiel Worley
Michael Huff	Richard Wells
John Enslow	James Fletcher
Walter Hoyle	Henry Schitlor
James Milliken	Guideon Richy
Robert Moore	George Kemble (affirmed)
Mathias Deatch	Daniel Loude

Petition of inhabitants of Air and Bethel Townships for road to begin at Stoney Batter thence to Daniel Royer's mill. Ordered William Kerney, Hugh Rankin, John McKinley, Jacob Casnor, Andrew White, and Brian Coyle to view, lay out, and make return next session.

Page 48 July 1773
Petition of inhabitants of Brothers Valley setting forth that township is too extensive. Ordered that the part of the township beginning where Chestnut Ridge crosses line dividing the Province from Maryland thence along summit of Chestnut Ridge to where it crosses the Great Road from Bedford to Fort Pitt thence along road to where it crosses Quemahoning Creek thence down the creek to the junction with Stoney Creek thence to the mouth of Little Conemaugh to where the line dividing Bedford from Westmoreland crosses it thence along the said line to the Provincial line thence along the Provincial line to the beginning. The new township called Turkey Foot Township.

James Spencer appointed Constable of said [Turkey Foot] Township.

On motion of Mr. Galbreath ordered that Honor Sullivan, servant of James McCashlan, serve her master one year over and above the time she is bound.

The King v. Degory Sparks. Recognizance taken by Robert Cluggage Esq. £40. Charles Magill junior of Dublin £40 and Benjamin Jolly of Barree £20 for appearance of Degory Sparks at this session to answer indictment found against him last session. Degory Sparks came not therefore recognizance forfeit until next Court.

Page 49 July 1773
Constables
Bedford Town	Samuel McCashland
Bedford Township	David Reynard
Air	Abraham Lowrey fined 20/ remitted Oct
Barree	Charles Caldwell fined 20/ remitted Oct
Brothers Valley	Philip Kemble discharged
Bethel	John Rush appointed in room of Peter Hum[ble?] deceased
Colerain	Robert Bradshaw
Cumberland	Evan Cessna
Dublin	John Bale fined 20/
Turkey Foot	James Spencer

Tavern Keepers recommended for license: Jane Woods, Jean Fraser, Frederick Nagle, George Funk, James Anderson, Charles Magill Dublin,

William Elliot Bedford, John Peters Brothers Valley, John Miller Edmunds Swamp, Moses Watson, Daniel McConnell, John Burd, Michael Cryder, Benjamin Jolly.

Page 50 [October 1773]
At Bedford second Tuesday in October 1773 before Benjamin Dougherty and Associate Justices.

Grand Jury: Robert Moore, foreman

Michael Diepert	Conrad Samuel
William McCall	Gabriel Rhoads (affirmed)
John Diepert	Peter Stifler
Samuel Drennin	Andrew Steel
Thomas Johnson	Adam Sams
Lawrence Koon	Joseph Shenywolf
George Wisegarber	Michael Feather (affirmed)

Constables:

Bedford Town	Samuel McCashlan
Bedford Township	David Rynhart
Barree	James Little appointed in room of Charles Caldwell
Air	Abraham Lowrey
Brothers Valley	Philip Kemble
Bethel	John Rush
Colerain	Robert Bradshaw
Cumberland	Evan Cessna
Dublin	John Bale
Turkeyfoot	James Spencer

That part of Barree Township including all the watershed emptying into the Raystown Branch of Juniata below the mouth of Yellow Creek up said creek to Tussey's Mountain is hereby erected into Hopewell Township. Michael Whetstone appointed Constable of Hopewell.

Page 51 October 1773
William Kerney, Hugh Rankin, John McKinley, Jacob Cavnor, Andrew White, and Bryan Coyle appointed last session to lay out road from Stoney Batten to Daniel Royer's mill made report [metes & bounds for road]. Ordered and confirmed as public road.

Petition from inhabitants of Bethel Township for road from the Provincial line by Read's mill to Branch Creek thence to the King's road leading to Bedford.

Page 52   [October 1773]
Ordered William Hart, Joseph Coomb, Edward Coomb, Obadiah Stillwell, James Graham, and Abraham Covalt view, lay out, and make report next session.

Petition of inhabitants of Barree for road to lead to that part of the township lying on the Frankstown Branch of Juniata between Water Street and the junction of the two branches to the Great Road at Bloody Run. And a road from Bloody Run to the crossings of Yellow Creek near James Pipers thence down Woodcock Valley to Bouquet's Spring thence to fork and one part to run to Water Street and the other part to run to the point of the island above Standing Stone and along the principal street of Huntingdon and cross Standing Stone Creek at the end of Standing Stone Mountain thence to the County line. Ordered John Piper Esq., Richard Long, Michael Cryder, Samuel Anderson, James Little, and William Shirley to view, lay out and report next session.

Page 53   [January 1774]
At Bedford second Tuesday of January 1774 before Bernard Dougherty Esq. and Associate Justices.

Grand Jury: Thomas Menzies, foreman
  Samuel Davidson   Timothy Ryan
  Adam Saam   William Elliott
  Thomas Woods   Robert Culbertson
  Jacob Saylor   Matthew McAllister
  Robert Henry   Thomas Croyle
  Charles Rubey   John Cessna
  John Mortimore   Andrew Steel
  George Milligan

The King v. Thomas Wilkins. Larceny. True Bill.
Defendant called; appears not. Process awarded.

The King. v. James Hughes. Ignoramus.

Page 54   January 1774
Petition of David Scott for road from Soaking Ridge to Samuel Kerr's thence to William Gaff's thence to John Cunningham thence to the Great Road leading from McConnels to Bedford. Ordered William Latta, Abraham Lowrey, Francis Patterson, John Wilson, James Cunningham, and John Cunningham to view, lay out, and make report next session.

William Hart, Joseph Coombs, Obadiah Stillwell, James Graham, Edward Coombs and Abraham Covalt appointed last session report on road from the Provincial line by Read's mill to Brush Creek Gap thence to the King's Road leading to Bedford make report. Road found agreeable and convenient and annex draft.
[report dated] 12 November 1773

Page 55 January 1774
[metes and bounds; no individuals named; road diagram]
Road ordered opened.

Page 56 January 1774 [includes March 1774]
Recognizances returned this session.

George Corn in £50 and William Colvin in £25 for the appearance of George Corn at this session to answer indictment.

George Corn does not appear and William Colvin called to bring in George Corn makes default. Recognizances forfeit until next session.

<u>Constables</u>
Bedford Town	Samuel McCashlan
Bedford Township	David Rynhart discharged
Air	Abraham Lowrey fined 20/ remitted 25 March
Barree	James Little fined 20/
Brothers Valley	Philip Kemble
Bethel	John Rush fined 20/
Colerain	Robert Bradshaw (affirmed)
Dublin	John Bale fined 20/
Turkey Foot	James Spencer fined 20/

At Bedford in private session 14 March [1774] before Bernard Dougherty, George Woods and Thomas Smith Esqs.

James McMullen recommended to license to keep Publick House.

At Bedford in private session 25 March [1774] before George Woods, Abraham Miley, and Thomas Coulter Esqs. the following persons were appointed Constable, Overseer of the Poor and Supervisor of Roads:

Page 57
Bedford Town: Constable, Samuel McCashlan.
Bedford Township: Constable, Michael Diepert; Overseer of the Poor, Conrad Samuels & Michael Sills; Supervisor of Highways, Thomas Kinton.

Air: Constable, James Cunningham; Overseers of Poor, James Galloway & Evan Philips; Supervisor of Highways, William Sloan & John McKinley.
Colerain: Constable, Gideon Ritchie; Overseer of the Poor, James Patterson & Ezekiel Worley.
Cumberland: Constable, William Dixon; Overseer of the Poor, Joseph Kelly & Thomas Jones; Supervisor of Roads, Matthew Kelly.
Brothers Valley: Constable, Frederick Ambroser; Overseer of Poor, George Kimel & Michael Byerley; Supervisor of Roads, Christian Spiker.
Hopewell: Constable, Philip Stoner.

This indenture 01 October 1773 between John Proctor High Sheriff of the one part and James Anderson, Abraham Miley, and John Miller, assistant judges and Henry Rhoads, John Fleetharty, James Little, Michael Divert, Charles Boyle, Jacob Rush, Thomas Hardistie, and James Bellows, inspectors of the other part. Charles Cessna elected Commissioner for County of Bedford.

Page 58
Evan Shelly, William Parker, Tuskin Death, Richard Long, Robert Moore, and Jacob Hendershot elected Assessors for County of Bedford.

Page 59   [April 1774]
[The penciled number on this page is 59. Some confusion in page numbers follows this page.]
At Bedford second Tuesday in April 1774 before Bernard Dougherty and associate Justices.

Grand Jury:
John Burd, foreman

Moses Watson	John McClellan
Timothy Ryan	Frederick Helm
Robert Culbertson	Frederick Reighart
Thomas Menzies	John Rhoads
Joseph Kelly	James Milligan
James Henry	James Barnet
Elijah Adams (affirmed)	Samuel Graves

Constable	Township	Appointed in their room this session
Samuel McCashlan	Bedford Town	appeared
Michael Diepert	Bedford Township	appeared
James Cunningham	Air	fined 20/
James Little	Barre	Robert Caldwell
Adam Stam	Brothers Valley	Adam Stam
John Rush	Bethel	James Graham
Gideon Richey	Colerain	
William Dixon	Cumberland	
John Bell	Dublin	John Latta
James Spencer	Turkey Foot	John P__ slay
Philip Stoner	Hopewell	

Reverse side of Page 59   April 1774
[This would be page 60, but the page following apparently was omitted when numbers were added. The page following this one was then numbered 59 ½, so this page is here denoted as the reverse side of the page numbered 59.]
Report of men petitioned to lay out road at last session petitioned for by David Scott. Returned the same as a public road therefore the petition is quashed.

Petition of inhabitants of Bedford County for road from mouth of Aughwick to the Great Road leading from Bedford to Baltimore and requesting persons to view the ground from Silver's ford on the Juniata about a mile from the mouth of Aughwick to the mill of Robert Cluggage Esq. thence to intersect the Great Road at Burnt Cabbins. Ordered James Galbrath, Samuel Thompson, Gaven Cluggage, Giles Stevens, Charles Boyle, Samuel Daniel to view, lay out, and report next session.

Petition of inhabitants of Barree Township who suffer from want of road from that part of the township lying on the Frankstown Branch of Juniata between Water Street and the two branches of the Great Road at Bloody Run that they be able to take their produce to market.

Page 59 ½   April 1774
[Apparently this page was skipped in the initial numbering, and, it being the right side page between 59 and 60, it was later numbered 59 ½.]
Petition asks for men to view a road from Bloody Run crossing Yellow Creek near James Piper's thence by Wookcock Valley to Bouquet's

Spring then to fork and one part to run to Water Street and the other to run to the Point of the Island above Standing Stone and along the Principal Street of Huntington and cross Standing Stone Creek thence to the County Line at the end of Standing Stone Mountain. Ordered John Piper Esq., Richard Long, James Little, Samuel Anderson, Michael Cryder, and John Mitchell to view, lay out, and make return next session.

The King v. Lorentz Counts. Felony. True Bill. Process awarded. July defendant appears pleads non Cul. October defendant discharged on proclamation and payment of costs.

The King v. Edward Henderson. Felony. Ignoramus.

The King v. Thomas Menzies. Fornication. Ignoramus.

The King v. Elizabeth Campbell. Fornication. Ignoramus.

Page 60   April 1774
The King v. Thomas Hay. Libel. True Bill.
Defendant pleads not guilty July Court. October continued. Jan 1775 continued. In April term jury of John Cessna, Thomas Woods, Jacob Mann, Benjamin Truax, John Melott, Henry Abrahams, Samuel Drennin, Peter Smith, James Fletcher, James Milligan, Thomas Crossen, and Thomas Johnston find defendant guilty. Fine £10 and costs. Recognizances: John Henry, William Elliot, Thomas Murphy each in £20 to give testimony against Thomas Hay. Thomas Hay of Bedford Township £40 and John Burd £20 for appearance of Thomas Hay to answer indictment. Thomas Hay £30 and John Mortimore £15 conditioned that Mary Hay keep the peace particularly towards Elinor Elliot and appearance at next court.

Page 61   [July 1774]
At Bedford second Tuesday in July 1774.

Constables and Supervisors of Highways.

Town	Constable	Supervisor of Highways
Bedford Town	Samuel McCashlin	
Bedford Twp.	Michael Dipert	James Kinton
Air	James Cunningham	William Sloan John McKinley
Barree	Robert Caldwell John Thorlton deputy	James Little Michael Cryder
Brothers Valley	Adam Stam (affirmed)	Christian Specher

Town	Constable	Supervisor of Highways
Bethel	James Graham	Andrew Man
Colerain	Gideon Ritchey fined 20/	Samuel Moore
Cumberland	William Dixon	Matthew Kelly
Dublin	John Latta fined 20/	John Ramsey James Foley
Turkeyfoot	John Pursley fined 20/	
Hopewell	Philip Stoner (affirmed)	Richard Long Samuel Thompson

Grand Jury:
    Richard Brown   John Creighton
    Benjamin Jolly   Robert Culbertson
    Robert Elliot   Henry Rhoades (affirmed)
    Charles Rubey   William McCall
    Timothy Ryan   Jacob Rine
    Benjamin Burd   Joseph Sapington
    John Peters   John Wensyel (affirmed)
    James McMullen

The King v. Lorentz Kuntz. Catherine Kuntz who entered recognizance to appear this court being called did not appear. Recognizance forfeit.

Page 62   July 1774
Recognizances taken since last returnable this session.

The King v. Lorentz Kuntz. Lorentz Kuntz £40 and John Friend £20 conditioned on appearance of defendant this session to answer.

The King v. James Gilmore. James Gilmore £20 and Abraham Kimberlin £10 conditioned on appearance of defendant this session to answer.

The King v. Henry Hall. Henry Hall £40 and John Galacher £30 conditioned on defendant's good behavior and appearance this session to answer. Defendant called and came not. Bail default.

The King v. Sarah Hall. Sarah Hall £40 and John Gallacher £30 conditioned on the same as the last.

The King v. Charles Stuart. Defendant in £20 and James Dalton in £10 conditioned on appearance of defendant to answer.

The King v. Aquila White. Defendant in £40 and Richard Brown £20 conditioned on appearance of defendant to answer.

The King v. Abraham Kimberlin and William Creechlow. Defendants in £20, John Kimberline in £10, and Richard Henry in £10 conditioned on appearance of the defendant to answer.

The King v. John McDonald. Defendant in £10 and William Holiday in £10 conditioned on appearance of defendant to answer.

The King v. Abraham Kimberlin and William Creechlow. James Black in £10 conditioned for his appearance to give evidence.

Page 63   July 1774
Recognizances taken in open court.

The King v. Lorentz Kuntz. Defendant £40 and Casper Davebaugh £20 for the appearance of the defendant next session.

The King v. Thomas Hay. Defendant £40 and John Mortimore £20 for appearance of defendant next session.

The King v. William Critchlow. William Critchlow £40 and John Kimberlin £20 for appearance of defendant next session.

The King v. Thomas Hay. William Elliot £20 and John Henry £20 for their appearance next session to give evidence.

The King v. Ludwick Sell. Samuel Anderson in £20, James Little in £20, Charles Cotswell £20, Michael Cryder £20, and John Thorlton £20 to give evidence next session.

The King v. John McDonald. Defendant in £20 and Robert Smiley in £10 for appearance of defendant next session.

Indictments this Session.

The King v. Ludwick Sell. Tipling House. True Bill.
Process awarded October Term. Defendant pleads guilty. Fine £5 to Governor and one half pound to the poor of Barree Township where the offence was committed and costs.

The King v. Charles Stuart. Assault. True Bill.
Defendant arraigned. Pleads guilty. Fine one shilling and costs.

Page 64   July 1774
The King v. Aquilla White. Assault. Ignoramus.

Motion of David Espy Esq. that William Montgomery indentured servant to Joseph Carroll serve his master for ten months above the time he is indentured by reason of expense to his Master from his running away and to make up the time his master lost by his so doing.

Ordered that tavern keepers who now have license be recommended to the Governor for license for the ensuing year provided they apply to the Clerk of Sessions before the next Court.

John Piper Esq., Richard Long, James Little, John Mitchell, Samuel Anderson, and Michael Cryder appointed last Court to lay out road from Bloody Run to Water Street & Standing Stone make return. [Metes and bounds.]

Page 65 July 1774
[Metes & bounds continue and name Charles Caldwell's Run, house of Henry Lloyd, Esq.]

Page 66 July 1774
[Metes & bounds continue mentioning Water Street at Lewis's house, hickory near George S[hacks?].

Page 67 July 1774
[Metes and bounds continue; mention James Pipers house, John Piper's Run a quarter mile below his house.]
Ordered that the same be confirmed as a Publick Road.

Page 68 July 1774
James Galbreath, Charles Boyle, Giles Stevens, Samuel Thompson, Samuel Daniel, and Gaven Clugage appointed last Court to view road from Mouth of Aughwick to the Great Road from Bedford to Baltimore make return [metes & bounds follow naming Robert Clugage Esq. mill and Wagon Road at Chas Magill].

Page 69 July 1774
Ordered the same confirmed as Publick Road.

Petition of Bartholomus Davis for road from Robert Clugage's mill to James Galbraiths thence to the Petitioners Mill. Ordered that James Galbreath, John Donough, John Ramsey, Robert Ramsey, James Clugage, and Samuel Thompson to view and lay out and report next Court.

Page 70 [October 1774]
At Bedford second Tuesday in October 1774 before Bernard Dougherty, William Proctor, and George Woods Esqs.

Grand Jury:
- Richard Brown, foreman
- Robert Henry
- Thomas Hay
- George Wisecarver
- Gabriel Rhoades (affirmed)
- Andrew Steel
- George Keller
- Casper Davebaugh
- David Rynhart
- Jacob Miller
- Peter Stiffler
- John Mortimore
- William Eceles
- Peter Smith
- Conrad Samuel

Recognizances taken returnable this session.

The King v. John Gallacher. Defendant in £50 and Benjamin Elloit in £25 for appearance of defendant this session.

The King v. Thomas Hay William Elliot in £10 and John Henry in £10 for their appearance next session to give evidence.

Page 71   October 1774

The King v. John Gallacher. William Beard of Cumberland County in £10 for his appearance to give evidence. Defendant in £25 and John Burd in £20 for appearance of defendant next session. Defendant in £100 and David McCrorey in £50 for good behavior for one year particularly to William Beard.

The King v. Thomas Hay. Defendant in £40 and John Burd of Littleton in £20 for appearance of defendant at next Session.

Indictments found this session by the Grand Jury.

The King v. John Gallacher. House Burning. True bill.
Motion the Court quash the indictment because the offence is not properly set forth in the indictment.

Petition of Bartholomew Davis of Dublin Township for road from the petitioner's to James Galbreath's thence to Patrick Kaman on the Great Road from Silver's Ford to the Burnt Cabbins. Court appoints James Galbreath, John Donough, John Ramsey, Robert Ramsey, James Clugage, and Samuel Thompson to view and lay out

Page 72   October 1774
and make report next session.

List of Tavern Keepers recommended for the ensuing year:

Frederick Nagle	William Elliot
James Anderson	John Burd
Benjamin Jolly	John Miller
Daniel McConnell	Ludwick Sells
Charles Magill	George Funk
Cornelius McAulay	Michael Huff
John Creighton	John Kimberlin
Timothy Ryan	John Burd Luking
Michael Cryder	Matthew McAllister

Page 73 [January 1775]

At Bedford second Tuesday in January 1775 before Bernard Dougherty, Arthur St. Clair, William Proctor, Robert Clugage, George Woods Esqs.

Grand Jury:

John Burd, foreman	Timothy Ryan
John Plummer	Robert Elliot
Elijah Rippy	John Mortimore
Shadwick Casteel	Mathew McAllister
William Henton	John Peters
Henderson Murphy	Andrew Mann
George Wolfe	James Henry
Jeremiah Stilwell	

Township	Constable
Bedford Town	Samuel McCashlan
Barree	Robert Caldwell, deputy John Thorlton fined 20/
Air	James Cunningham fined 20/
Bethel	James Graham
Brothers Valley	Adam Stam
Colerain	Gideon Ritchie
Dublin	John Latta
Cumberland	William Dixon
Turkey Foot	John [P]insley fined 20/
Hopewell	Philip Stoner

Page 74 January 1775

Recognizances taken returnable this session.

The King v. Thomas Hay. William Elliot in £10 and John Henry in £10 for their appearance to give evidence. John Henry being three times called came not; his recognizance forfeit until next term.

The King v. John Gallacher. William Beard in £10 for his appearance next session to give evidence. Discharged. Defendant in £25 John Burd Littleton in £20 for appearance of defendant to answer. Discharged.

The King v. Thomas Hay. Defendant in £40 and John Burd Littleton in £20 for appearance of defendant next session.

Recognizances taken since last sessions and returnable this session.

The King v. John McKiney. Defendant in £30 and Robert McKiney in £30 for appearance of defendant this session. Henry Salts in £30 and Sarah Rhoades in £10 for appearance this session to testify.

The King v. James McKiney. Defendant in £30, James Graham in £30, and Henry Warford in £30 for appearance of defendant this session. Henry Salts in £30, James Graham in £30, and Henry Warford in £30 for appearance of Henry Salts to give evidence.

The King. v. Joseph McKiney. Defendant in £30 and James McKiney in £30 for appearance of defendant this session. Henry Salts in £30 and James Graham in £30 for appearance of Henry Salts to give evidence.

Page 75 January 1775
The King v. Jacob Adams. Defendant in £50 and James Bella in £50 conditioned that defendant keep the peace, be of good behavior, and appear this session. Discharged.

The King v. William Scovel. Ja^s Witherspoon in £20 for appearance of defendant and that he keep the peace.

The King v. Edward Higgins. Defendant in £40 and Richard Brown in £20 for appearance of defendant this court. Daniel Hay in £10 to testify this session.

The King v. Richard Shee. Defendant in £40 and Frederick Nagel in £20 for appearance of defendant this session.

The King v. Alexander Miller & Richard Shee. Samuel McCashlan £20 for appearance of Margaret his wife to testify.

The King v. Alexander Miller. David Irwin £20, Samuel McCashlan £20, Abraham Miley Esq. £20, and Patrick McMullen £20 for their appearance this session to testify.

The King v. James McMullen. Defendant in £50, Patrick McMullen in £25, and William Parker in £25 for appearance of defendant this session.

The King v. Patrick Quin. Defendant in £40 and Samuel McCashlan in £20 for appearance of defendant this session.

The King v. David Irwin. Defendant in £40 and William Frederigill in £20 for appearance of defendant this session. Edward Henderson in £10 to testify this session.

The King v. Elijah Rippy. Defendant in £40 and Cornelius McAulay in £20 for appearance of defendant this session.

Page 76 January 1775
The King v. John Creighton. Defendant in £40 and John Ryan in £20 for good behavior of defendant and his appearance this session.

The King v. Patrick Mullen. Defendant in £40 and Elijah Rippy in £20 for appearance of defendant this session.

The King v. Patrick Hartford. Defendant in £40 and Timothy Ryan in £20 for appearance of defendant this session.

The King v. John Keller. Defendant in £40 and Matthew McAllister in £20 for appearance of defendant this session. David Irwin in £20 and Cornelius Maulay in £20 for their appearance to give evidence.

Recognizances taken in open court.

The King v. Edward Higgins. Defendant in £100, John Cessna in £50, and Thomas Jones in £50 that defendant will keep the peace for one year and especially toward Daniel May.

The King v. Thomas [torn]y. Defendant in £40 and John Burd Litt^n in £20 for appearance of defendant next session.

The King v. Thomas Hay. William Elliot in £20 and John Cessna in £20 for their appearance to testify.

The King v. Aquila White. Richard Brown in £20 for his appearance to testify.

The King v. Patrick Hartford. Defendant in £20 and Jonathan Cessna in £10 for appearance of defendant next session.

Page 77 January 1775
The King v. Alexander Miller & Richard Shee. Larceny. True Bill. Defendants arraigned and plead not guilty. Prosecutor Andrew Allen Esq. Jury of Charles Cessna, Thomas Jones, William Eckles, David Irwin, Casper Davebaugh, Rynhart Wolf, Adam Sam, Jacob Sailor, William McCall, David Rynhart, John Cessna, and James Milligan find

defendants guilty. Defendants to restore the stolen watch to owner James Williams or pay him the like sum of six pounds ten shillings and pay the like sum of six pounds ten shillings to the Governor and they be taken to the public whipping post Friday next being the twentieth inst. between the hours of one and two in the afternoon and Richard Shee to receive five stripes on his bare back well laid on and Alexander Miller to receive twenty one stripes on his bare back well laid on and they to pay costs.

The King v. Aquilla White, Pierce Noland, George Browner, Frederick Unsel, Paul Ernstberger, Jacob Morningstar, Daniel Morningstar, Adam Kefer, Henry Stegner, William Noland, Peter Bocher, and Frederick Vertress. Riot and Assault. True Bill.
Defendants being three times called came not. Process awarded.

The King v. Patrick Hartford. Assault & Battery. True Bill.
Defendant arraigned. Pleads not guilty. Andrew Allen Esq. for the King follows in like manner.

Page 78 January 1775
The King v. Broad Cole. Fornication. True Bill.
The defendant being three times called came not. Process awarded.

The King v. Delilah Whealler. Fornication. True Bill.
The defendant being three times called came not. Process awarded.

The King v. John Keller. Larceny. Ignoramus.

The King v. Edward Higgins. Fornication. Ignoramus.

George Woods Esq., Samuel Davidson Esq., and Frederick Nagel are appointed to be Rangers for the County of Bedford for one year only and subject to the following regulations:
1) When a stray horse or mare is brought they shall enter such in a Book kept for this purpose where they shall describe the age, color, brands, marks, shape, size, and gait of such and when brought and by whom brought and where taken up and with such description shall advertise such horse or mare in the Town of Bedford within three days and the said Book shall be free and open to inspection of all persons and shall be signed by said Rangers once every month.
2) They shall deliver a list of horses in their custody with description & if any such horses have been claimed and taken away; they mention when and by whom to the Clerk of Sessions.
3) Those who take up any stray horse or mare shall advertise them as aforesaid in the most public place in the Township where taken up within three days [bottom of page cut off]

Page 79   January 1775
three weeks such horse or mare is not legally claimed and taken away such person so taking up any horse or mare shall bring it to the said Rangers who are authorized to make such person a reasonable allowance for their trouble. Rangers accounts for such allowance shall be under control of the court.
4) Rangers shall settle their accounts once every quarter. If said Rangers of persons taking up as aforesaid shall omit or neglect to act agreeable to these Rules they shall have no allowance for their trouble.

Petition of inhabitants of Bethel Township for road to begin at John Mellot's at the Cove Road till it intersects the public road which leads from the Provincial Line in the said Township to Henry Warfords House. Ordered George Horse, John Mellot, Andrew Mann, John Fisher, Henry Rush, and Jacob Rush to view, lay out, and report next session.

Page 80   [March 1775]
At Bedford in private session 25 March 1775 before George Woods, Abraham Miley, Thomas Coulter, Samuel Davidson Esqs. the following persons were appointed:

Township	Constable	Overseer of Poor	Supervisor of Highways
Bedford Town	Samuel McCashlan		
Bedford Township	Thomas Hay	John Crissman James Fletcher	Thomas Kinton
Air	James Bella	James Galloway Evan Philips	William Sloan James Paxton
Bethel	James Graham	William Hart John Fisher	John Mellot
Barre	John Mitchell	Samuel Anderson Thomas Johnson	James Little Michael Cryder
Brothers Valley	Jacob Fisher	Jacob Cable William Wise	Christian Spicker
Colerain	John Fleeharty	James Patterson Achor Worley	Robert Elliot James Perrin
Cumberland Valley	Joseph Kelly	Andrew Price William Dickson	Joseph Kelly
Turkey Foot	John Pursley		
Hopewell	Philip Stoner		
Dublin	John Latta		

Page 81   [April 1775]
At Bedford second Tuesday in April 1775 before Bernard Dougherty, Arthur St. Clair, William Proctor junior, Esqs.

Township	Constable	Overseer of Poor	Supervisor of Highways
Bedford Town	Samuel McCashlan		
Bedford Township	Thomas Hay	John Crisman James Fletcher	Thomas Kinton
Air	James Bella fined 20/	James Galloway Evan Philip	William Sloan Thomas Paxton
Bethel	James Graham	William Hart John Fisher	John Melott
Dublin	Samuel Daniel appointed		
Hopewell	Walter Clark appointed	Benjamin Sanders Barkin Sharpe	Michael Whitestone Peter Hartstock
Barre	Jarnet Dean appointed	Samuel Anderson Thomas Johnson	James Little Michael Cryder
Cumberland Valley	Joseph Kelly	Andrew Rice William Dickson	Joseph Kelly
Colerain	John Fleharty	James Patterson Achor Worley	Robert Elliot John Parron
Brothers Valley	Jacob Fisher fined 20/	Jacob Cable William Ware	Christian Spiker
Turkey Foot	Aaron Rice apptd.		
Franks town	William Philips		
Quemahoning	Joseph Rhoads		

Page 82   April 1775
Grand Jury:
    Charles Cessna, foreman   Daniel Stoy
    Robert Culbertson   Allen Rose
    Moses Read   Joseph Johnston
    John Fisher   James Henry
    Obadiah Stillwell   Edward Coomb
    Benjamin Truax   Henry Warford
    John Wensyel (affirmed)   Michael Whetstone
    Samuel Paxton

The King v. Aquila White & al. Riot & Assault found last session. Aquila White, William Noland, George Browner, Frederick Unsel, Jacob Morningstar, and Daniel Morningstar plead not guilty. Andrew Allen prosecutor follows in like manner. Pierce Noland, Paul Ernstberger, Adam Kefer, Adam Stegner, Peter Bocher, Frederick Vertress being called came not. Process awarded.

The King v. Patrick Hartford. Assault & Battery found last Court. Jury of John Cessna, Thomas Woods, Jacob Mann, Benjamin Truax, John Melott, Henry Abrahams, Samuel Drennin, Peter Smith, James Fletcher, James Milligan, Thomas Crosier, and Thomas Johnston find defendant not guilty.

The King v. Aquila White.
Defendant in £100, Henry Rhoads in £50 Herman Husband in £50 for appearance of defendant next session and he shall keep [the peace?].
[Bottom of page cut off.]

Page 83 April 1775
The King v. William Noland, George Browner, Frederick Uncel, Jacob Morningstar, and Daniel Morningstar.
Defendants each in £50, Henry Rhoads £25, Herman Husband in £25, Wensyel in £25, John Pernod in £25 for appearance of defendants next session and they shall keep the peace and be of good behavior in the mean time.

The King v. Aquila White. Richard Brown in £20 to testify next session.

The King v. Herman Husband. Defendant in £1000, Henry Abrahams in £500, John Wenzel in £500, John Pinslay in £500 conditioned that defendant shall keep the peace and good behavior for one year and then shall appear.

The King v. Aquila White. Assault & Battery. True Bill.
Defendant being called came not. Process awarded.

The King v. Aquila White. John Pursley in £10 and Charles Cessna in £10 for appearance to testify next session.

The King v. William Scovel. Defendant in £20 and Cornelius McAuley in £10 for good behavior of defendant particularly toward James Henry.

Page 84 April 1775
On motion of David Espy Esq. Robert Stocks indentured servant of Benjamin Loan to serve his master two years beyond his indenture to satisfy his master for expenses & loss sustained by reason of servant running away from his master.

On motion of David Espy Esq. Margaret Reardon indentured servant woman to Samuel McCashlan to serve her master nine months over her indenture to satisfy her master for expenses and loss of time sustained by reason of her absenting herself from her masters service.

That portion of Brothers Valley and Turkey Foot Townships included in the following boundary [boundary given] is erected a new township by the name of Quemahoning Township.

That part of Bedford and Barree Townships within the following boundary [boundary given] is erected a new township by the name of Frankstown Township.

Page 85   April 1775
Return of George Horse, John Mellot, John Fisher, Henry Rush, and Jacob Rush for road from John Mellots to Henry Warfords in Bethel Township. [Sketch in margin with metes and bonds including following names: Great Cove Road at John Mellots, Rush and Pitmans, Henry Rushs place, Richard Mortons place, John Cormmings place, William Mortons place, Lims Run on Jeremiah Stillwell's place, Thomas Crossans place, Francis Reynoldses place, Thomas Barneys place, spring on James Mitchells place, John Fishers, Lawrence Slickers place, Jacob Man, Andrew Man, John McKinneys place, James McKinneys place, James Graham, and Henry Warford.]

Page 86   April 1775
Confirmed as a public road and Supervisors of Highways ordered to clear the same.

Petition of inhabitants of Bedford County. A Bridle Path from Dunnings Creek at Andrew Steels mill in Bedford Township is much used and petitioners request public road running from where the Great Road crosses Dunnings Creek to Andrew Steels mill. Ordered Frederick Nagel, William Parker, Thomas Woods, Thomas Kinton, Matthew McAllister, and Robert Elliot to view, lay out and report next session.

Page 87   [July 1775]
At Bedford on the second Tuesday of July 1775 before Bernard Dougherty, Arthur St. Clair, and William Proctor junior Esqs.

Township	Constable
Bedford Town	Samuel McCashlan
Bedford Township	Thomas Hay
Air	James Bella fined 20/
Barree	James Dean fined 20/
Bethel	James Graham fined 20/
Brothers Valley	Jacob Fisher
Colerain	John Fleharty
Cumberland Valley	Joseph Kelly fined 20/
Dublin	Samuel Daniel fined 20/
Hopewell	Walter Clark fined 20/
Turkey Foot	Aaron Rice
Frankstown	William Philips fined 20/
Quemahoning	Joseph Rhoads

Grand Jury:
   Thomas Ury, foreman   James Milligan
   Timothy Ryan   Samuel Thompson
   Samuel Armit (affirmed)   Henry Rhoads (affirmed)
   William Tod   James Wilson
   Samuel Tod   Henry Abarahms
   Christian Long   John Wensyel (affirmed)
   Cornelius McAulay   Jacob Ryne
   James Patterson

Page 88   July 1775
Recognizances taken last court returnable this session.

The King v. Aquila White. Defendant in £100, Henry Rhoads in £50, Hermon Husband in £50, John Wensyel in £50, John Pernod in £50 for defendant's appearance this session and to keep the peace and good behavior in the meantime.

The King v. William Noland, George Browner, Frederick Unsel, Jacob Morningstar, Daniel Morningstar. Defendants each in £50, Henry Rhoads £25, Hermon Husband £25, John Wensyel £25, John Pernod £25 for appearance of defendants next session and their good behavior and peace in the meantime. Forfeited as to the first three named defendants until next term.

The King v. Aquila White. Richard Brown in £20 for appearance this session to testify.

The King v. Jacob Morningstar and Daniel Morningstar. Riot found at January session. Arraigned April last having plead not guilty. Now retract former plea and plead guilty. Fine five shillings.

Page 89   July 1775
Indictments this session.

The King v. John Peters. Tipling House. True Bill.
Arraigned. Pleads guilty. Fine £5 and one half to the Governor and one half pound to the poor of Quemahoning Township where the offence was committed and costs.

The King v. John Mitchell. Tipling House. True Bill.
Defendant called and came not. Process awarded. Thomas Anderson in £10 to testify next session.

The King v. Sarah Kimberlin. Forcible Entry & Detainer. True Bill.
Defendant being called came not. Process awarded. James Gelmor in £10 for his appearance next session to testify.

The King v. Jacob Kimberlin. Assault. Ignoramus.

Page 90   [October 1775]
At Bedford the third Tuesday in October 1775 before Bernard Dougherty and associate justices.

Township	Constable
Bedford Town	Samuel McCashlan
Bedford Township	Thomas Hay
Air	James Bella
Bethel	James Graham
	deputy Stephen Leech
Barree	James Dean
Brothers Valley	Jacob Fisher
Colerain	John Fleeharty
Cumberland Valley	Joseph Kelly
Dublin	Samuel Daniel fined 20/
Hopewell	Walter Clark
Turkey Foot	Aaron Rice
Frankstown	William Philips
Quemahoning	Joseph Rhoads (affirmed)

Grand Jury:
    James Anderson, foreman   Timothy Ryan
    Thomas Stephenson (affirmed) William Eccles
    Moses Read   John Royce
    William Todd   James Francis Moore
    Jacob Sailor   Henry Rhoads [affirmed?]
    [bottom of page cut off]

Page 91   October 1775
Indictments

The King v. Pierce Noland, Frederick Unsel, Paul Ernstberger, Adam Kefer, Henry Stegman, William Noland, Peter Bocher, Frederick Vertress. Riot and Assault found last January. Frederick Unsel, William Noland, Adam Kefer, Henry Stegman, and Peter Bocher appear and plead guilty. Judgment that Frederick Unsel, William Noland, Henry Stegman, and Peter Bocher pay five shillings to the Governor and Adam Kefer pay the Governor five pence and that they and each of them pay costs.

Recognizances returnable this session.

The King v. Sarah Kimberlin. John Kimberlin of Turkey Foot Township in £20 for appearance of defendant this session.

The King v. John Mitchell. Defendant in £40 and Charles Megill in £20 for appearance of defendant this session.

The King v. William Hamilton. Defendant in £40, Bernard Dougherty in £20, and Hugh Brown in £20 for appearance of defendant this session.

The King v. James Culbertson. Defendant in £20 and Charles Cessna in £10 for appearance of defendant this session. James Henry in £10 to testify.

Page 92   October 1775
The King v. Ann Crawford. Defendant in £20 and John Wilkins in £20 for appearance of defendant this session.

The King v. James Francis Moore. Defendant in £20 and Oliver Drake in £20 for appearance of defendant this session. George Howard in £10 and Aaron Rice in £10 for George Howards appearance this session to testify.

The King v. Richard Phibs. Defendant in £100 and John Wilkins in £50 for appearance of defendant this session. Adam Samuel in £40 and Conrad Samuel in £40 for appearance of Adam Samuel to testify.

The King v. Thomas Dalton. Defendant in £40 and Moses Watson in £30 for appearance of defendant this session. William Lemmon in £40 and Cornelius McAuley in £40 for W. Lemmon to testify.

The King v. Timothy Ryan. Defendant in £40 and Charles Ruby in £20 for appearance of defendant this session. Thomas Hay in £40 to testify.

The King v. James Chambers. Defendant in £40 and John Wilkins in £20 for good behavior of the defendant.

Page 93 October 1775
The King v. Timothy Ryan. Assault & Battery. Ignoramus.

The King v. Timothy Ryan. Larceny. Ignoramus.

The King v. James Culbertson. Assault & Battery. True Bill
Defendant Arraigned. Pleads guilty. Fine thirty shillings and costs.

The King v. William Hamilton. Misdemeanor. True Bill.
Defendant arraigned. Pleads guilty. Fine thirty shillings and costs.

The King v. John Rice. Tipling House. Ignoramus.

Page 94 October 1775
Petition of residents of Colerain and Frankstown Townships for road from Robert Elloit's at the Snake Spring to the gap in the Dividing Ridge between Croyle's Cove and Morrison's Cove thence to Daniel Oulerys's mill thence to Frankstown Gap in Dunnings Mountain. Ordered that Jo__ Piper Esq., Thomas Ury, William McComb, John Moore, Samuel Moore, and Robert Culbertson view, lay out, and make report next session.

Petition of inhabitants of Air Township for road from Top of the Cove Mountain beginning at the Line which divides Cumberland County from Bedford continuing to the foot of Sidling Hill. Ordered William Latta Esq., Thomas Paxton, Alexander Query, James Liddle, Daniel Royer, and Edward Head to view, lay out and report next session.

Page 95 October 1775
Petition of David Scott of Air Township saying that the petitioner has opened a road separating from the Great Road which leads from the settlement of Concheocheague to the foot of Sidling Hill asks the road be laid out as a Road or Cart Way. Ordered William Latta Esq., Thomas

DOCKET 1: 1771–1789 53

Paxton, Alexander Query, James Liddle, Daniel Royer, and Edward Head to view, lay out, and report next session.

Page 96 [January 1776]
At Bedford third Tuesday in January 1776 before Bernard Dougherty Esq. and associate justices.

Township	Constable
Bedford Town	Samuel McCashlan
Bedford Township	Thomas Hay
Air	James Bella
Bethel	James Graham
	deputy Stephen Leech
Barree	James Dean fined 20/
Brothers Valley	Jacob Fisher
Colerain	John Fleeharty fined 20/
Cumberland Valley	Joseph Kelly
Dublin	Samuel Daniel
Hopewell	Walter Clark
Turkey Foot	Aaron Rice
Frankstown	William Philips
Quemahoning	Joseph Rhoads (affirmed)

Grand Jury:
  Robert Moore, foreman   Casper Defebaugh
  Henry Abrahams   Timothy Ryan
  Robert Culbertson   Jonathan Cessna
  John Bowser   Jacob Saylor
  Godfrey Kniper   Gabriel McKinzey
  George Keller   Richard Dunlap
  Arnst Baker   Peter Smith
  George Wolf

Page 97 January 1776
Recognizances returnable this session.

The King v. Jonathan Coats. Defendant in £20 and James Marton in £10 for appearance of defendant this session. Defendant being called came not and James Martin being called to produce the defendant came not therefore recognizance is forfeit until next term.

The King v. Jacob Feather. Defendant in £50 and John Bowser in £25 for defendant to appear this session.

The King v. John McNaullay. Larceny. True Bill.
Defendant arraigned. Pleads not guilty. Andrew Allen prosecutor. Jury of Thomas Urie, James Patterson, John Miller, Samuel Moore, William McComb, James Beaty, Joseph Morrison, Samuel Drennin, Thomas Johnston, Charles Ruby, Edward Rose, and Rynhart Wolf find defendant guilty. Ordered that defendant restore goods mentioned and pay fine of four pounds ten shillings to the Governor and fifteen lashes on his bare back well laid on tomorrow between ten and twelve in the morning and pay costs.

Page 98 January 1776
The King v. Nicholas Fitzsimmons & James Reeves. Larceny. True Bill. Defendants Arraigned. Plead not guilty. Andrew Allen prosecutor. Jury of Thomas Ury, James Patterson, John Miller, Samuel Moore, William McComb, James Beaty, Joseph Morrison, Samuel Drennin, Thomas Johnson, Charles Ruby, Edward Rose, and Rynhart Wolf find defendants guilty. Ordered that they restore goods stolen or value thereof fifty shillings, pay a fine of fifty shillings, Nicholas Fitzsimmons to receive twenty lashes on his bare back, and James Reeves to receive five lashes on his bare back tomorrow morning between ten and twelve.

The King v. Jonathan Coats. Forgery. True Bill.
Defendant being called came not. Process awarded.

The King v. Elizabeth Stockberger. Bigamy. True Bill.
Defendant being called came not. Process awarded.

The King v. George Feather. Bigamy. True Bill.
Defendant being called came not. Process awarded.

Page 99 January 1776
George Woods and Samuel Davidson Esqs. and George Funk are licensed as Rangers for the County of Bedford for one year.

At Bedford in private session 05 March 1776 before Thomas Coulter, Abraham Miley, and Samuel Davidson Esqs.

Township	Constable	Overseer of Poor	Supervisor of Highways
Bedford Town	Jacob Hersch		
Bedford Township	Jonathan Cessna	James Williams John Walt	Thomas Kinton
Air	James Galloway	Enoch Williams Jacob Alexander	Andrew White
Brothers Valley	John Walter	Jacob Cable William Dwire	Christian Spiker
Colerain	Joseph Friend	James Patterson Achor Worley	Robert Elliot
Cumberland Valley	James Culbertson	William Dixon Andrew Royce	Joseph Kelly
Hopewell	William Smart	Benjamin Saunders Bastian Shoupe	Peter Hartsock
Frankstown	William Barrick	Absolom Gray Samuel Jack	Mackem Coleman
Quemahoning	Henry Washenbaugh	James Black John Bridges	John Penrod

Page 100 [April 1776]
At Bedford third Tuesday in April 1776 before Bernard Doughtery Esq. and associate justices.

Township	Constable
Bedford Town	Richard Delap appointed
Bedford Township	Jonathan Cessna
Air	Evan Philips appointed
Brothers Valley	John Walter
Barree	David Lewis appointed
Bethel	Stephen Leech appointed
Colerain	Joseph Friend (affirmed)
Cumberland Valley	James Culbertson
Dublin	Samuel Thompson
Hopewell	William Smart
Turkey Foot	David Jones
Quemahoning	Henry Washenbaugh

Turkey Foot Township. Overseers of Poor: Enoch Abrahams and Henry Elon.

Grand Jury:
- Thomas Urie, foreman
- Thomas Buck
- Robert Bradshaw
- Abraham Covalt
- Charles Rubey
- James Fleming
- Timothy Ryan
- Henry Abrahams
- David Rynhart
- William Critchlow
- George Keller
- Peter Stiffler
- Christian Spiker (affirmed)
- John Penrod (affirmed)

Page 101   April 1776
Indictments proffered to the Grand Jury this court.

The King v. Christopher Johnson. Forcible Entry and Detainer. Ignoramus.

The King v. Herman Husband. Defendant in £1000, Benjamin Pursley in £500, Aaron Royce in £500, Frederick Weimer in £500 that defendant shall keep the peace and good behavior for one year and that he shall then appear before the court.

Petition of inhabitants of Bethel and Air Townships for road leading from Cumberland County to the foot of Sidling Hill beginning where the county line at the top of Cove Mountain crosses the Cove Road thence to the house of Daniel McConnell in the Great Cove thence to intersect the road leading from Littleton to Bedford at the foot of Sidling Hill. Ordered Edward Head, Nicholas Wilson, Matthias Amberson, Daniel Royer, John McClure, and William Sloan to view, lay out, and make return next session.

Page 102   April 1776
Petition of residents of Colerain and Frankstown Townships for road from the house of Robert Ellot at the Snake Spring in the Township of Colerain to the gap in the Dividing Ridge between Croyle's Cove and Morris's Cove thence to the Gap in Dunnings Mountain known as Frankstown Gap. Ordered John Teiters, Jacob Knause junior, Joseph Cellars, Joseph Morrison, John Moore, and Samuel Moore to view, lay out, and make return next session.

Petition of inhabitants of Bedford Township and Frankstown for road from the Town of Bedford to the New Bridge erected near Frankstown Old Town. Ordered William Proctor Esq., William Holiday, Michael Wallack, John Guilford, George Wisegarver, and Michael Sells to view, lay out, and report next session.

Page 103   April 1776
Petition of inhabitants of Barree Township for road to the Juniata Frankstown Branch and to Bedford and to Huntingdon Meeting & Market unto the saw and grist mill on the aforesaid Branch. Asking for road beginning at William McLeveys on Standing Stone Creek near to the Big Gap that leads into Kishacoquillis Valley thence down Shaver's Creek to the Mouth thereof unto Frankstown Branch thence down the aforesaid Branch to the upper end of Doctor William Smiths Island thence crossing Juniata to the public road to Bedford. And the other road beginning at the upper end of the aforesaid Island where the first mentioned road ends on the northeast side of said Branch thence down said Branch until it joins the aforesaid Public Road. Ordered William McLevey, Alexander McCormick, James Williams, Abraham Haines, Robert Smith, and Nathaniel Jarrard to view, lay out and make return next session.

Page 104 blank.

Page 105   September 1777
At a Court of Petty Sessions held at the House of Henry Wirts in the Town of Bedford 27 September 1777 before James Martin, William Parker, John Malott, and Martin Longstretch Esqs., Justices.

Constables appointed:

Township	Constable
Bedford Town	George Milligan
Bedford Township	John Todd
Air	Daniel McConnell
Bethel	Thomas Williams
Barree	William Riddle
Brothers Valley	William Dyer
Colerain	Samuel Moore
Cumberland Valley	Samuel Paxton
Dublin	John Walker
Hopewell	Joshua Davis
Turkey Foot	Henry Abrahams
Quemahoning	Adam Wright

Page 106   [October 1777]
At Bedford 14 October 1777 before James Martin, William Parker, and John Malott Esqs., Justices.

Bedford County Quarter Sessions

Constables Sworn:

Township	Constable
Bedford Town	George Milligan fined
	David Erwin appointed & sworn
Bedford Township	John Todd
Air	Daniel McConnell
Bethel	Thomas Williams
Barree	William Riddle fined
Brothers Valley	William Dyer fined
Colerain	Samuel Moore
Cumberland Valley	Samuel Paxton fined
	Daniel McMichael appointed
Dublin	John Walker fined
	Thomas Anderson appointed
Hopewell	Joshua Davis
	Felix Miller appointed
Turkey Foot	Henry Abrahams fined
Frankstown	Joseph Cellers
Quemahoning	Adam Wright fined

Recognizances taken in open court.

The Commonwealth v. John Bilyu. James Martin Esq. prosecutor. Defendant in £100, Thomas Buck in £100, Thomas Williams in £100 for appearance of defendant next court.

The Commonwealth v. Peter Whitesides. Thomas Woods prosecutor. Defendant in £40, Cornelius McAuley in £20, Samuel Mc___ in [cut off] for appearance of defendant next court.

Page 107   October 1777

Recognizances taken in open court.

The Commonwealth v. Joshua Davis, Thomas Chiffinton, John Chiffinton. Defendants each in £100, Shebastian Shoaf in £100, Michael Whetstone in £100 for defendants keeping the peace and being of good behavior.

The Commonwealth v. Morris Kean and Jacob Shoub. Defendants in £100, Sebastian Shoef in £100, Michael Whetstone in £100 for defendants keeping the peace and being of good behavior.

The Commonwealth v. Gasper Miller and Thomas Miller. Defendants in £100, Sebastian Shoaf in £100, Michael Whetstone in £100 for defendants keeping the peace and being of good behavior.

Tavern keepers recommended: Robert Culbertson, Richard Dunlap, Cornelius McAuley, Benjamin Martin.

Page 108 [January 1778]
At Bedford 30 January 1778 before James Martin, William Parker and John Malott Esqs., Justices.

Township	Constable
Bedford Town	David Erwin
Bedford Township	John Todd
Air	Daniel McConnell
Bethel	Thomas Williams
Barree	William Riddle
Brothers Valley	William Dyer
Colerain	Samuel Moore
Cumberland Valley	Daniel McMichael
Dublin	Thomas Anderson
Hopewell	Felix Miller
Frankstown	Joseph Cellers
Turkey Foot	Henry Abrahams
Quemahoning	Adam Wright

Grand Jury:
Gideon Ritchie, foreman   William Buman
Edward Rose   Israel Garrison
Robert Bradshaw   John Wilt
Christopher Miller   Ernest Baker
Robert Moore   Joseph Morrison
Thomas Bush   John Ferguson
[cut off]   Henderson Murphy
[cut off]   [cut off] Smith
Henry Holley [written alongside vertically]

Page 109 January 1778
Recognizances taken last Term returnable to this [session].

The Commonwealth v. John Wilt. John Wilt in £100, Abraham Miley in £50, Robert Bradshaw in £50 for John Wilt's being of good behavior and keeping the peace for one year and appearing at January Sessions.

The Commonwealth v. Abraham Miley. Abraham Miley in £50 and Richard Dunlap in £25 for Abraham Miley's appearing at this Court.

The Commonwealth v. John Bilyew. John Bilyew in £100 and Thomas Storey in £100 for John Bilyew's appearance this court.

Bills of Indictment Found by the Grand Jury this court.

The Commonwealth v. Abraham Miley. Tipling House. True Bill.
Defendant pleads not guilty. Jonathan Serjant Esq. for Commonwealth.
Continued next term.

The Commonwealth v. Abraham Miley. Felony. Ignoramus.

The Commonwealth v. John Young. Felony. True Bill.
Defendant pleads not guilty. Jonathan Serjant Esq. for Commonwealth.
Continued next term.

Page 110 January 1778
The Commonwealth v. John Young. Felony. True Bill.
Defendant pleads not guilty. Jonathan Serjant Esq. for Commonwealth.
Continued next term.

The Commonwealth v. Peter Whitesides. Felony. True Bill. The defendant came not. Process awarded.

The Commonwealth v. Timothy Ryan. Tipling House. True Bill. The defendant came not. Process awarded. April 1778 upon motion the order of Noleprosequiti be entered.

The Commonwealth v. Michael Huff. Tipling House. True Bill. The defendant came not. Process awarded. Upon motion of Mr. Smith the order of Noleprosequiti be entered.

The Commonwealth v. John Peters. Tipling House. True Bill. The defendant came not. Process awarded.

The Commonwealth v. Jacob Hoover. The defendant came not. Process awarded.

The Commonwealth v. Patrick Quin. The defendant came not. Process awarded.

Page 111 January 1778
The Commonwealth v. Henry Wirt. Tipling House. True Bill. The defendant came not. Process awarded. April 1778 upon motion the order of Noleprosequiti be entered.

The Commonwealth v. Henry Didier. The defendant came not. Process awarded.

The Commonwealth v. Jonathan Cessna and Stephen Cessna. Accessory to Escape of Richard Richardson out of gaol. Not guilty returned by the Grand Jury.

The Commonwealth v. William Bromfield. Horse Stealing. Not guilty returned by the Grand Jury.

The Commonwealth v. George Shingledecker. Larceny. Parties agreed before court. No prosecution.

The Commonwealth v. John Hatch and Elizabeth Hatch his wife. Samuel McCashlan in £50 for appearance of John Hatch and wife this term. Defendants called and appeared not. Recognizance forfeit.

Page 112 January 1778
Recognizances taken in open court.

The Commonwealth v. Abraham Miley.
Abraham Miley in £40 and Jonathan Cessna in £20 for Abraham Mileys appearance next term to answer.

The Commonwealth v. John Young.
Abraham Miley in £40 and Jonathan Cessna in £20 for above Miley's appearance to prosecute.

The Commonwealth v. John Young.
John Young in £40, John Tod in £40, and John Moore in £20 for appearance of John Young next term.

The Commonwealth v. John Young.
John Young in £40, John Moore in £20, and John Tod in £20 for appearance of John Young next term.

The Commonwealth v. Abraham Miley.
John Young in £40, John Moore in £20, and John Tod in £20 for appearance of John Young next court to prosecute.

Tavern Keepers recommended: David Ervin, Daniel McConnell, Samuel Tod, John Tod, Thomas Storey, Thomas Vicroy, George Summerville.

Page 113 [April 1778]
At Bedford on 13 April 1778 before James Martin, William Parker, John Mellott, Martin Longstretch, Thomas Paxton, Robert Scott, Henry Rhoads, David Jones and William Tyshee Esqs.

Township	Constable
Bedford Town	Jacob Saylor excused
	Charles Rubey sworn
Bedford Township	George Wisecarver
Air	Jacob Hoover
Bethel	William Pitman (affirmed)

Township	Constable
Barree	William Willson
Brothers Valley	Jacob Cable
Colerain	John Wilt
Cumberland Valley	
Dublin	William Winton appointed
Hopewell	
Frankstown	
Turkey Foot	Henry Abrahams
Quemahoning	

Grand Jury:
John Todd, foreman   John Morgan   Thomas Hay
Samuel Todd   William Elliot   Charles Rubey
James Dunlap   Jacob Saylor   Daniel McConnell
[last row of juror list cut off]
[written vertically in margin are Samuel Skinner, Shadwick Casteel, William Scofil. These names, however, do not match the remnants of the names in the cut off last row.]

Page 114   [March 1778]
At private sessions held at Bedford on 25 March 1778 before James Martin, John Malott, and William Parker Esqs.

Township	Constable	Overseer of Poor	Supervisor of Highways
Bedford Town	Jacob Sahlor		
Bedford Township	George Wisecarver	James Dunlap George Cills	William Proctor
Air	Jacob Hoover	James Galloway Evan Philips	Daniel McCurdy Charles Query
Colerain	John Wilt	Bernard Dougherty Abraham Miley	Joseph Morrison
Turkey Foot	Henry Abrahams	Enoch Abraham John Reed	James Spencer John Wayman

Page 115   April 1778
Recognizances returnable to this court.

The Commonwealth v. John Wilt. John Wilt in £100, Abraham Miley in £50, Robert Bradshaw in £50 for John Wilt's good behavior for one year and appearing at Janr[y] sessions.

The Commonwealth v. Abraham Miley. Abraham Miley in £50 and Richard Delap in £50 for Abraham Miley appearing at this court to answer.

The Commonwealth v. John Belyen. John Belyen in £100 and Thomas Story in £50 for John Belyen's appearing at this court to answer. April Term 1778 upon motion John Belyen is discharged from the recognizance.

Bills of indictment continued to this session:

The Commonwealth v. Abraham Miley. Tipling House. True Bill. Defendant pleads not guilty. Jonathan Serjant prosecutor. Continued.

The Commonwealth v. Abraham Miley. Felony. Ignoramus.

The Commonwealth v. John Young. Felony. True Bill. Defendant pleads not guilty. Jonathan Serjant prosecutor. Jury of James Anderson, John Crisman, James Patterson, Christopher Miller, Benjamin Jolley, Earnist Baker, Geddian Ritchey, Edward Rose, Henderson Murphy, George Funk, Samuel McCashlan junior, and John Wilt find guilty. On 20th June next John Young to receive 7 lashes, restore the goods of value thereof and pay a fine of like value and costs.

Page 116   April 1778
The Commonwealth v. John Young. Felony. True Bill. Continued.

The Commonwealth v. Peter Whitesides. Felony. True Bill. Continued.

The Commonwealth v. Timothy Ryan. Tipling House. True Bill. Noloprosequi entered.

The Commonwealth v. Michael Huff. Tipling House. True Bill. Noloprosequi entered.

The Commonwealth v. John Peters. Tipling House. True Bill. Noloprosequi entered.

The Commonwealth v. Jacob Hoover. Tipling House. True Bill. Continued. Noloprosequi entered.

The Commonwealth v. Patrick Quin. Tipling House. True Bill. Continued. Noloprosequi entered.

The Commonwealth v. Henry Wert. Tipling House. True Bill. Continued. Noloprosequi entered.

The Commonwealth v. Henry Didier. Tipling House. True Bill. Continued. Noloprosequi entered.

The Commonwealth v. Abraham Miley. Abraham Miley in £40 and Jonathan Cessna in £20 for defendant's appearance next term.

Page 117 April 1778
The Commonwealth v. John Young. Abraham Miley in £40 and Jonathan Cessna in £20 for Abraham Miley's appearance to prosecute.

The Commonwealth v. John Young. Abraham Miley in £40, John Cessna in £20 for appearance of Abraham Miley next court to prosecute.

The Commonwealth v. John Young. John Young in £40, John Todd in £20, and John Moore in £20 for defendant's appearance next court. [This entry repeated twice in the docket.]

The Commonwealth v. John Hatch and wife. Recognizance continued to this court. April Term on Motion defendants discharged for want of Prosecutor.

The Commonwealth v. Abraham Miley. John Young in £40, John Moore in £20, and John Todd in £20 for John Young's appearance next court.

Recognizance returnable to this term since last.

The Commonwealth v. John and James Curry. John Russel in £10, Christopher Miller in £10, John Hoover in £10, Christopher Beeman in £10, Jacob Miller in £10, James England in £10, and Henry Armstrong in £10 for appearance to prosecute in behalf of the state.

Page 118 April 1778
The Commonwealth v. John Curry. John Curry in £100 and Joseph Morrison in £50 for appearance of defendant to answer.

The Commonwealth v. James Curry. James Curry in £100 and Joseph Morrison in £50 for his appearance to prosecute.

The Commonwealth v. Richard Kimber. Richard Kimber in £150, George Elder in £100, and Felix Mellen in £100 for appearance of defendant. The Grand Jury returns Ignoramus.

The Commonwealth v. Richard Kimber. George Shoup in £40 for his appearance to give evidence.

The Commonwealth v. Hugh Skelley. Hugh Skelley in £150, George Elder in £100, Felix Mellen in £100 for appearance of defendant. The Grand Jury return Ignoramus.

The Commonwealth v. Elizabeth Keeler. Elizabeth Keeler in £100, Thomas Menzies in £50 for her appearance next court.

The Commonwealth v. George Burget. Nicholas Keck in £50 and David Ervin in £50 for Keck's appearance on behalf of the state.

Page 119 April 1778
The Commonwealth v. George Burget. George Burget in £40 and Thomas Menzies in £25 for Burgert's appearance to answer. The Grand Jury returned Ignoramus.

The Commonwealth v. John Chuck. John Chuck in £100, Gedion Richey in £100 and Abraham Miley in £100 for John Chuck's appearance next court to answer.

The Commonwealth v. John Chuck. John Kinkead in £50, Anne Kinkead in £50, and James Kinkead in £50 for Ann Kinkead and James Kinkead to testify next Court.

The Commonwealth v. John Chuck. Richard Delap in £50 and John Boyce in £50 for John Boyce's appearance next court to give evidence.

The Commonwealth v. Mary Garrison. Mary Garrison in £50 and William Barman in £50 for appearance of Mary Garrison next court to answer.

The Commonwealth v. Hans Hamilton. Hans Hamilton in £100, Thomas Menzies in £100, and Richard Delap in £100 for Hans Hamiltons appearance next court to answer.

Page 120 April 1778
The Commonwealth v. William Scofil. William Scofil in £100 and Cornelius McAulay in £50 for William Scofil being of good behavior for one year.

The Commonwealth v. Hethcock Picket, William Edwards, and Gavin Cluggage. Hethcock Picket in £1000, William Edwards in £1000, and Gavin Cluggage in £2000 for their appearance next court to answer. April Term 1778 motion discharged.

The Commonwealth v. Robison Chilcotte, Gilles Stephens, Barnet ____ [underline in place of surname in original]. Robison Chilcotte in £200,

Gilles Stephens in £200, and James Barnet in £200 for their appearance next court to answer. On motion discharged.

The Commonwealth v. John Young. Forcible Entry. True Bill. Defendant pleads not guilty. John Young in £100, Thomas Story in £100, and David Ervin in £100

Rangers appointed at April Sessions 1778: George Woods, George Funk, James Little, Frederick Ambrose, William G___.

Page 121 April 1778

The Commonwealth v. John Chuck. John Chuck in £50, Gigeon Ritchey in £25, and Abraham Miley in £25 for John Chuck being of good behavior and keeping the peace for one year.

The Commonwealth v. Hans Hamilton. Hans Hamilton in £50 and Richard Delap in £25 for Hans Hamilton's appearance next court to answer.

Tavern keepers recommended: James Anderson, John Burd, Francis Cluggage, Henry Wert, Casper Stattler, Timothy Ryan, Doctor John Peters, Henry Didier, Patrick Quin, and Robert Elliot.

Page 122 [July 1778]

Bedford 14 July 1778 before James Martin Esq. and associate justices.

Township	Constable
Bedford Town	Charles Rubey
Bedford Township	George Wisecarver
Air	Jacob Hoover
Bethel	William Pitman
Barree	William Willson
Brothers Valley	Jacob Cable
Colerain	John Wilt
Cumberland Valley	
Dublin	William Winton
Hopewell	
Frankstown	
Turkey Foot	Henry Abrahams
Quemahoning	

Grand Jury: Thomas Menzies, foreman, William Hunt, William Clark, James Henry, Samuel McCashlan senior, Jacob Rhine, Daniel Stoy, George Funk, William Compton, Timothy Ryan, Henry Wert, George Nixon, Patrick Hartford, Thomas Johnston, William McCall.

Page 123   July 1778
Recognizances and Indictments Returnable & Continued to July 1778

The Commonwealth v. Abraham Miley. Abraham Miley in £50 and Richard Delap in £50 for Miley's appearance this court to answer. Appeared.

The Commonwealth v. Abraham Miley. Tipling House. True Bill. Defendant pleads not guilty. On motion discharged on payment of costs.

The Commonwealth v. John Young. Felony. True Bill. Continued.

The Commonwealth v. Abraham Miley. Abraham Miley in £40 and Jonathan Cessna in £20 for Miley's appearance this court to answer.

The Commonwealth v. Abraham Miley. John Young in £40, John Moore in £20, and John Todd in £20 for Young's appearance this court to prosecute.

The Commonwealth v. John Young. Forcible Entry & Detainer. True Bill. Defendant pleads not guilty.

The Commonwealth v. John Young. John Young in £100, Thomas Story in £100, and David Ervin in £100 for Young's appearance at this court to answer. The defendant being called appeared not. Recognizance forfeit.

Page 124   July 1778
The Commonwealth v. Hans Hamilton. Hans Hamilton in £50 and Richard Delap in £25 for Hamilton's appearance this court to answer.

Bill of Indictment Returnable to This Court.

The Commonwealth v. Edward Higgins. Assault & Battery. True Bill. Defendant pleads not guilty. Jury of John Burd, Henry Didier, Samuel Drennan, Adley Hemphill, Christian Long, William Scofil, John Parran, William Ecles, Thomas Bradshaw, David Ervin, John Morgan and Thomas Woods find guilty. Fine five shillings.

The Commonwealth v. Barbara Elliott. Fornication. True Bill. Defendant pleads guilty.

The Commonwealth v. John Stanley. Forcible Entry & Detainer. True Bill. Defendant three times called came not. Process awarded.

The Commonwealth v. Peter Whitesides. Felony. True Bill. Defendant pleads not guilty. Jonathan Serjant Esq. prosecutor. Jury of John Burd, Henry Didier, Samuel Drennan, Patrick Quin, Christian

Long, William Scofil, John Parron, Robert Smiley, William Ecles, Thomas Bradshaw, David Ervin, and John Morgan find defendant guilty. A new trial is ordered in the above action.

Page 125 July 1778
Recognizance taken at July Court 1778.

The Commonwealth v. Justinus Hoeshill. Justinus Hoeshill in £100, Henry Wert in £50, and George Funk in £50 for Hoeshill appearing next session to answer. Upon motion Justinus Hoeshill discharged from his former recognizance.

The Commonwealth v. Peter Whitesides. Peter Whitesides in £100, Cornelius McAuley in £50, and Timothy Ryan in £50 for Whitesides appearing next court to answer.

The Commonwealth v. Hans Hamilton. Thomas Woods in £100 for Hamilton's appearing next court to answer.

Tavern keepers names that have taken out license to July 1778:
Benjamin Martin paid £3.10.0
William Black paid £3.0.0
Henry Wert paid £3.0.0

Pages 126–129 blank

Page 130 [April 1789]
At Bedford second Tuesday in April 1789 before Bernard Dougherty Esq. and associate judges.

Petition of inhabitants of Bedford Township for road from Town of Bedford to the Westmoreland County Line to Black Lick settlement and asking for road to be laid out from the Town of Bedford to or near big spring thence to the top of Allegheny Mountain at the head of Hills Branch thence to the place aforesaid. Court appoints William Clark junior, Adam Croyle, Frederick Reichart, Robert Adams, Thomas Blackburn, and Matthew Taylor to view, lay out, and make report next session.

Report of subscribers to view and lay out road from the Town of Bedford to the Westmoreland line thence to black licks settlement.

Page 131 [April 1789]
[Metes and bounds for road mention following names: George Wisegarver, James Clark]

Page 132–167 blank

Page 168   April 1771

Township	Constable	Supervisors	Overseers of the Poor
Air	Jacob Rush	John Burd	John Galloway William Lata
Armstrong	Edwd Cahil	George Leazer	William Styphel James Craig
Baree	William Shirley	Saml Anderson	James Siple John Wilson
Bedford	John Rodes	Thos Thornton	John Miller Saml Drennin
Brothers Valley	John Huff	Hen^y Rhode Senr	Richd Wells Gabriel Rhode
Colerain	John Moore	Saml Moore	Oliver Miller William Parker
Cumberland	Thos Davis	Thos Jones	Thomas Coulter Samuel Barrick
Dublin	James Foley	Ja^s Cluggage	Benj^a Elliot Charles Boyle
Fairfield	Robt Loughlin	John Campbell	Thomas Jamison Garrett Pendergrass
Hempfield	Wendal Urie	Joseph Erwin	Joshua Meek James Bird
Mount Pleasant	Willm Perry	Ja^s Fletcher	Joseph [Eine?] John Shepeard
Pitt	Willm Troop	William Elliot	Devereaux Smith Conrad Wendmiller
Ross Straver	Willm Lynd	Robert Thompson	Henry Spears Robt McConner
Spring Hill	Lewis Seltzer	Charles Burkham	John Willm Province Luke Collins
Tyrone	Saml Lyon	Saml Harrison	Ebenezer Lane John Stinson
Talleyleague	And^w Bogs	none	none

Docket 2: 1771–1801

Unlike Docket 1, Docket 2 uses folio page numbering (from page 3 onward) with a number penciled at the top right corner of facing pages.

At the formation of Bedford County, John Penn, Lieutenant Governor of the Province, issued a proclamation recorded 30 March 1771 giving John Fraser, Bernard Dougherty, and Arthur St. Clair, all of Bedford, the authority to administer oaths to all judges, justices, sheriffs, and civil and military officers for the County of Bedford.

Docket 2 begins with Penn's proclamation and records oaths of office and oaths of allegiance from the formation of Bedford County. Chronologically, the oaths in the first portion of Docket 2 are concurrent with court proceedings in Docket 1.

This work transcribes (rather than abstracting) the early oaths of office. The earliest oath swears allegiance to the ruler of Great Britain. Once independence was declared, officials used the oath on page 6R. Those taking an oath signed the docket, so the docket contains a large number of original signatures.

Docket 2 is not in the original binding and it is apparent that pages became loose and were re-bound, often out of order. The following table lists the information present in Docket 2, and, where possible, the corresponding dates. Since pages are known to be out of order, dates from the surrounding pages do not establish a date range for an undated page. The loose case papers may help establish to a date.

While Docket 2 contains session entries from 1777 through May 1801, it is not complete. Docket 3 contains overlapping entries from 1795–1801.

Docket 2	
Pages 1–32L	March 1771–1812 Oaths of Office and Allegiance
Page 32R	March 1773 Oaths of Office and Allegiance
Pages 33L–34L	Sept. 1810–1813 Oaths of Office and Allegiance
Page 34R	Cover "Quarter Sessions Docquet October 1777"
Page 35L	March 1778 oath of office
Page 35R–36L	September 1777 Magistrate Qualification and Constable Appointments
Page 36L	Continue Constable Appointments October 1777 Session begin
Page 36R	October 1777 Session

Docket 2	
Page 37L–39L	January 1778 Session
Page 39R	March 1778 Recognizances
Page 40L	March [1778?] Oaths & Qualifications
Pages 40R–41L	March 1778 Constable Court
Pages 41R–42L	April 1778 Session
Pages 42R–43R	Undated
Pages 44L–45L	April 1778 Session
Page 45R	Undated
Page 46L	Blank
Page 46R	October 1778 Session
Page 47L	Undated
Pages 47R–48R	October 1778 Session
Page 49L	Undated
Page 49R	Cover "Session Minutes April 1780"
Pages 50L–52L	April 1780 Session
Page 52R	Undated
Pages 53L–55R	July 1780 Session
Pages 56L–58L	October 1780 Session
Pages 58R–59L	Undated
Pages 59R–60L	October 1780 Session
Pages 60R–62R	January 1781 Session
Page 63L	April 1781 Session
Page 63R	Undated
Pages 64L–67L	April 1781 Session
Page 67R	Undated
Page 68L	July 1781 Session
Page 68R	Undated
Page 69L	July 1781 Session
Pages 70L–70R	Blank
Page 71L	Tavern Keepers July 1781
Page 71R	Tavern Keepers July, October 1780; July 1781
Page 72L	Tavern Keepers April [no year]
Pages 72R–73R	April 1786 Session
Pages 74L–76L	July, October 1786 Sessions
Pages 76R–77R	January 1887 Session
Page 78L	March 1787 private session
Pages 78R–81R	April 1787 Session
Page 82L	Undated
Page 82R	Election results entered July 1786

Docket 2	
Page 83L	Election results for October 1783
Page 83R	Election results for October 1785
Pages 84L–90R	July, October 1787 Sessions
Pages 91L–102L	January, April, July, October 1788 Sessions
Pages 102R–111L	January, April, July, October 1789 Sessions
Pages 111R–119R	January, April, July, October 1790 Sessions
Pages 120L–130L	January, April, July, October 1791 Sessions
Pages 130R–132L	Tavern Keepers 1788–1791
Page 132R	October 1779 Common Pleas case
Page 133L	Tavern Keepers 1792 and possibly 1793
Pages 134R–136L	October 1781 Session
Pages 136R–146R	January, April, July, October 1782 Sessions
Pages 147L–159L	January, April, July, October 1783 Sessions
Page 159R	January 1784 Session
Page 160L	Undated
Page 160R	Cover "Sessions Minutes"
Page 161L	Blank
Pages 161R–162L	Tavern Keepers 1786–October 1787
Page 162R	Tavern Keepers (fragment)
Pages 163L–163R	Blank
Page 164L	March 1786 Private Session
Pages 164L–165L	Cover (1786–1791) & reverse
Pages 165R–166L	Cover (commencing 1792) & reverse
Page 166R–167L	Fragment. Announcement for opening Court
Pages 167R–176L	January, April, August, November 1792 Sessions
Pages 176R–185R	January, April, August, November 1793 Sessions
Pages 186L–209L	January, April, August, November 1794 Sessions
Pages 290R–212L	Tavern Keepers January 1792–November 1794
Page 212R	Tavern Keepers January, April, September 1800
Pages 213L–213R	Blank
Pages 214L–214R	Cover (commencing 1790) & reverse
Page 215L	Blank
Page 215R	January 1795 Session
Pages 216L–218L	Undated
Pages 218R–220L	Loose papers from Martin Toomey murder trial
Page 220R–221L	April 1795 Session
Pages 221R–223L	Undated
Pages 223R–224R	August 1795 Session
Pages 225L–226L	Undated

Docket 2	
Pages 226R–227L	August 1795 Session
Pages 227R–228R	Undated
Pages 228R–229L	November 1795 Session
Pages 229R–232L	Undated
Pages 232R–233L	April 1796 Session
Pages 233R–234L	Undated
Page 234R	April 1796 Session
Page 235L	Undated
Page 235R	April 1796 Session
Page 236L	August 1796 Session
Pages 236R–239R	Undated
Page 240L	Possibly 1797 Session
Page 240R	Early 1797
Pages 241L–241R	Undated
Page 242L	January 1798? Crossed out Orphans' Court entry
Page 242R	August 1797 Session
Pages 243L–243R	Undated
Page 244L	November 1797 Session
Page 244R	January 1798 Session
Pages–245R	Undated
Page 246L	August 1798 Session
Pages 246R–252R	Undated
Page 253L	August 1799 Session
Pages 253R–257R	Undated
Pages 258L–258R	April 1800 Session
Pages 259L–259R	Undated
Pages 260L–260R	April 1800 Session
Pages 261L–261R	September 1800 Session
Pages 262L–262R	Undated
Pages 263L–263R	September 1800 Session
Page 264L	November 1800 Session
Page 264R	Undated
Pages 265L–265R	November 1800 Session
Pages 266L–266R	Undated
Pages 267L–268L	February, May 1801 Session
Pages 268R–269L	Cover & reverse (unknown year)
Pages 269R–271L	Tavern Keepers January, April, August, November 1795
Page 271R	Undated

DOCKET 2: 1771–1801

Docket 2	
Page 272L	Undated, refers to 1795 and 1796 cases
Page 272R	August 1797 Session
Page 273L	Undated, refers to 1796 case
Page 273R	February 1799 Session
Page 274L	May 1801 Session

Page 1 [Transcribed]
The Honorable John Penn Esquire Lieutenant Governor and Commander in Chief of the province of Pennsylvania and Counties of New Castle Kent and Sussex on Delaware TO [John] Fraser Bernard Dougherty and Arthur St Clair of the County of Bedford Esquires. Greeting. Reposing special Trust and Confidence in your Loyalty and Integrity I have authorized impowered and by these presents do authorize and impower the said John Fraser Bernard Dougherty and Arthur St Clair [or?] either of you to administer to all Judges Sheriffs and all other Officers civil and Military and all other Persons whatsoever within the County of Bedford as [well?] the Oath of Office also the Oaths of Allegiance and _____ and other the usual Declarations and Tests and Qualifications required by Law to be taken by the said several officers Civil and Military to qualify them every or any of them for the entering upon and executing their several respective offices to which they are or shall be commissioned or any other Occasion may make it requisite and proper to tender or administer the said several Oaths Tests and Qualifications or any of them to such officers and other persons until my Pleasure shall be further known therein. GIVEN under my hand and seal at Philadelphia the twelfth day of March in the Year of our Lord one thousand seven hundred seventy one.

John Penn

Recorded 30 March 1771

Page 2
[Oath of Allegiance at county formation.[6] Transcribed.]
I _____ do sincerely promise and swear that I will be faithful and bear true Allegiance to his Majesty King George the Third so help me God.
I ____ do swear that I do from my heart abhor detest and abjure as

---

[6] The Oath reflects the English political climate of the time and therefore repudiates Roman Catholic religious beliefs. References to James II and the "Person pretended to be the Prince of Wales" rule out loyalty to James II, the last Catholic King, and his supposed son, born late to James II's second wife, Mary of Modena. In 1688 William of Orange deposed James II. By 1771 the House of Hanover occupied the British throne. The oath contains an allegiance to the heirs of Princess Sophia of the House of Hanover.

impious and heretical that damnable Doctrine or Position that Princes excommunicated and deprived by the Pope or any other authority of the See of Rome may be deposed or murdered by their subjects or any other whomsoever and I also declare that no foreign Prince Person or Prelate State or Potentate hath or ought to have any Jurisdiction Power Superiority Preeminence or Authority Ecclesiastical or Spiritual within this Realm So help me God.

I ___ declare that I believe there is not any transubstantiation of the Sacrament of the Lords Supper or in the elements of Bread and Wine at or after the Consumption thereof by any Person or Persons whatsoever.

I ___ do truly and sincerely acknowledge posses testify and declare in my Conscience before God and the World that our Sovereign Lord King George the Third is lawful and rightful King of this Realm and other his Majestys Dominions ___ nts belonging and I do solemnly and sincerely declare that I do believe in my Conscience that not any of the Descendants of the Person pretended to be the Prince of Wales during the life of the Late King James the Second and since ___ pretending to be and took upon himself the title and ___ of King of England by the name of James the Third and of Scotland by the name of James the Eighth of the title king of Great Britain hath and [right?] ___ ___soever to the Crown of this Realm or any other ___ thereunto belonging ___ allegiance obedience ___ [lower portion of page damaged].

Page 3L

___ and true Allegiance to his Majesty King George the third and will defend to the utmost of my power against all traitorous conspiracies and attempts whatsoever which shall be made against his Person Crown and Dignity and I will do my endeavor to disclose and make known to his Majesty and his Successors all treason and traitorous Conspiracies which I shall know to be against him or any of them and I do faithfully promise to the utmost of my power to support maintain and defend the succession of the Crown against the Descendants of said James and against all other Persons whatsoever which succession (by an Act [entitled] an Act for the further Limitation of the Crown and better securing the Rights and Liberties of the Subjects) is and stands ___ to the Princess Sophia late Electoress and Duchess Dowager of Hanover and the heirs of her Body being [Protestant] and all these things do plainly and sincerely acknowledge and swear according to the express words by one spoken and according to the plain and common sense and understanding of the same words without any equivocation secret reservation or mental evasion whatsoever and I do make this Recognition Acknowledgement Abjuration Renunciation and promise heartily willingly and truly upon the true faith of ___ Christian. So help me God.

         Bernard Dougherty [sig.]
         Arthur St Clair [sig.]

Page 3R

02 April 1771 Robert Hanna subscribed to oath.

16 April 1771 George Wilson subscribed to oath.

___ April 1771 George Wood subscribed to oath.

17 April 1771 John Fraser subscribed to oath.

[blank date] William Lochery subscribed to oath.

[blank date] William Crawford subscribed to oath.

___ ____ 1771 Dorsey Penecost subscribed to oath.

16 April 1771 Robert Cluggage subscribed to oath.

Page 4L

02 Sep 1771 Alexander McKee subscribed to oath.

15 Oct 1771 Thomas Gist subscribed to oath.

Page 4R

Justice of the Peace oaths administered by Thomas Smith:

> 20 March 1773 Justice of the Peace oath administered to John Fraser and George Woods,
>
> 23 March 1773 same oath administered to Thomas Coulter.
>
> 23 March 1773 same oath administered to Elias Stilwell.
>
> 27 March 1773 same oath administered to Bernard Dougherty.
>
> 03 March 1773 same oath administered to William Proctor.

Page 5L

> 13 April 1773 same oath administered to Robert Clugage and William McConnell.
>
> 15 April 1773 same oath administered to John Piper.
>
> 13 July 1773 same oath administered to Richard Hougland.

Page 5R

03 May 1774 Justice of the Peace oaths administered by Thomas Smith

to George Woods, William Proctor, Thomas Coulter, Samuel Davidson, Bernard Dougherty, Arthur St. Clair.

03 May 1774 Justice of the Peace oath administered by Bernard Dougherty to Thomas Smith.

12 and 13 May 1774 Justice of the Peace oaths administered by Thomas Smith to Robert Cluggage, Elias Stillwell, Henry Stoy and John Piper.

Page 6L
12 September 1774 Justice of the Peace oath administered by Bernard Dougherty to Richard Hougland.

Page 6R
[Here appears the oath used after American independence. This oath is transcribed, not abstracted.]

> I _____ do swear that I renounce and refuse all allegiance to George the Third, King of Great Britain, his heirs and successors and that I will be faithful and bear true Allegiance to the Common Wealth of Pennsylvania as a free and independent State; and that I will not at any time do, or cause to be done, any matter or thing that will be prejudicial or injurious to the freedom and independence thereof as declared by Congress; and also that I will discover and make known to some Justice of the Peace of the said State al [sic] treasonous or traitorous conspiracies, which I now know or hereafter shall know, to be formed against this or any other of the United States of America. So help me God.

> I _____ do swear that I will faithfully execute the office of a Justice of the Peace for the County of Bedford, and will do equal right and Justice to all Men to the best of my Judgment and abilities according to law. So help me God.

September 1777. Robert Galbreath and James Martin take oath as Justices of the Peace before George Bryan Esq.

Page 7L
11 September 1777 Thomas Paxton takes oath as Justice of the peace before Robert Galbraith.

27 September 1777 William Parker, John Mallott, and Martin Longstretch take oath as Justices of the Peace before Robert Galbraith.

Page 7R
[No day] September 1777 Thomas Urie takes Oath of Allegiance and oath of office for the same before Robert Galbraith.

06 January 1778 John Cessna takes Oath of Allegiance and oath of office for the same before Robert Galbreath.

Page 8L
13 January 1778 Cornelius McAulay takes Oath of Allegiance and oath of office for the same before Robert Galbreath.

10 March 1778 Francis Moore takes Oath of Allegiance and oath of office for the same before Robert Galbreath.

Page 8R
12 April 1778 David Jones and Thomas Anderson take Oath of Allegiance and oath of office for the same before Robert Galbreath.

Page 9L
27 November 1777 Robert Scott takes Oath of Allegiance and oath of office as Justice of the Peace before James Martin.

14 April 1778 William Tyshee takes Oath of Allegiance and oath of office as Justice of the Peace before Robert Galbreath.

Page 9R
20 March 1778 Henry Rhoads and James Wells take Oath of Allegiance and oath of office as Justice of the Peace.

Page 10L [also penciled 22]
10 September 1778 Bernard Dougherty and James Martin take Oath of Allegiance and oath of office as two justices to inquire on the Oath of honest and lawful Men &c of a certain Murder and Treason before Robert Galbreath.

28 September 1778 Archibald McClean takes the same before Robert Galbreath.

Page 10R
30 November 1778 David Espy takes oath of office as Justice before Bernard Dougherty.

19 December 1778 Samuel Davidson takes oath of office as Justice of the Peace before David Espy.

22 December 1778 David Espy takes oath of office as Commissioner before Samuel Davidson.

Page 11L
27 November 1778 Thomas Wilson takes oath of office as Justice of the Peace before David Espy.

23 December 1778 William Todd takes oath of office as Justice of the Peace before David Espy.

09 January 1779 Abraham Cable takes oath of office as Commissioner before David Espy.

Page 11R
13 January 1779 James Coyle and James Carmichael take oath of office as Justice of the Peace before David Espy.

John Hains takes oath of office as Justice of the Peace before Bernard Dougherty.

Page 12L
21 January 1779 Cornelius McAullay takes oath of office as Coroner before David Espy.

12 February 1779 Matthew Dean takes oath of office as Justice of the Peace before David Espy.

14 April 1779 Abraham Cable takes oath of office as Justice of Bedford County before David Espy.

Page 12R
06 November 1779 Moses Reed takes oath of office as Justice of the Peace before David Espy.

01 September 1780 Jacob Saylor takes oath of office as Justice of the Peace before David Espy.

19 December 1780 John Wilt, gentleman, takes oath of office as Coroner before David Espy.

26 December 1780 George Ashman takes oath of office as Lieutenant of the County of Bedford before David Espy.

Page 13L
28 December 1780 Bernard Dougherty takes oath of office as President of the Quarter Sessions as Justice of the Peace before David Espy.

01 January 1781 John Cessna takes oath of office as Sheriff before David Espy.

Same day. Thomas Hay takes oath of office as under Sheriff before David Espy.

02 January 1781 Andrew Todd takes oath of office as Justice of the Peace before David Espy.

19 February 1781 Gideon Richey takes oath of office as Justice of the Peace before David Espy.

28 April 1781 John Cannon takes oath of office as Justice of the Peace before David Espy.

Page 13R
30 November 1781 George Funk takes oath of office as Coroner before David Espy.

17 April 1782 John Piper and James Martin take oath of office for special commission for trial of Peter Shaver charged with papering counterfeit Continental Money, and George M___ charged with accidentally shooting Frederick Mes__ly, before David Espy.

29 October 1782 Abraham Miley takes oath of office as Sheriff before David Espy.

29 October 1782 John Cessna takes oath of office as Justice of the Peace before David Espy.

Page 14L
02 November 1782 Thomas Hay takes oath of office as under Sheriff before David Espy.

21 November 1782 John Wilt takes oath of office as Coroner before David Espy.

18 December 1782 Robert Clugage takes oath of office as Justice of the Peace before Bernard Dougherty.

20 December 1782 William Proctor takes oath of office as Justice of the Peace before Bernard Dougherty.

06 January 1782 Bernard Dougherty takes oath of office as Justice of the Peace before David Espy.

Page 14R
04 November 1783 William Ward takes oath of office as under Sheriff before Bernard Dougherty.

06 February 1784 Hugh Barclay takes oath of office as Justice of the Peace before Bernard Dougherty.

16 June 1784 Abraham Miley takes oath of office as Sheriff before Bernard Dougherty.

16 June 1784 Cornelius McAulay takes oath of office as Coroner before Bernard Dougherty.

23 November 1784 Hugh Davison takes oath of office as Justice before David Espy.

Page 15L
29 November 1784 Abraham Miley takes oath of office as Sheriff before David Espy.

29 November 1784 Cornelius McAulay takes oath of office as Coroner before David Espy.

04 December 1784 George Woods takes oath of office as Lieutenant of Bedford County before David Espy.

13 December 1784 John Piper takes oath of office as Justice of Common Pleas before David Espy.

17 March 1785 James Martin takes oath of office as Justice of the Peace before David Espy.

13 August 1785 David Jones takes oath of office as Justice of the Peace before David Espy.

Page 15R
19 December 1785 Benjamin Elliot takes oath of office as High Sheriff before David Espy.

19 December 1785 Samuel Davidson takes oath of office as Coroner before David Espy.

20 December 1785 William Wood takes oath of office as under Sheriff and Gaoler before David Espy.

09 January 1786 Thomas Coulter takes oath of office as Justice of the Peace before David Espy.

16 May 1786 John Tait takes oath of office as under Sheriff before David Espy.

DOCKET 2: 1771–1801 83

Page 16L
19 June 1786 James Wills takes oath of office as Justice of the Peace before David Espy.

12 July 1786 Abraham Cable takes oath of office as Justice of the Peace before David Espy.

20 July 1786 John Little takes oath of office as Justice of the Peace before David Espy.

25 July 1786 Thomas Wilson takes oath of office as Justice of the Peace before David Espy.

31 July 1786 David Espy takes oath of office as Justice of the Peace and Justice of Common Pleas before Bernard Dougherty.

Page 16R
17 October 1786 William Patterson takes oath of office as Justice of the Peace before David Espy.

22 January 1787 John Coyle takes oath of office as under Sheriff before David Espy.

29 January 1787 Samuel Davidson takes oath of office as Coroner.

09 April 1787 Benjamin Elliot takes oath of office as Sheriff before David Espy.

22 June 1787 James Coyle takes oath of office as Justice of the Peace before David Espy.

Page 17L
07 September 1787 Samuel Crossan junior takes oath of office as Collector of Excise before David Espy.

22 October 1787 Arthur McGaughy takes oath of office as Sheriff before David Espy.

23 October 1787 Anthony Nagel takes oath of office as Coroner before David Espy.

24 October 1787 Bithul Covalt takes oath of office as Justice of the Peace before David Espy.

24 October 1787 Thomas McGaughey takes oath of office as under Sheriff before David Espy.

28 May 1788 Jacob Hartzel takes oath of office as Justice of the Peace and Common Pleas before David Espy.

Page 17R
05 June 1788 Michael Dewalt takes oath of office as Justice of the Peace and Common Pleas before David Espy.

13 December 1788 Thomas McGaughey takes oath of office as Coroner before David Espy.

15 December 1788 Arthur McGaughey takes oath of office as Sheriff before David Espy.

01 April 1789 Jacob Wink takes oath of office as Justice of the Peace and Common Pleas before David Espy.

01 June 1789 Thomas Buck takes oath of office as Justice of the Peace and Common Pleas before David Espy.

11 August 1789 Thomas Crossan takes oath of office as Justice of the County Court of Common Pleas before David Espy.

Page 18L
23 November 1789 Thomas Vickroy takes oath of office as Coroner before David Espy.

13 January 1790 Benjamin Burd takes oath of office as Justice of the Peace and Common Pleas before David Espy.

13 January 1790 Cornelius Devore takes oath of office as Justice of the Peace and Common Pleas before David Espy.

19 May 1790 George Woods takes oath of office as Justice of the Peace and President of the County Court of Common Pleas of the Court of General Quarter Sessions of the Peace and Jail Delivery and of the Orphans Court before David Espy.

18 September 1790 William Proctor takes oath of office as Justice of the Peace and Common Pleas before David Espy.

18 September 1790 John Cessna one of the Justices of the Peace and Common Pleas before David Espy.

Page 18R
02 November 1790 Benjamin Martin takes oath of office as Collector of Excise before David Espy.

29 November 1790 Thomas McGaughey takes oath of office as Sheriff before David Espy.

Oaths Under the New Constitution

I _____ do solemnly swear or affirm as the case may be that I will support the constitution of the United States. So help me God.

You do swear that you will support the Constitution of the Commonwealth of Pennsylvania, and perform the duties of the office of _____ in and for the County of Bedford, with fidelity. (So help you God).

Thomas Mifflin Governor of the Commonwealth of Pennsylvania confirms David Espy, George Woods, and James Martin all of the County of Bedford to administer oaths and commissions.

Page 19L
01 September 1791 George Woods Esq. takes oath as First associate Judge of the Court of Common Pleas & Court of Oyer & Terminer & General Gaol Delivery — also one of the Judges of Orphans Court of the Court of Quarter Sessions of the Register's Court and a Justice of the Peace before James Martin.

01 September 1791 James Martin takes oath as second associate Judge of the Court of Common Pleas & Court of Oyer & Terminer & General Gaol Delivery — also one of the Judges of Orphans Court of the Court of Quarter Sessions of the Register's Court and a Justice of the Peace before George Woods.

05 September 1791 David Espy takes oath as Prothonotary of the Court of Common Pleas Clerk of the Court of Quarter Sessions Clerk of the Orphans Court Register for Wills before George Woods.

Page 19R
19 September 1791 John Scott takes oath as Justice of the Peace for Town of Bedford before David Espy.

21 September 1791 William Ward takes oath as Justice of the Peace for Town of Bedford before David Espy.

23 September 1791 Thomas Coulter takes oath as Justice of the Peace for Township of Cumberland Valley before David Espy.

24 September 1791 Adam Miller takes oath as Justice of the Peace for Township of Brothers Valley before David Espy.

24 September 1791 Andrew Mann takes oath as Justice of the Peace for Township of Bethel before David Espy.

26 September 1791 William Proctor takes oath as Justice of the Peace for Township of Bedford before David Espy.

28 September 1791 John Friend takes oath as Justice of the Peace for Colerain Township before David Espy.

Page 20L
29 September 1791 Jacob Hartzel takes oath as Justice of the Peace for Turkeyfoot Township before David Espy.

01 October 1791 Cornelius Devore takes oath as Justice of the Peace for Londonderry Township before David Espy.

20 September 1791 Hugh Barclay takes oath as Judge of Court of Common Pleas, Judge of the Court of Oyer & Terminer, Judge of the Orphans Court, Justice of the Court of Quarter Sessions, and Judge of the Registers Court before David Espy.

04 October 1791 John Piper takes oath as Justice of the Peace for Hopewell Township before David Espy.

11 October 1791 John Hopkins takes oath as Judge of Common Pleas, Judge of the Court of Oyer and Terminer, Judge of Orphans Court, Judge of Quarter Sessions, Justice of the Registers Court, and Justice of the Peace before David Espy.

Page 20R
13 October 1791 Benjamin Burd takes oath as Justice of the Peace for Dublin Township before David Espy.

17 October 1791 John Moore takes oath as Justice of the Peace for Providence Township before David Espy.

10 October 1791 James Wells takes oath as Justice of the Peace for Quamahoning Township before David Espy.

12 October 1791 William Patterson takes oath as Justice of the Peace for Quamahoning Township before David Espy.

13 October 1791 Ebenezer Griffith takes oath as Justice of the Peace for Elk Lick Township before David Espy.

13 October 1791 Philip King takes oath as Justice of the Peace for Elk Milford Township before David Espy.

14 October 1791 Jacob Wink takes oath as Justice of the Peace for Elk Belfast Township before David Espy.

Page 21L
03 March 1792 Jacob Butterbaugh takes oath as Justice of the Peace for Woodberry Township before David Espy.

10 May 1792 David Espy takes oath as Clerk of Court of Oyer & Terminer before George Woods.

12 September 1792 Benjamin Burd takes oath as Lieutenant of the County of Bedford before David Espy.

29 January 1793 James Heydon takes oath as Coroner before David Espy.

06 June 1793 James Wells takes oath as Judge of Court of Common Pleas before David Espy.

Page 21R
04 November 1793 Jacob Bonnett takes oath as Sheriff before David Espy.

19 November 1793 John Lamp__ takes oath as Justice of the Peace for Stoney Creek Township before David Espy.

01 January 1794 David Espy takes oath as Justice of the Peace for the Town of Bedford George Woods.

20 January 1794 George Smith takes oath as under Sheriff and Gaoler before David Espy.

30 April 1794 Martin Reily takes oath as Justice of the Peace for the Town of Bedford before David Espy.

Page 22L
01 May 1794 John Ritchie takes oath as Justice of the Peace for Providence Township before David Espy.

06 May 1794 Daniel Stoy takes oath as Justice of the Peace for Quamahoning Township before David Espy.

30 May 1794 Andrew Dixon takes oath as Justice of the Peace for Woodberry Township before David Espy.

29 April 1795 John Rankin takes oath as Justice of the Peace for Air Township before David Espy.

Page 22R
13 June 1795 Thomas Mifflin, Governor, authorizes Hugh Barclay and George Woods junior to administer commissions.

25 June 1795 George Woods junior takes oath as Prothonotary, Clerk of Quarter Sessions, Clerk of Orphans Court, Register for Wills, Recorder of Deeds, and Clerk of Court of Oyer and Terminer before Hugh Barclay.

Page 23L
05 November 1795 John Anderson takes oath of Prothonotary, Clerk of Quarter Sessions, Clerk of Orphans Court, Register for Wills, Recorder of Deeds, and Clerk of Oyer & Terminer before Hugh Barclay.

26 January 1796 John Piper takes oath as Judge of Common Pleas before John Anderson.

Page 23R
03 February 1796 John Scott takes oath as Justice of the Peace for the town of Bedford before John Anderson.

25 October 1796 Isaac Bonnett takes oath as Sheriff before John Anderson.

29 December 1796 William Clark takes oath as Justice of the Peace for St. Clair Township before John Anderson.

Page 24L
04 October 1797 John Davis takes oath as Justice of the Peace for Air Township before John Anderson.

23 April 1798 John Dickey takes oath as Judge for the Court of Common Pleas before John Anderson.

10 May 1798 Henry Sicles takes oath as under Sheriff before John Anderson.

Page 24R
19 May 1798 Amos Evans takes oath as Justice of the Peace for Hopewell Township before John Anderson.

03 November 1798 Henry Wertz takes oath as Sheriff before John Anderson.

25 February 1799 John Scott takes oath as Judge for the Court of Common Pleas before John Anderson.

Page 25L
24 April 1799 Jacob Hart takes oath as Justice of the Peace for Belfast Township before John Anderson.

DOCKET 2: 1771–1801 89

24 April 1799 Henry Markley takes oath as Justice of the Peace for Belfast Township before John Anderson.

24 May 1800 Alexander Ogle takes oath as Brigade Inspector for the Second Brigade composed of the militia of the Counties of Bedford, Fayette, & Somerset before Jacob Bonnett.

Page 25R
06 June 1800 John Piper takes oath as the Major General of the Division comprised of the Counties of Bedford, Fayette & Somerset militia before Jacob Bonnett.

26 June 1800 Abraham Martin takes oath as Justice of the Peace for Providence Township before Jacob Bonnett.

26 June 1800 John Cessna takes oath as Justice of the Peace for Cumberland Valley Township before Jacob Bonnett.

Page 26L
06 July 1800 George Hardinger takes oath as Justice of the Peace for Cumberland Valley Township before Jacob Bonnett.

05 February 1801 Cornelius Devore takes oath as Justice of the Peace for Londonderry Township before Jacob Bonnett.

29 January 1801 Abendnego Stephens takes oath as Justice of the Peace for Air Township before Jacob Bonnett.

Page 26R
05 May 1801 John Stillwell takes oath as Justice of the Peace for Bethel Township before Jacob Bonnett.

29 April 1801 David Reiley takes oath as High Sheriff of Bedford County before Jacob Bonnett.

23 January 1802 Jacob Bonnett takes oath as Justice of the Peace for the Town of Bedford before Martin Reiley.

31 January 1803 Christopher Reiley takes oath as Justice of the Peace for the Borough of Bedford before Jacob Bonnett.

Page 27L
05 February 1803 John Kinton takes oath as Justice of the Peace for the Bedford Township before Jacob Bonnett.

09 February 1803 Thomas Robeson takes oath as Justice of the Peace for Dublin Township before Jacob Bonnett.

17 February 1803 Francis Welch takes oath as Justice of the Peace for Bethel Township before Jacob Bonnett.

27 January 1804 John May takes oath as Justice of the Peace for the District numbered 4 in the County of Bedford before Jacob Bonnett.

Page 27R
15 August 1804 Isaac Fickes takes oath as Justice of the Peace for the thirteenth District in the County of Bedford before Jacob Bonnett.

19 February 1805 Thomas Logan takes oath as Justice of the Peace for the ninth District in the County of Bedford before Jacob Bonnett.

22 April 1805 Robert Kenny takes oath as Justice of the Peace for the District N° [blank space for district number] in the County of Bedford before Jacob Bonnett.

29 April 1805 Thomas Fanagan takes oath as Justice of the Peace for the District N° 11 in the County of Bedford before Jacob Bonnett.

Page 28L
23 November 1805 Jacob Fletcher takes oath as Coroner of the County of Bedford before Jacob Bonnett.

06 February 1806 Joshua Johnson takes oath as Justice of the Peace for the District N° 6 in the County of Bedford before Jacob Bonnett.

13 February 1806 Amos Dicken takes oath as Justice of the Peace for the District N° f___ in the County of Bedford before Jacob Bonnett.

19 January 1807 George D. Foulke takes oath as Justice of the Peace for the District numbered one in the County of Bedford before Jacob Bonnett.

03 March 1807 James Anderson takes oath as Justice of the Peace for the District numbered one in the County of Bedford before Jacob Bonnett.

Page 28R
11 April 1807 William Davis takes oath as Justice of the Peace for the District N° 12 in the County of Bedford before Jacob Bonnett.

09 May 1807 Joshua Peirson takes oath as Justice of the Peace for the District N° 1 in the County of Bedford before Jacob Bonnett.

23 July 1807 John Hunter takes oath as Justice of the Peace for the District N° 9 in the County of Bedford before Jacob Bonnett.

14 September 1807 Joseph Williams takes oath as Justice of the Peace for the District N° 11 in Hopewell Township in the County of Bedford before Jacob Bonnett.

Page 29L
02 November 1807 John Fletcher takes oath as High Sheriff of the County of Bedford before Jacob Bonnett.

15 April 1808 Jacob Adams takes oath as Justice of the Peace for the District numbered five in the County of Bedford before Jacob Bonnett.

20 August 1808 Richard Baker takes oath as Justice of the Peace for the District numbered two in the County of Bedford before Jacob Bonnett.

23 March 1809 William Crisman takes oath as Justice of the Peace for the District N° [blank space for district number] in the County of Bedford before Jacob Bonnett.

04 May 1809 Tobias Hammer takes oath as Justice of the Peace for the District N° [blank space for district number] including the Township of St. Clair in the County of Bedford before Jacob Bonnett.

Page 29R
28 February 1809 David Mann takes oath as Prothonotary, Clerk of Quarter Sessions, Clerk of Oyer & Terminer, Register of Wills, Clerk of Orphans Court, and Recorder or Deeds before James Martin.

17 May 1809 Daniel Daniels takes oath as Justice of the Peace for the District N° [blank space for district number] including the Township of Belfast in the County of Bedford before David Mann.

Page 30L
07 August 1809 William Cessna takes oath as Justice of the Peace for the District N° [blank space for district number] including the Borough and Township of Bedford in the County of Bedford before David Mann.

30 August 18[09] Richard Silver takes oath as Justice of the Peace for the District N° 11 including Township of Hopewell in the County of Bedford before David Mann.

28 February 1810 Richard Shirley takes oath as Justice of the Peace for the District N° 13 including the Township of Greenfield in the County of Bedford before David Mann.

03 March 1810 Andrew Mann takes oath as Justice of the Peace for the District N° 7 including the Township of Bethel in the County of Bedford before David Mann.

Page 30R
21 March 1810 David Bonnett takes oath as Justice of the Peace for the District N° [blank space for district number] including the Township of Londonderry in the County of Bedford before David Mann.

26 March 1810 George Lingenfelter takes oath as Justice of the Peace for the District N° 13 including the Township of Greenfield in the County of Bedford before David Mann.

07 June 1810 Christian Snider takes oath as Justice of the Peace for the District N° 12 including the Township of Woodberry in the County of Bedford before David Mann.

08 March 1810 Thomas Hunt takes oath as Justice of the Peace for the District N° 1 including the Borough and Township of Bedford in the County of Bedford before David Mann.

09 March 1810 George Henry takes oath as Justice of the Peace for the District N° 1 including the Borough and Township of Bedford in the County of Bedford before David Mann.

Pages 31L and 31R are a copy of an early oath used prior to American independence. This oath is quite similar to, but not identical to, the oath found on page 2 of the docket.

Page 32L
11 April 1810 John Piper takes oath as Justice of the Peace for the District N° eleven including Township of Hopewell in the County of Bedford before David Mann.

08 November 1810 Joseph S. Morrison takes oath as Sheriff of Bedford County before David Mann.

03 June 18__ John Alexander takes oath as Justice of the Peace for the District N° eleven including Township of Hopewell in the County of Bedford before David Mann.

__ April 1812 William Alexander takes oath as Justice of the Peace for the District numbered nine including Township of Air in the County of Bedford before David Mann.

Page 32R [Out of chronological order.]
25 March 1773 Abraham Miley takes oath as Justice of the Peace before Thomas Smith.

13 April 1773 Abraham Cable takes oath as Justice of the Peace before Thomas Smith.

DOCKET 2: 1771–1801 93

Page 33L
12 September 1810 Anthony Shoemaker takes oath as Justice of the Peace for the District numbered nine including Township of Air in the County of Bedford before D. Mann.

21 November 1810 Nathan Wright takes oath as Justice of the Peace for the District numbered three including Cumberland Valley Township in the County of Bedford before D. Mann.

03 December 1810 Henry Hipple takes oath as Justice of the Peace for the District numbered twelve including Woodberry Township in the County of Bedford before D. Mann.

09 March 18__ John Noble takes oath as Justice of the Peace for the District numbered [blank] in Belfast Township before D. Mann.

Page 33R
27 March 1811 Christopher Waggoner takes oath as Justice of the Peace for the District numbered ten before D. Mann.

29 December 1812 Peter Schell takes oath as Justice of the Peace for the District numbered thirteen including Napier Township in the County of Bedford before D. Mann.

02 August 1813 John Davis takes oath as Justice of the Peace for the District numbered ten including Dublin Township in the County of Bedford before D. Mann.

Page 34L
17 November 1813 Thomas Moore takes oath as Sheriff before David Mann.

Page 34R
Cover reading "Quarter Sessions Docquet October 1777."

Page 35L [Much bleed through]
21 March 1778 Henry Roads and James Wells qualified as Magistrates.

Page 35R
September 1777 Robert Galbraith and James Martin qualified as magistrates for Bedford County.

26 September 1777 William Paxton qualified as Magistrate.

27 September 1777 William Parker, John Malott, and Martin Longstrolik qualified as Magistrates.

27 September 1777 at Court of Petty Sessions held at house of Henry Wertz in the Township of Bedford. Present: James Martin, William Parker, John Malott, and Martin Longstreck as Justices.

Persons appointed Constable for their respective Townships

Person	Township	Person	Township
George Milligan	Bedford Town	John Todd	Bed___
David E___			

[bottom of page torn & tattered additional line(s) not readable]

Page 36L

Person	Township
Daniel McConnel	Air
Thomas Williams	Bethel
John Walker Thomas Anderson in his room	Dublin
Adam Wright	Quamahoning
Henry Abrahams	Turkey Foot
William Dyer	Brothers Valley
Joseph Cellar	Frankstown
Joshua Davis Felix Miller in his room	Hopewell
William Riddle	Barree
Samuel Moore	Colerain
Daniel McMichael in room of S[amuel] Paxton	Cumberland Valley

At a Court of Quarter Sessions in the Town of Bedford 04 October 1777 before James Martin, William Paxton, and John Malott.

Page 36R [October 1777]

James Martin prosecutor v. John Bilyew.
John Bilyew held in £100, Thomas Buck of Colerain Township held in £100, Thomas Williams of Bethel Township held in £100, taken 05 October 1777 before Robert Galbraith.

Thomas Woods prosecutor v. Peter Whitesides.
Peter Whitesides held in £40, Cornelius McAuley in £20, Samuel McQuity in £20 taken 15 October 1777 before Robert Galbraith. 17 January 1778 forfeited.

Page 37L   January 1778
John Wilt bound in £100, Abraham Miley bound in £50, Robert Bradshaw bound in £50 for John Wilt keeping the peace and to appear January 1779.

The Commonwealth v. Abraham Miley.
Abraham Miley bound in £50 and Robert Dunlap bound in £25 conditioned to answer.

The Commonwealth v. John Bilyew.
Defendant in £100 and Thomas Story in £100 for defendant appearing next court to answer.

Page 37R   January 1778
1. The Commonwealth v. Abraham Miley. Tipling House. True Bill.

2. Pennsylvania v. Abraham Miley. Felony. Ignoramus.

3. Pennsylvania v. John Young. Felony. True Bill.

4. Pennsylvania v. John Young. Felony. True Bill.

Page 38L
The Commonwealth v. Abraham Miley.
Defendant in £40 and Jonathan Cessna in £20 conditioned for his appearance next court to answer.

The Commonwealth v. John Young.
Abraham Miley in £40 and Jonathan Cessna in £20 for Miley to appear to prosecute.

The Commonwealth v. John Young.
Abraham Miley in 40 and Jonathan Cessna in £20 for Miley to appear and prosecute.

The Commonwealth v. John Young.
Defendant in £40, John Tod in £20, and John Moore in £20 for defendant's appearance next court.

The same v. the same. The same for the same.

The Commonwealth v. Abraham Miley.
John Young in £40, John Moore in £20, and John Tod in £20 for John Young to appear next court and prosecute.

Page 38R   January 1778
[5.] The Commonwealth v. Peter Whitesides. Felony. True Bill.

[6.] Pennsylvania v. Timothy Ryan. Tipling House. True Bill.

[7.] Pennsylvania v. Michael Huff. Tipling House. True Bill.

8. Pennsylvania v. John Peters. Tipling House. True Bill.

9. Pennsylvania v. Jacob Hoover. Tipling House. True Bill.

10. Pennsylvania v. Patrick Quin. Tipling House. True Bill.

Page 39L January 1778
11. Pennsylvania v. Henry Wert. Tipling House. True Bill

12. Pennsylvania v. Henry Didier. Tipling House. True Bill

13. Pennsylvania v. Jonathan Cessna, Stephen Cessna, John Hatch and Elisabeth his wife. Recognizance for accessory to escape of Richard Anderson out of Gaol. Grand Jury find Jonathan Cessna and Stephen Cessna not guilty.

14. Pennsylvania v. William Bromfield. Recognizance for being an accessory to Horse Stealing. The Grand Jury find him not guilty.

15. Pennsylvania v. George Shingledecker. Recognizance for Larceny. The parties agreed before the court.

[16.] Pennsylvania v. John Hatch. Samuel McCashlin bound in £50 for appearance of Hatch. [date torn off] 1778 forfeit until next term.

Page 39R [March 1778]
March ye 10th 1778.

Pennsylvania v. Henry Didier. Defendant in £40, John Todd Bail in £40 for appearance of Henry Didier next court the second Tuesday in April.

Pennsylvania v. Martha Ramsay. Defendant in £40 and James Fletcher in £40 for Martha Ramsay being of good behavior and keeping the peace until next term.

Pennsylvania v. Timothy Ryan. Defendant in £40 and Abraham Miley in £40 conditioned for Ryan appearing next term.

Page 40L
Colonel John Piper has taken oath as Lieutenant of Bedford County before Willm Parker.

Colonel Robt Moore has taken oath as Judge of the Appeal before Willm Parker.

21 March Henry Roads qualified as Magistrate.

21 March James Wills qualified as Magistrate.

~~Pennsylvania v. Robert Eliott. Tipling House. True Bill.~~

~~Thomas Menzies v. George Smith. Conditioned for George Smith appearance to answer 03 April 1776. George Smith in £40 and Samuel Moore in £40.~~

Page 40R [March 1778]
At a Constable Court held at Bedford 25 March 1778 before James Martin, John Mellott, William Parker.

Township	Constable	Overseer Poor	Supervisor Highways
Bedford Town	George Wisecarver	James Dunlop George Cells	Wm Proctor
Air	————	John Wilson Enoch Williams	Daniel McCardie
Colerain	John Wills	Bernard Dougherty Abraham Miley	[cut off]

Page 41L

Township	Constable	Overseer Poor	Supervisor Highways
Bethel	Wm Pittman	Samuel Truax Peter Smith	Benjn Truax Jacob [Mooney?]
Barree	Wm Wilson	Samuel Anderson Thomas Johnson	Michael Cryder James Little
Brothers Valley	Jacob Cable	Fred^k Ambrose Philip Wagerlin	Jacob Wingerd Jacob Glasner

Page 41R [April 1778]
At Bedford 13 April 1778

Township	Constable
Bedford Town	Jacob Saylor excused, Charles Rubey
Air	Jacob Hoover
Bethel	Wm Pittman
Barree	William Wilson
Brothers Valley	Jacob Cable
Colerain	John Wilt
Dublin	William Winton
Turkey Foot	Henry Abrahams

Page 42L   April 1778

Grand Jury:
    John Tod, foreman   Charles Rubey
    Samuel Tod   Daniel McConnell
    James Dunlap   George Milligan
    Thomas Blair   Samuel Skinner
    John Morgan   Shadwick Casteel
    William Elliott   William Scovil
    Jacob Sahlor   Nicholas Keg
    Thomas Kay

Recognizances returnable this court.

The Commonwealth v. John Wilt. John Wilt in £100, Abraham Miley in £50, and Robert Bradshaw in £50 for John Wilt's good behavior and keeping the peace until January session.

The Commonwealth v. Abraham Miley. Abraham Miley in £50, Richard Dunlop in £50 for Miley's appearance this court to answer.

The Commonwealth v. John Bilyew. John Bilyew in £100, Thomas Storey in £100 for John Bilyew appearing this court to answer. April 1778 on motion John Bilyew discharged from recognizance.

Indictments found last court and continued to this.

The Commonwealth v. Abraham Miley. Tipling House. True Bill. Defendant pleads not guilty. Jonathan Serjant to prosecute. Continued to next term.

Page 42R
The Commonwealth v. Abraham Miley. Felony. Ignoramus.

The Commonwealth v. John Young. Felony. True Bill. Defendant pleads not guilty. Jury of James Anderson, John Chrisman, James Patterson, Christopher Miller, Banjamin Jolley, Ernest Baker, Gideon Ritchie, Edward Rose, Henderson Murphey, George Funk, Samuel McCashlan, and John Wilt who find [verdict left blank].

The Commonwealth v. John Young. Felony. True Bill. Continued.

The Commonwealth v. Peter Whitesides. Felony. True Bill. Continued.

The Commonwealth v. Timothy Ryan. Felony. True Bill. Continued. Noleprosequiti entered.

The Commonwealth v. Michael Huff. Tipling House. True Bill.
Continued. Noleprosequiti entered.

The Commonwealth v. John Peters. Tipling House. True Bill.
Continued. Noleprosequiti entered.

The Commonwealth v. Jacob Hoover. Tipling House. True Bill.
Continued. Noleprosequiti entered.

The Commonwealth v. Patrick Quin. Tipling House. True Bill.
Continued. Noleprosequiti entered.

Page 43L

The Commonwealth v. Henry Wert. Tipling House. True Bill.
Continued. Noleprosequiti entered.

The Commonwealth v. Henry Didier. Tipling House. True Bill.
Continued. Noleprosequiti entered.

The Commonwealth v. Abraham Miley. Defendant in £40 and Jonathan Cisna in £20 for Miley's appearance to answer.

The Commonwealth v. John Young. Abraham Miley in £40 and Jonathan Cisna in £20 for Miley's appearance to prosecute.

The Commonwealth v. John Young. Abraham Miley in £40 and Jonathan Cisna in £20 for appearance of Abraham Miley to prosecute.

The Commonwealth v. John Young. Defendant in £40, John Todd in £20, John Moore in £20 for appearance of John Young to answer next session.

Page 43R

The Commonwealth v. John Young. Defendant in £40, John Todd in £20, John Moore in £20 for appearance of John Young next court.

The Commonwealth v. John Hatch & wife. Recognizance continued to this term. On motion defendant discharged for want of prosecutor.

The Commonwealth v. Abraham Miley. John Young in £40, John Moore in £20, John Todd in £20 for John Young's appearance next court.

Recognizances returned to this term since last.

The Commonwealth v. John & James Curry. John Russell in £10, Christopher Miller in £10, John Howe in £10, Chrisley Beeman in £10, Jacob Miller in £10, James England in £10, Henry Armstrong in £10 for their appearance to prosecute. Upon motion defendant discharged from recognizance.

The Commonwealth v. John Curry. John Curry bound in £100, Joseph Morrison in £50 for his appearance to answer.

The Commonwealth v. James Curry. James Curry in £100, Joseph Morrison in £40 for his appearance to prosecute.

The Commonwealth v. Richard Kimber. Defendant in £150, George Elder in £100, Felix Miller in £100 for his appearance this court. Grand Jury returns ignoramus.

Page 44L April 1778
The Commonwealth v. Richard Kimber. George Shoup in £40 for his appearance to give evidence.

The Commonwealth v. Hugh Skelly. Hugh Skelly in £150, George Elder in £100, Felix Miller in £100 for Skelly's appearance to answer. The Grand Jury returns ignoramus.

The Commonwealth v. Elizabeth Keller. Elizabeth Keller in £100 and Thomas Menzies in £50 for defendant's appearance to answer. Agreed before Court.

The Commonwealth v. George Burket. Nicholas Hay in £50, David Ervin in £50 for Keg's appearance to give evidence.

The Commonwealth v. George Burket. George Burket in £40 and Thomas Menzies in £25 for Burket's appearance this court to answer. The Grand Jury returned ignoramus.

Page 44R April 1778
The Commonwealth v. John Cheeck. John Cheeck in £100, Gideon Ritchie in £100, Abraham Miley in £100 for John Cheeck's appearance next court to answer.

The Commonwealth v. John Cheeck. John Kinkead £50, James Kinkead in £50, Ann Kinkead in £50 for James Kinkead and Ann Kinkead to appear next court.

The Commonwealth v. John Cheeck. Richard Dunlap in £50 and John Boyce in £50 for John Boyce's appearance next court to give evidence.

The Commonwealth v. Mary Garrison. Mary Garreson in £50, William Beeman in £50 for Mary Garrison's appearance next court to answer.

The Commonwealth v. Hance Hamilton. Hance Hamilton in £100, Thomas Menzies in £100, Richard Dunlop in £100 for Hance Hamilton's appearance next court to answer.

Page 45L　　April 1778
The Commonwealth v. William Scovil. William Scovil in £100 and Cornelius McAuley in £50 for Scovil being of good behavior.

The Commonwealth v. Hethcote Picket, William Edward, Gavin Cluggage. Hethcote Picket in £1000, William Edward in £1000, and Gavin Cluggage in £2000 for defendants appearance to answer. On motion discharged.

The Commonwealth v. Robison Chilcotte, Gilles Stephens, James Barnet. Each in £200 for their appearance to answer. On motion discharged.

Page 45R
The Commonwealth v. John Young. Forcible Entry. True Bill. Pleads not guilty. John Young in £100, Thomas Story in £50, David Ervin in £50.

Rangers appointed at April Sessions 1778. George Woods, George Funk, James Little, Frederick Ambrose, William Ga__.

The Commonwealth v. John Cheeck. John Cheeck in £50, Gideon Ritchey in £25, Abraham Miley in £25 for Cheek being of good behavior for one year.

The Commonwealth v. Hans Hamilton. Hans Hamilton in £50 and Richard Dunlap in £25 for Hans Hamilton to appear next court to answer.

Page 46L　Blank.

Page 46R　　[October 1778]
At Bedford 13 October 1778 before James Martin, William Parker, and John Mellott.

Page 47L
Recognizances continued to this term.

The Commonwealth v. Hans Hamilton. Hans Hamilton in £50, Richard Delap in £25 for Hamilton's appearance to answer. Being three times called forfeited.

The Commonwealth v. John Stanley. Forcible Entry and Detailer. True Bill. Defendant three times called came not. Process awarded.

The Commonwealth v. Peter Whitesides. Felony. True Bill. Defendant pleads not guilty. On motion new trial ordered. Defendant three times called came not therefore forfeited until next term. April term defendant appeared and being ready for trial no prosecution. On motion defendant discharged from his recognizance.

The Commonwealth v. Justinius Hoeshill [Hoerhill?]. Justinius Hoeshill [Hoerhill?] in £100, Henry Wert in £50, George Funk in £50 for Hoeshill [Hoerhill?] appearing next session. Oct on motion defendant is discharged.

Page 47R October 1778

The Commonwealth v. Peter Whitesides. Peter Whitesides in £100, Cornelius McAuley in £50, Timothy Ryan in £50 for Whitesides appearing this court. Found guilty. Forfeit until next term.

The Commonwealth v. Hans Hamilton. Thomas Woods in £100 for Hans Hamilton appearing at this court to answer. Thomas Woods being three times called came not. Recognizance forfeit.

Recognizance returnable to this court.

The Commonwealth v. Mary Hays. Assault and Battery. Ignoramus. Mary Hays in £30, Thomas Hays in £15, Saml McCashlan in £15 for Mary Hays appearance at the Court.

The Commonwealth v. Mary Hays. Patrick Quin in £30, Richard Delap in £15 for Patrick Quins appearance to prosecute Mary Hays for an Assault & Battery.

Page 48L October 1778

The Commonwealth v. William Kennedy. William Kennedy in £50, John Todd in £25 for Kennedy to appear at this court. Defendant not appearing recognizance continued.

The Commonwealth v. George Sills. Assault and Battery. True Bill. George Sills in £40, Barnard Dougherty in £20 for Sills appearance at this court. William Murphy indorsed prosecutor. Defendant pleads guilty Fine six pence.

The Commonwealth v. George Sills. William Murphy in £40, James Dolton in £20 for Murphy to prosecute Geo Sills.

The Commonwealth v. Dorothy Sills. Dorothy Sills in £40, John Cessna in £20 for Dorothy Sills appearance. Defendant being called came not. Bail entered for her appearance next court.

The Commonwealth v. Dorothy Sills. Margaret Dolton in £40, Charles Rubey in £20 for Margaret Dolton to prosecute.

Page 48R   October 1778
The Commonwealth v. Samuel Laton. Felony.
Samuel Laton in £50, Asher Laton in £50 for Samuel Laton to appear this court. Jury of Moses Read, George Enslow, John Rush, Saml Moore, William Martin, Samuel McCahslan, Daniel Hay, Andrew Diving, William Scovil, Timothy Ryan, Charles Cessna, and W^m McCoomb find defendant guilty.

The Commonwealth v. Samuel Laton. James Trench in £25, John Whipkey in £25, Adam Ash in £25, John Smith in £25 for James Trench appearance to prosecute Samuel Laton in above action.

The Commonwealth v. Dorothy Cills. George Cills in £40 for Dorothy Cills appearance next court to answer.

The Commonwealth v. Hans Hamilton. Thomas Woods in £100 for appearance of Hans Hamilton next session to answer.

The Commonwealth v. Samuel Layton. Felony. True Bill.

Page 49L
The Commonwealth v. Samuel Layton. Samuel Layton in £50, Obiah Layton in £25, Robert McKenzie in £25 for Layton's appearance next court to answer.

The Commonwealth v. Dorothy Cills. James Dolton in £40 for appearance of Margaret Dolton next court to prosecute.

The Commonwealth v. Samuel Layton. James French in £50, William Stockw__ in £50, James Whipkey in £50, Adam Ash in £50 for appearance next court to prosecute Samuel Layton.

Page 49R
Cover reading "Session's Minutes April 1780."

Page 50L
Reverse side of cover. At the bottom, probably overflow from page 50R:

	Constable	Overseer of Poor	Supervisor Highways
Milford Township	Christian Anthony	Harmon Husbands	Frederick Weimer John Penrod

Page 50R [April 1780]
At Bedford 07 April 1780 before James Martin, President; Thomas Paxton; James Croyle; Sam¹ Thompson; Thomas Wilson; Samuel Carmichael; Abraham Cable; David Jones; Robert Scott.

	Constable	Overseer of Poor	Supervisor Highways
Bedford Town	Henry Wertz Thoˢ Anderson	James Dunlap Michael Sill	John Evalt Thomas Kenton
Colerain	John Moore Thomas Hall	Abraham Miley Ernest Baker	Casper Diffebaugh Joseph Friend
Bethel	John Dart	Benjamin Truax Thomas Crossan	Henry Rush Benjamin Abbot
Bedford Township	James Fletcher	James Dunlap Michael Sill	John Ewalt Thomas Kenton
Air	Enoch Williams Jacob Hoover Deputy	Joseph Bell Abraham Lowry	Daniel Royer Evan Shelby
Dublin	James Morton	Hugh Davison John Walker	James Coyl Esq John Ramsay
Barre	Robert Wasson	Alexander McCormick John Glenn	James Anderson Jeremiah Rickets
Hopewell	Benjamin Sanders	William Shirley Levi Moore	Solomon Sell Hugh Skelly
Brothers Valley	Henry Washbaugh Jacob Barkey	Clement Angle Benedict Leman	Peter B____ Frederick Oldfather
Huntingdon	George Reynolds Isaac Worrel Deputy	Archibald Fletcher James Gibson	Ludwig Sells Joshua Lewis
Frankstown	Jacob [B/Rowler?]	Patrick McGuire David Lowry	Jacob [Rowler?] Abraham G____
Turkey Foot	George Reiff Henry Abrahams	John Reed Henry Abram	James Spencer
Cumberland Valley	Frederick Touchman		

Page 51L   April 1780
Grand Jury:
    Abraham Miley (affirmed)
    John Bonnet
    Henry Abram
    William Kenny
    George Enslow
    Thomas Rhea
    Sam¹ Hall
    Sam¹ Borland
    Jacob Fisher (affirmed)
    John Elder
    Michael Bughly
    Thomas Johnson (affirmed)
    William Shirley
    George Imler (affirmed)
    Andrew Mann

Pennsylvania v. Matthias Judah. Assault and Battery. True Bill. Defendant pleads guilty.

Pennsylvania v. Mary [S/I]wales. Felony. Ignoramus.

Pennsylvania v. Thomas Edmonton. Forcible Entry and Detainer. True Bill.

Pennsylvania v. Martha Clem. [No charge,] Defendant being arraigned pleads guilty.

Page 51R April 1780
Pennsylvania v. John Reynolds. John Reynolds in £1__[torn away], Francis Reynolds in £500, Thomas Crossan in £500 for good behavior of John Reynolds for one year.

Pennsylvania v. Samuel Hall, Sarah Hall, and John Cessna. True Bill. Defendants plead guilty. Samuel Hall fined $6, Sarah Hall fined $6 and John Cessna fined $12.[7]

Pennsylvania v. Elizabeth Ferguson. Fornication. True Bill.

Pennsylvania v. William Martin [S/I]wales [name partially scraped away] and Mary his wife. Defendants bound in £700

Abraham Cable is appointed Ranger in the place of Frederick Ambrose.

Pennsylvania v. William [S/I]wales. Felony. True Bill.

Pennsylvania v. Daniel McGuire. Counterfeiting Paper Money. Ignoramus.

Pennsylvania v. John Young and Hugh Mitchell. Felony. True Bill.

Page 52L April 1780
Pennsylvania v. Grace Justice. Fornication. True Bill.

Pennsylvania v. Mary Shaver. Fornication. True Bill.

Pennsylvania v. James McDonald. Felony. True Bill.
James McDonald in £__, Sam[l] Anderson in £__ for James McDonald appearance to answer.

Pennsylvania v. John Young and Hugh Mitchell. ~~John Young in £500~~, ~~Hugh Mitchell in £500~~, James McGuiness in £500, Sam[l] Anderson in £500 conditioned as above.

---

[7] This page of the docket shows both dollar and pound units for currency.

Pennsylvania v. John Young and Hugh Mitchell. James S___ in £__ to appear and prosecute the above.

Page 52R
Pennsylvania v. James McDonald. James S___ in £[800] to appear and prosecute.

Pennsylvania v. Rebecca Squires. George Squires in £1000, Abraham Cable in £500 for Rebecca Squires to appear next court to answer to indictment for felony.

Page 53L [July 1780]
At Bedford 11 July 1780

Grand Jury:
Samuel Davidson	Jacob Hersch
George Funk	Charles Ruby
Henry Wirtz	Frederick [Nelson?]
John Fleeharty	Casper Davibaugh
John Hamilton	George Elder
Samuel Skinner	William Morrow
John _____	John Andrewmay
	[John Andrew May]

Entry of recognizances.

Pennsylvania v. Martha Mountain. Martha Mountain in £5_ to give evidence against James Hendricks for begetting a bastard child on the body of her the said Martha Mountain. Forfeited to next term.

Pennsylvania v. Nicholas Iler. Nicholas Iler in £500, Peter Smith in £500 for appearance of Nicholas and his good behavior. Settled.

Page 53R July 1780
Pennsylvania v. Emanuel Smith. Defendant in £1400, Obadiah Layton in £600 for appearance of Emanuel Smith. Forfeited.

Pennsylvania v. Thomas Moorehead. Defendant in £500, Philip Edington in £500 for appearance of Thomas Moorehead to answer.

Pennsylvania v. Peter McMullan. Defendant in £500, James Johnston in £500 for appearance of Peter McMullan to prosecute Thomas Moorehead.

Pennsylvania v. Elizabeth Ferguson. Pleads guilty. Fined £10.

Entry of Indictments.

Pennsylvania v. Ephraim Wallace. Felony. Ignoramus.

Pennsylvania v. Thomas Ferguson. Fornication. True Bill.

Page 54L July 1780
Pennsylvania v. Thomas Moorehead. Felony. True Bill.

Pennsylvania v. Leonard Karns. Fornication. True Bill.

Pennsylvania v. Thomas Moorehead. Thos Moorehead in £100, George Elder in £100 for defendant to answer next court.

Pennsylvania v. Peter McMullan. Peter McMullin in £100 to appear next session to prosecute Thomas Moorehead for Felony.

Pennsylvania v. Margaret Rush. Pleads guilty. Fined £10.

Pennsylvania v. Charles Rubey. Fornication. Ignoramus.

Page 54R July 1780
Pennsylvania v. Phebe Wolf. Bastardy.

Pennsylvania v. Henry Amorine. Henry Amorine in £500, John Cessna in £500 for appearance of Henry Amorine next session to answer for Assault & Battery upon William Bell.

Pennsylvania v. Charles Rubey. Charles Rubey in £500, Henry Wirtz in £50, William ____ in £50.

The court proceeded to regulate the Price of Labor and are of Opinion that the same shall be estimated and rated 26 Dollars each Man Day. October Sessions Court at the same rate.

Pennsylvania v. Nicholas Iler. Nicholas Iler in £1000, Peter Smith in £500, Thomas Croyle in £500 for the good behavior and his appearance next court.

Pennsylvania v. Nicholas Iler. Nicholas Iler in £500, Peter Smith in £250, Thomas Croyle in £250 for Ilers appearance next court to answer Assault & Battery upon Michael Bowser.

Pennsylvania v. Nicholas Iler. Michael Bowser in £500 to appear and prosecute and give evidence.

Page 55L [facing pages 55L and 55R not numbered] July 1780
Pennsylvania v. Henry Amorine. William Bell in £500 to appear next Court and prosecute and give evidence against Henry Amorine for an Assault & Battery committed upon him by Henry Amorine.

Pennsylvania v. Nicholas Iler. Defendant in £1200, Peter Smith in £600 for the appearance of Nicholas Iler next court to answer for erazing [sic[8]] the mark off of a State Gun.

Pennsylvania v. Charles Rubey. Charles Rubey in £500, Thomas Anderson in £500, William ____ in £50 for appearance of Charles Rubey next session to answer.

Pennsylvania v. Ellinor Torrence. Ellinor Torrence £[no amount].

Adjourned to 07 November next.

Page 55R Blank.

Page 56L [numbered "55"]   [October 1780]
At Bedford 17 October 1780 before James Martin, James Carmichael, William Farin, Moses Reed.

Grand Jury:
    Doct[r] John Peters   James Dunlap
    Abraham Covalt   George Wisecarver
    Frederick Reicher   John Fleeharty
    John Rhoads   Timothy Ryan
    Earnest Baker   Daniel Stoy
    Charles Cessna   Francis Reynold
    John Mortimor   William Kerney
    Jacob Tarwater

Page 56R [numbered "56"]   October 1780
Pennsylvania v. Thomas Moorehead. Felony. Testified for prosecution: Peter McMullin, Samuel Anderson, Patrick McGuire, John Mitchell, James Little. For the defense: Jacob Smith, Charity Edington. Jury of Jacob Hendershot, Jacob Markley, John Hendrickson, Abraham Covalt, George Enslow, Jacob Hersh, Evan Jenkins, James McDonald, Benjamin Vanmater, Casper Durst, Abraham Nelson, and Wallace find defendant guilty. Judgment that Thomas Moorehead return goods stolen or the value thereof, that he pay fine equal to value of goods stolen, and on Saturday next preceding the next General Quarter Sessions that he be taken to the Common Whipping Post and receive three lashes on his Bare Back.

Pennsylvania v. Gavin Eddy. Fornication. True Bill.
Gavin Ody the elder in £1000 for defendant to appear next session.

---

[8] erasing.

DOCKET 2: 1771–1801 109

Page 57L   October 1780
Pennsylvania v. Edward Gray. Edward Gray in £1000, James Little of Bedford County in £500 for appearance of Edward Gray next court to answer for Felony.

Pennsylvania v. Gavin Eddy junior. Elizabeth Duval in £500, John Duval in £500 to appear and give evidence against Gavin Eddy junior for Fornication.

Pennsylvania v. Thomas Kelly. Felony. True Bill. Defendant pleads guilty. Sentence to restore goods stolen of value thereof, pay fine equal to value of goods, and be taken to the Public Whipping Post and receive fifteen lashes.

Page 57R   October 1780
Pennsylvania v. Arthur McGaughey. Assault & Battery. True Bill. Defendant pleads guilty. Fined £20.

Pennsylvania v. John McGaughey. Assault & Battery. True Bill. Defendant pleads guilty. Fined £20.

Pennsylvania v. William Neimier. Forcible Entry. True Bill.

Pennsylvania v. James Stevens. Tipling House. True Bill. John Paxton in £500 to give evidence in the above prosecution.

Pennsylvania v. Nicholas Iler. Assault & Battery. True Bill.

Pennsylvania v. Gavin Eddy. Bastardy. True Bill.

Pennsylvania v. Elizabeth Dibol. Bastardy. True Bill.

Page 58L   October 1780
Pennsylvania v. Nicholas Iler. Assault & Battery. True Bill.

Pennsylvania v. John Bonnet. Assault & Battery. Ignoramus.

Entry of Recognizances

Pennsylvania v. Elizabeth Devol and John Devol. Bound in £2000 to prosecute Gavin Eddy.

Pennsylvania v. Gavin Eddy and Gavin Eddy junior. Bound in £2000 to answer.

Pennsylvania v. Zachariah Smith and Emanuel Smith. Bound in £2000 to answer.

Pennsylvania v. Jacob Rush junior and Henry Rush senior. Bound in £2000 to answer.

Pennsylvania v. Nicholas Liech, George Horse, William Pitman. Bound in £2000 each to answer.

Pennsylvania v. Bernard Money, Peter Smith and John Shaver. Bound in £2000 each to prosecute.

Page 58R
Pennsylvania v. William Jones. Bound in £500 to prosecute.

Pennsylvania v. Benjamin Vanvater, Joseph McKinney. Defendants in £1000. Bail £500.

Pennsylvania v. James Anderson and Benjamin Vanvater. Defendant in £1000, Bail £500.

Pennsylvania v. Moses Gordon and Joseph McKinney. Defendant in £1000, Bail £500.

Pennsylvania v. [Morris?] Gibbons, Philip Gelliland and Martin Longstreth. Defendant in £1000, Bail each £500.

Page 59L
Pennsylvania v. Benjamin Vanvaiter and Joseph McKinney. Defendant in £1000, Bail £500.

Pennsylvania v. Nicholas Leech. Misprison of Treason. True Bill. Barnard Money in £1000 to prosecute. John Shaver in £1000.

Pennsylvania v. Edward Grey. Felony. True Bill.

Pennsylvania v. Nicholas Cline. Felony. True Bill.

Pennsylvania v. John Bonnet. Defendant in £6000, Charles Cessna in £3000, Henry Wertz in £3000.

The same v. the same. John Bonnet in £4000, Chas Cessna in £2000, Henry Wertz in £2000.

Pennsylvania v. John McGaughey. Elazir David in £200.

Page 59R   October 1780
Pennsylvania v. John McGaughey. Defendant in £500, George Milikin in £250.

Pennsylvania v. Arthur McGaughey. Defendant in £500, Hugh Simpson in £250.

The same v. the same. John Hite in £500

Pennsylvania v. Abraham Covalt and John Reeves. Abraham Covalt in £500, Thomas Reeves in £500, Henry Livingston in £500. No persons s___ discharged upon proclamation.

Pennsylvania v. Thomas Moorehead. Thomas Moorehead £3000, James Carmichael £2500, James Little £2500, Samuel Anderson £2500 for Thomas Moorehead to appear at Bedford Saturday next preceding the next Quarter Sessions between the hours of nine and twelve in the fore noon and then and there to abide and receive the sentence of this Court passed this session. Pardoned by Council as to the Whiping.

Page 60L October 1780
On motion and by consent rule to take the depositions [of] Thomas Montgomery, John McNaman, and David Caldwell on behalf of Defendants Hugh Mitchell and John Young, Jacob Hall, and Francis Clugage.

Pennsylvania v. John Bonnet. John Bonnet in £4000, John Cessna in £2000 for peace and good behavior of said John and his appearance next court. Discharged by proclamation.

Pennsylvania v. Nicklas Cline. Hugh Robison and William Jones held each in £200 to prosecute Nicklas Cline. Forfeited into Jan.

Pennsylvania v. Nicholas Leech. Nicholas Leech in £3000, John Bonnet in £500, Henry Wertz in £500 for appearance of defendant next court to answer for Misprison of Treason. 20 Oct 1780. Forfeit till next session.

Page 60R [January 1781]
At Bedford 16 January 1781 before Barnard Dougherty, President, and James Martin, Thomas Paxton, David Jones, John Hain, Jacob Saylor, Andrew Todd, Justices.

Grand Jury:
    William Simonton   Joseph Bell
    John Fittrees   Nicholas Ruff
    James Foley   Michael Cryder
    Benjamin Winkfield   John Rankin
    James McDaniel   Joseph Kelly
    Benson Lickey   John Killpatrick
    Barnard Money   Jacob Hoover
    Patrick Hartford

Page 61L   January 1781
Pennsylvania v. Gavin Eddy junior. Gavin Eddy in £40 to appear next court.

Pennsylvania v. Gavin Eddy junior. Elizabeth Devol in £40 and John Devol in £40 for Elizabeth to appear and prosecute Gavin Eddy.

Pennsylvania v. William Neimier. George Wisecarver in £40 to give evidence and prosecute defendant for Forcible Entry.

Pennsylvania v. Brice Blair. Forcible Entry & Detainer. Thomas Pannel in £40 to appear and prosecute.

Pennsylvania v. Mary Conner. Felony. Ignoramus.

Page 61R   January 1781
Pennsylvania v. Edward Gray. Edward Gray in £80, James Little in £40 for defendant to appear next court to answer to Felony.

Pennsylvania v. William Satorius. Forcible Entry. True Bill. Michael Divirt in £40 to prosecute above next session.

Pennsylvania v. Mary Connor. Mary Connor in £500, John Kirkpatrick surety £500.

Same v. same. Richard Pinkerton bound to give evidence.

Page 62L   January 1781
Pennsylvania v. Mary Connor. Richard Pinkerton in £50 to give evidence against Mary Connor. Henry Brown surety in £500. Henry Abrahams in £500 to give evidence. Henry Broen £500 to give evidence.

Pennsylvania v. John Young. John Young in £80. James Little in £40 for appearance of defendant next court to answer for Felony.

Pennsylvania v. William Sartorius. Defendant in £80 to answer indictment for Felony. Doct^r John Peters in £40.

Pennsylvania v. Edward Gray. Edward Beatty in £40. James Little in £20 for his appearance next court to give evidence against the defendant for Felony.

Page 62R   January 1781
Pennsylvania v. Nicholas Cline. Hugh Robinson in £40 for his appearance next session to give evidence against defendant for Felony.

Pennsylvania v. Nicholas Leech. Barnard Money in £40, John Shaver of Colerain Township in £40 for their appearance next court to give evidence against Nicholas Leech.

Pennsylvania v. John Young. James Spencer in £40 to appear next court to prosecute.

Pennsylvania v. James McDonald. On motion rule to take deposition of Rebecca Spencer on the part of the State. James McDonals in £80, James Little in £40 for the appearance of defendant next court to answer indictment for felony.

Page 63L [April 1781]
At Bedford 02 April 1781 before Bernard Dougherty and Justices.

Township	Constable	Overseer Poor	Supervisor Highways
Bedford Township	Reynart Wolf	James Dunlap Michael Sill	Samuel Davidson George __
Colerain	Edward Rose	Robert Moore John Friend	John Wilt Thomas Hall
Cumberland Valley	Frederick Rice	Edward Evans Jacob Fox	Joseph Kelly William Purdue
Bethel	John Dart	Thomas Crossan John Stilwell	Benjamin Abbit Jacob Mooney
Air	Frederick Humbugh	Daniel McCurdy Jacob John	Daniel Royer John Harrod
Dublin	James Barnet	Hugh Davison John Walker	James Coyle John Ramsay
Shirley	George Clugage	James Galbraith James Clugage	James Carmichael Jacob Sharra
Barree	David Ralston	Joseph Oburn Benjamin McGuffay	William Nelson Archibald Glen
~~Hopewell~~	~~Absolom Gray~~	~~Samuel Rhea~~ ~~James Johnson~~	~~Ulrich __~~ ~~Edward Beatty~~
Frankstown	Absolom Gray	Samuel Rhea James Johnston	Ulrich __ Edward Beatty
Brothers Valley	John Markley	Benidict Laman Clement Angle	Valentine Lant Walter Hile
Turkeyfoot	Joseph Donohow	John Read Henry Brown	John Jones William Rush
Providence	Henry Livingston	Joseph Morison Robert Culbertson	James Martin Thomas Woods
Milford	John Penrod	Herman Husband John Sho__	Frederick Weimer Christian Anthony
Huntingdon	Ludwick Sills	Henry Loyd Michael Cryder	Joseph Prigmor Moses Donaldson

Page 63R
Grand Jury:

Martin Longstraith
Richard Delapt
David Irwin
John Graham
Samuel Skinner
James Henry
George Wisecarver
George Milligan

Thomas Faris
George Funk
Brice Blair
John Kenton
Henry Armstrong
James McDonald
Samuel Graves

1. Pennsylvania v. George Amorine. Felony True Bill.

2. Pennsylvania v. John Fleeharty. Assault & Battery. True Bill. Parties have agreed and each is to pay half the costs.

3. Pennsylvania v. Cornelius McAulay. Assault & Battery. True Bill. Testify for prosecution Mary Hay; for defense John Hamilton, John Boyer. Defendant pleads guilty.

On motion of Wm Smith the Order for Review of road from the three Links through the Glades to the top of Laurel Hill be cont[inued].

Page 64L   April 1781
3. Pennsylvania v. Gavin Eddy junior. Fornication.
Testify for prosecution Elizabeth Devol, John Devol; for defendant Gavin Eddy, David Carlisle, David Eddy. Jury of Abraham Miley, John Friend, John Shaver, Nicholas Livingston, William Proctor, Earnest Baker, Casper Davebaugh, John Haggans, John England, Anthony Nagel, Adam Young, and J___ Patterson find defendant guilty.

4. Pennsylvania v. Andrew Ludz. Felony. True Bill.
Tried and not guilty.

5. Pennsylvania v. Mary Connor. Felony. Ignoramus.

6. Pennsylvania v. Bartholomew Davis. Forcible Entry. True Bill. Defendant pleads guilty and fined 20/.

7. Pennsylvania v. Moses Reed. Tipling House. True Bill.

Page 64R   April 1781
8. Pennsylvania v. Andrew Ludz. Felony. True Bill.
Found to be Petit Larceny and struck off by the Court.

9. Pennsylvania v. Andrew Ludz. Felony. Ignoramus.

10. Pennsylvania v. Andrew Ludz. Felony. Ignoramus.

11. Pennsylvania v. John Bonnet. Assault & Battery. True Bill. John Bonnet in £100 to appear and answer. John Bonnet in £200 and John Cessna in £100 for John Bonnet to appear next court and in the mean time be of good behavior especially toward James Martin. Discharged as to his good behavior.

12. Pennsylvania v. William Hart. Tipling House. True Bill

Page 65L   April 1781

Pennsylvania v. James Trench. James Trench in £100 and David Ervin in £50 for good behavior.

Pennsylvania v. John Bonnet. John Bonnet in £100, John Wilt in £50 for good behavior.

Pennsylvania v. John Bonnet. James Martin in £40, Richard Dunlap in £20.

Pennsylvania v. Cornelius McAulay. Cornelius McAulay in £40, Samuel Moore in £20 for good behavior

Pennsylvania v. William Neimier. Forcible Entry & Detainer. Testify for state George Wisecarver; for defense James Dunlap, Frederick Helm. Jury of Abraham Miley, John Friend, John Shaver, Nicholas Livingston, William Proctor, Earnest Baker, Casper Davebaugh, John Haggans, John England, Anthony Nagel, Adam Young, and James Patterson find defendant guilty. Defendant fined ___.

Pennsylvania v. Bartholomew Davis. Defendant in £50. Giles Stephens in £25. Jury of Abraham Miley, John Friend, John Shaver, Nicholas Livingston, William Proctor, Ernest Baker, Casper Davebaugh, John Haggans, John England, Anthony Nagel, Adam Young, and James Patterson find defendant £50 and Giles Stephens in £25.

Page 65R   April 1781

Pennsylvania v. John & Margaret Thompson. Defendant in £50, George Buchannan in £30.

Pennsylvania v. Cornelius McAulay. Thomas Hay in £40, Samuel Skinner in £20.

Pennsylvania v. Brice Blair. Brice Blair in £40, James Stewart in £20.

Pennsylvania v. Thomas David. Thomas David in £40, David Carlisle in £20.

Pennsylvania v. George Amrine. John Cessna in £40, Michael Ruff in £20, George Amrine in £200, Henry Wertz in £100.

Pennsylvania v. John Goble. George Nixon in £20, David Erwin in £10.

Page 66L April 1781
Pennsylvania v. David Organ. David Organ in £40, Hector McNeill in £20, Leonard Swigart in £20.

Pennsylvania v. Brice Blair. Brice Blair in £500, James Stuart in £250.

Pennsylvania v. Andrew Ludz. Andrew Ludz in £100, Henry Wertz in £50.

Pennsylvania v. Patrick Conner and Mary his wife. Richard Pinkerton in £100, William Greathouse in £50.

Pennsylvania v. John Fleeharty. John Fleeharty in £50, Thomas Bradshaw in £25.

Pennsylvania v. John Young. Defendant in £80, Nathaniel Ja__t in £40 for appearance of defendant next October court to answer Felony indictment.

Pennsylvania v. James McDonald. Defendant in £80, Samuel Thompson in £40 for defendant to appear next October court to answer [bottom of page missing].

Page 66R April 1781
Pennsylvania v. Brice Blair. Defendant in £80, Thomas Johnston in £40 for appearance of defendant next October session to answer indictment for Forcible Entry. Thomas Pannel in £40, John Friend in £20 for his appearance to prosecute and give evidence against defendant.

Pennsylvania v. Morris McNamar. Morris McNamar in £200, William Wilson in £100, Bartholomus McGuire in £100. Discharged by Proc.

Pennsylvania v. Andrew Ludz. Felony. Jury of Abraham Miley, John Friend, John Shaver, Nicholas Livingston, William Proctor, Ernest Baker, Casper Davebaugh, John Haggan, John England, Anthony Nagel, Adam Young and James Patterson find defendant not guilty.

Page 67L April 1781
Pennsylvania v. Gavin Eddy junior. Judgment of the court for the Maintenance of a Bastard child begotton [sic] upon the Body of Elizabeth Devole and also for finding the said child in clothing £23. Charges of the lying in of the said Elizabeth £7.0.0.

Thomas Faris being sworn upon the Grand Jury departed the Court without leave before the session ended. Fined according to law.

Pennsylvania v. James McDonald. James Spencer in £50 to appear at next October session to prosecute defendant for Felony.

Pennsylvania v. John Young. James Spencer in £50 as above.

Pennsylvania v. George Amorine. George Amorine in £50, Henry Amorine in £50 for appearance of said George next court to answer indictment for Felony. Appeared.

Doodle at bottom of page 67L.

Page 67R
Pennsylvania v. William Satorius. William Satorius in £50, Doctor John Peters in £30 for appearance of said William next court to answer indictment for forcible entry. Forfeit until next term.

Page 68L   [July 1781]
At Bedford, third Tuesday, 17 July 1781 before Barnard Dougherty, Jacob Saylor, Gideon Richey.

Pennsylvania v. George Goosehorn. George Goosehorn in £40, Thomas Anderson in £20 for appearance of said George. Forfeited to Jan 1782.

Pennsylvania v. Jacob Brown. Jacob Brown in £40, Thomas Anderson in £20. Discharged by Proclamation.

Pennsylvania v. David Bell. David Bell in £10, David Bradshaw in £10.

Page 68R
Pennsylvania v. George Swigart & John Swigart. Defendants in £50, Samuel Davidson and George Burket in £50. Settled. David Organ in £50 to give evidence and prosecute.

Pennsylvania v. Margaret Simpson. Hugh Simpson in £50 for her appearance.

Page 69L   July 1781
Pennsylvania v. Margaret Simpson. Hugh Simpson in £40 for his wife Margaret to appear at next court to answer indictment for Assault and Battery upon Katherine David the younger. Eliezer David in £20 for the appearance of Katherine David the younger at next court to give evidence in the Assault and Battery upon her by Margaret Simpson.

Pennsylvania v. George Amorine. George Amorine in £50, Henry Amorine in £50 for appearance of said George next court to answer.

Pennsylvania v. David Bates, Richard C[omp?], and Wm Turner. Defendants each in £50. Michael Huffnagel, John Cessna and John Cummins Esq. each £25 for defendants appearance next session to answer.

Page 69R
John Cessna in £100 and Henry Abrahams in £100 for [appearance] of John Bonnett next session to answer.

Pages 70L and 70R Blank.

Page 71L [erroneously penciled number 70]   [July 1781]
Persons recommended for Tavern Keepers July Court 1781.
Thomas Anderson, David Ervin.

Page 71R [Left side of page deteriorated; Most given names not readable.]   [1780]
Tavern Keepers recommended July 1780 ___ Anderson, ___ Irwin, Anthony Nagel, Frederick Marstaller.

Tavern keepers recommended October session 1780: Saml McCashlan, Richard Delapt, ___ Bonnet, ___ Wallace, ___ McConnell, ___ McGaughy, ___ ___, ___ McAulay.

Recommended for Tavern keepers at July 1781: Ludwick Sills, ___ Anderson, __is Clugage, [Henry?] Livingstone, ___ Anderson, [Elizabeth?] Burd, ___ Wilson, ___ __tz.

Page 72L
April Sessions [no year] Tavern Keepers recommended: Samuel Anderson, Benjamin Elliot, William Watson, John Parkison, William Jones license to be taken out after 10th of August next, George Enslow, Gideon Read.

Page 72R   [April 1786]
At Bedford 11 April 1786 before Bernard Dougherty and Justices.

DOCKET 2: 1771–1801 119

Township	Constable	Overseer Poor	Supervisor Highways
Colerain	William Farmer	Arnet Baker John Friend	James Patterson Joseph Friend
Bether	Samuel Graves	Thomas Stafford Benjamin Abbot	Adam Linn Bethuel Covalt
Dublin	Benjamin Burd	John Ramsay Hugh Orlton	Robert Ramsay George Hudson
Barre	Abraham Nelson		
Fransktown	Absalom Gray	William Diviney Thomas McC___	Samuel Davis Michael Feather
Brothers Valley	William Vought	Philip Keble Joseph Johnes	John Miller Henry Pittinger
Cumberland Valley	Charles Wall	Joseph Kelly Henry Williams	Thomas Leasure John Elder
Turkey Foot	Jacob Hartzel	Richard Green Benjamin Pursel	Edward Hamet
Quamahoning	John Rhoads	Jacob Yoder	Daniel Hay Jacob Thi___mel
Milford	Moses Rambo	George Brenner James Gilmore	John Penrod Adam Keffer
Providence	William Boyd	John Ritchey Uriah Bilew	
Huntingdon	John Biddle	John ___ Jacob Laird	Henry [Neff?] George Reynolds
Shirley	Nicholas Coons	Jacob Ashman Jacob Sharrah	Charles __olye James Galbraith
Belfast	Peter Rush		
Elk Lick	Jacob Merkley	John Griffith Christian Hostatler	John Markley William ___
Londonderry	John _ail	Joseph Rhoads George Liberger	John Haines Nicholas Liberger
Woodberry	Edward [Crossin?]	Joseph Collay Christian Whetstone	
Hopewell	Solomon Sill	James Hale Felix Miller	William Shirley Hugh Skelly

On motion Mr. Smith, James Carson admitted attorney.

Page 73L April 1786
Grand Jury:

Thomas Paxton	David Calwell	Hugh Orrenton
John Williams	James Mortimore	Wendal Ott
William Patterson	George Wilson	Henry Rush
Thomas Leasure	Peter Smith	Gabriel Rhoades
John Galbreath	Peter Reiley	Thomas Blackburn
Patrick Heney	John Davebaugh	George Kimble
John Shaver	Michael Dibert	Robert Gibson

Pennsylvania v. Peter Augustine. Defendant in £100, Michael Beeghley in £50.

Pennsylvania v. William Neimier. Defendant in £20, Jacob Helm in £20.

Pennsylvania v. Peter Augustine. Assault & Battery. True Bill.

Pennsylvania v. Charles Boyle & John Carmichael. Forcible Entry & Detainer. True Bill. Testify for prosecution: B___ Luckey, James Davis, Margaret Davis, William Laughlan, John Latta; for defense: Bartholomew Davis, E___ Evans, Peter Reily, __mes Carmichael, ___t Galbreath [bottom left of page torn off]. Jury of George Wisecarver, Thomas Buck, Alexander McConnell, Michael Sill, Benjamin Truax, William McMoultrie, Ludwick Sills, Frederick R___, Jacob Berkey, John Lafferty, John Car___, and George Jackson find defendant guilty. On motion judgment fine 5/.

Page 73R April 1786
Pennsylvania v. John Edwards & Jacob Berkey. Indictment for Not Repairing Highways. True Bill.
James Black Quamahoning Township in £20, John Weimer Milford Township in £20 for appearance of James Black and John Weimer at next July session to give evidence.

Pennsylvania v. Eleanor Rubey. Indictment N° 1 Oct Session 1785. Defendant retracts her former plea and submits to the court. Fined six pence. Testify for prosecution: Ann C___, Mary Night, Elizabeth Knight.

Pennsylvania v. John Edwards & Jacob Berkey. Jacob Berkey in £20, David Jones in £20 for appearance of defendant next court to answer indictment for not repairing highways.

Page 74L [July 1786]
At Bedford second Tuesday in July 1786 before Bernard Dougherty and Justices.

Grand Jury:
 Martin Riley   John Walker
 Henry Hoover   Thomas Blair
 Philip Izor   Andrew Boyd
 John ___burgh   John Spensor
 John Jenkins   Jacob Laird
 Michael McKerney John Patton
 John Fisher   Samuel Davis
 George May   Thomas McGaughy
 Jonathan Buck

Pennsylvania v. William Alexander. Assault & Battery. True Bill. Defendant submits to court. Fined £4.

Pennsylvania v. Jonathan Prigmore. Assault & Battery. True Bill.

Pennsylvania v. Edwards & Berkey. Indictment for Not Repairing Highway. Defendants submit to Court. Fined /4^d.

Pennsylvania v. John Jacobus. Forcible Entry & Detainer. True Bill.

Page 74R   July 1786
Pennsylvania v. Ephraim Wallace & Michael Fink & Thomas Knox. Assault & Battery. True Bill.
Ephraim Wallace in £50, Alexander McConnel in £50 for appearance of defendants at next October session to answer.

Pennsylvania v. Arthur McGaughy. Nuisance. True Bill.
Arthur McGaughy in £20, Allen McCombe in £20 for appearance of defendants October session to answer.

Pennsylvania v. Duncan McDonald. Assault & Battery. Ignoramus.

Pennsylvania v. Ephraim Wallace et al. Duncan McDonald in £20 to appear at next October session and prosecute.

Pennsylvania v. Jonathan Prigmore. John Fee in £20 to appear at next October session to give evidence.

Pennsylvania v. William Alexander. Defendant in £20, Joseph Alexander in £10. Ended on defendants submission.

Pennsylvania v. Duncan McDaniel. Defendant in £25, Baltzer Dishong in £25, Charles McHenry in £25. ____ Bill being found Ignoramus.

Page 75L   July 1786
Pennsylvania v. John Fee senior & ~~John Fee junior~~. John Fee senior in

£50, ~~John Fee junior in £50~~, Peter Reiley in £50. October appeared & discharged.

Pennsylvania v. John Fee junior. Defendant in £50, David Caldwell in £50. Appeared & discharged.

Pennsylvania v. John Fee junior & John Fee senior. Jonathan Prigmore in £50, Peter McMullin in £50. October 1786 on motion recognizance set aside.

Pennsylvania v. Jonathan Prigmore. Defendant in £50, William McMuthrie in £50

Page 75R [October 1786]
At Bedford third Tuesday in October 1786 before James Martin & associate justices.

Grand Jury:
>   John Dickey   Michael Bigehley
>   Robert Hammel   Cornelius Reiley
>   William Gaff   Abraham Good
>   Jacob Hellem   Jacob Kebler
>   William Porter junior   Richard Pitman
>   Walter Criswell   William Morton
>   Casper Stotler [Hoker?]   William McIlwain
>   Solomon Penrod   Benjamin Drake

Pennsylvania v. John Jeffery. Assault & Battery. Ignoramus.

Pennsylvania v. John Tait. Assault & Battery. True Bill.

Pennsylvania v. John Hangin. Felony. True Bill.

Pennsylvania v. Ephraim Wallace, Thomas Knox & Michael Fink. Ephraim Wallace in £40, Arthur McGaughey in £40 for appearance of defendant next court.

Page 76L   October 1786
Pennsylvania v. John Peck. Tipling House. True Bill.

Pennsylvania v. John Hangin. John Huston in £20, Robert Huston in £20 for appearance of Jesse Huston to give evidence against John Hangin for Felony.

Pennsylvania v. Arthur McGaughy. Arthur McGaughy in £20, Samuel Davidson in £20 for appearance of A^r McGaughy at next January court to answer for Nuisance.

Pennsylvania v. John Hangin. John Hangin in £20, Philip Hangin in £20 for appearance of John Hangin next January to answer for Felony. January 1787 appeared and new Bail.

Pennsylvania v. Ephraim Wallace et al. Duncan McDonald in £20, John Tate in £20 for appearance of said Duncan next January to give evidence.

David McLean committed for want of security for good behavior. Discharged by proclamation.

Pennsylvania v. John Peck. Defendant in £20, John Tate in £20 for appearance of said John Peck next court to answer for Tipling House.

Page 76R [January 1787]
At Bedford the third Tuesday in January 1787 (16th day) before Bernard Dougherty, Hugh Barclay, William Proctor, Robert Galbraith, John Cessna, Jacob Saylor, James Wells, Thomas Coulter, &c.

Grand Jury:

George Ashman	John Graham
John Coyle	Joseph Kelly
James Gordon	John Loge
Isaac Thompson	Thomas Paxton
George Clugage	Henry Houser
Abraham Lingenfelter	Michael Sills
Hugh Logan	John Riggle
John Elder	Lot French
William Anderson	William Gibson
George Smith	Silas Lockhart
George Imler	John Reed

Pennsylvania v. William Holliday junior. William Holiday junior in £40, William Holiday senior in £40. Discharge by proclamation.

Pennsylvania v. Elizabeth Williams. William William in £10, Wm Wilson in £10. Ended.

Pennsylvania v. Leonard Na__. Defendant in £200, Peter Cap in £200. Discharged by proclamation.

Page 77L January 1787
1. Pennsylvania v. Bryce McWhinney. Horse Stealing.
Testify for prosecution: James Williams and Ephraim Williams. Jury of Robert Riddle, William Kerr, Thomas Brackenridge, Ernest Baker, John McLemans, James McMullin, Abraham Overhholtz, Allen McComb,

Michael Hay, Valentine Ripley, John Richey, Henry Cline find defendant guilty. Judgment that Brice McWhinney restore the horse stolen or the value thereof, pay fine of £2, that he be taken tomorrow between the hours of nine and twelve to the Common Whipping Post and receive thirty nine lashes on his bare back well laid on, to have both his ears cut off and nailed to the pillory, and stay therein for one hour, and be committed until this sentence is complied with.

Pennsylvania v. John Hangin. Defendant in £20, Jacob Roads in £20 for appearance of defendant next session to answer for Felony.

Pennsylvania v. John Hargor. Larceny. Ignoramus.

Pennsylvania v. Moses Kelly. Defendant in £50, Robert Watsworth in £25, Thomas Kelly in £25.

Page 77R   January 1787
Pennsylvania v. John Jacobus. John Jacobus in £40. John Cessna junior in £40 for appearance of defendant next April session to answer for Forcible Entry and Detainer.

Pennsylvania v. Arthur McGaughy. Arthur McGaughy in £40 to appear next April session to answer for Nuisance. Ended.

Pennsylvania v. John Hanger. Thomas Coulter in £20 for appearance of Jesse Huston next April session to prosecute for Felony. April appeared.

Page 78L   [March 1787]
At Private Session held at the house of William Wood 26 March 1787 before Hugh Barclay, James Wells, and David Espy.

Township	Constable	Overseer Poor	Supervisor Highways
Bedford Town	Anthony Nagel Adam Crise		
Bedford Township	Michael Sill	Arthur McGaughy Thomas Anderson	George Funk James Gordan
Hopewell	Zebulon Moon	George Elder Felix Miller	William Shirley Hugh Skelly
Quamahoning	George Khemal George Boyer	Philip Khemel jr William Boyd	Jacob Smoker Christian Spiker
Providence	William Boyd junior	John Elliot John Tate	John Moore George Barton
Belfast	William Pittman	Morris Dishong Peter Swartzwalder	William K___ William Morton
Woodberry	Martin Loy	Joseph Cellars Godfrey Painter	Henry Wi___ William Dilts

Page 78R [April 1787]

At Bedford second Tuesday in April 1787 before Bernard Dougherty, Hugh Barclay, John Cessna, Thomas Coulter, William Proctor, Abraham Cable, Robert Galbreath, William Patterson, John Little, Thomas Watson, Ruben Skinner, & Jacob Saylor justices.

Township	Constable	Overseer Poor	Supervisor Highways
Barree	William Nelson	James Anderson John Dickey	John Wilson James Hannan
Brothers Valley	Frederick Ambrosier	Walter Hoyle George Coleman	Henry Bittinger
Colerain	John Paron	Abraham Miley John Friend	James Patterson Joseph Friend
Cumberland Valley	John Dick__	Joseph Kelly Henry Williams	Thomas Lazer John Elder
Dublin	John Ramsay	James Barnet Hugh Davidson	Robert Ramsay George Hudson
Turkey Foot	Jacob Hartzel	John Millick John Mitchell	Edward Camp Edward Hartzel
Huntingdon	John Bittle	John Fee George Reynolds	Henry Niff Nathaniel Jarrot
Shirley	John Armstrong	George Wilson John Morgan	James Galbreath William Morris
Milford	Abraham Faith	George Paron John Weimer	John Penrod Adam Shaffer
Londonderry	William Workman	George Lebarger Jacob Rhoad	John Hains Nicholas Lebarger
Elk Lick	Shafit Devore	Abraham Berkey Clements Engle	John C___ John ___
Tyrone	David Lowry	John Smith Thomas McC__	Robert Stewart Thomas K__

Page 79L   April 1787
Grand Jury:
James Jamison, foreman
William Carter
William Wilson
George McCullough
David John
David Shelby
Benjamin William
Michael Oswald
Joseph Morrison
James Patterson
Israel Penrod
Matthias Whetstone
Christian Heible (affirmed)
Joshua Lewis
David Caldwell
James Hunter
James Anderson
William Shirley

Pennsylvania v. John Haugher. Larceny. True Bill. Appeared.

Pennsylvania v. James Martin, Gavin Beagle & William Williams. Nuisance. True Bill. Process awarded & bail entered.

Pennsylvania v. Pennsylvania v. John Mitchell. John Mitchell in £50, Ludwic Sills in £50.

Pennsylvania v. John Fee senior. John Fee senior in £50, Matthiu Daul__ in £50.

Pennsylvania v. Benjamin Stevens. Defendant in £50, Jacob Rush in £25.

Pennsylvania v. John Tate. John Tate in £50, Thomas Norton in £25.

George Ensley and Peter Bark__ elected Appraisers for Providence. Township.

Page 79R   April 1787

1. Pennsylvania v. Alexander Murphy. Defendant in £40, William Farmer & Fergus Higgins in £20. Joseph McDonald and Daniel Means bound to prosecute in £40.

2. Pennsylvania v. John Albright. John Albright in £20, Nichols Leiberger in £10.

3. Pennsylvania v. John Mitchell. Assault & Battery. True Bill.

4. Pennsylvania v. Charles Gordon. Larceny. True Bill.

5. Pennsylvania v. Robert Filson. Tipling House. True Bill.

Pennsylvania v. Charles Gordon. Larceny. True Bill.

Pennsylvania v. Jacob Helm. Defendant in £40, John Helm in £20. William Williams in £20.

Pennsylvania v. Charles Gordon. Defendant in £40, George James in £10, Jacob Chamberlain in £10 for appearance of defendant next court to answer of Felony.

Page 80L   April 1787

Pennsylvania v. John Hauger. Felony. Testify for prosecution: Henry Liberger, Nicholas Liberger, John Smith, Robert Huston, Thomas Coulter; for defense: Isaac Hardin, Rebecca Rhoads, Jacob Rhoads. Jury of William Nelson, Anthony Smith, John Dough__, Henry Neff, John Williams, Francis Clugage, George Buchan__, Laban Purdue, John Cornelius, John Neff, Samuel Montgomery, and Henry Williams find defendant guilty. Sentence: Between the hours of ten and two tomorrow John Haugen to be taken to the Common Whipping Post and receive ten lashes on his bare back well laid on and return the goods of value thereof and pay a fine equal to their value and pay costs. Fine £3.0.0.

Pennsylvania v. Margaret Coal. Bastardy. Ignoramus.

Pennsylvania v. Elizabeth S_ade. Bastardy. True Bill.

Page 80R   April 1787

Pennsylvania v. John Mitchell. Defendant in £20, Abraham Miley in £20 for appearance of defendant next July session to answer for Assault & Battery.

Pennsylvania v. Robert Filson. Matthias Carpenter in £20 to appear at July session to prosecute Robert Filson for keeping a Tipling House.

Pennsylvania v. Ebenezer Griffith & John Clink. Ebenezer Griffith in £40, John Clink in £40, William Tisue in £20.

Pennsylvania v. Hugh Robison. Defendant in £20, James Black in £10. Appeared.

Pennsylvania v. John Haugher. John Hauger in £10, Philip Hauger in £10. Appeared. John Albright in £10 to prosecute. Michael Oswalt and Valentine Barker in £5 each to give evidence for the state.

10. Pennsylvania v. William Gultrie. Tipling House. True Bill.

11. Pennsylvania v. Hugh Robison. Assault & Battery. True Bill.

Page 81L   April 1787

Pennsylvania v. John Haugar. Felony. Testify for prosecution: John

Albright, Michael Oswalt, Valentine Baker; for defense: Jacob Rhoads, Jacob Hagar. Jury of Henry Williams, John Cornelius, John Williams, Anthony Smith, Samuel Montgomery, L___ Purdew, William Nelson, John Doughman, John Neff, George Buchanan, Matthew Kelly, Francis Clugage find defendant guilty. Sentence that between the hours of ten and two John Haugar to be taken to the Common Whipping Post and receive four lashes to his bare back well laid on, to return goods stolen of value thereof, pay a fine of like value, pay costs.

Pennsylvania v. Derry Ryan. Defendant in £20, Timothy Ryan in £20 for appearance of Derry Ryan at next session to answer for Fornication.

Pennsylvania v. Jacob Hellem. Defendant in £40, Felix Mellan in £40 for appearance of defendant at next July session to answer. July 1787 discharged.

Pennsylvania v. Alexander Murphy. Abraham Miley in £40 for good behavior of defendant until next July session particularly toward Joseph McDonald.

Page 81R April 1787
Pennsylvania v. Hugh Robison. Defendant pleads guilty and submits to the court. Fined 7/6.

Pennsylvania v. John Mitchell. John Fee in £10 for his appearance at July session to give evidence against defendant for Assault & Battery.

Pennsylvania v. Benjamin Stevens. Benj[n] Stevens in £40, Benjamin Williams in £40 for appearance of defendant to answer. July 1787 discharged by proclamation.

Pennsylvania v. Ebenezer Griffith & John Clink. Ebenezer Griffith in £20, John Clink in £20 for their appearance next session to answer. Appeared and gave Bail.

Pennsylvania v. James Martin, Gavin Beagle & William Williams. James Martin in £20, John Richey in £20 for appearance of defendant next session to answer for Nuisance on the Highway.

Page 82L
Pennsylvania v. Robert Philson. Defendant in £15, Terrence Campbell in £15 for appearance of defendant to answer for Tipling House.

Pennsylvania v. Thomas Abrams. Thomas Abrams in £25, Arthur McGaughy in £10, Thomas McGaughy in £10 for appearance of defendant next session to answer for Forcible Entry.

Page 82R [July 1786]
To certify the subscribers, two of the Commissioners of Bedford have appointed William Ward of the Town of Bedford to be Commissioner in the place of Hugh Barclay, excused. 13 July 1786
William Proctor
Thomas Crossan

The above mentioned William Ward duly sworn 14 April 1786 before Bernard Dougherty and Hugh Barclay.

Page 83L [October 1783]
Certification that William Proctor was elected Commissioner the second Tuesday of October 1783. Thomas Coulter, John Friend, James Sommerville. W^m Ki_ley, Hugh Orlton, James Martin.

21 October 1783 said William Proctor took Oath of Allegiance and General oath of office before David Espy and Bernard Dougherty.

Certification that Hugh Barclay was elected Commissioner the second Tuesday of October 1783. William Anderson, Michael Longnecher [German script], John Friend, Thomas Coulter.

Page 83R [October 1785]
Election of Thomas Crossan as Commissioner entered 14 October 1785. John Friend, William Gaff, William Philip, Reuben Skinner.

Election of Harman Husbands as Commissioner entered 13 October 178_. Hugh Barclay, Samuel Thompson, William Jones, Robt Clugage, David Stewart.

Page 84L [July 1787]
At Bedford 17 July 1787 before Bernard Dougherty, James Martin, Hugh Barclay, Abraham Cable, James Wells, Richard Galbreath, William Proctor, John Cessna, Jacob Saylor, David Jones, Thomas Coulter.

Grand Jury:
Cornelius McAulay
Charles Rubey
Martin Reiley
James Francis
Henry Wise
Samuel McCashlan
Robert Hopper
John Andrew May

Michael Cryder (affirmed)
Alexander Dean
Jonathan Priestly
George Falker (affirmed)
Balzer Copenhover
Peter McMullen
Alexander McConnell
John Fee

Recognizances.

Pennsylvania v. Derry Ryan. Defendant in £40, Timothy Ryan in £20 for appearance of defendant next session to answer for Bastardy.

Pennsylvania v. Moses Donnaldson. Defendant in £50, Henry Canan in £50.

Page 84R   July 1787
Pennsylvania v. John Chilcot, Josiah Franklin, Umprey Chilcot, John Machanel, William Price. Defendants in £200 each, George Ashman £200. Bail. Thos Blair in £200 to prosecute. Ignatius Gad in £200 to give evidence.

Pennsylvania v. Philip Ketchim. Philip Ketchim in £50. John Rush in £50.

Pennsylvania v. Asaph Moore Colgate, Charles Prossor, Joseph Parish, & Thomas Morgan. Defendants in £200 each. Jacob Shara £200 for each. Bail entered. Thomas Blair in £200 to prosecute. Ignatius Gad in £200 to give evidence.

Pennsylvania v. David Stevens, Benjamin Brown & William Stevens. Defendants in £200 each. Jacob Shara in £200 for each.

Pennsylvania v. Hugh Orlton, George Nanzant, W^m McClean & Benjamin Chilcot. Defendants in £200 each. George Ashman in £200.

Pennsylvania v. John Moore, Merryman Price, & Benjamin Mackane. Defendants in £200 each. George Ashman in £200.

Pennsylvania v. Andrew McFarran. Defendant in £50. Moses Donnaldson & Ludwic Sells in £50 to prosecute.

Page 85L   July 1787
1. Pennsylvania v. Derry Ryan. Fornication. True Bill. Bail entered.

2. Pennsylvania v. Philip Ketchim. Fornication. True Bill. Bail entered.

3. Pennsylvania v. Humphrey Chilcot, John Mackane, Josiah Franklin, William Price, Hugh Orlton, George Nanzant, William McClean, Benjamin Chilcot, David Stevens, William Stevens, John Moore, Merryman Price, Benjamin Mackane, Charles Prosser, Asaph Moore Colgate, Thomas Morgan, Joseph Parish, Benjamin Brown, Nathaniel Rockwell, Samuel Wheeler, William Long, Robison Chilcot, William Cotton, William Cornelius, Daniel Brown, Joshua Brown, John Chilcot. Riot & Forcible Entry. Bail entered to Jan. Jacob Sharran, Hugh Orlton,

jointly and individually in £500 for appearance of above twenty seven persons to answer for Riot & Forcible Entry.

Page 85R   July 1787
Pennsylvania v. Henry Thomas & Abednego Stevens. Henry Thomas in £50, Abednego Stevens in £25. Ended.

Pennsylvania v. Robert Hamilton. Defendant in £50, Matthew Arter in £25. Ended.

Pennsylvania v. Edward & Jane Taylor. William Boyd in £20 to give evidence.

Same v. same. Thos Norton to prosecute in £20. James Martin in £10. John Tate in £10. Bail entered.

Pennsylvania v. Thos Norton. Edward Taylor in £20 to prosecute.

Pennsylvania v. Andrew McFarren. Assault & Battery. True Bill. Bail Entered.

Pennsylvania v. Thomas Blair, John Blair, John Campbell & William Gadd. Riot & Forcible Entry. Ignoramus.

Pennsylvania v. Moses Donnaldson. Assault & Battery. True Bill.

Pennsylvania v. Andrew McFerran. Defendant in £40, Joseph McFerran in £40 for appearance of defendant October session to answer for assault & battery. Forfeited. Bail entered to January 1788.

Page 86L   July 1787
Pennsylvania v. Hugh Orlton, David Stevens, Asaph Moore Colgate, Josiah Franklin, William Price, Benjamin Brown, Daniel Brown, Joshua Brown, William McClean, Jacob Shearer, Giles Stevens, Samuel Wheeler, Robison Shillcoat, John Shillcoat, Benjamin Shillcoat, Humphrey Shillcoat & William Stevens. Riot & Forcible Entry. True Bill. Bail returned to July 1787. Jacob Sharran & Hugh Orlton jointly & severally in £300 for appearance of defendants at next October session to answer.

Pennsylvania v. Alexander Murphy. Defendant in £20. Abraham Miley in £10, Samuel Davis of Frankstown in £10 for good behavior of defendant until next October session especially toward Joseph McDonald. Discharged by proclamation.

Pennsylvania v. Philip Ketcham. Philip Ketcham in £50. John Rushin in £25 for appearance of defendant next session to answer for Fornication.

Page 86R   July 1787

Pennsylvania v. Philip Ketcham. Benjamin Abbot in £20 for appearance of Elizabeth Abbot at next October session to prosecute and give evidence against defendant for Fornication.

Pennsylvania v. Cristine Countz. James Robinson of Brothers Valley in £40 for appearance of defendant next October session to answer. Bail entered to January 1788.

Pennsylvania v. Moses Donaldson. Defendant in £20, John Canan Esq. in £20 for appearance of defendant next October session to answer for Assault & Battery.

~~Pennsylvania v. Hugh Orlton. Robert Galbreath Esq. in £40 for appearance of Thomas Blair at next session to prosecute.~~

Pennsylvania v. Edward Taylor & James Taylor. James Norton in £10, James Martin Esq. in £10 for appearance of Thomas Norton at next session to prosecute and give evidence against Edward Taylor and James Taylor for Assault & Battery. Bail to January 1788.

Pennsylvania v. Ebenezer Griffith & John Klink. Ebenezer Griffith in £20, Abraham Cable in £20 for appearance of defendant next court to answer. Bail to January 1788.

Page 87L   July 1787

Pennsylvania v. Ebenezer Griffith & John Klink. Abraham Cable Esq in £20 for appearance of William V___ at next court to give evidence against the defendants for not assisting him in the execution of his office as Constable.

At Bedford 01 October 1787 at a meeting of a number of Justices of the Peace for Bedford: William Proctor, Thomas Coulter, James Martin, Hugh Barclay, Abraham Cable, and John Cessna Esqs. in pursuance of instrument of writing from Thomas Crossan, one of the Commissioners of the County of Bedford:

> To Bernard Dougherty, David Espy, Hugh Barclay, Tho[s] Coulter, John Cessna, James Martin, William Peterson, James Coyle, Robert Galbraith, Tho[s] Wilson, John Little, William Proctor, Abraham Cable, James Wells, David Jones, and William Skinner, Justices of the Peace and Court of Quarter Sessions. Take notice that the subscriber, one of the Commissioners of Bedford County calls you to meet on Monday the first day of October next at the court house to make enquiry into the under return of two

Commissioners (Herman Husband and David Stewart) made last October term [bottom of page torn away]

Page 87R [July 1787]

and then and there determine and distinguish which of those two persons above is and was the Commissioner who served in the stead of Hugh Barclay so that it may be known which of the two above mentioned Herman Husband or David Stewart will be the Legal Commissioner after the next election.

  dated at Bedford this   James Crossan
  12 September 1878

And whereas it appeared to the Justices present that a notice has been served on all Justices of the Peace it is the opinion of said Justices that Herman Husband is the Commissioner for three years from his being elected which was the second Tuesday in October 1786.

Page 88L [October 1787]
At Bedford 16 October 1787 before William Proctor Esq., President, and associate Justices. Present: William Proctor, Hugh Barclay, Thomas Coulter, John Cessna, James Martin.

Grand Jury:

John Reed	John More
Daniel McConnel	Henry Sides
William Johnson	Thomas Laz__
Moses Reed	John Jones
George Eby	Frederick Dibert
Thomas Norton	Balzer Hesse
Benjamin Martin	John Ewalt junior
Joseph Warford	Philip Wagerlin (affirmed)
James Mortimore	George Coleman

Pennsylvania v. John Imlir. Davis Moore of Cumberland in £20 for his appearance at October session 1787 to be held at Carlisle for the County of Cumberland to give evidence against John Imlir for Horse Stealing.

Indictments.

Pennsylvania v. John Cravens. Stopping up the Way. Bail entered.

Page 88R October 1787
2. Pennsylvania v. William Hartley. Assault & Battery. True Bill. Defendant pleads guilty. Fined six pence.

3. Pennsylvania v. William Ramsay. Assault & Battery. True Bill.

4. Pennsylvania v. William Ramsey. Justinius Horsal in £20 for appearance of said Justinius at next July session to give evidence and prosecute Wm Ramsay for assault & Battery. Appeared.

5. Pennsylvania v. Humphrey Chilcot, John Mackerel, Jonah Franklin, William Price, Hugh Orlton, George Nanzant, William McClean, Benjamin Chilcot, David Stevens, William Stevens, John Moore, Merryman Price, Benjamin Mackerel, Charles Prosser. Asaph Moore Colegate, Thomas Morgan, Joseph Parish, Benjamin Brown, Nathaniel Rockwell, Samuel Wheeler, William Long, Robison Chilcot, William Cotton, William Cornelius, Daniel Brown, Joshua Brown, John Chilcot. Jacob Sharra, and Hugh Orlton jointly and severally in £500 for appearance of the above twenty seven next January session to answer for Riot and Forcible Entry.

Page 89L   October 1787
Pennsylvania v. Hugh Orlton, David Stevens, Asaph Moore Colgate, Josiah Franklin, William Price, Banjamin Brown, Daniel Brown, Joshua Brown, William McClean, Jacob Sharran, Giles Stevens, Samuel Wheeler, Robison Chilcot, John Chilcot, Benjamin Chilcot, Humphrey Chilcot, William Stevens. Hugh Orlton, and John Sharra jointly and severally in £300 for the appearance of the named seventeen persons to appear next January session to answer for Riot and Forcible Entry.

4. Pennsylvania v. Jacob Taylor and Jane his wife. Assault & Battery. True Bill. Bail entered. April 1879 submitted & fined.

5. Pennsylvania v. Thomas Smith Esq. Indictment by Presentment. Assault & Battery. True Bill.

Pennsylvania v. Philip Ketchim. Fornication. Found at July session. Pleads guilty. Judgment is fine of £10, pay Elizabeth Abbet £5 for lying in expenses and 3/ per week for the maintenance of the child from the time of birth of the child until it reaches the age of [blank space for age] if it lives so long and shall also indemnify the ___ where the child was born & give security for the obedience of the order of the court.

Page 89R   October 1787
Pennsylvania v. Thomas Downy. Assault & Battery. True Bill. Defendant pleads guilty. Fined 2/6.

Pennsylvania v. William Hartley. Defendant pleads guilty. Fined six pence.

Pennsylvania v. George Nixon. Defendant in £10, James Patterson in £10. Forfeit until January 1788.

Pennsylvania v. Edward Taylor & Jane his wife. Edward Taylor in £20, Timothy Ryan in £10 for appearance of defendant next session to answer for Assault and Battery on Thomas Norton. Forfeit to October 1788. Forfeit Absolute.

Pennsylvania v. Edward Taylor & Jane his wife. Thomas Norton in £10 for his appearance to give evidence against Edward Taylor & Jane his wife for Assault & Battery.

Pennsylvania v. Ebenezer Griffith & John Clink. Thomas Vickroy in £20, Abraham Cable Esq. in £20 for appearance of defendant next court. to answer. January 1788 discharged by proclamation.

Page 90L October 1787
Pennsylvania v. Christina Countz. Defendant in £20, James Robison of Brothers Valley Township in £20 for appearance of defendant next session to prosecute John Griffith for Fornication and Bastardy.

Pennsylvania v. Ebenezer Griffith & John Clink. William V__ht in £10 for appearance of W^m V__ht at next session to give evidence against defendant for not assisting him in the execution of his office as Constable.

Pennsylvania v. Andrew McFerran. Defendant in £20, Joseph McFerran in £20 for appearance of defendant next court to answer for Assault & Battery. Forfeit to January 1788. July forfeit absolute.

Pennsylvania v. Andrew McFerran, Mary Donnaldson in £20, Henry Cannan in £20 for appearance of Mosis Donnaldson next session to prosecute and give evidence against defendant Assault & Battery. January 1788 forfeit & reposted.

Pennsylvania v. Charles Gordon. Charles Gordon in £30, Robert Gibson in £30 for appearance of defendant next session to answer two indictments. Appeared.

Pennsylvania v. John Cra_m_. John Cra_m_ in £20, William Ward in £20 for appearance of defendant next July to answer for Nuisance on the Highway. Ended.

Page 90R [October 1787]
Recording of certificate dividing townships for election of justices.

In Council, Philadelphia Saturday 08 September 1787. Certificates of the division of the townships of Cumberland Valley, Bethel, & Brothers Valley each into two distinct districts for election of Justices of the Peace and the division of Frankstown into three distinct districts for the same. Extract from the Minutes
> James Trimble for John Armstrong
> Recorded & Compared. David Espy, Clerk.

October Sessions 1787.

Pennsylvania v. Derry Ryan. By argument of attorneys matter referred to Thomas Coulter, Thomas Vickroy, William Todd, Robert Gibson, and William Hartley or any three of them who are to hear the matter and make report therein ex parte Rule in half an hours notice. Same session report read. Derry Ryan to pay £3 to Hannah Bateson and one shilling per week for one year to the support of the said Hannah Bateson's child and six pence to the state. Judgment of the court is the same.

Page 91L [January 1788]
At Bedford the third Tuesday in January 1788 before Bernard Dougherty, William Proctor, Hugh Barclay, James Martin, William Patterson, and John Cessna.

Grand Jury:
- Thomas Burk
- Robert Gibson
- Frederick Swartz
- Abraham Bullman
- William Beatty
- William Frazer
- Adam Smith
- John Ogden
- Philip Coleman
- William Gibson
- Michael Wallock
- Jacob Myers
- John Livingstone
- George Johnston
- Nathaniel Titus
- John Andrew May
- John Barger

Pennsylvania v. Humphrey Chilcot and others. Testify for prosecution: Ignatius Gad, David Logan, Thomas Blair. For defense: Baltzer Covenhoven, Giles Stevens. Indictment for Riot and Forcible Entry fount at July session 1787. Jury of Thomas Hay, Benjamin Loan, Frederick Allehouser, Duncan Morrison, John Hamilton, Henry Rigar, Wm Anderson, Edward Taylor, William Todd, James Anderson, John Paxton, and George Burket find defendants guilty.

Page 91R   January 1788
Pennsylvania v. William Boyd. Assault & Battery. True Bill. Bail entered to April next.

Pennsylvania v. John Kennard. Forcible Entry & Detainer. True Bill. Bail entered.

Pennsylvania v. Thomas Norton. Assault & Battery. True Bill. Bail entered.

Recognizances.

Pennsylvania v. John Longstreath & Benjamin Stevens. Jno Longstreath in £50, Benjn Stevens in £25. Discharged by proclamation.

Pennsylvania v. Joseph Lily & George Elder. Joseph Lily in £50, George Elder in £25. Discharged by proclamation.

Pennsylvania v. Charles Gordon. Larceny found at April 1787, Testify for prosecution: William Hartley, John Andrew May, John Dougherty, John Lafferty, William Fraser. For defense: John Cessna, George Iams. Jury of Thomas Woods, Anthony Smith, William Baker, James Fletcher junior, Robert Culbertson, Henry Whetstone, John McGaughey, Thomas Kenton, Michael Barndollar, John Graham, Philip Deal, and Thomas McGibbon find defendant not guilty.

Page 92L   January 1788
Pennsylvania v. Charles Gordon. Larceny found at April session 1787. Testify for prosecution: William Hartley, John Andrew May, John Dougherty, John Lafferty, William Fraser. For defense: John Cessna Esq., George James. Jury of Thomas Woods, Anthony Smith, William Baker, James Fletcher junior, Robert Culbertson, Henry Whetstone, John McGaughey, Thomas Kenton, Michael Barndollar, John Graham, Philip Deal, and Thomas McGibbon find defendant not guilty.

Pennsylvania v. John Paxton and John Paxton junior. John Paxton in £20, John Paxton junior in £20, Daniel McCortney in £20. Appeared and bail entered.

Pennsylvania v. Willm Boyd. Assault & Battery. True Bill. Bail entered.

Pennsylvania v. William Boyd junior. Assault & Battery. Ignoramus.

Pennsylvania v. William Boyd junior. William Boyd junior in £20, John Cravens in £20 for appearance of defendant April session to answer for Assault & Battery. April appeared and submitted to the court.

Pennsylvania v. William Boyd. William Boyd junior in £20, John Cravens in £20 for appearance of defendant April session to answer for Assault & Battery. April appeared and submitted to the court.

Page 92R　　　January 1788
Return for road from Stattl_ to Berlin in the Glades and it appeared that only five had viewed so order to view is continued.

Pennsylvania v. Michael Port, Michael Port in £20, Martin Loy in £20 for good behavior.

Pennsylvania v. Charles Gordon. Larceny from April 1787. Tried and continued to January 1788. Judgment that defendant return goods or value thereof to owner and pay a fine of like value and he be taken to the public whipping post on this Sunday between the hours of ten and twelve and receive five lashes on his bare back well laid on and pay costs of prosecution.

Pennsylvania v. John Kennard. John Kennard in £20, William Pitman in £20 for appearance of defendant next April to answer for Forcible Entry and Detainer. April 1788 appeared in custody.

Pennsylvania v. Charles Gordon. Charles Gordon in £40, George James in £20, Robert Gibson in £20 for appearance of defendant next April session to answer.

Page 93L　　　January 1788
Pennsylvania v. Thomas Norton. Thomas Norton in £10, Felix Melan in £10 for appearance of defendant next April session to answer of Assault & Battery.

Pennsylvania v. Humphrey Chilcot, John Mackarel, Josiah Franklin, William Price, Hugh Orlton, George Nanzant, William McClean, Benjamin Chilcot, David Stevens, William Stevens, John Moore, Merryman Price, Benjamin Mackarel, Charles Prosser, Asaph Moore Colgate, Thomas Morgan, Joseph Parish, Benjamin Brown, Nathaniel Blackwell, Samuel Wheeler, William Long, Robison Chilcot, William Cotton, William Cornelius, Daniel Brown, Joshua Brown, and John Chilcott. Hugh Orlton and Asaph Moore Colgate jointly and severally in £500 for appearance of above twenty seven persons next April to answer for riot and Forcible Entry.

Page 93R　　　January 1788
Pennsylvania v. Hugh Orlton, David Stevens, Asaph Moore Colgate, Josiah Franklin, William Price, Benjamin Brown, Daniel Brown, Joshua Brown, William McClean, Jacob Sharran, Giles Stevens, Samuel

Wheeler, Robison Chilcot, John Chilcot, Benjamin Chilcot, Humphrey Chilcot, William Stevens. Hugh Orlton, Asaph Moore Colgate jointly and severally bound in £300 for appearance of above seventeen persons at next April session to answer for Riot & Forcible Entry, &c.

Pennsylvania v. John Paxton. John Paxton in £20, Thomas Coulter Esq. in £20 for appearance of defendant next April session and in the meantime be of good behavior particularly toward Samuel Price.

Page 94L [March 1788]
At the house of William Ward in the town of Bedford 25 March 1788 before Bernard Dougherty, Hugh Barclay, James Martin & David Espy.

Township	Constable	Supervisor Highways	Overseer Poor
Bedford Town	George Funk		
Bedford Township	Allen McCoomb	~~Samuel Davidson~~ ~~Henry Werth~~	Allen Rose Adam Croyle
Colerain	Philip Deal	Abraham Miley John Friend	James Patterson Joseph Friend
Cumberland Valley	Christopher Mea__	Henry Williams Amos Dickens	Thomas Ray Jonathan Cessna
Turkey Foot	John Meloch	Henry Eberly Edward Harnet	John Skinner Richard Green
Providence	William Gibson	Amos Jones John Gibson	Joseph Morrison George Barton
Woodberry		John Snyder Philip Knee	John Ferguson Valentine Easter

Page 94R [April 1788]
At Bedford the third Tuesday in April 1788 before Bernard Dougherty, William Proctor, James Martin, Abraham Cable, John Cessna, Hugh Barclay, David Jones, James Wells, Thomas Coulter, James Coyle, &c.

Township	Constable	Supervisor Highways	Overseer Poor
Bedford Township		Solomon Adams Henry Wirth	
Air	Matthew Caldwell	William Alexander James Balla	Benjamin Stevens William Gaff
Bethel	Isaac Cowel	John Stilwell Andrew Hornler	Samuel Graves John Fisher
Brothers Valley	Casper Hoover	Michael Bieghley Jacob Glasner	Andrew Borndrager John G__ing
Quamahoning	Daniel Hoy	James Black	Jacob Smoker

Township	Constable	Supervisor Highways	Overseer Poor
		William Boyd	Christian Spiker
Milford	Henry Bruner	Philp B___gh	
		John Penrod junior	Adam Keffer
Elk Lick	Frederick Sap	Abraham Beechey	John Clink
		Clemens Ingle	John Syler
Londonderry	Casper Albright	Jacob Rhoads	John Harris
		Godfrey Welfair	Nicholas Liberger
Belfast	Jacob Poorman	Morris Dishong	William Kerney
		Peter Swartzwelder	William Morton
Woodberry	Martin Loy		
Hopewell	Benjamin Cherry	Sebastian Shoup__	Jeremaih D___
		Philip ___	Thomas B___

[Bottom of page faint.]

Page 95L   April 1788
Grand Jury: James Black, foreman

    Jacob Nave   George Kimbel (affirmed)
    Henry Armstrong   Valentine Fillebaugh (affirmed)
    Adam Croyle (Affirmed)   George Rough
    John Cra__ (affirmed)   Jacob Keifer (affirmed)
    Jacob Good (affirmed)   Michael Beighley (affirmed)
    George Imbler   John Miller
    George Wisegarver   Henry Bruner
    Joseph Barcidol (affirmed) George Bruner (affirmed)
    Gabriel Rhoads (affirmed) Samuel Spiker
                                      John Spiker (affirmed)
                                      John Richey
                                      Samuel McAshlan

Indictments.

1. Pennsylvania v. Edward Warren. Felony. Ignoramus

2. Pennsylvania v. John Davis. Adultery. True Bill.

3. Pennsylvania v. John Tait. Assault & Battery. Submitted to the court and fined.

4. Pennsylvania v. Grace Justice. Fornication. True Bill.

5 Pennsylvania v. Henry Beam. Tipling House. True Bill.

6. Pennsylvania v. John Hopkins. Tipling House. True Bill.

DOCKET 2: 1771–1801   141

Page 95R   April 1788
Recognizances.

Pennsylvania v. Edward Warren. Edward Warren in £30, Anthony Assher in £30

[Between these recognizances appears the notation "Bill of Indictment Returned. Ignoramus." The case that the notation refers to is not apparent.]

Pennsylvania v. Archibald Lemmon. Archibald Lemon in £40. Ended.

Pennsylvania v. Richard Pinkerton. Richard Pinkerton in £50, John Kilpatrick in £50. Discharged by proclamation.

Pennsylvania v. Grace Justice. Grace Justice in £50.

Pennsylvania v. John Davis. John Davis in £50, Abraham Faith in £50.

Pennsylvania v. Humphrey Chilcot et al. Riot and Forcible entry found at July session 1787. Testify for prosecution: Ignatius Gad, James Logan, Robert Galbreath Esq. Testify for defense: Balser Copenhoven, Giles Stevens, John Stevens. Jury of Thomas Paxton, Derry Ryan, George Croyle, Samuel McCashlan, Frederick Humberg, James Williams, Henry Sides, James Smith, Abraham Teetor, Henry Swagar, Philip Stoner, and Philip Longstrath find defendants guilty of Riot and not guilty of Forcible Entry. Each defendant fined 2/6.

Page 96L   April 1788
Pennsylvania v. William Boyd. Assault & Battery found January 1788. Defendant pleads guilty. Fined 1/-.

Pennsylvania v. John Tate. Assault & Battery found this session. Defendant pleads guilty. Fined 1/6.

Pennsylvania v. Hugh Orlton, Davis Stevens, Asaph Moore Colgate, Josiah Franklin, William Price, Benjamin Brown, Daniel Brown, Joshua Brown, William McClean, Jacob Sharrow, Giles Stevens, Samuel Wheeler, Robeson Chilcot, John Chilcot, Benjamin Chilcot, Humphrey Chilcot, William Stevens. Riot & Forcible Entry found July 1787. April 1788. Defendants retract plea of not guilty as to the Riot and submit to court protesting their innocence and pray to be admitted to a small fine. Each fined 1/6 except Asaph Moore Colgate fined 2/6.

Page 96R   April 1788
Pennsylvania v. John Kennard. Defendant retracts his former plea

protesting his innocence prays to be admitted to a small fine. Fined 1s. Defendant in gaol.

Pennsylvania v. Elizabeth Paxton. Fornication. True Bill.

Pennsylvania v. Michael Cuntz. Tipling House. Ignoramus.

Pennsylvania v. John Colepenny. Tipling House. Ignoramus.

Pennsylvania v. William Boyd junior. Assault & Battery found January 1788. Defendant submits to court protesting his innocence and prays to be admitted a small fine. Fined £1.0.0.

Pennsylvania v. Samuel Moss et al. Riot & Assault. Ignoramus.

Pennsylvania v. Edward Conner and Samuel Crossan. Forcible Entry & Detainer. True Bill. Samuel Crossan in £20, Thomas Crossan in £20 for appearance of Samuel Crossan at next court to answer. Edward Conner in £20, Edward Taylor in £20 for appearance of Edw[d] as above.

Page 97L April 1788
Pennsylvania v. L___ Cuntz. Defendant in £20, George Funck in £20 for appearance of defendant and for good behavior. Discharged by proc.

Pennsylvania v. John Hopkins. Defendant in £20, Sam[l] Davidson in £20 for appearance of defendant next session to answer for Tipling House. July session ended Nole Prosequti.

Page 97R [July 1788]
At Bedford the third Tuesday of July 1788 before Bernard Dougherty, Hugh Barclay, David Jones, James Martin, William Proctor, Abraham Cable, James Wells, John Cessna, Michael Oswalt, Jacob Hartzel, Thomas Coulter, Bethuel Covalt.

Grand Jury: Benjamin Burd, foreman
  James Jamison   Adam Ballam
  Joseph McFarren   Christian Fritz
  Daniel Anderson   Jacob Flick
  Godfrey Panter   Henry Baker
  William McClemens   Jacob Heffer
  Henry Livingston   Cornelius McAuley
  Philip Isor   Samuel Plummer
  Ludwic Bean   William Henry

1, Pennsylvania v. David Evans. Fornication & Bastardy. True Bill.

2. Pennsylvania v. Michael Imfelt. Assault & Battery. True Bill.

3. Pennsylvania v. Thomas Smith. Assault & Battery. True Bill. Bail Ent^d. Oct submitted to Court & fined 6 pence.

4. Pennsylvania v. James Martin Esq. Assault & Battery. Ignoramus.

5. Pennsylvania v. David Jones Esq. Felony. True Bill.

6. Pennsylvania v. Thomas Hays. Assault & Battery.

Page 98L   July 1788

7. Pennsylvania v. Daniel Royer. Assault & Battery. Ignoramus

8. Pennsylvania v. ~~Daniel Royer~~ David Griffith. Misdemeanor. True Bill. David Griffith in £40, Ebenezer Griffith in £40 for appearance of defendant next session to answer.

Recognizances.

Pennsylvania v. Thomas Hay. Adam Crise in £20, John Tate in £10. Appeared.

Pennsylvania v. Samuel Able. Robert McIntire in £10. Forfeited.

Pennsylvania v. Michael Imfelt. Michael Imfelt in £40, George Wisecarver in £40. Forfeited.

Pennsylvania v. David Jones, Esq. Isaac Jones in £50, Daniel Stoy in £50. Bail entered.

Pennsylvania v. James Martin Esq. Samuel Crossan junior in £20. Appeared and discharged.

Pennsylvania v. David Jones Esq. Defendant in £40, Jacob Hartzell Esq. in £40 for appearance of defendant next term to answer for Larceny. William Blair in £20 to testify and give evidence.

Page 98R   July 1788
Pennsylvania v. David Jones Esq. Isaac Jones of Fayette County Yeoman in £200 for appearance of said Isaac Jones at next Court of Oyer & Terminer to be held at Philadelphia for the state of Pennsylvania on 24 September next there give evidence against David Jones Esq. for Felony. On motion that the prosecutor give evidence for his appearance to prosecute defendant at next Supreme Court, James Gilmore in £100 conditioned that said James and Margaret his wife appear at next Court of Oyer & Terminer in Philadelphia 24 September next to give evidence against David Jones Esq. for Felony.

Thomas Crossan and William Ward, Commissioners, present accounts of County of Bedford. Court appointed Hugh Barclay, David Jones and James Martin as Committee with the Grand Jury to examine the accounts. Committee reported books and receipts justly kept.

Page 99L   July 1788
Pennsylvania v. Edward Conner & Samuel Crossan. Samuel Crossan in £20, George Ensley in £20 for appearance of said Saml Crossan at next session to answer for Forcible Entry & Detainer found last April. Edward Connor in £20, Jacob Rush in £20 for appearance of Edward Connor as above.

Pennsylvania v. Thomas Smith. Thomas Smith in £10 for his appearance next October session to answer for Assault & Battery.

Page 99R   [October 1788]
At Bedford second Tuesday October 1788 before Bernard Dougherty, Hugh Barclay, James Martin, Willm Patterson, Michael Oswalt, Abraham Cable, David Jones, William Proctor, & John Cessna.

Grand Jury: Thomas Blackburn, foreman
    Michael Divert   Elisha Grady
    John Divert   Jonathan Potts
    Frederick Divert   Matthew Taylor
    John Fiske   Thomas Smith
    George Enslow   William Patterson
    Ephraim Wallace   George Enslow junior
    Willm Carter   George Dantzdell

Recognizances.

Pennsylvania v. David Eage. Frederick Eage surety in £20. Ended.

Pennsylvania v. Catherine Eage. Frederick Eage surety in £20. Ended.

Pennsylvania v. Wm Cowan junior. Eve Reppleogle in £10, Peter Ruff in £10 to prosecute. Settled.

Pennsylvania v. John Graham. John Graham in £40, Samuel McAshlan in £40, James Anderson in £20 to prosecute. Approved.

Pennsylvania v. Samuel McCausland & Daniel McMichael. Saml McCashlan in £20, Daniel McMichael in £20. Approved.

Pennsylvania v. Henry Wirth & Solomon Adams. Defendants bound £10 each. James Ker bound in £10 to prosecute. Forfeited.

Page 100L   October 1788
1. Pennsylvania v. David Eage. Assault & Battery. True Bill. Defendant submits to court and prays to be admitted a small fine. Fine 1/-.

2. Pennsylvania v. Catherine Eage. Assault & Battery. True Bill. Defendant submits to court and prays to be admitted a small fine. Fine -/6.

Pennsylvania v. Thomas Smith. Assault & Battery found last session. Defendant submits to court protesting his innocence and prays be admitted to a small fine. Fine 6 pence.

Pennsylvania v. Peter Swope. Defendant in £50, Philip Coleman in £25 to appear and answer. Settled.

3. Pennsylvania v. John Tait. Assault & Battery. True Bill.

4. Pennsylvania v. John Tait. Assault & Battery. True Bill.

5. Pennsylvania v. William Cowan junior. Fornication. True Bill. Defendant pleads guilty. Fined ten pounds.

6. Pennsylvania v. John Graham. Felony. True Bill.

Pennsylvania v. James Gilmore. Adam Keffer in £20.0.0 to prosecute. Forfeit. Bail entered.

Pennsylvania v. Benj^m [struck out] & Garret Wafeld. Benj^m P___ in £50, Garret Wafeld in £25. Discharged by proc.

Page 100R   October 1788
Pennsylvania v. Matthew Caldwell & Benjamin Stevens. Matthew Caldwell in £50, Benj^m Stevens in £25.

Pennsylvania v. Samuel Stevens & Benjamin Stevens. Saml Stevens in £50, Benj^m Stevens in £25.

Pennsylvania v. William [Ferrol?] & Benj^m Stevens. William [Ferrel?] in £50, Benj^m Stevens in £25.

Pennsylvania v. Benj^m Stevens & Matthew Caldwell. Benj^m Stevens in £50, Matthew Caldwell in £25.

Pennsylvania v. David Griffith. Defendant in £50, William Ti___ in £50 for appearance of defendant next April session to answer for Misdemeanor.

Pennsylvania v. John Graham. Felony found this term. Testify for prosecution: James Anderson junior. Testify for defense: George Graham, John Allen, Milly Graham. Jury of John Penrod, Michael Stall, James Gilmore, Peter Rush, David Slegart, Christian Study, Reinhart Wolf, Peter Stiffler, William Boyd, Adam Keffer, Peter Uries, Jacob Rush find defendant not guilty.

Page 101L October 1788
7. Pennsylvania v. Samuel McCausland. Tipling House. True Bill. Bail entered. Nole Prosq.

8. Pennsylvania v. Peter Swope. Assault & Battery. True Bill. Defendant pleads guilty. Fined £10.

9. Pennsylvania v. James Gilmore. Assault & Battery. True Bill. Process Awarded. Bail entered. Jany 1789 fined £6.

10 Pennsylvania v. Samuel McCausland. Assault & Battery. Ignoramus.

11. Pennsylvania v. Daniel McMichael. Assault & Battery. True Bill. Defendant pleads guilty. Fined £6.

Pennsylvania v. Samuel McCashlin. Samuel McCashlin in £20 and John Cessna junior in £20 for appearance of defendant Jany session to answer for Tipling House. Jany 1789 Noli Proseiqui entered.

Pennsylvania v. Edward Conner and Samuel Crossan. Edward Connor in £10 and Samuel Crossan in £10 for their appearance next Jany session to answer for Forcible Entry & Detainer.

Pennsylvania v. William Gibson. Contempt and Neglect of Duty as a Constable. Process Awarded.

Page 101R October 1788
Pennsylvania v. John Tate. Thomas Crossan in £20 for his appearance next session to prosecute defendant for Assault & Battery.

Pennsylvania v. John Tate. Thomas Crossan in £20 for his appearance as above. Ended.

Pennsylvania v. John Gilmor. James Gilmor in £20 and Arthur McGaughey in £20 for appearance of defendant next session to answer for Assault & Battery. Ended.

Pennsylvania v. Samuel McCashlan. John McDonald in £10 and Henry R_gar in £20 for appearance of John McDonald next session to prosecute and give evidence against Samuel McCashlan for Tipling House. Ended.

Pennsylvania v. Thomas Norton. Defendant in £10 for appearance next session to answer for Assault & Battery.

Pennsylvania v. Edward Taylor & Jane his wife. Thomas Norton in £10 for his appearance next session to prosecute and give evidence against defendant for Assault & Battery.

Pennsylvania v. James Gilmore. Adam Keffer in £10 and Arthur McGaughey in £10 for appearance of said Keffer next session to prosecute and give evidence against the defendant for Assault & Battery.

Page 102L October 1788
Anthony Nagle elected Commissioner, certified 16 October 1788 by Thomas Tait, Abraham Miley, and Peter Swarzwilder.

Page 102R [January 1789]
At Bedford 13 January 1789 before Bernard Dougherty, Hugh Barclay, James Martin, William Patterson, Bethuel Covalt, Michael Oswalt.

Grand Jury:
William Scovil

Nathaniel Hart	Jacob Davibaugh
James England	Philip Wolf
David Bradshaw	Jacob Cline
Henry Smith	Jacob Springer
William Drennan	John Hoover
Robert Hemphill	James Ferrel
Simon Hoch	
John Helsel	
George Imler	
Godfrey Huff	

On motion of John Woods Esq., Daniel St Clair admitted an Attorney of this Court.

Commonwealth v. James Black. Jacob Keefer in £20 and Jacob Keefer jr in £20 to prosecute.

Pennsylvania v. John Tate. Assault & Battery found last session.
14 January 1789 rule that Sheriff bring in John Tate by tomorrow 4 PM.

Page 103L   January 1789
1. Pennsylvania v. George Masters. Felony. True Bill.
Defendant pleads guilty and sentenced agreeably.

2. Pennsylvania v. James Black. Assault & Battery. True Bill
Process awarded. Bail entered.

Pennsylvania v. James Gilmore. Assault & Battery found October 1788. Defendant submits to the court protesting innocence and prays a small fine. Fined /6.

Pennsylvania v. John Helsel. Recognizance. Defendant in £50, Henry Werth in £25, George Imler in £25. Discharged by Proc.

Pennsylvania v. Christian Whetstone. Recognizance. Martin Loy in £10, Michael Hildebrand in £10.

Pennsylvania v. George Masters. Felony found this session. Defendant pleads guilty. Judgment servitude of nine months, restore money to the owner, that is 25 pounds & nine pence Lawful money of Pennsylvania & pay same sum to Commonwealth, this being the amount stolen.

Page 103R   January 1789
Pennsylvania v. John Tait. Assault & Battery found last session. Defendant pleads not guilty. Defendant withdraws prior plea and submits to Court. Fined £2.10.-

Pennsylvania v. John Tait. Assault & Battery found last session. Defendant pleads not guilty. Defendant withdraws prior plea and submits to Court. Fined £20.

~~Pennsylvania v. George Martin. Felony found this session. Defendant pleads guilty. Judgment is~~

Pennsylvania v. William Gibson Constable. Defendant in £20 for his appearance next session to answer for Neglect of Duty as Constable.

Page 104L   January 1789
Pennsylvania v. James Black. Adam Keffer in £20 for appearance of Jacob Keefer next session to give evidence against defendant for Assault & Battery. Ended.

Pennsylvania v. James Black. Defendant in £20 and Arthur McGaughey Esq. in £20 for appearance of defendant next session to answer for Assault & Battery on Jacob Keefer.

Page 104R [March 1789]
At Private Sessions at the house of William ____ [page cut off] in the Town of Bedford ___ [page cut off] March 1789 before William Proctor, Hugh Barclay, & David Espy.

Township	Constable	Supervisor Highways	Overseer Poor
Bedford Township		William Drenning John Divert	William Beatty Peter Steffer
Bethel	James McKinney	Peter Smith Jacob Hart	Timothy Fidler Joseph Warford
Colerain	John England		
Cumberland Valley		Andrew Boreland John Elder	
Brothers Valley	Christian Stoner	Michael Bighley Jacob Glassner	Andrew Bur___ John K___
Turkey Foot	Isiah Strawn	John Reed Edward Kemp	Reuben Skin___ James McMu___
Milford	Adam Krimer	Christian Anthony Adam Keeffer	John Penrod Philip King
Providence	John Ritchy	Jacob Studdybaker Edward Daniels	Abiah Akers John Gibson
Hopewell	Joseph Shoupe	Sebastian Shoupe Andrew Lewiston	Lewis Foster Frederic Swar___
Woodberry	Daniel Ullery Edward Cowan to serve for him		

Page 105L [April 1789]
At Bedford the second Tuesday of April 1789 before William Proctor, James Martin, Thomas Coulter, David Jones, Bethul Covalt, Michael Oswalt, Jacob Hartzell, James Wells, William Patterson, John Cessna.

Township	Constable	Supervisor Highways	Overseer Poor
Bedford Town	Baltzer Hesse		
Bedford Township	Ludwic Samuel		
Air	Christian Study	Philip Isor James Ballah	Benjamin Stevens William Gaff
Colerain		John Friend John Flegherty	James Patterson Joseph Friend
Cumberland Valley	Christopher M___		Thomas Rhay Jonathan Cessna
Quamahoning	Philip Kimmel	Simon Shaver James Black	Jacob Smoker Christian Spiker
Elk Lick	Joseph Gundy	Abraham Puchy Clemens Ingle	John Clink John Syler
Londonderry	Duncan McVicker	Cornelius Devore Nath[1] Critchfield	Luke Devore John Masters
Belfast	Jacob Poorman	Peter Swartzwilder Ephraim Wallace	William Kerney William Morton
Woodberry		John Croll John Snyder	John Furguson Valentine Easter
Dublin	William Wilson	Philip Iler George Wilds	Robert Ramsey James Shields

Page 105R   April 1789
Grand Jury:

                William Hartley, foreman

     James Mortimer   James Patterson
     George Croyle   William Gardner
     Daniel Croyle   Anthony Smith
     John Snyder   John Carver (affirmed)
     Francis Hay   Abraham Clevenger
     Peter Smith   Peter Swartzwilder
     Henry Bush   Andrew Boreland

1. Pennsylvania v. Philip Gelliland. Assault & Battery. True Bill. Process awarded. Submitted and fined.

Pennsylvania v. Edward Taylor & Jane his wife. Indictment for Assault & Battery at October Session 1787. Defendant submits to Court & fined.

Pennsylvania v. Thomas Norton. Indictment for Assault & Battery at January session 1788. Defendant submits to Court & fined three pence.

DOCKET 2: 1771–1801 151

2. Pennsylvania v. Hugh Fulton & Edward [Tool?]. Assault & Battery. Defendants plead guilty and submit to Court. Fined 6 pence each.

3. Pennsylvania v. John Mackay. Assault & Battery. True Bill.

Pennsylvania v. Daniel McIntosh. Edward [Tool?] in £10 to prosecute. Ended.

Recognizances.

Pennsylvania v. Henry Hess. Henry Hess in £30. Daniel Stoy in £30. Henry [Keller? Heller?] in £30. Martin [Keller? Heller?] in £30.

Page 106L   April 1789
Pennsylvania v. John Mackay. John Mackay in £10 and Samuel McCashlan in £10 for appearance of defendant next July session to answer for Assault & Battery.

Pennsylvania v. John Mackay. Peter Swartzwilder in £20 to prosecute and give evidence next July session.

Pennsylvania v. William Trimble. William Trimble in £20, John Trimble in £20, and James Trimble in £20. Edward Warren bound to prosecute in £10.

Pennsylvania v. John Mackey. Defendant in £40. Patrick Haney in £20.

4. Pennsylvania v. John Chapman, Nathaniel Chapman, Henry Chapman Jr., Samuel Thomson, Theopolis Bell, Mary John & David John. Assault & Battery. Ignoramus.

5. Pennsylvania v. John Chapman and Samuel Thompson. Assault & Battery. True Bill.

6. Pennsylvania v. Donald McIntosh. Assault & Battery. Ignoramus.

7. Pennsylvania v. Samuel Thomson, Henry Chapman, Henry Chapman Jr., John Chapman & John Anderson. Riot, Assault & Battery. True Bill. Sam[l] Thomson, Henry Chapman, & John Chapman, Henry Chapman Jr., & Jn° Anderson ent[d] Bail. Oct 1789 Defendant John Anderson submits to the Court protesting his innocence. Fine five shillings.

Page 106R   April 1789
Pennsylvania v. John Anderson et al. John Anderson in £4_[cut off] and Betheul Covalt in £40 for appearance of John Anderson next J__[cut off] session to answer for Riot Assault & Battery.

Pennsylvania v. Samuel Thompson. William Carlisle in £20 for appearance of said William Carlisle next Court to prosecute and give evidence against Samuel Thompson for Assault & Battery.

Pennsylvania v. Henry Chapman. Defendant in £100. Edwd Conner in £50.

Pennsylvania v. David John. Defendant in £100. George McCullock in £50,

8. Pennsylvania v. Henry Livingston. Tipling House. True Bill.

9. Pennsylvania v. John Cravens. Tipling House. True Bill.

10. Pennsylvania v. Wm Trimble. Assault & Battery. True Bill.

11. Pennsylvania v. Samuel Thompson, Nathaniel Chapman, Henry Chapman Jr., John Chapman. Riot & Assault. True Bill.

Page 107L April 1789

Pennsylvania v. Edward Conner and Samuel Crosan Jr. Edward Conner in £20 and Samuel Crosan Jr. in £20 for their appearance next July session to answer for Forcible Entry and Detainer.

12. Pennsylvania v. Nancy Fredrigle. Indictment by Presentment. Fornication.

13. Same v. Sarah Fredrigal. Indictment by Presentment. Fornication.

14. Same v. Elizabeth Hall. Indictment by Presentment. Fornication.

15. Same v. Catherine Tantlinger. Indictment by Presentment. Fornication. Oct 1789 Defendant pleads guilty and submits to Court. Fined agreeably to Act of Assembly.

16 Same v. Rebecca Hillock. Indictment by Presentment. Fornication.

Pennsylvania v. Henry Chapman. Henry Chapman in £50, Edward Connor in £25, Daniel Anderson in £25 and Cornelius McAulay in £25 for appearance of Henry Chapman next July session to answer for Riot, Assault & Battery.

Thomas Kennedy sworn in as Constable for the Town of Bedford until next July Session.

Page 107R [July 1789]
At Bedford July 1789 before William Proctor, Hugh Barclay, James Martin, Jacob Wink.

Grand Jury:

William Hartley, foreman
Abraham Whetstone
George Brouch
William Henry
Peter Miller [affirmed]
Jacob Fox
John Andrew May
John Cravens
Henry Livingston
William Wilson
John Paxton
George Barton
Bernard Blue
William Aker
Nicholas Crivingstone

Recognizances.

Pennsylvania v. Nicholas Crivingstone. Defendant in £20 and John Dibert in £10 to appear.

Pennsylvania v. John Souders. James Wells Esq. in £10 to prosecute.

Pennsylvania v. John Cravens. Defendant in £25 and Henry Liviston in £12 to appear.

Pennsylvania v. Henry Liviston. Defendant in £25. John Cravins in £10.

Pennsylvania v. Jonathan Hamilton. Defendant in £40 and Thomas Hamilton in £20 to answer. Discharged by proc.

Same v. Same. John Fleeharty Jr. in £40 John Fleeharty Sr. in £20.

Pennsylvania v. Mary wife of William Scovil. Henry Wertz in £40 to appear.

Page 108L July 1789
Pennsylvania v. William Henry. William Henry in £20. Thomas Anderson in £20.

Pennsylvania v. William Satorus. Defendant in £20. Leonard Kline in £20.

Pennsylvania v. Frederick Crise. Jacob Lambert in £40 to prosecute.

Pennsylvania v. George Burke. Defendant in £20. Thomas Smith in £20. Discharged by Proc.

Indictments.

1. Pennsylvania v. William Sartorius. Tipling House. True Bill. Nolle Prosiqui entered.

2. Pennsylvania v. Frederick Crise. Felony. True Bill. Defendant pleads not guilty.

3. Pennsylvania v. Nicholas Crivingstone. Assault & Battery. Ignoramus.

4. Pennsylvania v. David Root. Assault & Battery. True Bill.

5. Pennsylvania v. John Bonnet. Tipling House. True Bill. Noli Prosequti

6. Pennsylvania v. John Souders. Felony. True Bill. Pleads guilty. Ordered to hard labor &c

Page 108R   July 1789
Pennsylvania v. William Satorius. Ind^t at this session N. 1. Defendant in £20, Frederick Hill in £20 for appearance of defendant at next session to answer for Tipling House.

Pennsylvania v. Frederick Crise. Jacob Lambert in £100, George Funk in £50 for appearance of Jacob Lambert next October session to give evidence against defendant for Felony.

Pennsylvania v. Daniel Rynhart. Assault & Battery. True Bill.

Pennsylvania v. Ephraim Wallace. Nuisance. Ignoramus.

Pennsylvania v. Philip Gilliland. Indictment for Assault & Battery found last session N 1. Defendant pleads guilty and submits to the Court. Fined two shillings and six pence.

Pennsylvania v. John Souders. Indictment for Felony found this session N. 6. Defendant pleads guilty. Judgment to restore to the owner the stolen property if not already done or pay him twenty five pounds the value thereof, pay a fine of twenty five pounds to the Commonwealth, be put to hard servitude for three weeks, and pay costs.

Page 109L   July 1789
Pennsylvania v. John Cravins. Defendant in £20 and Henry Liviston in £20 for appearance of defendant next October session to answer for keeping a Tipling House. Oct 1789 forfeited.

Pennsylvania v. Henry Liviston. Defendant in £20 and John Cravens in £20 for appearance as above. July 1790 forfeit absolute.

Pennsylvania v. David Root. Defendant in £40 for good behavior.

Pennsylvania v. Henry Chapman et al. David Carlisle in £40 for appearance of David Carlisle and William Carlisle at October session to provide evidence against the defendants for Riot Assault &c.

Pennsylvania v. Edward Conner. Edward Conner in £20 and Samuel Crosan Jr in £20 for their appearance at October session to answer for Forcible Entry and Detainer.

Page 109R   [October 1789]
At Bedford second Tuesday of October (13th) 1789 before Bernard Dougherty, Thomas Coulter, Hugh Barclay, John Cessna, Bethuel Covalt, Jacob Hartzell, William Patterson, Jacob Wink, Thomas Buck, James Martin.

Grand Jury:
John Cessna junior
John Hamlin   George Coffman
Adam Burtnet   Jacob Rhoads
George Wisecarver   Andrew Americk
William Boyd   Joseph [Beyer?]
John Nucham   John Albright
Jacob Lambert   Peter S_____
Gabriel Rhoads [affirmed] Duncan McPharran
                           John Black

Recognizances

Pennsylvania v. Nichel Friend. Nichel Friend in £100 and Andrew Mann in £50 to appear and answer.

Pennsylvania v. Peter Smith. Defendant in £50 and Andrew Mann in £25 to appear and answer.

Pennsylvania v. John Horse. Defendant in £50 and Andrew Mann in £25 to appear and answer.

Page 110L   October 1789
Pennsylvania v. Peter Smith, John Horse, and Nicholas Friend. Peter Smith in £40, John Horse in £40, Nicholas Friend in 40, and Andrew Mann in £40 for appearance of defendants next April to answer for Riot Assault & Battery.

Same v. Same. John Dady in £40 for his appearance next April session to prosecute and give evidence against defendants.

Pennsylvania v. John Curtz. Defendant in £20 for his appearance next session to answer for Tipling House.

Indictments.

1. Pennsylvania v. Thomas McGaughey. Assault & Battery. True Bill.

2. Pennsylvania v. Conrad Hartzel. Assault. True Bill. Defendant submits to the Court protesting his innocence. Fined /6.

3. Pennsylvania v. Michael Po_t. Assault & Battery. True Bill. Defendant submits to the Court protesting his innocence. Fined fifteen shillings.

4. Pennsylvania v. Sarah [Hess? Hoff?]. Tipling House. True Bill.

5. Pennsylvania v. John D[ivert] and William Drenning Supervisors in Bedford Township. Neglect of Duty. True Bill.

Page 110R October 1789

Pennsylvania v. Frederick Bea_ley. Indictment by presentment. Tipling House.

Pennsylvania v. John Hoover. Tipling House. True Bill.
Oct 1790 bail entered to July 1791.

Pennsylvania v. Jacob Cline. Tipling House. True Bill.

Pennsylvania v. Peter Smith, John Horse, Nicholas Friend. Riot, Assault & Battery. True Bill.

Pennsylvania v. John Curtz. Tipling House. True Bill.

Pennsylvania v. Mary Cashman. Indictment by presentment. Fornication.

Pennsylvania v. Samuel Thompson, Henry Chapman, Henry Chapman Jr., John Chapman, John Chapman Jr., John Anderson. Isaac C____ in £20 and John Hill in £20 for appearance of Isaac Cor___ at next January session to give evidence against defendant for Riot, Assault & Battery.

Pennsylvania v. Frederick Crise. Jacob Lambert in £100 for appearance of Jacob Lambert next January session to give evidence and prosecute defendant for felony.

Pennsylvania v. Mary Cashman. Discharged by Proc.

Page 111L   October 1789

Pennsylvania v. John Divert and William Drennen Supervisors of Highways Bedford Township. William Drennen in £20 and John Dibert in £20 for appearance next January session to answer for Neglect.

Page 111R   [January 1790]

At Bedford the second Tuesday in January (12th) 1790 before Thomas Coulter, Hugh Barclay, David Espy, Thomas Buck, James Wills, Abraham Cable, Benjn Burd, Cornelius Devore, Jacob Hartzell.

Grand Jury:

        Andrew Boreland, foreman

Michael Sill	John Divert
Michael Kimble	George Earnest
George Enslow	Christopher King
Robert Boyd	Martin Cable
Jacob Feather	Robert Adams
Michael Hammond	Michael Divert
James Fletcher	George Croyle
	Adam Croyle

William M. Brown and John Cadwalader Esq^s were on motion of James Riddle Esq. admitted as Attornies of this and other Courts.

Indictments.

1. Pennsylvania v. Benjamin Martin. Assault True Bill. Nole prosequi entered by Atty Genl.

2. Pennsylvania v. Francis Gibbs. Assault. Ignoramus.

3. Pennsylvania v. Hugh Robison. Tipling House. True Bill.

Page 112L   January 1790

Pennsylvania v. Catherine Tantlinger. Ind^t No 15 found at April session 1789. Defendant pleads Guilty and submits to Court. Judgment that she pay fine of ten pounds and costs.

Pennsylvania v. John Fry. Jacob Boor in £20 to prosecute.

Pennsylvania v. Benjamin Martin. Francis Gibbs in £20 and George Ensley in £20 for their appearance next April session to prosecute and give evidence against the defendant.

Pennsylvania v. Benjamin Martin. Defendant in £40 and Joseph Shoupe in £40 for appearance of defendant next April session to answer for Assault & Battery and in the mean time to be of good behavior especially toward Francis Gib.

Page 112R   January 1790

4. Pennsylvania v. Israel Burkhart. Tipling House. True Bill.

5. Pennsylvania v. David Penrod. Tipling House. Ignoramus.

6. Pennsylvania v. Philip Smith. Tipling House. True Bill. Nole Prosequi.

7. Pennsylvania v. Jacob Smith. Tipling House. True Bill. Nole Prosequi.

8. Pennsylvania v. John [Lashey]. Ind^t for same. True Bill.

9. Pennsylvania v. Ephraim Wallace. Ind^t for same. True Bill.

10. Pennsylvania v. Jane Mc__eary. Fornication. Ignoramus.

Page 113L [Blank]

Page 113R   [April 1790]

At Bedford 12 April 1790 before Hugh Barclay, Thomas Coulter, David Jones, Abraham Cable, Jacob Hartzell, Cornelius Devore, James Wilt, William Patterson, Benjamin Burd, Jacob Wink.

Township	Constable	Supervisor Highways	Overseer Poor
Bedford Town	William Beaty		
Bedford Twp.	Frederick Reighart	Thomas Blackburn Peter Wirth	Samuel McCashlin Anthony Blackburn
Air	Benjamin Williams	William Gaff Christian Study	Benjamin Stevens Barnard Ford
Bethel	James McKinny	Addis Linn Conrad Rush	John Brothead Christian Kowel
Colerain	Nicholas Roof	John Friend John Fleharty	James Patterson Joseph Friend
Cumberland Valley	John Addison	Andrew Borland John Elder	Thomas Rhay Jonathan Cessna
Brothers Valley	John Gulick	Michael Beighley Jacob Glassner	Tilman Sheets John Elinger
Turkeyfoot	James Mitchell	John Reed Henry Hartzell	Robert Coleburn Isaac Dwire
Quamahoning	John Good	Alexander Hunter Adam Hellem	John Rhoads Christian Heiple

Township	Constable	Supervisor Highways	Overseer Poor
Milford	Frances Phillipy	Frederick Weimer Henry Shaver	Philip King John Corpenny
Elk Lick	William Tissue	Jacob Markley John Burger	John Keg_y John Lyler
Londonderry	Duncan McVicker	John Nemier Robert Huston	John Masters Joseph Boyer
Providence	Joseph Morrison	Jacob Studdybecker Abiah Akers	John Gibson George Barton
Belfast	Jacob Poorman Jr	Ephraim Wallace Peter Swartzwilder	John Milburn Jacob Shock
Hopewell	Joseph McFerran	Andrew Livingston Felix Miller	Benjamin Cherry George Nixon
Woodberry	Michael Poel	John Snyder John Croll	John Ferguson John Teitor
Dublin	George Dandsdell	Philip Isor George Wilds	Robert Ramsey James Shields

Page 114L   April 1790
Grand Jury:
   James Jamison, foreman   Thomas Bradshaw
   William Drenning   William Paxton
   John Friend   Francis South
   William Williams   Conrad Haverstack
   Hugh Robison   James Lafferty
   John Riddle   William Gardner
   Michael Ruff   Elijah Adams Jr.
   Matthias Ruff   Solomon Sparks

Indictments.

1. Pennsylvania v. John Lafferty. Fornication. True Bill.
Bail entered. July 1790 tried and verdict for Deft.

Pennsylvania v. Ezekiel Worley. Sarah Fleharty in £20 and John Fleharty in £20 for appearance of Sarah Fleharty next July session to prosecute and give evidence against defendant for Fornication.

Same v. Same. Defendant in £20 and Thomas Bradshaw in £20 for appearance of defendant next July session to answer for Fornication.

Pennsylvania v. Peter Smith, John Horse & Nicholas Friend. John Dady in £10, Matthias Swartzell in £10, Sally Swartzell £10, Conrod Hopkearn for their appearance next July session to prosecute and give evidence against defendant for Riot, Assault & Battery.

Page 114R April 1790

2. Pennsylvania v. Ignatius Elder. Tipling House. True Bill.

Pennsylvania v. Rachel Carter. Tipling House. True Bill.

Pennsylvania v. Hugh Robison. Defendant in £20 and Robert Smiley in £20 for appearance of defendant next July session to answer indictment for Tipling House.

Pennsylvania v. George Kauffman. Defendant in £20 and Conrad Hite in £20 to appear and answer &c.

Pennsylvania v. Jacob Smith. Defendant in £20 and Henry Everly in £20 to appear and answer &c.

Pennsylvania v. James Lafferty. Defendant in £40 and Wm Fraser in £40 to appear and answer &c.

Pennsylvania v. Rachel Carter. William Wilson in £20 for his appearance next July session to prosecute and give evidence against defendant.

Pennsylvania v. Benjamin Martin. Defendant in £20 and Peter Smith in £20 for appearance of defendant next session to answer for Assault & Battery.

Page 115L April 1790

Pennsylvania v. Jacob Smith Defendant in £20 for appearance next July to answer for Tipling House.

Pennsylvania v. Ezekiel Worley. Sarah Fleharty in £10 and John Fleharty in £10 to appear and prosecute.

Same v. Same. Defendant in £40 and Thomas Anderson in £40 to appear and answer &c.

Pennsylvania v. George Kauffman. George Kauffman in £20 and Thomas Blackburn in £20 for appearance of defendant at next July session to answer for Assault & Battery committed on Jacob Smith.

Pennsylvania v. George Kauffman. Jacob Smith of Bedford Township in £10 and Philip Knight in £10 for appearance of above Jacob next July session to prosecute and give evidence against George Kauffman for Assault & Battery upon Jacob Smith.

Pennsylvania v. Benjamin Martin. Francis Gibbs in £20 for his appearance next July session to prosecute and give evidence against defendant for Assault & Battery.

Page 115R   April 1790
Pennsylvania v. James Lafferty. Defendant in £40 and Thomas McGaughey in £40 for appearance of defendant next July session to answer for Fornication.

Page 116L   [July 1790]
At Bedford 12 July 1790 before George Woods, Hugh Barclay, Cornelius Devore, Thomas Coulter, Thomas Buck, David Jones, James Wells, Abraham Cable, Benjamin Burd.

Grand Jury:
                Thomas McGaughey, foreman
   John McGaughey   William Williams
   Martin Fifer   Conrad Hite
   David Potts   William Henry
   Robert Spencer   John Davibaugh
   Felix Millan   Samuel Skinner
   Robert Gibson   Adrian Hoplitz
   Henry Reiger   John McGaghan

Pennsylvania v. James Hardy. James Hardy in £50 and William Nixon in £50 for good behavior &c.

Pennsylvania v. William Garner. Defendant in £10 to appear and answer. Geo. Smith in £10 that Rebecca McCall appear and prosecute.

On motion of W. Smith, Jacob Nagle Esq. was admitted Attorney of this Court & the Court of Common Pleas.

Page 116R   July 1790
Pennsylvania v. Samuel Paxton. Defendant in £20 and Wm Hartley in £20 to appear and answer &c.

1. Pennsylvania v. William Gardner. Assault & Battery True Bill. Defendant pleads guilty and submits to Court. Defendant to pay fine of five shillings and costs.

2. Pennsylvania v. John Paxton. Assault & Battery. True Bill. Defendant pleads guilty and submits to Court. Defendant to pay fine of ten shillings and costs.

3. Pennsylvania v. Wm Wilson. Assault & Battery. Ignoramus.

Page 117L   July 1790
4. Pennsylvania v. Henry Shaffer. Assault & Battery. True Bill.

Pennsylvania v. James Lafferty. Fornication found last session No. 1. Jury of William Ward, John Black, Richard Wolf, John Dickey, Adam Stigers, Henry Wirth, Frederick Dubbs, Christopher [Cowell?], William Scovil, Conrad Hartzell, James Hardy, and Peter Fisher find defendant not guilty of Fornication.

Pennsylvania v. Peter Smith, John Horse, & Nicholas Friend. Riot, Assault & Battery found at Octr session 1789. Testify for prosecution: John Dady, Benj^m Smith, Conrad Hoppinger, Matthias Swartzill, __my Bishop, Sarah Swartzill. Testify for defense: Barbara Hendershot, J___m Lemon, Christ___ Hayle, David Slei___, Christopher Cowell, Jacob Hendershot. Jury of Frederick Dubbs, John Dickey, George Funk, Ezekial Worley, James Gilmore, John Andrew May, Anthony Nawgel, Peter Fisher, John Black, Henry Wirt, Conrad Hartzell, and Thomas Norton find the defendants are not guilty of the Riot, Assault & Battery but that Nicholas Friend is guilty of the Assault & Battery only. Nicholas Friend to pay fine of one penny and costs.

Page 117R July 1790
Pennsylvania v. Rachel Carter. William Carter in £20 for appearance of defendant next session to answer for Tipling House

Pennsylvania v. Henry Goble. Defendant in £40 and Robert Adams in £40 for appearance of defendant next session and in the meantime to be of good behavior particularly toward John Levear.

Page 118L [October 1790]
At Bedford 11 October 1790 before George Woods, Willm Proctor, Thomas Buck, John Cessna, Abraham Cable, Thomas Coulter, Jacob Hartzell, Bethuel Covalt.

Grand Jury: Jacob Saylor foreman
    John Gibson   Jacob Fisher
    John Humbert   Michael May
    Philip Coleman   Saml Hall
    Joseph Fraser   Peter Baker
    Henry Rush   John Smouse
    John Hart   George Smouse
    John Hoover   Nicholas Ott
    Henry Everly   Valentine Co__

Pennsylvania v. Rachael Hardy. Defendant in £20 and William Nixon in £10 for good behavior.

Pennsylvania v. John Ch__ington. Defendant in £20 for good behavior.

DOCKET 2: 1771–1801 163

Pennsylvania v. Dan[l] Rush. Dan[l] Rush in £25 and Conrad Rush in £25 to appear and answer &c.

Pennsylvania v. Levi Reed. Levi Reed in £20 and M___ Reed in £20 to appear & answer &c.

Page 118R   October 1790
1. Pennsylvania v. William Hartley. Assault & Battery. True Bill. Jany 1791 defendant fined 6^d.

2. Pennsylvania v. George Kaufman. Assault & Battery. Ignoramus.

3. Pennsylvania v. Daniel Rush & Levy Reed. Felony. Ignoramus.

4. Pennsylvania v. John Piper et al. Forcible Entry. True Bill. Rule for trial next April session.

5. Pennsylvania v. William Colbert. Assault. True Bill. Jany 1791 defendant fined 6 pence.

6. Pennsylvania v. Elizabeth North. Bigamy. True Bill.

7. Pennsylvania v. Samuel Wallace. Bigamy. True Bill.

8. Pennsylvania v. Ann Hunt. Fornication. True Bill.

Page 119L   October 1790
Pennsylvania v. John Piper Esq. Defendant in £40 for his appearance next April session to answer for Forcible Entry.

Pennsylvania v. William Piper, Ignatius Hardin, John Hardin, and John Boyce. John Piper Esq. in £40 for appearance of defendants next April session to answer for Forcible Entry.

Pennsylvania v. Will[m] Colbert. Defendant in £20 and Joseph Morrison in £20 for appearance of defendant next session to answer for assault.

Pennsylvania v. Will[m] Hartley. William Colbert in £20 and Joseph Morrison in £20 for appearance of W[m] Colbert next session to prosecute and give evidence against W[m] Hartley for Assault & Battery.

Pennsylvania v. John Piper et al. James Hardy in £20 for his appearance next April session to prosecute defendants for Forcible Entry.

Pennsylvania v. Same Defendants. James Hardy in £20 for appearance of Rachel Hardy & Rebecca Nixon next to give evidence against defendants for [page cut off].

Page 119R October 1790
9. Pennsylvania v. Mary Gandy. Bigamy. True Bill.

10. Pennsylvania v. James McCoy. Bigamy. True Bill.

11. Pennsylvania v. Catherine David. Presentment for Fornication.

Pennsylvania v. Daniel Rush & Levi Reed. John Fisher in £20 to appear and give evidence &c.

Pennsylvania v. Same. Peter Rush in £20 to appear and give evidence.

Pennsylvania v. John Hoover. Defendant in £40 and Abraham Cable, Esq., in £40 for appearance of defendant at next January session to answer for Tipling House.

Page 120L [January 1791]
At Bedford 10 January 1791 before George Woods. William Proctor, William Patterson, Jacob Hartzell, David Jones, James Wells.

Grand Jury: James Heydon, foreman
John Sailor	David Brannan
Neil McMullen	Jacob Easter
Alex^r McGrygar	Henry Whitstone
John Divart	James England
Frederic Divert	Adam Croyle
Philip Rhinehart	Peter Morgert
Philip Wegerline	Jacob Wians
Anthony Smith	Samuel ___ ner
	Henry _ides

Recognizances returned.

Pennsylvania v. Ezekiel Ogden and Albert Ogden. Ignatius Hardin in £10 and John Boys in £10 to appear and prosecute &c.

Same v. Elizabeth Hall. Defendant in £40 and Patrick Haney in £20 to appear and answer &c.

Pennsylvania v. Daniel Royer. Defendant in £100 and Saml Kerr in £50 to appear and answer &c.

Pennsylvania v. Robert Hamilton. Defendant in £50 and _____ _____ in 25 for [bottom of page cut off].

Page 120R January 1791
1. Pennsylvania v. Ezekial Ogden and Albert Ogden. Felony. True Bill. Defendants plead guilty. Ended next page.

DOCKET 2: 1771–1801 165

2. Pennsylvania v. Ezekial Ogden and Albert Ogden. Felony. True Bill. Defendants plead guilty. Ended next page.

Same v. Sarah Fredrigal. Ind^t for Fornication found at April session 1789 No. 13. Defendant pleads guilty and fined according to Act of Assembly.

Same v. Elizabeth Hall. Ind^t for Fornication found at April session 1789 No. 14. Defendant pleads guilty and fined according to Act of Assembly.

Benjamin Peck confined under Habeas Corpus in order that he may give evidence to the Grand Jury.

Pennsylvania v. Daniel Royer. Ludwick Waldeck in £20 for appearance of said Ludwick and Mary his wife at next April session to prosecute Daniel Royer for Forcible Entry & Detainer.

3. Pennsylvania v. Daniel Royer, James Wilson & Wm Jack. Forcible Entry & Detainer. True Bill.

4. Pennsylvania v. Benjmin Peck. Assault & Battery. Ignoramus.

Page 121L January 1791
Pennsylvania v. Ezekiel Ogden and Albert Ogden. Horse Stealing. Defendants plead guilty. Judgment that defendants restore goods stolen to the owner or pay the owner or owners the value thereof and moreover pay to the Commonwealth the like value of the goods stolen, and for the term of five years shall be confined and kept at hard labor.

Pennsylvania v. Ezekiel Ogden and Albert Ogden. Horse Stealing. Defendants plead guilty. Same judgment.

5. Same v. John Miller. Tipling House. True Bill.

6. Same v. Gillian Geery & Hugh Linn. Indictment by Presentment for Nuisance.

7. Same v. Robert Hamilton. Assault & Battery. True Bill.

Page 121R January 1791
Pennsylvania v. Robert Hamilton. Defendant in £20 and Benjn Stevens in £20 for appearance of defendant next April session to answer for Assault & Battery.

8. Pennsylvania v. David McClean. Indictment by Presentment. Tipling House.

Pennsylvania v. Daniel Royer &c. Defendant in £40 for appearance of defendant next April session to answer for Forcible Entry & Detainer.

Pennsylvania v. Gillian Geery & Hugh Linn. Peter Anthony in £40 and Gillian Geery in £40 for appearance of Gillian Geery and Hugh Linn next April session to answer for Nuisance.

Pennsylvania v. John Miller. John Miller in £20 for appearance of defendant next Court to answer for Tipling House.

Page 122L [March 1791]
In Private Session at the house of Henry Wirth in the town of Bedford 25 March 1791.

Township	Constable	Supervisor Highways	Overseer Poor
Bedford Township	Thomas Smith		
Colerain	July 1791 John Hagan is appointed Constable to serve in room of Ezekial Spurgeon Excused.		
Cumberland Valley	Christopher Mease		
Providence	Michael Barndollar		
Belfast	Jacob Boerman		

Page 122R April 1791
At Bedford 11 April 1791 before George Woods, Will[m] Proctor, Bethuel Covalt, Cornelius Devore, Jacob Wink, Thomas Coulter, Thomas Burk, William Patterson, Jacob Hartzell, James Martin, Benj[n] Burd, David Jones.

Township	Constable	Supervisor Highways	Overseer Poor
Bedford Town	Felix Mellan		
Bedford Township		James Anderson Jr George Funk	John MgCaughey W[m] Griffith
Air	Robert Hamill	Will[m] Alexander Benj[n] Williams	Adidnego Stevens Barnard Ford
Bethel	Moses Graham	Jacob Hart George Bishop	George Horse Peter Smith
Colerain	~~Ezekiel Spurgeon~~	John Cessna Patrick Haney	Ernest Baker Edward Rose
Cumberland Valley		John Elder Christopher Ferguson	Thomas Ray Jonathan Cessna
Brothers Valley	Benedict Leman	Jacob Fisher Jacob Good	Adam Palm Francis Hay

DOCKET 2: 1771–1801   167

Township	Constable	Supervisor Highways	Overseer Poor
Turkeyfoot	James Mitchell	John Nick___ Jacob Smith	William Nicholson Samuel Smith
Quamahoning	Jacob Baker	Michael Zimerman John Noseaker	James Black C___ Swink
Milford	~~John Colpenny~~ Herman Husband	James Wilson Jonathan B___	John Colpenny Samuel Wright
Elk Lick	Peter [Miller?]	Joseph Markley Willm Tissue	Peter Livengood Yost Zook
Londonderry	George Keller	Nathaniel S___ field John___	John Lydick James Thomson
Providence		Peter Morgert Jacob Davibaugh	John Moore Joseph Sparks Jr
Belfast		Jacob Shock Obadiah Mellot	Ephraim Wallace John Strait
Hopewell	John White	John Ryland Andrew __iston	John Piper George Nixon
Woodberry		John Snyder John Croll	John Ferguson John___ or
Dublin	William Wilds	Robert Ramsey James Shields	Joseph Bell William Carter

Page 123L   April 1791

On motion of Mr. Smith, Samuel Riddle Esq. admitted as Attorney of this Court and the Court of Common Pleas.

On motion of Mr. Smith, John Clark Esq. admitted as Attorney of this Court and the Court of Common Pleas.

Recognizances returned.

Republica v. Philip Strawbill. Defendant in £40 and Baltzer Hesse in £20 to appear and answer &c.

Same v. James Anderson Jr. Defendant in £50 to appear and answer &c.

Pennsylvania v. Mary Waldecker. Defendant in £50 to appear and answer &c.

Pennsylvania v. John Miller. Defendant in £24 and Abraham Clevenger in £12.

Pennsylvania v. Daniel Royer. Defendant in £50 and John T___ Licking Creek in £25.

Pennsylvania v. Daniel & Samuel Royer. Defendant Daniel in £40, Defendant Samuel in £40, Jacob Poorman in £20, [cut off] in £20.

168   BEDFORD COUNTY QUARTER SESSIONS

Page 123R   April 1791
Grand Jury:
George Kimmel, foreman

Simon Shader (affirmed)	John Mortimer
Jacob Kimble (affirmed)	Joseph Sparks
James Ross (affirmed)	George [Fochs]
Jacob Barnhart	William Carter
John Penrod	Nathaniel Hart
George ___ crow	Henry Ash
Abraham Faith	George Swartz (affirmed)
James Mortimore	John Johnston

Indictments.

1. Pennsylvania v. Philip Shopell. Assault & Battery. True Bill.

2. Pennsylvania v. James Anderson. Assault & Battery. True Bill. Defendant pleads guilty. Fined six pence.

3. Pennsylvania v. Samuel Moss, Joseph Moss, N___ Moss, Mary Moss, Euphemia Moss & Christina Moss. Assault & Battery upon a Constable in the execution of his Office. True Bill.

4. Pennsylvania v. Samuel Royer, Daniel Royer, William Jack & John Milton. Riot. True Bill.

5. Same v. Samuel Royer, Daniel Royer, William Jack & Esther Royer. Assault & Battery. True Bill.

Page 124L   April 1791
Pennsylvania v. Philip Shopell. Baltzer Hess in £40 for appearance of defendant next session to answer for Assault & Battery.

Pennsylvania v. Robert Hamilton. Defendant in £20 and Jacob Rush in £20 for appearance of defendant next July session to answer for Assault & Battery.

Pennsylvania v. John Webster. John Johnson in £20 for his appearance next July session to give evidence against defendant for Tipling House.

Same v. Stephen Bruner. Abraham Faith in £20 for his appearance next July session to give evidence against defendant for Tipling House.

Same v. Henry Shaver. George Tidrow in £20 for his appearance next July session to give evidence against defendant for Tipling House.

Pennsylvania v. Casper Stotler. John Johnson in £20 for his appearance next July session to give evidence against defendant for Tipling House.

Page 124R April 1791
Pennsylvania v. Benjamin Elliot. William Carter in £20 for appearance of said William next July session to give evidence against defendant for Tipling House.

Pennsylvania v. Samuel Moss et al. Jacob Poorman in £20 for his appearance next July session to give evidence against defendant for Assault & Battery.

Pennsylvania v. Susanna Brunner. Simon Shaver in £20 for appearance of said Simon next July session to give evidence against defendant for Fornication.

Pennsylvania v. Catherine Smith. Simon Shaver in £20 ut supra.

Pennsylvania v. Samuel Royer & Daniel Royer. Defendants in £40 and Jacob Rush in £20 and Jacob Poorman in £20 for appearance of defendants next July session to answer for Assault & Battery, Forcible Entry &c also to keep the peace.

Page 125L April 1791
6. Pennsylvania v. Samuel Royer, William Jack & Daniel Royer. Forcible Entry & Detainer. True Bill.

7. Pennsylvania v. John Webster. Indictment by Presentment. Tipling House.

8. Pennsylvania v. Stephen Bruner. Indictment by Presentment. Tipling House.

9. Pennsylvania v. Henry Shaver. The same.

10. Pennsylvania v. Casper Stotler. The same.

11. The same v. Benjamin Elliot. The same.

12. Same v. Susana Brunner. Indictment by Presentment. Fornication.

13. Same v. Catherine Smith. Indictment by Presentment. Fornication.

Page 125R April 1791
Pennsylvania v. Samuel Wallace. Bigamy found at October session 1790 N° 7. Testify for prosecution: Wm Proctor Esq., John Cessna Esq., George Funk. Jury of Ernest Baker, Jacob Poorman, Jacob Rush, Henry Rush, Peter Smith, John Nickham, William Wilson, Paul George,

William Baker, Michael Stall, John Mason, and Peter Seeman find not guilty.

Pennsylvania v. John Piper, William Piper, Ignatius Hardin, John Hardin & John Boyce. Forcible Entry & Detainer found at October session last N° 4. Testify for prosecution: George Swartz, Rachel Hardy, Th° Buck Esq. Jury of Saml Graves, Jacob Poorman, Jacob Rush, John Nickham, Earnest Baker, Patrick Haney, Michael Stall, William Baker, William Griffith, John Mason, Thomas Bradshaw, and Peter Smith find defendants not guilty.

Pennsylvania v. Samuel Royer, James Wilson & Wm Jack. Samuel Wood in £20 and Robert ___ton in £20 for appearance of the said Samuel and Robert at next July session to testify and give evidence against defendants for Forcible Entry and Detainer.

Page 126L April 1791
Pennsylvania v. Samuel Royer, Daniel Royer et al. Ludwick Waldeck in £20 for his appearance and the appearance of his wife Mary next July session to testify and give evidence against defendants for Assault & Battery &c.

Pennsylvania v. Henry Shaver. John Co__nning in £20 and John Shaver in £20 for appearance of defendant next July session to answer for Tipling House.

Page 126R July 1791
At Bedford 11 July 1791 before George Woods, James Wells, James Martin, Bethuel Covalt.

Grand Jury:
Terrence Campbell, foreman

John McGaughey	Daniel Diffebaugh
Henry Wert	Thomas Anderson
Anthony Nagle	Eliezer David
George Funk	Thomas Kennedy
Samuel Paxton	David McKlean
Francis Gibbs	John McGahagan
Abraham Martin	Thomas Norton
John Dieffebaugh	Martin Fritz

Recognizances returned.

Pennsylvania v. Phillip Ott. Defendant in £40 and Joseph Sparks in £20 to appear and answer &c.

Pennsylvania v. Susanna Brunner. Jacob Brunner in £40 for appearance of defendant to answer &c.

Same v. Stephen Brunner. Henry Abram in £40 for appearance of defendant to answer &c.

Page 127L July 1791

Pennsylvania v. Catherine Smith. Philip Smith in £40 for appearance of defendant.

Same v. Casper Stotler. Defendant in £20 to appear and answer &c.

Indictments.

1. Pennsylvania v. David Penrod. Tipling House. True Bill.

2. Pennsylvania v. John Faith, Abraham Amorine, Andrew Wolford, Frederick Wolford, Frederick Amorine, Margaret Snyder. Assault & Battery. True Bill.

3. Pennsylvania v. John Ward. Assault & Battery. True Bill.

Page 127R July 1791

4. Pennsylvania v. John Ward. Tipling House. True Bill.

5. Same v. Same. Felony. Ignoramus.

6. Same. v. Philip Oats. Fornication. True Bill.

7. Pennsylvania v. Jesse Rutlidge. Tipling House. True Bill.

8. Pennsylvania v. Ephraim Wallace. Indictment by Presentment. Tipling House.

9. Pennsylvania v. Thomas Prather. Indictment by Presentment. Tipling House.

Recognizances for next Court.

Pennsylvania v. Philip Ott. James Dalton in £20 for appearance of ~~defendant~~ Mary Miller next Oct session to prosecute and give evidence against defendant for Fornication &c.

Page 128L July 1791

Pennsylvania v. John Ward. William Neill in £40 for his appearance next Oct session to prosecute and give evidence against defendant for Tipling House.

Pennsylvania v. John Ward. William Neill in £40 for his appearance next Oct session to prosecute and give evidence against defendant for Assault and Battery.

Pennsylvania v. Susanna Brenner. Defendant in £20 and Jacob Barnhart for appearance of defendant next Oct session to answer for Fornication &c.

Pennsylvania v. Robert Hamilton. Defendant in £20 and James Bell in £20 for appearance of defendant next Court to answer for Assault & Battery.

Pennsylvania v. Philip Ott. Nicholas Ott in £40 for appearance of defendant next Oct session to answer for Fornication &c.

Page 128R [October 1791]
At Bedford 10 October 1791 before Thomas Smith Esq. and his Associate Judges.

Township	Constable
Bedford Town	Felix Millan
Bedford Township	Thomas Smith
Air	Samuel Hammel
Bethel	Moses Graham
Colerain	John Harkleroad
Brothers Valley	Emmanuel Penrod
Milford	Herman Husband
Londonderry	George Keller
Providence	William Paxton
Belfast	Jacob Poorman Jr.
Hopewell	John White Leave of absence
Woodberry	John Mitchell [affirmed]

Grand Jury:
    Thomas Blackburn
    Christian Livingood
    Robert Smiley
    Elizer Penrod
    Charles Dibert
    Lewis Hershiser
    Nathan Hammon
    Jacob Reigher
    Abraham Whitstone
    Jacob Hoover
    Joseph Markly
    David Penrod
    Geo. Michael Grove
    Peter Stiffler
    Simon Kinton
    Conrad Haverstook
    Jacob Saltzgaver

Page 129L October 1791
Pennsylvania v. John Sells. Defendant in £40 and Robert Smiley in £40 for appearance of defendant the 4th Monday of January next to answer for Assault & Battery and in the mean time to keep the peace.

Pennsylvania v. John Sells. Simon Shaver to appear and prosecute the above.

1. Pennsylvania v. John Sells. Assault & Battery. True Bill.

2. ~~Pennsylvania v. John Faith et al. Assault & Battery. True Bill.~~

2. Pennsylvania v. Christian White. Assault & Battery. Ignoramus. Defendant in £50, Jacob Butterbaugh in £25 and Michael [Pact? Poit?] in £25 for good behavior of defendant for one year.

Pennsylvania v. John Smith, Abraham Amorine, Andrew Wolford, Frederick Wolford, Frederick Amorine, and Margaret Snyder. Defendants each in £40, Luke Devore in £40, and Duncan McVicker in £40 for appearance of defendants next Court to answer for Assault & Battery.

Page 129R October 1791
Pennsylvania v. Philip Ott. Defendant in £40 and Nicholas Ott in £40 for appearance of defendant next Court to answer to Fornication.

Pennsylvania v. John Ward. William Neal of Franklin County for appearance next Court to give evidence against defendant for Tipling House.

Pennsylvania v. Catherine Smith. Indictment for Fornication found last April Session. Defendant pleads guilty and fined agreeably to Law.

William McDermot appointed Ranger in Room of Jacob Hartzell and Anthony Nagel in room of George Woods Esq.

John Woods Esq. and Jacob Cadawallader Esq. admitted Attornies of the County of Bedford severally.

Page 130L [Blank]

Page 130R [1788]
Tavern Keepers recommended Jany Sessions 1788.
    John Bonnet 05 Feb 1789 Rec^d by his son Jacob.

Tavern Keepers recommended April Sessions 1788.
    1. James Jamison   2. Philip Breight
    3. James Anderson   4. James Black

Tavern Keepers recommended July Sessions 1788.
1. Jacob McClean
2. Anthony Nawgel
3. Peter Barnet
4. John B Webster
5. Jacob Cline
6. Arthur McGaughey
7. Marcus Metzgar
8. Peter Wertz
9. John Hoover
10. James Black
11. Benjamin Burd
12. Henry Shaver
13. Thomas McGaughey
14. Thomas Anderson
15. William Ward.

October Sessions 1788
Michael Barndollar

Page 131L [1789–1790]
Tavern Keepers recommended at Jany Sessions 1789.
Peter Morgert
John Ensle not ____ed because not paid
John Dickey   Abraham Martin
Samuel McCashlan   William Todd
Ignatius Elder   Run away

Tavern Keepers Recommended July Sessions 1789.
Anthony Nawgel   Thomas McGaughey
John Bonnet   Peter Werth
Henry Werth   Thomas Anderson

Tavern Keepers recommended October Sessions 1789.
Jacob McClean   Marcus Metsgar
John Webster   George Wilds
George Burkher   Derry Ryan
John Dickey   William Todd

January Sessions 1790 Recommended for Tavern Keepers.
William Satorious   Samuel Coyle
John McGaughey   Thomas __ther
Benjamin Burd   John Curtz
Peter Morgert   Michael Barndollar
Casper Statler

Page 131R [1790–1791]
April Sessions 1790 Recommended for Tavern Keepers.
Philip Smith   Abraham Martin
James Jamison   John Davibaugh

July Sessions 1790 Recommended for Tavern Keepers
1. John Anderson
2. Anthony Nagle
3. John Skinner
4. Jacob Smith
5. Thomas McGaughey
6. ~~Derry Ryan~~
7. Thomas Anderson
8. John Bonnet
9. Henry Wirth
10, Rachel Carter

October Sessions 1790.
1. John Sailor
2. William Todd
3. Marcus Metsgar
4. John Davis
5. Peter Wirth
6. George Barkher

Recommended for Tavern Keepers Jany 1791.
John Dickey
George Rise
Derry Ryan
Peter Morgert
John McGaughey
William Hartley

Page 132L [1791]
Tavern Keepers Recommended April 1791.
Jacob McClean
William McDermot
Duncan McVicker
Michael Barndollar
John Miller
George Wilds
Samuel Coyle
Benjamin Burd
James Jamison

Tavern Keepers Recommended July 1791.
1. John Webster
2. Casper Statler
3. John Bonnet
4. Abraham Martin
5. David Penrod
6. John Kimmel
7. Anthony Nagel
8. ~~John Bridges~~

October Sessions 1791 Tavern Keepers Recommended
1. John Davibaugh
2. Peter Didier
3. Marcus Metzgar
4. John Skinner
5. George Burkher
6. John Davies
7. Ephraim Wallace
8. William Todd

Page 132R [1779]
[Likely a Common Pleas case]
To October Term 1779. N° 41.
January Term 1772.
Charles Moore v. David Ervin. Testify for Plaintiff: Rebecca Smith, Joseph M. Ferran [McFerran], John Graham, David Espy. Testify for Defendant: E___ David, Jn° Dougherty, Th° Hays, Catherine David. Jury of Benjamin Eliott, Joseph McDaniel, Henry Devee, Charles Ruby,

Edward Taylor, Nicholas Grivingston, John England, Earnest Baker, John Friend, John Mortimore, Joseph Morrison, and John Wilt find for the Plaintiff. Five pounds damages & six Pence costs.

Page 133L [1792 and possibly 1793]
Tavern Keepers recommended October 1792.
    1. James McCune   2. Daniel McConnel
    3. Thomas Lemon

Tavern Keepers Recommended at July Sess [page cut off]
    Thomas Anderson   Cornelius McCaulay
    Samuel McCashlan   Anthony Nagel
    James Black   John C__vin
    John Paxton   John Bonnet
    Rachel Carter   John Elliot

Tavern Keepers Recommended at October [page cut off]
    George Ensle   John Tate
    Daniel McConnell   John Fee
    Duncan McDonald   William [Kirby?]
    Abraham Wallis   [cut off] Gilmor

Page 133R [October 1781]
At Bedford third Friday in October 1781 before Bernard Dougherty, James Martin, James Carmichael, Jacob Saylor, Moses Reid, Gideon Richey, Abraham Cable, David Jones.

Grand Jury:
    Henry Abraham   Benson __key
    James Cluggage   Joseph Kelly
    Cornelius Devore   Obadiah Layton
    Nicholas Liberger   Gabriel Rhoade (affirmed)
    John Johnson   Samuel Skinner
    Thomas Lazier   Casper Davibaugh
    Nathaniel S___field   George Liberger

Pennsylvania v. John Young. Testify for prosecution: James Spencer. Testify for defense: William Holiday Jr., Samuel Anderson. Jury of Abraham Miley, George Enslow, Daniel McCurdy, John McClellan, James Gibson, William Gaff, Daniel McConnel, Jacob Dagay, John Peters, Martin Longstradth, Samuel Anderson, and John Bonnet find not guilty.

Page 134L October 1781
Entry of Recognizances
1. Pennsylvania v. Samuel Layton. Samuel Layton in £10.

2. Same v. Samuel Layton. Emmanuel Smith in £10.

3. Pennsylvania v. John _rimly. John _rimley in £50, John [Bonner?] in £50 and John Wean in £50.

4. Pennsylvania v. Matthias Myers. Matthias Myers in £20, George Ensley in £10 and George Ensley Jr. in £10.

5. ~~Same v. Henry Abrams. Henry Abrams in £500.~~

5. Same v. Martin Longstreth. Martin Longstreth in £40.

6. Same v. William Elder. George Elder in £40 for appearance of William Elder.

7. Same v. Martin Longstreth. Matthias [Cerly?] in £20.

Page 134R
Indictments [Inconsistent numbering on this page]

1. Pennsylvania v. John Breathead. Assault & Battery. True Bill.

2. Same v. George Miles. Felony. True Bill.

Pennsylvania v. George Amorine. Felony. Testify for prosecution: Joseph Morrison, Ezekiel Worley, Thomas Hays, Elizabeth Right. Testify for defendant: Abraham Miley, Gideon Richey, Ann [Kinner?]. Jury of Abraham Miley, George Enslow, Daniel McCurdy, John McClellan, Ja__[cut off] Gibson, William Gaff, Daniel McCon_[cut off], Jacob Dagay, John Peters, Martin Longstr_[cut off], John Bonnet, and John Casebeer find not guilty.

5. Pennsylvania v. Justices Henry Kencerin. Felony. True Bill.

3. Same v. Martin Longstreth. Misprison of Treason. Ignoramus.

Page 135L October 1781
Pennsylvania v. Justius Henry Kinerin. Defendant in £60 and Frederick _____ in £60 for appearance of defendant next Court to answer for Felony.

Pennsylvania v. William McKenzie. Felony. True Bill

Pennsylvania v. Patrick Hartford, Assisting and Escape. Ignoramus.

Pennsylvania v. Ge° Miles. Defendant in £100 and Richard Johnson in £50 for appearance of George Miles next Court to answer for Felony.

Page 135R   October 1781
Pennsylvania v. John Bonnet. Defendant in £100 for his appearance next session to answer.

Pennsylvania v. John Bonnet. James Martin in £40 for his appearance to prosecute the above Jn° Bonnet.

Pennsylvania v. James McDaniel. Ja^s McDaniel in £40 and Samuel Anderson in £40 for appearance of defendant next Court to answer for Felony.

~~Pennsylvania v. William Elder. William Elder in 40 and Samuel McCashlan in ____ for peace and good behavior in the mean time.~~

Page 136L   October 1781
Pennsylvania v. Justis Henry Kenerin. David Griffiths in £40 and Abraham Cable in £40 conditioned that Rachel the wife of the said David appear next Court to give evidence against the defendant.

Page 136R   [January 1782]
At Bedford 15 January 1782 before James Martin, Jacob Saylor, Gedeon Richey, John C____n.

Grand Jury:
Hugh Davison	James Gilmore
Jacob Laird	Jacob Hendershot
John Fee	James Mortimore
John Rush	Henry Whitstone
John Richey	Thomas Blair
Christian Coyle	John Graham
James Wilson	Jacob Holtz
John Hamilton	

Pennsylvania v. George Miles. Giles Stevens in £30 and Joseph Franklin in £30 for their appearance next July session to give evidence against George Miles for Felony.

Page 137L
Pennsylvania v. George Miles. John Orbison in £30 for his appearance next July session to give evidence against George Miles for Felony.

Pennsylvania v. Jacob Miller, Joseph Morrison, Henry Armstrong. Felony. Ignoramus.

DOCKET 2: 1771–1801 179

Pennsylvania v. William Satorius. Indictment for Forcible Entry and Detainer found at Jany Session 1783. Testify for prosecution: [cut off]__ael Divert, [cut off]__il Rhoads. Jury of Benjamin Elliot, Earnest Baker, Joseph McDaniel, Joseph Morrison, John England, Edward Taylor, Henry Devee, Ephraim Wallace, Charles Rubey, Nicholas Crivingstone, John Friend, David Irwin find guilty of the Forcible Entry but not the Detainer. Defendant fined 16^d and costs.

Page 137R   January 1782

Pennsylvania v. Brice Blair. Thomas Pennel in £40 and Shederick Casteel in £20 for appearance of Thomas Pennel next session to prosecute Brice Blair for Forcible Entry and Detainer.

1. Pennsylvania v. Stephen Goble. Stephen Goble in £20 and William McCall in £10.

2. Pennsylvania v. Jacob Miller, Joseph Morrison and Henry Armstrong. Jacob Miller in £20, Joseph Morrison in £30, Henry Armstrong in £20 and George Woods in £20.

3. Pennsylvania v. John Mortimore. John Mortimore in £20.

4. Pennsylvania v. Stephen Goble. Stephen Goble in £20 and William Mc__ll in £10.

5. Pennsylvania v. Eliezer Davis. Eliezer Davis in £20.

Page 138L   January 1782

Pennsylvania v. Stephen Goble. Indictment for Assault & Battery. Defendant pleads guilty. Fined 7/6 and costs.

6. Pennsylvania v. Patrick Leonard. George Jackson in £50 and William Wilson in £50.

Pennsylvania v. John Bonnel. Testify for defendant: ~~Bernard Dougherty~~, John Cessna Esq., Rinehart Wolf, Frederick Helm, Jacob Helm. Jury of Benjamin Elliot, Earnest Baker, Joseph McDaniel, David Ervin, John England, Edward Taylor, Henry Devee, Ephraim Wallace, Charles Rubey, Nickolas Grivingstone, Thomas Buck, and John Friend find John Bonnel guilty of the Assault.

Page 138R   January 1782

Pennsylvania v. Patrick Leonard. Jacob Laird of Bedford County in £50 for appearance of Patrick Leonard next session to answer for Treasonable Words Expressions and Other Misdemeanors.

Pennsylvania v. John Brathead. Edward Brathead of Bethel Township in £40 for appearance of John Brathead next session to answer for Assault & Battery committed on Robert Gray.

Pennsylvania v. John Bonnet. John Bonnet in £40, Charles Rubey in £20 and Jacob Saylor Esq. in £2 for appearance of Jn° Bonnet to answer for an assault upon James Martin, Esq.

Page 139L [Blank]

Page 139R [April 1782]
At Bedford 16 April 1782 before James Martin and his Associate Justices.

Township	Constable	Overseer Poor	Supervisor Highways
Bedford Town	Hugh Simpson		
Bedford Township	George Sills	James Dunlap Michael Sill	Samuel Davidson John Ewalt
Colerain	Abraham Miley Abraham Miley Jr deputy	Robert Moore John Friend	Robert Bradshaw Jr. Joseph Johnstone
~~Cumberland Valley~~	~~Frederick Rice~~	~~Samuel Paxton~~ ~~Joseph Kelly~~	~~Cornelius Devore~~ ~~Shadwick Casteel~~
Brothers Valley	Yost Luck Matthias __ger	Jacob Good Peter Livingood	Christian Knagy Jacob Keffer
Turkeyfoot	~~Joseph~~ Peter Everly	John Reed Henry Brown	William Rice John Jones
Milford	John Penrod	John Shofe Nicholas Parone	Herman Husbands Jacob Morningstar
Barre	Chaen Rickerts	Henry Ferguson James [Carswell?]	William McLevy Alexander McCormick
Huntingdon	William Travers	Michael Cryder Henry Lloyd	Joseph Prigmore Jacob Laird
Dublin	William Justice	Hugh Davison John Walker	James Coil John Ramsay
Shirly	Giles Stevens		
Air	John Anderson	William Gaff James Billow	William Hunter Daniel Royer
Bethel	John Dart	~~Jacob Mann~~ ~~Samuel Layton~~	Jacob Mann Samuel Layton
Providence	George Enslow	Joseph Morrison Robert Culbertson	James Martin Esq. Thomas Woods
Cumberland Valley	Cornelius Devore	Jacob Fox Edward Moran	Samuel Paxton Joseph Kelly

Page 140L [April 1782]
Grand Jury:
John Reid	Joseph Cornelius
Reubin Skinner	William Long
Benjamin Jennings	Christian Anthony
Henry Enslow	George Brunner
James Spencer	Samuel Anderson
William Greathouse	John Divert (affirmed)
John Morgan	Michael Divert (affirmed)
Hugh Orlton	

Pennsylvania v. John Penrod. John Penrod in £200 and George Shaver in £100.

Same v. Same. John Penrod in £200, Peter Bucher in £100, and William Greathouse in £100 for peace and good behavior of defendant until next term.

Pennsylvania v. Patrick Leonard. Defendant in £100 and Benjamin Elliot in £50 for appearance of defendant to answer such things as may be objected against him on behalf of the Commonwealth for Immoral Words.

Page 140R [April 1782]
1. Pennsylvania v. Hugh Simpson. Assault & Battery. Defendant pleads guilty and submits to Court. Fine two and six pence with costs and five shillings for getting drunk.

2. Pennsylvania v. Brice Blair. Indictment for Forcible Entry. Testify for prosecution: Thomas Pennal, Shadrick Casteel, Joshua Burton, Hannah Murphy. Testify for defense: John Cessna Esq., Brice Blair Jr., John [Spurgeon?]. Jury of Samuel Graves, John Bridges, David Noble, James Hendrickson, James Patterson, William Boyd, Robert Adams, James Warford, Robert Gibson, John Spurgeon, Clemens Ingle and Joseph Mountain find Brice Blair not guilty of Forcible Entry and Detainer.

Pennsylvania v. James Graham. Felony. Ignoramus.

Pennsylvania v. John Allen_on. Tipling House. True Bill.

Page 141L [April 1782]
Pennsylvania v. James McDonald. Felony. Jury of Samuel Graves, John Bridges, David Noble, James Hendrickson, James Patterson, Wm Boyd, James Warford, Thomas Coulter, Samuel McCashlan, Clement Ingle, Joseph Mountain, and Robert Adams find James McDonald not guilty of Felony.

Pennsylvania v. Justis Henry Knerin. Indictment for Felony. Testify for prosecution: Rachel Griffith, David Griffith. Testify for defense: [cut off]__est Baker, [cut off]__derick _____, [cut off]__cob Saylor. Jury of John Bridges, David Noble, James Hendrickson, James Patterson, William Boyd, James Warford, James Brown, Samuel McCashlan, Clemant Ingle, Joseph Mountain, and Robert Adams find defendant not guilty of the Felony.

Page 141R [April 1782]

~~Pennsylvania v. James Graham. Felony. Ignoramus.~~

Pennsylvania v. George Rumick. Assault & Battery. True Bill.

Pennsylvania v. Moses Donnaldson. Moses Donnaldson in £40 and John Carnivan in £20 for peace and good behavior of defendant until next session.

Page 142L [Blank]

Page 142R [July 1782]
At Bedford 16 July 1782 before James Martin, Gideon Richey and John Harris.

Grand Jury:

Robert Moore	Robert Bradshaw
Abraham Miley	Robert Elliot
David Carlisle	Benjamin W___field
John Parkison	Anthony Nagle
Valentine Easter	James Foley
Samuel Anderson	Moses Donaldson
Joseph Morrison	James Brown
William Holliday	

Entry of Indictments July Sessions.

Pennsylvania v. John Boyd. Forcible Entry. True Bill.

Same v. Robert Adams. Assault & Battery. True Bill.

Same v. Robert Adams. Assault & Battery. True Bill.
[Two identical entries]

Page 143L   July 1782
The petition for the road called Jones's Road is continued.

Pennsylvania v. John Thompson. Bartholomew Davis in £20 and Giles Stephens in £10 for appearance of B. Davis at next Court to prosecute defendant for an Assault.

Same v. Same. John Thompson in £20 and John Cessna Esq. in £10 for appearance of defendant at next Court to answer for assault upon B. Davis and in the mean time be of good behavior.

Pennsylvania v. John [Danilap?]. Defendant in £20 and Evan Cessna in £20.

Same v. ____ Davibaugh. Defendant in £20 and Casper Davibaugh in £20.

Same v. Patrick Leonard. Thomas Brackenridge, bound to prosecute Patrick Leonard in £50. Jacob Laird in £25 to give evidence.

Page 143R July 1782
Pennsylvania v. Bartholomew Davis. Defendant in £20 and Giles Stevens in £10 for good behavior of defendant and his appearance next Court.

Pennsylvania v. Patrick Leonard. Thomas Brackenridge in £50 to prosecute defendant. Jacob Laird in £25 to give evidence.

Pennsylvania v. Robert Adams son of Robert Adams. Defendant in £20 and George Funk in £10 for appearance of defendant next session to answer for Assault & Battery upon Patrick Hartford.

Pennsylvania v. Same. Defendant in £20 and George Funk in £10 conditioned as above for Assault & Battery upon John Hartford.

Page 144L [Blank]

Page 144R [October 1782]
At Bedford 15 October 1782 before James Martin, David Jones, James Coil, John Carnivan, Thomas Paxton.

Grand Jury:
William Jones	Daniel McConnell
James Wilson	Joshua Davies
Hugh Robinson	David Irwin
Hugh Robinson Jr.	James Patton
John Friend	John Johnston
Alexander McConnel	Timothy ONeal
James Elderton	James Nelson

(see over) [Notation in original.]

Indictments.

1. Pennsylvania v. Daniel Palmer. Felony True Bill.

2. Pennsylvania v. Valentine Wyrick. Assault & Battery. True Bill. Settled.

3. Same v. Hugh Alexander. Assault. True Bill. Settled.

Page 145L　　October 1782

Pennsylvania v. Daniel Palmer. Horse Stealing. Testify for prosecution: [Frederick?] Fridline, Ludwick Fridline. Jury of Hugh Barclay, Daniel Rhoads, John Johnston, John Graham, [Dickey Berkshire?], Robert Wadsworth, Thomas Conway, George Elder, Shadwick Casteel, Joshua Davis, Samuel Skinner, and Robert Gibson find defendant guilty. Daniel Palmer will be taken tomorrow morning to the whipping post between the hours of eight and ten and shall receive thirty nine lashes on his bare back and then shall be placed in the pillory where he shall stand one hour and have his ears cut off and nailed to the pillory and shall forfeit to the Commonwealth the sum of fifteen pounds that being the value of the Goods of Ludwick Fridline of which Daniel Palmer is convicted of stealing and pay the costs of prosecution.

Pennsylvania v. Hugh Alexander. John [McKinley?] in £20 for appearance of G____ [McKinley?] next April session to give evidence against the defendant for Assault.

Page 145R　　October 1782

Pennsylvania v. Valentine Wyrick. Robert Wadsworth in £20 for his appearance next session to prosecute and give evidence against the defendant for Assault & Battery.

4. Pennsylvania v. Henry Washabaugh. Assault & Battery. True Bill. Agreed by Parties. Defendant to pay costs.

5. Same v. Mary Longstrath. Fornication. True Bill.

Pennsylvania v. Robert Urie. Robert Urie in £50 and Arnest Baker in £25.

Pennsylvania v. John Hamilton. John Hamilton in £50 and Joseph Cummins in £25.

Same v. Thomas Bush. Defendant in £50.

Same v. John Boyd. Defendant in £40 and Wm Boyd in £20.

Same v. William Davies. Defendant in [£20?] and Joseph Davies in ____.

Page 146L October 1782

Pennsylvania v. Thomas Paxton Esq. Defendant in £100 and John Paxton in £50. Agreed defendant for costs.

Pennsylvania v. George Elder. Defendant in £20 and Abraham Miley in £10.

Pennsylvania v. Barbara B___, Elizabeth Z___ and Mary Z___. Hugh Simpson in £20, David Noble in £20. Discharged by Proc.

Same v. John King. Defendant in £20 and Charles Taggert in £20. Ended by agreement. Defendant to pay ½ cost.

Indictments.

9. Pennsylvania v. Catherine Errat. Bigamy. True Bill.

Same v. Henry Amorine Jr. Felony. True Bill.

Page 146R [Blank]

Page 147L [Numbered 146]   January 1783
At Bedford 14 January 1783 before Bernard Dougherty, James Martin, Thomas Paxton, Moses Reed, William Proctor.

14 Jany 1783 George Thompson Esq. admitted Attorney of this Court.

Grand Jury:
    Thomas Coulter   Amos Jones
    William Todd   Saml Drennin
    George Milligan   Thomas Buck
    Michael Sills   William Fraser
    Thomas Kenton   Michael Divert
    John Ewalt   John Boyd
    John Divert   Cornelius Simmons
    Joseph Kelly

1. Pennsylvania v. Thomas Winton. Assault & Battery. True Bill. Defendant pleads guilty. Fine five Shillings. Testify for State: Saml McCashlan, John Johnston, Robert Boyd.

2. Pennsylvania v. William Winton. Assault & Battery. True Bill. Defendant pleads guilty and fined 10/ and costs.

Page 147R [Numbered 147]   January 1783
3. Pennsylvania v. Thomas Winton. Assault & Battery. True Bill. Defendant pleads guilty. Fined 5/.

4. Same v. Emmanuel Smith. Assault & Battery. True Bill. Defendant pleads guilty. Fined £3.

5. Same v. William Winton. Assault & Battery. True Bill.

6. Same v. John Johnston. Assault & Battery. True Bill. Defendant pleads guilty. Fined /6^d.

7. Same v. John [Burge?]. Assault. True Bill.

8. Same v. Peter Smith. Tipling House. True Bill. Defendant pleads guilty. Fined £5 and costs.

Pennsylvania v. Nicholas Luck. Defendant in £10 and George Burket in £10.

Same v. George Sills. Defendant in £30 and Bernard Dougherty in £15 for good behavior &c and especially towards Ludwick Samuel.

Page 148L　　January 1783
Pennsylvania v. Henry Amorine Jr. and Henry Amorine. Thomas Davis in £20. William Tucker and Thomas Davis each in £20 to appear and prosecute and give evidence. [Thomas Davis listed twice in this entry.]

Same v. Henry Amorine Jr. Henry Amorine the elder and Adam Young each in £40 for defendant to appear and answer.

Pennsylvania v. Henry Amorine. Defendant in £40 and Adam Young in £40 for defendant to appear and answer.

Indictments.

9. Pennsylvania v. Catherine Errat. Bigamy. True Bill.

10. Pennsylvania v. Henry Amorinr Jr. Felony. True Bill.

11. Same v. Philip Fisher. Bigamy. True Bill. Discharged by Proc.

Page 148R　　January 1783
12. Pennsylvania v. John Buck. Presentment by Grand Jury [no charge].

Pennsylvania v. William McIntire. Defendant in £20 conditioned for peace and good behavior especially toward his wife Sarah for the span of one year.

13. Pennsylvania v. Thomas Carter. Tipling House. True Bill.

14. Pennsylvania v. John Todd. Felony. Ignoramus.

Pennsylvania v. Peter Smith. Peter Smith in £50 and Ralph Hunt in £25.

Pennsylvania v. Samuel McCashlan and John Johnston. Thomas Winton in £50 and George Ensle in £25.

Page 149L   January 1783
Pennsylvania v. James Anderson. James Anderson in £40 and John Jenton in £20.

Pennsylvania v. John Todd. John Todd in £100 and Allen McCoomb in £50.

Pennsylvania v. Simon Kenton. Simon Kenton in £40 and William Proctor Esq. in £20.

Pennsylvania v. William Weston. William Weston in £50 and George Ensle in £25.

Pennsylvania v. Thomas Weston. Thomas Weston in £50 and George Ensle in £25.

Same v. William Weston. William Weston in £50, George Ensle in £25.

Indictments.

15. Pennsylvania v. William Kennedy. Assault & Battery. True Bill.

16. Pennsylvania v. Sarah McKinney. Bastardy. True Bill. Nolo Prosequi.

Page 149R   January 1783
17. Pennsylvania v. Elizabeth Standley. Bastardy. Ignoramus.

18. Pennsylvania v. William Holliday. Assault & Battery. True Bill.

19 Pennsylvania v. John Burd Esq. Assault & Battery. True Bill.

Pennsylvania v. William Kennedy. Defendant in £40 and John Todd in £20 for appearance of defendant next session to answer for Assault & Battery.

Same v. Same. Timothy Ryan in £20 for appearance next Court to give evidence and prosecute in the above.

Pennsylvania v. John Boyd. Defendant in £40 and Tho[s] Bush in £20 for appearance of defendant next Court to answer for Forcible Entry.

Page 150L   January 1783
Pennsylvania v. Thomas Weston. Defendant in £20 and William Weston in £20 for appearance of defendant next session to answer.

Pennsylvania v. William Weston. Defendant in £20 and Thomas Weston in £20 for appearance of defendant next session to answer.

Pennsylvania v. Henry Amorine Jr. Thomas Davis in £20 to appear at next session and give evidence against defendant for Felony.

Pennsylvania v. Henry Amorine Jr. Henry Amorine in £40 for appearance of defendant next session to answer for Felony.

Page 150R   April 1783
At Bedford 15 April 1783 before Bernard Dougherty, David Jones, Robert Clugage, Thomas Paxton, John Cessna, James Martin, Moses Reed, and William Proctor.

Township	Constable	Overseer Poor	Supervisor Highways
Bedford Town	John [Canber?]		
Bedford Township	~~William Todd~~ George Imler	James Dunlap Michael Sill	Thomas Kenton Gabriel Rhoads
Colerain	Michael Ruff	Robert Moore John Friend	Robert Bradshaw Joseph Johnston
Bethel	Jacob Bush Jr.	Jacob Wink Thomas Crossan	Andrew Mauer Moses Reed Esq.
Air	Joshua Davis	William Gaff James Billow	William Hunter Daniel Royer
Dublin	James McKee	Hugh Davison John Walker	John Burd George Hudson
Shirley	James Clugage	James Galbreath Matthew Patton	John Morgan Francis Clugage
Barre	William Long	Benjamin McGaffin	David Ralston Gilbert Cheny
Huntingdon	George Jackson	Henry Lloyd Michael Cryder	George Reynolds Samuel Daniel
Turkeyfoot	Thomas Smith		Oliver Drake Jacob Hartzel
Providence	George Ensle	Joseph Morrison John Moore	James Martin Esq. Thomas Woods
Milford	Peter Ankeny	[two names scraped away]	Nicholas Parone Ludwick Fredline
Brothers Valley	Michael Beghley	George Shinefelt Michael Tryer	John Berger Henry Glasner
Cumberland Valley	Shadwick Casteel	Thomas Coulter Nathaniel __tchfield	A___ Bole Jacob Fox

Page 151L　　April 1783
Grand Jury:
　　Robert Culbertson　　　　Jacob Holtz
　　William Hart　　　　　　　John Livingston
　　William Boyd　　　　　　　Nicholas Crivingstone
　　Adam Miller　　　　　　　 Joseph Sparks
　　John _annard　　　　　　　John McKenney
　　Thomas Norton　　　　　　 Joseph McDonald
　　Edward Harnet　　　　　　 Jacob Hendershot
　　James Brown.

Indictments.

1. Pennsylvania v. Lovey Ha__m_s_. Fornication. True Bill

2. Pennsylvania v. Joshua Fleeharty. Fornication. True Bill.

Pennsylvania v. John Boyd. Forcible Entry and Detainer. True Bill. Testify for prosecution: Margaret Bogart, David Buck, Edward Taylor, George Woods Esq. Jury of Hugh Barclay, Frederick Weimer, Wm Patterson, John Ramsay, David Walker, Hugh Logan, Hill Wilson, Reynhart Wolf, George Wiscarver, Valentine Wyrick, Charles Wilson, and Robert Bradshaw find John Boyd not guilty.

Page 151R　　April 1783
3. Pennsylvania v. Thomas Mitchell. Assault with an Attempt to Ravish. True Bill. Tried & verdict for defendant.

4. Pennsylvania v. Grace Justice. Bastardy. True Bill.

5. Pennsylvania v. Job Clark. Assault with Attempt to Ravish. True Bill.

6. Pennsylvania v. Andrew Friend. Assault with Attempt to Ravish. True Bill.

7. Pennsylvania v. Reuben Abrahams. Assault with Attempt to Ravish. True Bill.

8. Pennsylvania v. Susanna Dean. Bastardy. True Bill.

9. Pennsylvania v. B___ Abrahams. Assault with Attempt to Ravish. True Bill.

Page 152L　　April 1783
10 Pennsylvania v. Margaret Williams. Bastardy. Ignoramus.

11. Pennsylvania v. John McKewn & W^m McGill. Felony. Ignoramus.

12. Pennsylvania v. James Mitchell. Bastardy. True Bill.

13. Same v. Sarah Jennings. Bastardy. True Bill.

Same v. John [Cravens?]. Tipling House. True Bill.

Pennsylvania v. Thomas Mitchell. Assault with an Attempt to Ravish. Testify for prosecution: Elizabeth [Rush?], Joseph Skinner. Testify for defense: Jeremiah Friend, John Gaff, Jonathan Lochberger, William ___ Esq. Jury of Hugh Barclay, Frederick Weimer, William Patterson, John Ramsay, David Walker, Hugh Logan, Hill Wilson, Reynhard Wolf, George Wisecarver, Valentine Wyrick, Charles Wilson, and Robert Bradshaw find Thomas Mitchell not guilty.

Page 152R   April 1783

Pennsylvania v. Sarah Layton. Sarah Layton in £25 and James McKinney in £15.

Pennsylvania v. James Layton. James Layton in £15 and Lewis Meeks in £15.

Pennsylvania v. Sarah Jennings. Sarah Jennings in £50.

Pennsylvania v. James Mitchell. James Mitchell in £50.

Same v. John McKewn and Will. McGill. Defendants in £20 and Thomas Burd in £10.

Same v. Reuben Abrahams. Defendant in £500 and Henry Abrahams in £500.

Same v. Barzel Abrahams. Defendant in £500 and Henry Abrams in £500.

Same v. Thomas Mitchell. Defendant in £500, Charles Friend in £500.

Page 153L   April 1783

Pennsylvania v. Job Black. Defendant in £500 and Joseph Mountain in £500.

Same v. Elizabeth Rush. Defendant in £50 and William Rush in £50.

Same v. William Boyd. Defendant in £40 and Thomas Buck in £20.

Same v. Jacob Anderson. Defendant in £100.

Same v. Hugh Simpson. Defendant in £10 and Conrad Samuel in £10.

Same v. William Orr. Defendant in £20 and John Moore in £10.

DOCKET 2: 1771–1801 191

Same v. Mary Sa__age. Defendant in £10.

Same v. Isaac [Nelon?]. David Espy Esq. in £10.

Same v. William Doc. Defendant in £20 and Sam[l] Skinner in £10.

Same v. Same. An__ Adams in £10 and Jacob Miller in £10.

Page 153R   April 1783
Pennsylvania v. Thomas Weston. Assault & Battery. Testify for prosecution: Robert Boyd. Jury of Hugh Barclay, Frederick Weimer, William Patterson, John Ramsey, David Walker, Hugh Logan, Hill Wilson, Rynhart Wolf, George Wisecarver, Valentine Wyrick, Charles Wilson, and Robert Bradshaw find Thomas Weston not guilty.

Pennsylvania v. Nicholas Luck. Defendant in £100 and Henry Wertz in £100 for appearance of defendant next session to answer for Misprison of Treason. July 1783 Nolo Prosequi by order of the Court. The Court will proceed no further.

Pennsylvania v. William Weston. Assault & Battery. Testify for prosecution: Robert Boyd. Testify for Defense: Thomas Weston. Jury being called (ut supra) find W[m] Weston guilty.

Page 154L   April 1783
Pennsylvania v. James Mitchell. Defendant in £50 and James McKinney in £50 for appearance of defendant next session to answer for Bastardy.

Pennsylvania v. Reuben Abrams, Barzel Abrams, Andrew Friend & Job Clark. William Rush in £50 for appearance of Elizabeth his Dau[cut off] next session to give evidence against defendants for Assault with Intention to Ravish.

Same v. Same. Reuben Abrams in £40, Barzel Abrams in £40, Andrew Friend in £40, Job Clark in £40 and Henry Abrams in £100 for appearance of Reuben, Barzel, Andrew and Job next session to answer for Assault with Intention to Ravish.

Pennsylvania v. John Cravens. Benj[n] Elliot and Cor. McAulay in £40 for appearance of defendant next session to answer for Tipling House. Noli Prosequi entered.

Page 154R   July 1783
At Bedford 15 July 1783 before Bernard Dougherty and his Associate Justices.

On motion of Robert Galbreath Esq. Hugh Montgomery Brackenridge Esq. admitted as Attorney of this Court.

Grand Jury:
  Hugh Barclay
  Cornelius McAulay
  Thomas Anderson
  Henry Abrams
  Daniel Stoy
  Samuel McCashlan
  Samuel Skinner
  Robert Elliot
  Anthony Nagel
  George Campbell
  Charles Ruby
  Henry Wertz
  Richard Johnston
  John Bonnet
  George Sills

Pennsylvania v. Loruhanna Moss. Defendant in £20 and Samuel Moss in £20 for appearance of defendant next session to answer for Bastardy.

Page 155L   July 1783
1. Pennsylvania v. John Wilt. Assault & Battery. True Bill. Defendant pleads guilty. Fined six Pence.

2. Pennsylvania v. Michael Imfelt. Assault & Battery. True Bill. Defendant pleads guilty. Fined six Pence.

3. Pennsylvania v. Reubin Abrams et al. Riot & Assault.

4. Pennsylvania v. Reubin Abrams et al. Riot & Assault.

5. Pennsylvania v. Felix McCanna. Assault & Battery. Defendant pleads guilty. Fined one Shilling.

6. Pennsylvania v. George Elder. Felony. True Bill.

Page 155R   July 1783
Pennsylvania v. John Cravens. Defendant in £40. George Ensle in £20.

Same v. Michael Feather Jr. Defendant in £40. Michael Feather Sr. in £20.

Same v. Philip Countz. Defendant in £10 and Henry Wertz in £10.

Same v. Jacob Crivistone. Defendant in £20. Robert Culbertson in £20.

Same v. David Organ. D. Organ in £40, Charles Rubey in £20 and Hector McNeal in £20.

Same v. John Wilt. Defendant in £10. Hector McNeal in £10.

State v. George Elder. Defendant in £40 and Adam Miller in £25.

Same v. John Lafferty. Defendant in £40. Philip Wolf in £20.

Page 156L   July 1783
Pennsylvania v. Cor^s Simmons. Jacob Wiley in £20 to prosecute.

Same v. Same. Defendant in £40 and George Ensle in £20.

Pennsylvania v. George Elder. George Elder in £50 and Saml McCashlan in £25 for appearance of defendant next session to answer for Felony.

Same v. Same. Benjamin Cherry in £10 and Matthias Myers in £10 for appearance of both next Court to give evidence against George Elder.

Pennsylvania v. Paul Martin alias Black Paul. Defendant in £500, Michael Fetter in £250 and Frederick Helm in £250 for good behavior of Paul Martin for one year.

Page 156R
Pennsylvania v. William Nicholson, Jeremiah ___ind, Drusilla McCullough, Ann Spenser, Ruben Abraham, Bezil Abraham, Charles Friend, Andrew Friend Jr., Henry Abrahams in £20 and Thomas Johnston in £20 for appearance of each of the defendants next Court in October to answer for Riot.

Page 157L   October 1783
At Bedford second Tuesday in October 1783 before Bernard Dougherty, Saml Thompson, John Cessna.

Grand Jury:
    Edward Rose   Hugh Logan
    James Patterson   John Dipert
    Thomas Johnson   Samuel Carr
    Robert Adams   James French
    George Wisecarver   Patrick Leonard
    John Ewalt   George Buchannon
    Philip Wagerline   John Tate
                                   John McKinney

Indictments.

Pennsylvania v. Benjamin Burd. Forcible Entry. True Bill.
Upon motion Indictment quashed.

Pennsylvania v. Joshua Davis. Felony. ~~True Bill.~~

Page 157R   October 1783
Pennsylvania v. John McCashlan. Assault & Battery. True Bill.

Pennsylvania v. John Mitchell and Thomas Mitchell. Assault & Battery. True Bill.

Pennsylvania v. Elizabeth Rush. Bastardy. True Bill.

Pennsylvania v. Job Clark, Andrew Friend, Reuben Abrams, Barzil Abrams. Assault with Intent to Ravish. Jury of Charles Rubey, George Wirt, John Graham, Nicholas Roof, Patrick Haney, Saml Anderson, John Fee, William Elliot, George Wilson, Daniel Rhoads, Frederick Reicher who find defendants not guilty.

Hugh Logue appeared at this session in consequence of recognizance and no one appearing to prosecute he is discharged.

Page 158L   October 1783
Pennsylvania v. George Elder. Felony. Jury of Charles Rubey, George Wertz, John Rynhart, John Graham, Nicholas Roof, Patrick Haney, Samuel Anderson, John Fee, William Elliot, George Wilson, Daniel Rhoads, and Frederick Reicher find defendant is guilty of a bushel and a half of corn at 3/ per bushel and not guilty as to the ____ mentioned in the indictment.

Pennsylvania v. Benjamin Burd. Robert Clugage Esq. in £40 for appearance of defendant next Court to answer for Forcible Entry and Detainer.

Pennsylvania v. James Mitchell and Thomas Mitchell. James Mitchell in £40 and William Nicholson in £40 for appearance of defendants next Court to answer for Assault & Battery.

Page 158R   October 1783
Charles Rubey a juror in the case Commonwealth v. George Elder because he was upon the Grand Jury is fined six pence.

Pennsylvania v. George Elder. Defendant in £40 and Samuel McCashlan in £40 for appearance of defendant next Court to answer for Felony.

Pennsylvania v. George Elder. Benjamin Cheny in £20 and Shadwick Casteel in £20 for appearance of Edwd Chaney at next Court to prosecute and give evidence in the above indictment.

The v____ for the road from Rays Hill to Bedford Narrows is continued.

Pennsylvania v. William Nicholson et al. James Anderson in £40 and David Jones in £40 for appearance of defendants at next Court.

Page 159L   October 1783
Pennsylvania v. William Nicholson, Jeremiah Friend, Drusilla McCullouch, Ann Spencer, Reubin Abrams, Barzil Abrams, Charles Friend, Andrew Friend. Henry Abrams in £20 and Thomas Johnston in £20 for appearance of each of the defendants next Court to answer for Riot.

Pennsylvania v. John McCahslan [sic]. Samuel McCashlan of Bedford Township in £20 for appearance of defendant next session to answer for Assault & Battery.

Page 159R   [January 1784]
At Bedford second Tuesday in January 1784 before James Martin, William Proctor, James Shaler, John Cessna, John C____ Esqs.

On motion of Mr. Smith John Woods Esq. admitted Attorney for Court of Quarter Sessions and Court of Common Pleas.

Grand Jury:
    John Burd   William Fraser
    Benjamin Burd   Henry Armstrong
    James Anderson   George Reynolds
    James Anderson Jr.   John Ashbaugh
    George Burgat   John Bittle
    Timothy Ryan   Joseph Bell
    Thomas Blackburn   Benjamin Stephens

On motion Mr. Hamilton and Mr. Galbreath that Benjmin Burd and John Burd were interested in the consequences of a bill sent to the Grand Jury the Court orders two more jurors to be sworn and added to the panel Thomas Rush and William Scovill.

Page 160L
Pennsylvania v. Moses Reed Esq. Defendant in £40 for appearance of defendant next April Court to answer for Libel.

Page 160R   Cover reading "Sessions Minutes."

Page 161L [Blank]

Page 161R [1786–January 1787]
Tavern Keepers Recommended at [torn off] session 1786
 [torn off] McGaughey
 [torn off] _lack
 [torn off] ____ Jr.

Tavern Keepers recommended July 1786
 Samuel McCashlan
 George Steckleather
 John Bonnet
 Anthony Nagel
 William Ward
 Thomas McGaughey
 Henry Wertz
 ~~Cornelius McAulay~~
 Thomas Anderson
 James Anderson

Tavern Keepers recommended October 1786
 John Dickey
 Daniel McConnel
 ~~David Mc_____~~
 Henry Livingston
 Peter M____
 William Todd

Tavern Keepers recommended January 1787
 Jacob McClean
 William Jones
 D____ McDonald
 [scratched out and unreadable]
 _____ Wallace

Page 162L [April 1787–October 1787]
Tavern Keepers recommended April 1787
 ~~Thomas Mc_____~~   Peter Wertz
 John Davibaugh   James Gilmore

Tavern Keepers recommended July 1787
    Anthony Nawgel
    Casper Stotler
    Thomas Prether
    William Ward
    Peter Barnet
    Thomas McGaughey
    Ignatious Elder
    Ludwic Sill
    John & Alexander Dean
    Thomas Anderson
    Robert Philson
    John Tate
    Michael Barndollar
    John Wells
    Samuel McCashlan

Tavern Keepers recommended October 1787
    Willm Todd
    Peter Morgert
    Daniel McConnel
    Abraham Martin
    John Dickey

Page 162R [Fragement]
[Context of list not apparent from what remains.]
    Daniel Anderson
    George Enslow
    Thomas Anderson
    John Paxton
    Cornelius McAulay
    Anthony Nagel

Page 163L [Blank]

Page 163R [Blank]

Page 164L [numbered 163]   [March 1786]
At Private Session in the house of A___[torn off] 25 March 1786 before Bernard Dougherty, David Espy, [torn off]___ Saylor and Hugh Barclay Esqs.

Township	Constable	Supervisor Highways	Overseer Poor
Bedford Town	John Andrew May		
Bedford Township	John Chrisman	Samuel McCashlan George Imler	Frederick Divirt Big. Robert Adams
Air	Benjamin Stephens	Thomas Davis William Alexander	William Hunter David Evans
Frankstown	~~Leonard Wolfe~~		
Providence			Joseph Morrison Robert Culbertson
Belfast		Jacob Wink Ephraim Wallace	Henry Rush Morris Dishong

Page 164R [numbered 164]
Cover titled "Sessions Minutes from 25th March 1786 Until the 13th October 1791 Inclusive."

Page 165L [Blank]

Page 165R
Cover titled "Sessions Minutes Commencing Jan[y] Sessions 1792."

Page 166L [Blank]

Page 166R [Fragment]
"Oye Oye Oye
All Persons who sue or implead or have other wise here to do before the Judges of the Honorable Court of Common Pleas at a Court of Common Pleas, & all Persons who stand bound by Recognizances or have other wise here to do before the same Judges at a Court of Quarter Sessions of the Peace & Gaol Delivery here holden for the County of Bedford may now draw near & give there attendance & they shall be heard for now the Courts are sitting."

Page 167L [Blank]

Page 167R   [January 1782]
At Bedford 23 January 1782 before Thomas Smith, George Woods, James Martin, Hugh Barclay, & John Hopkins Esqs.

Township	Constable
Bedford Town	Felix Mellan
Bedford Township	Thomas Smith
Air	Samuel Hamill
Bethel	Moses Graham
Colerain	John Harkleroad
Cumberland Valley	Christopher Mease
Brothers Valley	Emanuel Penrod
Turkey Foot	James Mitchell
Quamahoning	Jacob Baker
Milford	Hermon Husband
Elk Lick	Peter Miller
Londonderry	George Keller
Providence	William Paxton
Bellfast	Jacob Poorman Jr.
Hopewell	John White
Woodberry	John Mitchell
Dublin	William Wilds

Grand Jury:
- William Hartley, foreman
- Nicholas Ruff
- John Wolf
- Philip Rhinehart
- John Elder
- Michael Dibert
- George Croyle
- Jacob Good
- William Nixon
- Robert Anderson
- Derry Ryan
- James Davibaugh
- Frederick Dibert
- Gabriel Rhoads
- George Imler
- Jacob Studybaker
- Henry Brown
- William Todd
- Andrew Sheets

Page 168L January 1782

Richard Smith Esq. admitted as Attorney of this Court and Court of Common Pleas.

Pennsylvania v. John Tate. John Tate in £40 and George Lucas in £50 to appear and answer &c.

Pennsylvania v. John Tate. Defendant in £50 and Aaron Donnald in £25 to appear and answer &c.

Pennsylvania v. William Henry. Defendant in £40 and James Taylor in £20 to appear and answer &c.

Same v. Same. Thos Anderson in £40 to appear and prosecute.

Pennsylvania v. John Johnson. Dr. John Anderson in £40 to appear and prosecute.

Pennsylvania v. Alisha Budget. Defendant in £24 and George Ensley in £12 to appear and answer &c.

Pennsylvania v. Peter Swartswilder. Tipling House. True Bill.

Page 168R January 1782

Pennsylvania v. Peter Swartzwilder. Jacob Poorman Jr. in £40 for his appearance next Court to give evidence against defendant for Tipling House.

Pennsylvania v. John Sill. Defendant in £40 for good behavior of the defendant and for his appearance next session and particularly for his good behavior toward Simon Shaver.

Pennsylvania v. Philip Ott. Indictment for Fornication and Bastardy found July 1791 N° 6. Defendant retracts his former plea of not guilty and pleads guilty. Judgment is that defendant pay fine of £10.0.0 for support of the Government and that he also pay to Mary Miller the prosecutrix £5 for lying in charges and five shillings P [per] week from the 14th day of April 1791 (on which day the child was born) until the 14th April 1792 and 3 shillings 6^d P week from 14 April 1792 until 14 April 1793 and two shillings and six pence P week from 14 April 1793 for five years if the child shall live so long; that he pay costs of prosecution and give security for performance of this judgment.

Page 169L   January 1782
2. Pennsylvania v. John Tate. Assault & Battery. True Bill.
Defendant pleads guilty and submits to Court. Fined 2/6 and costs and to give security for his good behavior fore three months.

3. Pennsylvania v. John Tate. Assault. True Bill.
Defendant pleads guilty and submits to Court. Fined 2/6 and costs and to give security for his good behavior for three months.

4. Pennsylvania v. William Henry. Assault & Battery. True Bill.
Defendant pleads guilty and submits to Court. Fined 5/ and costs and to give security for his good behavior for one year.

5. Pennsylvania v. John Johnston. Assault & Battery. Ignoramus.

Susanna Brown. Jacob Barnhart in £40 for appearance of defendant next Court to answer for Fornication.

Page 169R
Pennsylvania v. Alisha Bludget. Defendant in £40 and George Ensley in £40 for good behavior of defendant particularly toward John Tate until the next Court and also his appearance at next Court to answer.

Pennsylvania v. John Tate. Defendant in £40 and Martin Longstrath in £40 for his appearance next Court and in the meantime to keep the Peace & Good Behavior to all Citizens of this Commonwealth.

Pennsylvania v. William Henry. Defendant in £40 and James Taylor in £40 for good behavior of defendant for one year and to appear 4th Monday January next to answer.

Page 170L   [April 1782]
At Bedford 23 April 1792 before George Woods, James Martin, Hugh Barclay and John Hopkins.

Township	Constable	Supervisor Highways	Overseer Poor
Bedford Town	Martin Reiley	~~James Anderson Sr.~~ ~~Adam Croyle~~	
Bedford Township	James Williams	James Anderson Sr. Adam Croyle	Nathan Hammond Thomas Anderson
Air	James Gibson	William Alexander Jr. Benj[n] Williams	Abadnigo Stevens Adam Bam
Bethel	Moses Graham	George Bishop Adam Stigers	Christopher Cowell Andrew Young
Colerain	Patrick Haney	George Easter John Perrin	Earnest Baker Edward Rose
Cumberland Valley	Valentine Wyrick	Abraham Miley Michael Fox	Ezekiel Cox Abraham Miley Jr.
Brothers Valley	Frederick Oldfather	Jacob Kiffer Jacob Countryman	John Knipper Peter Switzer
Turkey Foot	James Mitchell	Peter Augustine Andrew [Reems?]	Henry Everly Stephen Bruner
Quamahoning	Frederick Marstaller	John Reed ~~Abraham Kimble~~ David Wright	[Christian?] Hipple ~~James Black~~ Casper Swink
Milford	John Shofe	John Kooser Adam Snyder	William Jones Samuel Wright
Elk Lick	Christian Knagey	Joseph Gundy John Houghstaller	Joseph Forney John Sailor
Londonderry	George Keller	Andrew McConnell John Shaver	Rob[t] McConnell Paul Wilker
Providence	William Paxton	Abia Akers Michael Barndollar	Will[m] Hartley Elisha Barton
Belfast	William Wilkins	Jacob McClean Peter Rush	Adam W___man John Mellot
Hopewell	Mordecai Williams	William Nixon Marton Stoler	Adam Young Sebastian Shope
Woodberry	Martin Houser	John Snyder Jacob Neave	John Ferguson John __tor
Dublin	David Jordan	James Jamison Bigger Head	George Wilds Azariah McClean
Stoney Creek	Jacob Kemble	Abraham Kemble John Lambert	James Black John Zigler

Page 170R April 1782
Grand Jury:
John Stewart	George Coleman
Thomas Royle	Cornelius Martinus
Daniel McCarty	Martin Luter
Elisha Grady	Martin Loy
Robert Wright	Samuel Chance
John Inglebright	Henry Buckley
Cornelius Myers	John Mill [Miller?]
John Holtz	Jacob Holtz

1. Pennsylvania v. James Lafferty. Fornication. True Bill.

2. Pennsylvania v. Sarah Blair, Elizabeth Langdale & Nancy Blair. Assault & Battery. True Bill.

3. Pennsylvania v. Peter Short. Fornication. True Bill.

4. Same v. John Gardner. Felony. True Bill.

5. Same v. John Black, Janet Black, Samuel McCashlan and Robert McCashlan. Riot and Assault & Battery. True Bill.

Page 171L April 1782
Recognizances Returned

Pennsylvania v. Henry Fisher. Samuel McCashlan in £40 to appear and answer.

Pennsylvania v. Sarah Blair. Thomas Blair in £40 to appear and answer.

Pennsylvania v. John Gardner. John Williams in £20 to appear and prosecute.

Recognizances to August Court.

Pennsylvania v. John Black & others. John Black in £40 and Sam[l] McCashlan in £40 for appearance of John Black, Jennet Black, Samuel McCashlan & Robert McCashlan next Court to answer for Riot, Assault & Battery.

Page 171R
Pennsylvania v. Elizabeth Langdale & Henry Blair. Thomas Blair in £40 for appearance of defendants next Court to answer for Assault & Battery.

Pennsylvania v. John Black et al. Christopher Means in £20 for appearance of said Christopher next Court to prosecute and give evidence against defendant for Riot, Assault & Battery.

Page 172L   [August 1782]
At Bedford fourth Monday in August 1792 before Thomas Smith, George Woods, Hugh Barclay, Samuel Martin, John Hopkins.

Township	Constable
Bedford Town	Martin Reiley
Bedford Township	James Williams
Air	James Gibson
Bethel	Moses Graham
Colerain	Patrick Haney
Cumberland Valley	Valentin Wyrick
Brothers Valley	Frederick Oldfather
Turkey Foot	James Mitchell
Quamahoning	Frederick Marstaller
Milford	John Shofe
Elk Lick	Christian Knagey
Londonderry	George Keller
Providence	William Paxton
Bellfast	William Wilkins
Hopewell	Moredecai Williams
Woodberry	Martin Houser
Dublin	David Jordan
Stoney Creek	Jacob Kimble

Grand Jury:
    Jacob Saylor, foreman   William Gaff
    Benjamin Pitman   Jacob Rush
    John Nickham   Charles Bee__l
    Jacob Heron   Daniel May
    Anthony Ling   Jacob Ritchey
    Michael R____d   John Ewalt
    Robert Hempill   Christian Livingstone
    Michael Mour   Jacob Barnhart
    Yost Miller   Gasper Stattler
    Arthur Wray

Page 172R   August 1782
Henry Woods Esq. for motion of John Woods Esq. admitted Attorney of Court of Common Pleas, Quarter Sessions, Orphans Court.

Indictments.

Pennsylvania v. John Black, Jennett Black, Samuel McCashlan and Robert McCashlan. Testify for prosecution: Christopher Mease. Testify for defense: Patrick Haney. Jury of George Johnson, Henry Williams, James Fletcher, William Horse, George Sills, Jacob McClean, George Wisecarver, William McDonald, James Black, Robert Philson, John Bonnet, and Jacob Feather find John Black is not guilty; Jennett Black guilty of Assault only; Samuel McCahshlan not guilty; Robert McCashlan guilty of Riot and Assault ~~& Battery~~ with two others unknown. Judgment is that Jennett Black pay fine of fifteen shillings; Robert McCashlan pay fine of three pounds and he enter surety for his good behavior for one year.

Page 173L   August 1782
Recognizances Returned.

Pennsylvania v. Nicholas Ferrence. Ludwick Young in £20 to prosecute

Same v. James Burd. Defendant in £50 and David Jordan in £25 to appear and answer.

Indictments Tried.

Pennsylvania v. Mary Groves. Larceny N° 3. Testify for prosecution: Robert Orbison. Jury of George Sill, John Kimmell, James Fletcher, Andrew Work, William Horse, Jacob McClean, Michael Roof, Jacob Feather, John Davibaugh, Anthony Smith, Elijah Adams, and David Stoy find defendant not guilty.

Same v. Henry Myers. Assault & Battery N° 2. Testify for prosecution: Mary Thompson, Mary__ [Foster?]. Defendant being arraigned pleads guilty. Judgment is fine of fifteen shillings.

Page 173R   August 1782
Indictments Returned by the Grand Jury.

1. Commonwealth v. Anna Williams. Assault & Battery. True Bill.

2. Same v. Henry Myers. Assault & Battery. True Bill. Fined 15/.

3. Same v. Mary Groves. Larceny. True Bill. Tried & not guilty.

4. Same v. John Bridges. Tipling House. True Bill.

Page 174L   August 1782
Pennsylvania v. Anna Williams. Sarah McConnor in £20 and James

McConnor in £20 for their appearance 3rd Monday of November to prosecute defendant for Assault & Battery.

Pennsylvania v. Robert McCashlan. Samuel McCashlan in £20 for good behavior of defendant for one year.

Pennsylvania v. John Black & Samuel McCashlan. John Black in £20 and Samuel McCashlan in £20 for appearance next Court to answer.

The Court appoints Thomas Vickroy, Henry Woods, & Jacob Nagle Esqs. auditors to settle the accounts of the Treasurers & Commissioners of Bedford County.

Page 174R   [November 1782]
At Bedford 19 November 1792 before Thomas Smith, George Woods, James Martin, & John Hopkins.

David McKeehan Esq. on motion of Mr. Hamilton admitted Attorney of this Court.

Grand Jury:
  Joseph McCartney   Thomas Blair
  Joseph Garner   Daniel Davibaugh
  Valentine [Cow?]   Aaron Donnaldson
  David Keefer   Charles Debert
  William Swager   Michael May
  ~~Godfrey Pa~~___   John McClemens
  Derry Ryan
  Hermon Persons   Jacob Helm
  Daniel Smith   Samuel McCashlan

Indictments Returned by the Grand Jury.

1. Pennsylvania v. Benjamin Smith & Henry Smith. Larceny. True Bill.

2. Same v. David Brown, Benjn Smith & Fred^k K___ns. Riot, Assault & Battery. True Bill.

Page 175L   November 1782
3. Pennsylvania v. Nicholas Ferrence. Larceny. Ignoramus.

4. Pennsylvania v. Adam Bower. Tipling House. True Bill.

5. Same v. Moses Graham. Nuisance. Ignoramus.

6. Same v. Luke Fetter. Nuisance. Ignoramus.

Recognizances Returned by Justices.

Pennsylvania v. Benjamin Smith. Defendant in £50 and Benjn Martin in £25 to appear and answer.

Same v. John Mellot & William Clevenger. Defendants each in £50 to appear and answer. Peter Swartswilder in £50 to prosecute.

Same v. Michael Stuff. Defendant in £20 and Joseph Walter in £10 to appear and answer.

Pennsylvania v. Benjamin Smith. Samuel Park in £40 and Christopher Cornel in £20 to appear and prosecute.

Pennsylvania v. Nicholas Ferrence. John Putnam in £15 to prosecute.

Pennsylvania v. John Hart. William Wilson in £40 to prosecute.

Page 175R November 1782
Indictments Tried.

Pennsylvania v. Benjamin Smith. Larceny N° 1. Testify for prosecution: Saml Parker, Conrod Rush. Testify for defense: Peter Peck. Jury of William Wilson, Philip Wolf, James Beaty, George Wert, Michael Dibert, George Ensley, Peter Morgert, James Taylor, John Andrew May, John Cessna Jr., James Gordon, and Thomas Kenton find defendant not guilty.

Indictments Returned Cont.

7. Pennsylvania v. John Mellot & Wm Clevenger. Killing a Dog. True Bill.

8. Pennsylvania v. James Hart. Larceny. True Bill.

9. Same v. Hector McNeal. Indictment by Presentment for Tipling House.

10. Same v. Catherine Saylor. Indictment by Presentment for Tipling House.

Page 176L November 1782

~~Commonwealth v. Adam Bower. John Shaver in £20 for his appearance next Jany Court to prosecute and give evidence.~~

On motion Jacob Nagle Esq. Samuel Selby 3rd Esq. admitted as Attorney of this Court.

Commonwealth v. Anna Williams. Sarah McCannon in £20 and James McCannon in £20 for their appearance next April Court to prosecute & give evidence against defendant for Assault & Battery.

Same v. John Mellot. Abraham Clevenger in £20 and John Crossan in £20 for appearance of defendant next April Court to answer for Killing a Dog.

Pennsylvania v. Hector McNeal. Defendant in £200, Martin Riley in £50 and George Funk in £50 to appear and answer.

Page 176R [January 1793]
At Bedford 28 January 1793 before James Martin, ~~George Woods, Hugh Barclay,~~ and John Hopkins.

Pennsylvania v. Mary Murry. Mordecai Williams in £40 for his appearance next April Court to testify and give evidence against defendant for Fornication & Bastardy.

Pennsylvania v. Benjamin Ferguson. Defendant in £50 and Thomas Buck in £25 to appear and answer. Philip Swartzwilder in £50 to prosecute.

Same v. Andrew Dougherty. Jacob Hoffman in £50 to appear and prosecute.

Page 177L January 1793
Pennsylvania v. Benjamin Ferguson. Defendant in £40 and Thomas Buck in £40 for appearance of defendant next April session to answer for Receiving Stolen Goods.

Same v. Robert Dougherty. Jacob Hoffman in £[cut off] for his appearance next April Court to prosecute and give evidence against defendant for Horse Stealing.

~~Pennsylvania v. Nathaniel Ames. Defendant in £10.~~

Page 177R [April 1793]
At Bedford 22 April 1793 before Thomas Smith, George Woods, James Martin, and Hugh Barclay.

Township	Constable	Supervisor Highways	Overseer Poor
Bedford Town	Henry Sides		
Bedford Township	Thomas Kenton	John Bonnett Wm Griffith	
Air	Philip Coleman	Wm Alexander Benjamin Williams	Christian [Study?] William Hunter
Bethel	Joseph Warford	Adam Stigers George Bishop	Christian Cowell Addis Lynn
Colerain	John Cessna Jr.	Joseph Friend Thomas Bradshaw	
Cumberland Valley	John Wimer	Frederick Rice Jonathan Cessna	Ezekial Cox Abraham Miley Jr.
Brothers Valley	Cornelius Martinus	Simon Hay Peter Leap	Jacob Glessner Jacob Winger
Turkey Foot	James Mitchell		
Quamahoning	John Noffsinger	Conrod Lint Robert Smiley	Wendal Emment Michael Zimmerman
Milford	Michael Tedrow	Thomas Wilson John Weimer Jr.	William Jones Henry Brown
Elk Lick	Henry Miller	John Fike John Hendrickson	John Houghstatler Shaphat Dwire
Londonderry	James Robinson	Nicholas Libarger Andrew Emerick	John Hynes Peter Shekley
Providence	George May		
Belfast	William Morton	John Straight Francis Welch	Jacob Wink William Hart
Hopewell	Jeremiah French	Thomas Buck Alex^r Alexander	Edward Cheney John Rynard
Woodbury	Christopher Markle	William Hart John Sook	Henry Brown Andrew [Dixon?]
Dublin	Frederick Dubbs	James Shields Christian Kiser	George Dansdell John Olinger
Stoney Creek	Albright Ginklesberger	Christian Miller John Musser	John Zigler Godfrey Raman

Page 178L   April 1793
Grand Jury:
James Wilson, foreman

Jacob Haines	John Hiple
Frederick Weimer	Jacob Fisher
Moses Rambo	Jacob Glassner
Jacob Baker	Jacob Cable
George Weymer	Christopher Miller
Abraham Faith	Andrew Bower
Abraham Good	Christopher Stoner

Indictments Returned by the Grand Jury

1. Commonwealth v. Catherine Brandon. Fornication. True Bill.

2. Same v. John Cessna. Assault. True Bill.
Defendant submits to Court, protesting his innocence. Fined 5/.

3. Same v. Sarah McCanan. Assault & Battery. True Bill.
Defendant submits to Court, protesting her innocence. Fined 5/.

4. Same v. John Cessna, Elizabeth Cessna, & Wm Hall. Forcible Entry & Detainer. True Bill.

Page 178R   April 1793
Pennsylvania v. Anna Williams. Assault & Battery found August 1792 N° 1. Testify for prosecution: Sarah McCannan, James McCanan, James Gibson, Wm Patterson Esq. Defendant submits to Court protesting innocence. Fined 10/.

5. Commonwealth v. William Gardner. Assault & Battery. True Bill. Defendant being arraigned submits to Court protesting his innocence. Fined 2/6.

6. Same v. William Gardner and John Gardner. Assault & Battery. True Bill. Defendant Wm Gardner submits to Court protesting his innocence. Fined 2/6.

7. Same v. Tobias Helsel. Assault & Battery. Ignoramus.

8. Same v. Robert Dougherty. Larceny. True Bill.
Jacob Hoffman in £20 to appear and prosecute in the above next August Term.

9. Same v. Caleb Hill. Larceny. True Bill.

Page 179L April 1793
Pennsylvania v. Catherine Brandon. Moses Graham in £20 for appearance of said Moses next August to testify and give evidence against defendant for Fornication.

Pennsylvania v. James Hart. Nicholas Wilson in £20 for his appearance next August to testify and give evidence against defendant for Larceny.

Pennsylvania v. James Hart. Defendant in £40 and William Gaff in £40 for appearance of defendant next August to answer for Larceny.

Pennsylvania v. John Cessna, Elizabeth Cessna & Wm Hall. Philip Drollinger in £[cut off] and John Bower in £[cut off] for appearance of Philip Drollinger next August to testify and give evidence against defendants for Forcible Entry & Detainer.

Page 179R
Pennsylvania v. John Cessna, Elizabeth Cessna & Wm Hall. John Cessna in £20 and Abraham Miley in £20 for appearance of John Cessna and Elizabeth Cessna fourth Monday in August to answer for Forcible Entry & Detainer. John Cessna in £20 and Wm Hall in £20 for appearance of Willi^m Hall to answer as above.

Pennsylvania v. Benjamin Williams. Susanna Coons in £20 and Valentine Wyrick in £20 for appearance of Susanna Coons to testify and give evidence against defendant for Adultery the fourth Monday of August next.

Same v. Susanna Coons. Defendant in £20 and Valentine Wyrick in £20 for appearance next August Court to answer for Fornication.

Page 180L April 1793
10 Pennsylvania v. Peter Swartzwilder. Larceny. True Bill.

11. Pennsylvania v. Peter Swartzwilder. Larceny. True Bill.

12. Pennsylvania v. Samuel Price. Assault & Battery. True Bill.
Testify for prosecution: Wm Paxton. Defendant being arraigned submits to court protesting his innocence. Fined 10/ and give security for his good behavior for one year.

13. Pennsylvania v. Benjamin Williams. Adultery. True Bill.

14. Pennsylvania v. Mary Murray. Fornication. True Bill.

15. Pennsylvania v. Susanna Coons. Fornication. True Bill.

Page 180R April 1793
Commonwealth v. Caleb Hill. Larceny N° 9 this Court. Defendant pleads guilty. Sentence of the Court as follows: the said Mare having been restored to the owner thereof Caleb Hill shall pay the value thereof being twelve pounds to the Commonwealth and shall undergo servitude of five years and shall be confined and kept at hard labor and pay costs. And it is also ordered that Caleb Hill the Felon now in the Gaol of the County be removed agreeably to the 34th section of The Act to Reform the Penal Laws[9] to the Gaol of the County of Philadelphia.

Pennsylvania v. Samuel Price. Defendant in £20 and John May in £20 for the good behavior of the defendant for one year.

Pennsylvania v. Peter Swartzwilder. Defendant in £40 and Benjn Martin in £40 for appearance of defendant next August session to answer two indictments for Larceny.

Page 181L
Pennsylvania v. Adam Bower. Indictment for Tipling House N° 4 1792. Defendant pleads not guilty. Jury of Henry Hoover, Charles Tagert, William Alexander, Abednego Stevens, Robert Gibson, Daniel McConnell, James Agnew, Rhinehart Wolf, Frederick Rohrer, John Davis, Samuel Bechtel, and William Gaff find defendant guilty. Fined £10 and costs.

16. Pennsylvania v. John Elder and James Elder. Misdemeanor. True Bill.

Page 181R April 1793
Pennsylvania v. James & John Elder. Peter Bush in £40 for his appearance next August session to testify and give evidence against defendant for misdemeanor.

Same v. Same. John Elder in £20, James Elder in £20 and John Anderson in £20 for appearance of defendants next session to answer for misdemeanor.

Same v. Peter Swartzwilder. Jacob Poorman in £20, George Ke___ in £20, and Jacob McClean in £20 for their appearance next session to

---

[9] *The Statues at Large of Pennsylvania from 1682 to 1801*, volume XII 1787—1790 (Harrisburg, Pennsylvania: Harrisburg Publishing Company, State Printer, 1908), "An Act to Reform the Penal Laws of the State," page 511. While the docket refers to the 34th section of the Act, it is the third section (revision to punishment for horse stealing) that applies here.

testify and give evidence in 2 Bills of Indictment against defendant for Larceny.

Page 182L   April 1793
Same v. John & James Elder. John Elder in £15, Jacob Oster in £15, James Elder in £15 and Jonathan Cessna in £10 to appear and answer. Peter Bush in £5 and Jonathan Cessna in £5 to prosecute.

Same v. William Hall. Defendant in £40 and Faithful Creton in £20 to appear and answer. Philip Dollinger in £40 to prosecute.

Same v. Abram Cashman. Defendant in £50 for his appearance this Court to answer.

Same v. John Fouzer. Defendant in £50 and Abraham Clevenger in £25 to appear and answer. Peter Swartzwilder in £50 to prosecute.

Page 182R   [August 1793]
At Bedford 26 August 1793 before Thomas Smith, George Woods, Hugh Barclay, James Martin, James Wells.

Derry Ryan appointed Supervisor in place of John Bonnett deceased.

Township	Constable
Bedford Town	Henry Sides
Bedford Township	Simon Kenton
Air	Philip Coleman
Bethel	Joseph Warford
Colerain	John Cessna Jr.
Cumberland Valley	John Wimer
Brothers Valley	Cornelius Martinus
Turkey Foot	James Mitchell
Quamahoning	John Noffsinger
Milford	Michael Tedrow Jr.
Elk Lick	Henry Miller
Londonderry	Jonas Robinson
Providence	George May
Belfast	William Morton
Hopewell	Jeremiah French
Woodberry	Christopher Markle
Dublin	Frederick Dubbs
Stoney Creek	Albright Ginklesberger

Grand Jury:
- Peter Bugh
- Peter Fox
- John Ulster
- John Sapp
- John Elder
- Nicholas Bodder
- Henry Holler
- Joseph Lilly
- Jesse Vaughn
- Joseph Adam
- Valentine Wyrick
- William Baker
- Henry Stover
- Abraham Fry
- Philip Drolinger
- John Mortimore Jr.
- Jacob Martin
- Peter Baker
- W^m McDaniel
- Joseph Brindle

Page 183L
[No case name] Benjamin Williams in £100 and Barnet Ford in £100 for appearance of Benjamin Williams next session to answer.

Pennsylvania v. Catherine Brandon. Moses Graham in £20 for his appearance next session to give evidence against defendant for Fornication.

Pennsylvania v. Peter Swartzwilder. 2 Indictments. Jacob Boreman in £20, Jacob McClean in £20, and George K__niger in £20 to appear next Court to give evidence in two Bills of Indictment found against defendant for Felony.

Pennsylvania v. Peter Swartzwilder. Defendant in £50 and Andrew Mann Esq. in £50 for appearance of defendant next Court to answer two indictments for Felony.

Page 183R   August 1793
On motion John Clark Esq. Jonathan Henderson Esq. admitted as Attorney for Court of Common Pleas, Quarter Sessions &c.

Ordered by the Court that Robert Dougherty the Felon before mentioned now in the Gaol of the County be removed agreeably to the 34th section of the Act to Reform the Penal Laws to the Gaol of the County of Philadelphia. [The preceding paragraph was inserted in different hand.]

Pennsylvania v. Robert Dougherty. Indictment for Larceny N° 8 April session 1793. Testify for prosecution: Jacob Hoffman, James Wells Esq. Testify for defense: Philip Kimmel, Thomas McGaughey Esq., George Nixon. Jury of George Coleman, Francis Hay, Peter Maugh, John Wolford, Adam Stull, John Fletcher, Michael Ingle, Allen Rose, John Kimmel, George Shenafeld, George Earnest, Philip Rhinhart find Robert

Dougherty guilty. Judgment that he restore the horse stolen, pay a fine of like value, undergo a servitude of three years at hard labor.

4. Pennsylvania v. Benjamin Ferguson. Larceny. Ignoramus.

2. Pennsylvania v. James Hart. Larceny. Testify for prosecution: Nicholas Wilson, William Wilson, George Woods Esq. Testify for defense: John Hart, James [McKenna?], Alexander Waugh. Jury of John Hoover, John Wolford, Jacob Curtz, John Himmel, Allen Rose, Henry Baker, John Fletcher, John Bowser, George Shenefelt, Peter Maugh, George Coleman, Henry A___ find defendant not guilty.

Page 184L August 1793
Pennsylvania v. John Cessna, Elizabeth Cessna, William Hall. Indictment for Forcible Entry & Detainer. Testify for prosecution: Philip Drolinger, Margaret Bower, Mrs. Drolinger. Testify for defense: George Woods Esq., John Cessna, and Elisabeth Cessna retract their plea and submit protesting their innocence. Fine two shillings and fifteen pence each.

Republica v. John Elder & James Elder. Misdemeanor. Defendants plead not guilty. Witnesses sworn: [P]eter Bush, [V]alentine Wyrick, [Th]omas Coulter Esq., [N]athan Wright, [A]braham Miley Jr. Jury of John Kimmel, George Shinefeldt, George Earnest, Philip Rinehart, William Scovill, John ____, Henry A__, John Bower, Thomas Hay, Peter Mauk, George Coleman, and Jacob Kurtz find defendants not guilty.

Edward Evans in £50 and Michael Murphey in £25 for his good behavior especially toward his wife Rachel Evans and his appearance at next November Court to answer.

Page 184R [November 1793]
At Bedford 18 November 1793 before Thomas Smith, George Woods, Hugh Barclay, James Wells.

Township	Constable
Bedford Town	Henry Sides
Bedford Township	Simon Kenton
Air	Philip Coleman
Bethel	Joseph Werford
Colerain	John Cessna Jr.
Cumberland Valley	John Wimer
Brothers Valley	Cornelius Martinus
Turkey Foot	James Mitchell

Township	Constable
Quamahoning	John Noffsinger
Milford	Michael Tedrow Jr.
Elk Lick	Henry Miller
Londonderry	Jonas Robinson
Providence	George May
Belfast	William Morton
Hopewell	Jeremiah French
Woodberry	Christopher Markle
Dublin	Frederick Dubbs
Stoney Creek	Albright Ginklesberger

Grand Jury:
    Jacob Saylor, foreman   John Colepenny
    Philip Harmon   Peter Covar
    Lewis [Cizer?]   James Husband
    Joseph Covanhoven   Joseph Johns
    Samuel Masters   Valentine Easter
    Arthur Wray   Thomas Wray
    William Swager   Michael Mourer
    Nathan Chany   Abraham Buzzard
    Martin Loy

Page 185L   November 1793
No 1. Pennsylvania v. Samuel Hall Jr. et al. Indictment against defendant and John Am___ for Larceny. Witnesses: Jacob Herron, Conrod Smith, John Cessna. Saml Hall pleads guilty. Judgment to return goods stolen or value thereof, pay fine of like amount, and be confined to hard labor for one month.

Pennsylvania v. John Ammor_. Same witnesses. Defendant pleads guilty. Same judgment as above.

Pennsylvania v. Peter Swartzwelder. Defendant in £40 and Conrad Rush on £20 for appearance of defendant next January to answer two indictments for Felony.

2. Pennsylvania v. Andrew Hay____. Assault & Battery. True Bill. Witnesses: Henry [Harradar?], James Porter, Thomas Spencer, John Jones, John Mitchel, Stephen Bruner. Defendant pleads not guilty. Jury of Valentine Ripley, Abraham Miley Jr., Henry Bruner, Robert Anderson, William M___, David Kimmel, Jacob ____, Henry Libarger, David Kershner, William Drenning, ____ Williams, and Joseph Oyler find defendants guilty. Fined 14/0.

Pennsylvania v. Enoch Leonard. Assault & Battery. True Bill.

Page 185R   November 1793
Pennsylvania v. Matthew McGinnis. Assault & Battery. Ignoramus.

5. Pennsylvania v. Rachel Ingland. Fornication. True Bill.

Pennsylvania v. Peter Swartzwilder. 2 Indictments. Jacob Boremand, John McClean and George Kisinginger each in £20 that the said Jacob Boreman, John McClean, and George Kis^{gn} appear next Jany session to prosecute.

Pennsylvania v. Andrew Hayrader. Defendant in £40 and John Hayrader in £40 for good behavior of defendant for one year.

Page 186L   [January 1794]
At Bedford 27 January 1794 before George Woods, James Martin, and James Wells.

Township	Constable	
Bedford Town	Henry Sides	
Bedford Township	Simon Kenton	
Air	Philip Coleman	
Bethel	Joseph Warford	
Colerain	John Cessna Jr.	
Cumberland Valley	John Wimer	
Brothers Valley	Cornelius Martinus	James Spraige appointed in place of Cornelius Martinus
Turkey Foot	James Mitchell	
Quamahoning	John Noffsinger	
Milford	Michael Tedrow Jr.	
Elk Lick	Henry Miller	
Londonderry	Jonas Robinson	
Providence	George May	
Belfast	William Morton	
Hopewell	Jeremiah French	
Woodberry	Christopher Markle	Jacob Broombach appointed in the place of Christopher Markle
Dublin	Frederick Dubbs	
Stoney Creek	Albrigh Ginklesberger	

Page 186R
Pennsylvania v. Jacob Devore. Defendant in £20 and Cornelius Devore in £20 for appearance of defendant next April session to answer for Assault against John Tomlinson.

Pennsylvania v. Jacob Devore. John Tomlinson in £10 and John Haines in £10 for appearance of said Jn° Tomlinson next April to prosecute the above.

Pennsylvania v. Joseph Buck. John Briges in £10 and David Penrod in £10 for appearance of John Bridges next April to prosecute and give evidence against defendant.

Pennsylvania v. Jacob Evarts. Daniel Moor in £20 for appearance of Daniel Moor next April to prosecute and give evidence against defendant Jacob Everts.

Pennsylvania v. Joseph Buck. Joseph Buck in £10 and William McDermott in £10 for appearance of Joseph Buck [next] April session to answer for Misdemeanor.

Page 187L [January 1794]
At Bedford January 1794. Petition of Michael Rein of Cumberland Valley Township resident and Freeholder of that township about one mile from the Great Road leading from Bedford to Fort Cumberland. Lands of John Cessna and John Deakins and Bernard Bower intervene between him and the Great Road and John Cessna has fenced up the Woods intervening in such a manner as to make it impossible for the petitioner to use the High Way except circuitous one and one half mile in Hills impassible to sledges & waggons. Petitioner asks for private road from the Great Road to petitioner's house to be kept open and repaired at the private expense of petitioner and those neighbors who may partake of advantages of the private road. Court appoints John Lazar, John Coulter, John Elder, Peter Bough, Henry B__res, & James Crosby to view and examine the ground and make report. We the subscribers appointed to view and lay out a road in issuance of the above petition lay out the road as follows: Beginning at Michael Rines land [metes and bounds follow mentioning Henry Miley's land and running on the dividing line between Abraham Miley Jr. and Barnet Bower's land] viewed 21 February 1794 and witnessed 04 May 1794.

John Lazare	Henry Burress	John Elder
James Crosby	John Coulter	Peter Bough

Page 187R [Sketch of above road.]

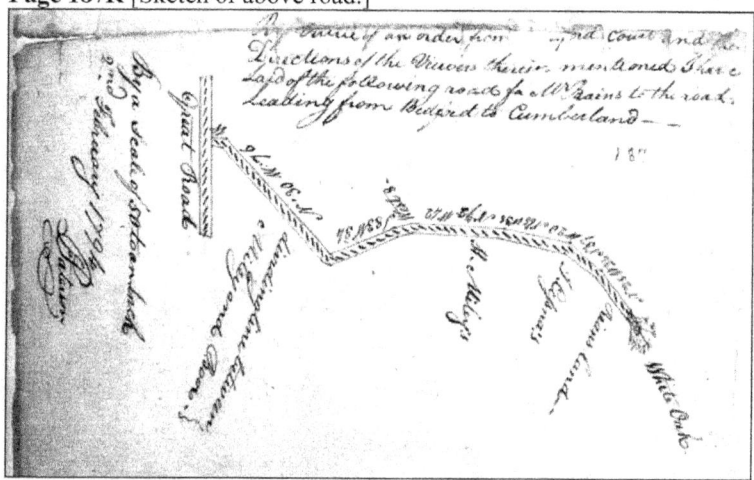

Page 188L [Blank]

Page 188R [April 1794]
At Bedford 28 April 1794 before James Riddle, George Woods, James Martin, Hugh Barclay, James Wells.

Township	Constable	Supervisor Roads	Overseer Poor
Bedford Town	Faithful Creton		
Bedford Township	John Dibert	Wm Wilson Baltzer Hesse	
Air	John Kendal	Wm Alexander Benjn Williams	Enoch Williams Abednego Stevens
Bethel	David ____	Adam Stigers George Bishop	Christian Cowell Addis Lynn
Colerain	George Waltman	Jacob Bear John May	
Cumberland Valley	Jonathan Cessna	Nathan Wright Christian Mease	Ezekial Cox Abraham Miley Jr.
Brothers Valley	Christian Fritz	Martin Dively Michael Fryer Sr.	John Olinger Jacob Blough
Turkey Foot	Thomas Spencer	John McClean John Nicholas	Edward Kemp James Spencer
Quamahoning	Moses Frame	Henry Stall John Furray	Wendal Emment Philip Kimmel
Milford	Adam Flick	George Weimer Moses Rambo	Henry Bruner Christian Ankney
Elk Lick	John Burger	Jacob Houghstaller Michael Engle	Solomon Claudfelty Christian Burntrager

Township	Constable	Supervisor Roads	Overseer Poor
Londonderry	David McVicker	Matthias Croy Robert McConnell	Joshua Wright Andrew McConnell
Providence	~~Edward Daniels~~ Michael Ritchie	Michael Barndoller Benjn Martin	
Belfast	Michael Stall	John Straight Francis Welch	Samuel Truax Jacob Shark
Hopewell	Jeremiah French	Thomas Buck Alex^r Alexander	Edward Cheny John Rynard
Woodbury	John Ullerick	Henry Clapper John Engel	George Rhoad John M___
Dublin	Thomas Carter	James Shields David Fields	Azariah McClean Bigg___ He___
Stoney Creek	John Zigler	Henry Hess David Kimmel	George Gro___ Jacob Inglesburger

Page 189L   April 1794
Grand Jury:
      William Hartley, foreman

- Peter Morgert
- William McCally
- Thomas Blair
- Isaac Bonnett
- James Taylor
- Valentine Cow
- Joseph Springer
- Benjamin Williams
- Adam Croyle
- Charles Croyle
- Duncan McVicker
- Francis Hay
- John Rush
- Andrew Young
- Joseph Murray
- David Beckwith
- Ephraim Wallace
- Adam Russ
- James Balla
- William McDermod
- Derry Ryan

Indictments returned by the Grand Jury.

1. Commonwealth v. Joseph Buck. Assault. Ignoramus

2. Same v. Joseph Buck. Assault & Battery. Ignoramus

3. Same v. Jacob Frownheiser. Tipling House. Ignoramus.

4. Same v. John Anderson. Assault & Battery. True Bill.

Page 189R   April 1794

5. Commonwealth v. John Waggoner. Assault. Ignoramus

6. Same v. Jacob Hains. Assault & Battery. Ignoramus.

7. Same v. Richard Pinkerton. Assault & Battery. True Bill. Defendant submits to Court protesting his innocence. Fined £3.

8. Same v. Susannah Flick, Assault & Battery. True Bill.

9. Same v. John Tomlinson. Assault. Ignoramus.

10. Same v. Jacob Devore. Forcible Entry & Detainer. True Bill. Trial put off on affidavit of defendant. Aug 1794 removed by Certiorari.

11. Same v. Benjn Burd Esq. Assault. True Bill.

Page 190L April 1794

12. Commonwealth v. Jacob Everts. Felony. True Bill.

13. Same v. George Kellerman. Felony. Ignoramus.

14. Same v. John Erich. Assault. True Bill. Defendant pleads guilty protesting his innocence. Fined 2/6.

15. Same v. Richard Pinkerton Jr. Fornication. True Bill.

16. Same v. Robert Means. Presentment of Grand Jury for Tipling House.

17. Same v. Frederick Hill. Same Presentment.

18. Same v. Jacob Grindle. Same Presentment.

19. Same v. Duncan Morrison, John Fletcher, Elazer Walford. Same Presentment.

20. Same v. John Peck & Isaac Rutledge. Same Presentment.

21. Same v. Peter Didier. Same Presentment.

22. Same v. David Jordan. Same Presentment.

Page 190R April 1794

Pennsylvania v. Peter Swartzwilder. Indictment N° 11 Apr 1793 for Larceny. Testify for prosecution: Jacob Boorman, Jacob Kessinger, Jacob Wink. Testify for defense: Danl Swartzwilder, James Martin, Andrew Mann. Jury of Henry Brown, John Snider, Joseph Snider, Christopher Uirke, George Ensley Jr., Adam Kuntz, William Paxton, John Hendricks, James Black, Conrod Haverstock, Peter Stiffler, and J___ P___ find defendant not guilty.

Louisa H__genbug discharged by Proc.

John, James & Robert Anderson discharged from their Recognizances.

Pennsylvania v. Peter Swartzwilder. N° 10 April Term 1793 for Larceny. Testify for prosecution: Jacob McClean, George Kessinger. Testify for defense: And^r Mann Esq. Jury of Christopher Uirke, Joseph McFerren, William Paxton, James Black, Henry Bush, John Snyder, Peter Weaverling, John Brits, Henry Brown, John Hendricks, Jacob Buterbaugh, John Bauman find defendant not guilty.

Page 191L
Henry Whetstone appointed Constable of Colerain Township in room of George Waltman.

Pennsylvania v. Derry Ryan. Indictment N° 1 July 1787. Defendant in £50 and Robert [Means?] in £25 for his appearance and to abide further orders of the Court.

Pennsylvania v. Benjamin Burd Esq. Defendant in £20 to appear next August Court to answer for Assault and Battery on Michael Houk.

Page 191R April 1794
Pennsylvania v. Jacob Devoure. Defendant in £40 and Cornelius Devore in £40 for appearance of defendant next August Court to answer.

Michael Houk bound in £50 to appear at next Court to give evidence.

Michael Richey appointed Constable of Providence Township in room of Edward Daniels.

Daniel Moore, James Sprauge, John Tomlinson, and John Haines bound in £20 to appear at next session to give evidence.

Matthias Zimmerman in £30 and George Kimmell in £25 for appearance of Matthias Zimmerman next Court and in the meantime to keep the peace particularly Wm Short.

Page 192L April 1794
Commonwealth v. Joseph Higgins Sr. Joseph Higgins Jr. in £25 for appearance of Joseph Higgins Jr. to prosecute Joseph Higgins Sr. Capias D^t £25 _ferred to Nov Term 1794 in the Common Pleas upon this Recognizance. Forfeited.

Page 192R [August 1794]
At Bedford 25 August 1794 before James Riddle, George Woods, and James Wells.

Township	Constable
Bedford Town	Faithful Creighton
Bedford Township	John Dibert
Air	James Kendal
Bethel	David Sliger
Colerain	Henry Whitstone
Cumberland Valley	Jonathan Cessna
Brothers Valley	Christian Fritz
Turkey Foot	Thomas Spencer
Quamahoning	Moses Frame
Milford	John Lynch
Elk Lick	John Burger
Londonderry	David McVicker
Providence	Michael Ritchie
Belfast	Michael Stall
Hopewell	Jeremiah French
Woodberry	John Ulbrick
Dublin	Thomas Carter
Stoney Creek	John Zigler
St Clair	Anthony Blackburn

Grand Jury:
    Jacob Saylor foreman
    Frederick Dibert
    Solomon Adams
    Robert Adams
    Peter Oyler
    George Imbler
    Benjamin Stine
    John Clarke
    Robert Moore
    David Jordan
    James Anderson
    George Wild
    John A May
    William Small
    Thomas Norton
    George Beeler
    Thomas Anderson
    Stephen Clarke
    Francis Gibbs
    John Davibaugh
    William Scovill

Page 193L   August 1794
Pennsylvania v. Edward Stoy. John Bridges bound in £20 for appearance of Margaret Bridges November session 1794 to give evidence against Edward Stoy for Fornication.

Abraham Morrison Esq. on motion Richard Smith admitted as Attorney of the Courts of Common Pleas, Quarter Sessions, &c.

Pennsylvania v. Edward Stoy. Daniel Stoy Esq. in £20 for appearance of Edward Stoy at November session to answer for Fornication.

Pennsylvania v. Susannah Flick. Alexander Thomas in £20 for appearance of defendant Sussanah Flick November session 1794 to answer for Fornication. James Spraig in £20 to appear November session 1794 and give evidence in the above.

Aaron Collins in £20, Francis Morr___ in £20, Henry Collins in £20 Moses Collins in £20, Rachel Collins in £20 and John Lynn in £100 for appearance of said Morr___ at November 1794 session to give evidence.

Page 193R August 1794
Pennsylvania v. Ruleph Rickets. Defendant bound in £50 that he shall be of peace and good behavior toward Hannah, a negro wench lately in his custody, and now liberated by the Court for the space of one year. Mr Griffith and Elijah Adams are trustees for the said Hannah until guardians are appointed.

Pennsylvania v. Michael Zimmerman. Michael Zimmerman in £20 and Michael Mauer in £20 for appearance of Michael Zimmerman to appear at November 1794 session to answer.

Pennsylvania v. James McCashlan. James Anderson of Bedford Township in £40 in lieu of Thomas Anderson of Bedford Township for Felony said to be committed by the said James.

Pennsylvania v. Michael Zimmerman. Daniel Stoy and Moses Frame each in £20 for their appearance at November 1794 session to give evidence.

Matthias Zimmerman in £100, George Kimmel in £50, and George Imler in £50 that Matthias Zimmerman be of good behavior particularly to Adam Miller Esq. for one year.

Page 194L August 1794
Indictments returned by the Grand Jury

1. Commonwealth v. Michael Zimmerman. Assault & Battery. True Bill.

2. Commonwealth v. Daniel Stoy Esq. Assault & Battery. Ignoramus.

3. Commonwealth v. Adam Miller. Assault. True Bill.
Defendant pleads guilty. Fined one penny and costs.

4. Commonwealth v. Frederick Long, Christian E____, [Jacob?] Arndt, Nicholas Lyenburger & Sarah Zimmerman. Riot & Assault. Ignoramus.

DOCKET 2: 1771-1801   225

5. Commonwealth v. Thomas Coulter Esq. Assault & Battery. True Bill.

Page 194R   August 1794

Pennsylvania v. Jacob Devoure. Defendant in £50 and Cornelius Devore in £50 for appearance of Jacob Devoure at November 1794 session to answer. John Tomlinson in £50, John Hains in £50, and Duncan McVicker in £50 for their appearance at November 1794 session to give evidence in the above.

Henry Woods Esq., Jacob Nagle Esq., and Thomas Vickroy appointed auditors for settling the public accounts for the ensuing year.

6. Pennsylvania v. James McCashlin. Larceny. Ignoramus.

7. Pennsylvania v. John Hartzel & others. Riot and Assault & Battery. True Bill.

Page 195L   August 1794

8. Pennsylvania v. Hartzel & others. Riot, Assault & Battery. True Bill.

Pennsylvania v. Benjamin Burd. No 11 April term 1794. Assault. Testify for prosecution: Michael Hook. Defendant submits to Court. Fined /6.

Pennsylvania v. Catherine Burket. Discharged on payment of costs.

9. Pennsylvania v. Frederick Hill. Tipling House. True Bill.

Page 195R   August 1794

Pennsylvania v. John Hartzel, George Williams, and Adam Davibaugh. N° 7 of this session. Riot, Assault & Battery.
Same v. Same. N° 8 of this session. Riot, Assault & Battery.
Testify for prosecution: Elizabeth McSurley, David Espy Esq., Jacob Earnest. Testify for defense: George Devebaugh, Jacob Davebaugh, George Woods Esq., Henry Werth. Jury of John Mallot, Wm Griffith, John Williams, Michael Sill, George Graham, Thomas Smith, James Beaty, Anthony Ling, Frederick Reickart, Henry Sides, Samuel McCashlan, and John Garrison find defendant guilty. Sentence continued to November session.

John Jones & Robert Coleburn each in £50 for appearance of Robert Coleburn November 1794 session to answer.

Commonwealth v. Thomas Coulter Esq. Thomas Coulter Esq. in £20 for his appearance November 1794 session to answer for Assault & Battery on Nicholas Knight and in the meantime to be of good behavior.

Page 196L [Blank]

Page 196R [November 1794]
At Bedford third Monday in November 1794 before James Riddle, George Woods, Hugh Barclay.

Township	Constable
Bedford Town	Faithful Creighton
Bedford Township	John Dibert
Air	James Kendal
Bethel	David Sliger
Colerain	Henry Whitstone
Cumberland Valley	Jonathan Cessna
Brothers Valley	Christian Fritz
Turkey Foot	Thomas Spencer
Quamahoning	Moses Frame
Milford	John Lynch
Elk Lick	John Burger
Londonderry	David McVicker
Providence	Michael Richie
Belfast	Michael Stall
Hopewell	Jeremiah French
Woodberry	John Ullrick
Dublin	Thomas Carter
Stoney Creek	John Zigler
St Clair	Anthony Blackburn

Grand Jury:
    Thomas Coulter, foreman   Henry Williams
    Wm Proctor   Robert Adams
    George Anderson   Thomas Royal
    William Ward   John Friend
    John Steward   Henry Smith
    Lewis Hessler   Edward Rose
    John Ritchey   Peter ONeal
    John Williamson   David Potts (affirmed)
    William Griffith (affirmed)

Page 197L
Recognizances returned.

Negro Peter bound in £20 and John Garretson bound in £20 conditioned that said Peter keeps the peace and be of good behavior particularly toward William Lafferty until next Court of Quarter Sessions.

Commonwealth v. Edward Stoy. Daniel Stoy in £20 for appearance of said Edward Stoy next January session to answer for Fornication.

Commonwealth v. Edward Stoy. John Bridges in £20 for appearance of Margaret Bridges next January session to prosecute against Edward Stoy.

Page 197R November 1794
Commonwealth v. Michael Zimmerman. No 1 August Session 1794. Assault & Battery. Testify for prosecution: Daniel Stoy Esq., Moses Frame. Testify for defense: Michael Mowrer, Jacob Barnhardt, James Wells. Jury of Conrod Rush, Joshua Purron, Samuel Truax, William Le___ket, Isaac Martin, George James, William Rassler, Asher Leaton, Arthur Rhay, George Mardes, Andrew Sl___, and John Brewer find defendant guilty. Fine $10 and costs.

Recognizances.

Pennsylvania v. Isaac Sh___man. Isaac Sh___man in £20 and Emanuel Brayler in £20.

Pennsylvania v. Frederick Hill. April session Tipling House. Defendant pleads guilty and submits to Court. Fined £10 and costs.

Same v. Same. August session 1794 Tipling House. Defendant pleads guilty and submits to Court. Fined £10 and costs.

14th April 1802 remission of above fines. J. Bonnett.

Page 198L November 1794
1. Commonwealth v. Daniel McCarty. Assault & Battery. True Bill. Witnesses for state: William Philips, Richard L Carmack, Doc[t] Auld. Testify for defense: Nathan Chaney. Defendant pleads not guilty. Defendant retracts his plea and submits to Court. Fined £0.15.0.

2. Pennsylvania v. Daniel McCarty. Assault & Battery. True Bill. Defendant pleads not guilty. Defendant retracts his plea and submits to Court. Fined. Daniel McCarty bound in £50 and Jonathan Woodside in £50 conditioned that Daniel McCarty appear at 3 o'clock in the afternoon of 19 November 1794 to answer.

Pennsylvania v. Doctor John Kimmel. John Bridges in £20 to appear next January session to give evidence against defendant.

Robert Coleburn is discharged by Proclamation on payment of costs.

Page 198R November 1794
Commonwealth v. Daniel McCarty. Witnesses for state: William Philips, Richard L Carmack, Doc^t Auld. Testify for defense: Nathan Chaney, Jacob Hartzel. Defendant pleads not guilty. Defendant retracts his plea and submits to Court. Fined £3 and costs.

Pennsylvania v. Daniel McCarty. N° 2 November 1794. Defendant pleads not guilty. Defendant retracts his plea and submits to Court. Fined £0.15.0 and costs.

3. Pennsylvania v. Wm Henry. Assault & Battery. Accomodated.

Page 199L [November 1794]
Recognizances Returned to November Session 1794.

1. Commonwealth v. Simon Kenton. Defendant in £200 and George Funk. Bail in £100 for appearance of Simon Kenton third Monday in November for Riot and other Treasonable proceedings in assisting and abetting the setting up of a seditious pole in opposition to the Laws of the United States. Recognized to January. John Kenton bail.

2. Commonwealth v. Simon Kenton. You Simon Kenton acknowledge to owe the Commonwealth £200. You John Kenton acknowledge to owe the Commonwealth £100 to be Levied on your Goods & Chattels Land & Tenements respectively on the condition that you Simon Kenton be and appear at the Court of General Quarter Sessions of the Peace to be held at Bedford for the County of Bedford fourth Monday in January next to answer.

3. Commonwealth v. John McGaughey. Defendant bound to appear in November £200. Samuel Davidson Esq. bail in £100. Conditioned as above. Recognized to January 1795 Christopher Riley bail.

Page 199R November 1794
4. Commonwealth v. John Linn. Defendant in £200 and Michael Dipert in £100. Recognized to January 1795. James Anderson bail.

5. Same v. George Sills. Defendant in £200 and John Dipert in £100. Recognized to January 1795. George Bowser bail.

6. Commonwealth v. Baltzer Hess. Defendant in £200 and Peter Stifler in £100. Recognized to January 1795. Robert Adams of Bedford bail.

7. Same v. John Cochran. Defendant in £200 and Joshua Persons in £100. Recognized to January 1795. Same Joshua Person bail.

8. Same v. William Todd. Defendant in £200 and Anthony Nagle in £100. Recognized to January 1795. Same bail Anthony Nagle.

9. Same v. Ludwick Samuel. Defendant in £200 and Martin Riley Esq. in £100. Recognized to January 1795. Nicholas Knight bail.

10. Same v. Thomas Smith. Defendant in £200 and Wm Ward Esq. in £100. Recognized to January 1795. Wm Todd bail.

Page 200L   November 1794

11. Commonwealth v. Peter Morgret. Defendant in £200 and John Ritchey in £100. Recognized to January 1795. John Ritchey bail.

12. Same v. William Willson Hopewell Township. Defendant in £200 and Wm Nixon in £100. Recognized to January 1795. Jacob McClean bail.

13. Same v. Isaac Bonnett. Defendant in £200 and Jacob Bonnett in £100. Recognized to January 1795. Martin Riley Esq. bail.

14. Same v. Martin Fritz. Defendant in £200 and Peter Stiffler in £100. Recognized to January 1795. Jacob Stifler bail.

15. Same v. James Doyle. Defendant in £200 and David Espy Esq. in £100. Recognized to January 1795. Henry Wertz bail.

16. Same v. Wm Wilson Bedford Township. Defendant in £200 and James Dalton in £100. Recognized to January 1795. James Dalton bail.

17. Same v. Joseph Scullnot. Defendant in £200 and Solomon Adams in £100. Recognized to January 1795. Robert Adams bail.

Page 200R   November 1794

18. Commonwealth v. Hill Wilson. Defendant in £200 and Samuel Davidson in £100. Recognized to January 1795. Nicholas Wilson bail.

19. Commonwealth v. Nicholas Wilson. Defendant in £200 and Samuel Davidson in £100. Recognized to January 1795. Wm Wilson bail.

20. Same v. Jacob Rickard. Defendant in £200 and Frederick Rickard in £100. Recognized to January 1795. Conrad Haverstick bail.

21. Same v. Conrad Haverstock. Defendant in £200 and Frederick Richard in £100. Recognized to January 1795. Jacob Rickard bail.

22. Same v. Neal McMullin. Defendant in £200 and James Taylor in £100. Recognized to January 1795. Daniel [surname blank] bail.

23. Same v. Michael Barndollar. Defendant in £200 and James Martin Esq. in £100. Recognized to January 1795. Andrew Mann bail.

24. Same v. Joseph Lilly. Defendant in £200 and James Martin in £100. Recognized to January 1795. Anthony Smith bail.

Page 201L [November 1794]

25. Commonwealth v. Thomas Moore. Defendant in £200 and David Espy Esq. in £100. Recognized to January 1795. Henry Wertz bail.

26. Commonwealth v. Barnabas Blue. Defendant in £200 and James Martin Esq. in £100. Recognized to January 1795. Wm Wilson Hopewell Township bail.

27. Commonwealth v. Henry Reikard. Defendant in £200. Recognized to January 1795. Nicholas Knight bail.

28. Commonwealth v. Andrew Sheets. Defendant in £200 and Michael Sill in £100. Recognized to January 1795. John Christman bail.

29. Commonwealth v. John Paxton Sr. Defendant in £200 and Wm Hartley in £100. Recognized to January 1795. John McClimans bail.

30. Commonwealth v. Adam Ritchey. Defendant in £200 and Michael Ritchey in £100. Recognized to January 1795. Earnest Baker bail.

31. Commonwealth v. Joseph Sparks. Defendant in £200 and John Martin in £100. Recognized to January 1795. John Rush bail.

Page 201R [November 1794]

32. Commonwealth v. John Kinton. Defendant in £200. Recognized to January 1795. Simon Kinton bail.

33. Commonwealth v. John Foster. Defendant in £200 and David Espy Esq. in £100. Recognized to January 1795. Wm Scovil bail.

34. Commonwealth v. Jacob Chamberlain. Defendant in £200 and Michael Ritchey in £100. Recognized to January 1795. Michael Irons bail.

35. Commonwealth v. John Mackey. Defendant in £200 and Saml McCashlin in £100. Recognized to January 1795. Same bail.

36. Commonwealth v. Henry Beeckley. Defendant in £200 and Faithful Creighton in £100. Recognized to January 1795. John Christman bail.

37. Commonwealth v. George Bastion. Defendant in £200 and John Martin in £100. Recognized to January 1795. Jacob Saltzgiver bail.

DOCKET 2: 1771–1801   231

38. Commonwealth v. Frederick Hill. Defendant in £200 and Jacob Studebaker in £100. Recognized to January 1795. Nicholas Knight bail.

Page 202L [November 1794]

39. Commonwealth v. John Britz. Defendant in £200 and Jacob Studebaker in £100. Recognized to January 1795. John Davibaugh bail.

40. Commonwealth v. John Utsler. Defendant in £200 and Wm Baker in £100. Recognized to January 1795. Same bail.

[41.] Commonwealth v. Peter _oras. Defendant in £200 and John Boys in £100. Recognized to January 1795. John Davebaugh bail.

[42.] Commonwealth v. Jacob Earnest. Defendant in £200 and Wm Baker in £100. Recognized to January 1795. Wm Nickum bail.

[43.] Commonwealth v. George Croyle. Defendant in £200 and Christopher Reiley in £100. Recognized to January 1795. Same bail.

[44.] Commonwealth v. George Bowser. Defendant in £200 and George Imbler in £100. Recognized to January 1795. Same bail.

[45.] Commonwealth v. James Smith. Defendant in £200 and John Boys in £100. Recognized to January 1795. Same bail.

Page 202R   November 1794

46. Commonwealth v. Michael Iron. Defendant in £200 and Wm Hartley in £100. Recognized to January 1795. George Weymer [bail].

47. Commonwealth v. John McClimans. Defendant in £200 and Valentine Hollar in £100. Recognized to January 1795. James French [bail].

48. Commonwealth v. Jacob Nagle. Defendant in £200. Recognized to January 1795. Andrew Mann Esq. bail.

49. Commonwealth v. Robert Moore. Defendant in £200 and Andrew Mann Esq. in £100. Recognized to January 1795. Andrew Mann Esq. bail.

50. Commonwealth v. David Ford. Defendant in £200. Recognized to January 1795. Adam Ritchey bail.

51. Commonwealth v. Simon Ford. Defendant in £200 and Adam Young in £100. Recognized to January 1795. David Ford bail.

52. Commonwealth v. Wm Kagg. Defendant in £200 and Nicholas Kagg in £100. Recognized to January 1795. Same bail.

BEDFORD COUNTY QUARTER SESSIONS

Page 203L [November 1794]

53. Commonwealth v. Jacob Way. Defendant in £200 and Nicholas Cagg in £100. Recognized to January 1795. Same bail.

54. Commonwealth v. Michael Samuel. Defendant in £200 and Martin Pfeifer in £100. Recognized to January 1795. Ludwick Samuel bail.

55. Commonwealth v. John Wisecarver. Defendant in £200 and Faithful Creaton in £100. Recognized to January 1795. John Christman bail.

56. Commonwealth v. Jacob Hellum. Defendant in £200 and James Dalton in £100. Recognized to January 1795. Same bail.

57. Commonwealth v. William McCauley. Defendant in £200 and James Harford in £100. Recognized to January 1795. Thomas Blair bail.

58. Commonwealth v. John Sills. Defendant in £200 and John Brady in £100. Recognized to January 1795. Jacob Stiffner bail.

59. Commonwealth v. George Cardue. Defendant in £200 and James French in £100. Recognized to January 1795. Same bail.

Page 203R November 1794

60. Commonwealth v. Philip Wolf. Defendant in £200 and Hector McNeal in £100. Recognized to January 1795. Same bail.

61. Commonwealth v. John Mortimore. Defendant in £200 and Wm Henry in £100. Recognized to January 1795. Samuel McCashlin bail.

62. Commonwealth v. James Mortimore Jr. Defendant in £200 and Wm Henry in £100. Recognized to January 1795. John Mortimore bail.

63. Commonwealth v. Peter Countz. Defendant in £200 and David Smouse in £100. Recognized to January 1795. William Hartley bail.

64. Commonwealth v. Peter Countz Jr. Defendant in £200 and David Smouse in £100. Recognized to January 1795. Wm Hartley bail.

65. Commonwealth v. Conrod Hartzel. Defendant in £200 and Earnest Baker in £100. Recognized to January 1795. Same bail.

66. Commonwealth v. Daniel McCarty. Defendant in £200 and William Lafferty in £100. Recognized to January 1795. [cut off] bail.

Page 204L [November 1794]

67. Commonwealth v. Samuel Counts. Defendant in £200 and David Smouse in £100. Recognized to January 1795. William Cagg bail.

68. Commonwealth v. Adam Davebaugh. Defendant in £200 and Nicholas Cogan in £100. Recognized to January 1795. John Davebaugh bail.

69. Commonwealth v. Jacob Davebaugh. Defendant in £200 and Peter Stiffler in £100. Recognized to January 1795. Michael May bail.

70. Commonwealth v. William Nickum. Defendant in £200 and John May in £100. Recognized to January 1795. William Hartley bail.

71. Commonwealth v. John Peck. Defendant in £200 and Nicholas Cogan in £100. Recognized to January 1795. Anthony Smith bail.

72. Commonwealth v. George Williams. Defendant in £200. John May bail. In custody.

73. Commonwealth v. Thomas Blair. Defendant in £200 and William Lafferty in £100. Recognized to January 1795. W^m McCally bail.

Page 204R   November 1794

74. Commonwealth v. Wm Paxton. Defendant in £200 and John Ruch in £100. Recognized to January 1795. George Hinish bail.

75. Commonwealth v. Martin Utslar. Defendant in £200 and Conrod Hartzel in £100. Recognized to January 1795. Same bail.

76. Commonwealth v. John Hartzel. Defendant in £200 and Conrod Hartzel in £100. Recognized to January 1795. Same bail.

77. Commonwealth v. John Peck. Defendant in £200 and Nicholas Cogan in £100. Recognized to January 1795. Anthony Smith bail.

Judge Wells's Recognizances Conditioned as before

77. Commonwealth v. Adam Bowers. Defendant in £30. Recognized to January 1795. Daniel Bowers bail.

78. Commonwealth v. Doct^r John Kimmell. Defendant in £30. Recognized to January 1795. Adam Keffer bail.

79. Commonwealth v. George Swarts. Defendant in £30. Recognized to January 1795. John Fletcher bail.

80. Commonwealth v. Michael Kunts. Defendant in £30. Recognized to January 1795. John Fletcher bail.

Page 205L   [November 1794]

81. Commonwealth v. Nicholas Cover. Defendant in £30. Recognized to January 1795. Jacob Hoof bail.

82. Commonwealth v. Jacob Hill. Defendant in £30. Recognized to January 1795. Thomas Norton bail.

83. Commonwealth v. Daniel Lindle Smith. Defendant in £30. Recognized to January 1795. Jacob B__z bail.

84. Commonwealth v. Jacob Hoil. Defendant in £30. Recognized to January 1795. Recognizance forfeited.

85. Commonwealth v. John Miller. Defendant in £30. Recognized to January 1795. Adam Keffer bail.

86 Commonwealth v. Abraham Cable Jr. Defendant in £30. Recognized to January 1795. Daniel Bower bail.

Page 205R   November 1794

87. Commonwealth v. Daniel Bowers. Defendant in £30. Recognized to January 1795. George Kimmell bail.

88. Commonwealth v. Adam Stall. Defendant in £30. Recognized to January 1795. George Kimmell bail.

89. Commonwealth v. William [no surname]. Defendant in £30. Recognized to January 1795. Philip Cocher bail.

90. Commonwealth v. Jacob Cuffman. Defendant in £30. Recognized to January 1795. Adam Hoyl bail.

91. Commonwealth v. Joseph Dugle. Defendant in £30. Recognized to January 1795. Peter Bowers bail.

92. Commonwealth v. James Smith. Defendant in £30. Recognizance forfeited.

93. Commonwealth v. Peter Bower. Defendant in £30. Recognized to January 1795. George Weymer bail.

94. Commonwealth v. George Weymer. Defendant in £30. Recognized to January 1795. Joseph Douglass bail.

95 Commonwealth v. Benjamin Brown. Defendant in £30. Recognized to January 1795. Jacob Hoof bail.

Page 206L   [November 1794]

96. Commonwealth v. Michael Browler. Defendant in £[cut off]. Recognizance forfeited.

97. Commonwealth v. George Switcher. Defendant in £30. Recognized to January 1795. Frederick Mattock bail.

98. Commonwealth v. John Hemminger. Defendant in £30. Recognizance forfeited.

99. Commonwealth v. George Ankeny. Defendant in £30. Recognized to January 1795. George Tedrow bail.

100. Commonwealth v. Jacob Cysor. Defendant in £30. Recognizance forfeited.

101. Commonwealth v. Jacob Huff. Defendant in £30. Recognized to January 1795. Benjamin Brown bail.

102. Commonwealth v. John Armstrong. Defendant in £30. Recognized to January 1795. Jacob Huff bail.

103. Commonwealth v. Abraham Miller. Defendant in £30. Recognized to January 1795. Nicholas Miller bail.

104. Commonwealth v. George Tedrow. Defendant in £30. Recognized to January 1795. George Ankeny bail.

Page 206R November 1794
105. Commonwealth v. Michael Mourer. Defendant in £30. Recognized to January 1795. John Sills bail.

106. Commonwealth v. John Seel. Defendant in £25, Michael Zimmerman in £25, and Israel Burket in £25. Recognized to January 1795. Michael Mourer bail. Daniel Stoys recognizance.

Philip King Esq. Recognizances.

107. Commonwealth v. James Connor. Defendant in £30. Recognized to January 1795. Jacob Hartzel Esq. bail.

108. Commonwealth v. John Killpatrick. Defendant in £30. Recognized to January 1795. Jonathan Woodsides bail.

109. Commonwealth v. Jonathan Woodsides. Defendant in £30. Recognized to January 1795. John Killpatrick bail.

110. Commonwealth v. Daniel McCarty. Defendant in £30. Recognized to January 1795. Jonathan Woodsides bail.

111. Commonwealth v. John Martin. Defendant in £30. Recognized to January 1795. James Conner bail.

Page 207L [November 1794]
112. Commonwealth v. William Pinkerton. Defendant in £30. Recognized to January 1795. John Miller bail.

113. Commonwealth v. John Miller Jr. Defendant in £30 and Jacob [Gosua?] in £3[cut off]. Recognized to January 1795. Same bail.

114. Commonwealth v. Peter Augustine. Defendant in £30. Recognized to January 1795. Henry Everly bail.

115. Commonwealth v. Henry Everly. Defendant in £30. Recognized to January 1795. Peter Augustine bail.

116. Commonwealth v. Henry Foust. Defendant in £30. Recognized to January 1795. Anthony Nawgel bail.

117. Commonwealth v. Adam Hoil. Defendant in £30. Recognized to January 1795. Jacob Cuffman bail.

Judge Martin's Recognizances.

118. Commonwealth v. Jonathan Pollard. Defendant in £[cut off]. Recognized to January 1795. Michael Blue bail.

Page 207R   November 1794

118. Commonwealth v. Robert Culbertson. Defendant in £200 and Abraham Martin in £100. Recognized to January 1795. Henry Reynard bail.

120. Commonwealth v. Nathaniel Chaney. Defendant in £200. Recognized to January 1795. William Paxton bail.

121. Commonwealth v. Michael Blue. Defendant in £200. Recognized to January 1795. John Rush bail.

122. Commonwealth v. Benjamin Lupton. Defendant in £200. Recognizance forfeited.

123. Commonwealth v. Francis Reynolds. Defendant in £20[cut off] and Edward Connor in £10[cut off]. Recognized to January 1795. William Willson of Hopewell bail.

124. Commonwealth v. Samuel Chance. Defendant in £200 and Abraham Martin in £100. Recognized to January 1795. George Hinish bail.

125. Commonwealth v. George Bower. Defendant in £200 and Henry Leader in £100. Recognized to January 1795. Michael Blue bail.

Page 208L November 1794
We the Judges from the different Election Districts do certify that William Ward was elected Commissioner for the County of Bedford 17 October 1794

    David Espy, Clerk   Sam McCashlin
    John Groner   John Philips
    Martin Loy   John Marshdollar
    Robert McConnell   Christian Meese
    Alex^r Scott Lowrey   Joseph Hunt

Page 208R November 1794
Commonwealth v. Wm Hartley. Presentment for Tipling House. Nolli Prosequi.

Commonwealth v. Abagail Weimer & Edward Cavener. Presentment for Fornication.

Commonwealth v. William Wilson and Baltzer Hess, Supervisors of Bedford Township. Presentment for Neglect of Duty as Supervisors of Roads.

Page 209L [Blank]

Page 209R [1792]
Tavern Keepers Recommended January Session 1792
    Peter Werth   Arthur McGaughey
    Peter Morgart   George Hamburgh
    Derry Ryan   James Anderson
    John McGaughey   William Hartley

Tavern Keepers Recommended April Session 1792
    Michael Barndollar   Conrod Rush
    John Dickey   George [Bryner?]

Tavern Keepers Recommended August Session 1792
    Duncan McVicker   John Miller
    Peter Barnets   John Kimmell
    Adam Kinder   James Gilmore
    John Bonnett   Anthony Nawgel
    Casper Stotler   Thomas Anderson
    William Jack   Henry Werth
    Arthur McGaughey   James Jamison
    Samuel Coyle

Page 210L [1792–1793]
Tavern Keepers Recommended November Session 1792
    John Skinner   Valentine Werth
    John Webster   Jacob Katz
    David Penrod   Peter Didier
    Joseph Strain

[Tavern Keepers Recommended] January Session 1793
    Marcus Metzgar   George Dansdill
    Peter Morgert   James Bridges
    William Todd

[Tavern Keepers Recommended] April Session 1793
    Derry Ryan   Jacob Snyder
    Ephraim Wallace   George Burkher
    Jacob Wiand   George Humburgh
    William Hartley   John McGaughey
    Michael Barndollar

Page 210R [1793–1794]
Tavern Keepers Recommended August Session 1793
    Peter Barndt   John Miller
    Lewis Fluick   Conrod Rush
    Adam Kinder   John Dickey
    George Wilds   James Jamison
    Jacob McClean   Arthur McGaughey
    Anthony Nawgel   John Kimmell

[Tavern Keepers Recommended] November Session 1793
    John Colepenny   Joseph Covenhoven
    Isaac Bonnett   Enoch Skinner
    Casper Stotler   Jacob Katz

[Tavern Keepers Recommended] January Session 1794
    David Penrod   ~~John Webster~~
    George Dansdill   Valentine Werth
    John Bridges   Jacob Shocks
    Peter Morgret   Joseph Buck

Page 211L [1794]
Tavern Keepers Recommended April Session 1794
    Marcus Metzger   George Humburger
    George Beyman   Joseph Lilly
    Michael Barndollar George Burkher
    William Hartley

Tavern Keepers Recommended August Session 1794
- John Cochran
- Cornelius Martinus
- George Ensley Jr.
- John McGaughey
- John Kimmell
- Peter Dedier
- Jacob Snyder
- William McDermitt
- John Lowry
- John Dickey
- Peter Barnet
- John Miller
- Lewis Fluick
- Casper Stotler
- John Fletcher
- Benjamin Burd
- William Todd
- Derry Ryan
- David Jordan

Page 211R [1794]

Tavern Keepers Recommended November Session 1794
- John Colepenny
- Jacob Katz
- Enoch Skinner
- Conrod Rush
- John Covenhoven

Page 212L [Blank]

Page 212R [1800]

Tavern Keepers Recommended Jamuary Session 1800
  Frederick Roderock, William Davis, Benjamin Martin

At April Session 1800
  John Devenbaugh, James Burns, Jacob Stevenson

Jacob Burse, John Davis, Andrew Smith, Daniel Bo[cut off], Jacob Blocher, Conrod Appleman.

At September Session 1800 [not clear if this applies to preceding or following list.]

John Head, George Ritchie, George Wilds, James Jamison, Benjamin Burd, Henry Deck, James Longstreath, Jacob McCain, John Graham, Robt Spencer, John Park, James Parsons, Christopher Ensloe, Henry Miller, William Ward, W^m McCulloch, James Taylor, David Field, Jane Ryan, John Noble, Joshua Wright, Jacob Fore, John Kniesly, Daniel Coyle, John Miller, Robt Moore, Valentine Wertz, William Hartley, Samuel Sel[cut off], Wm Vickroy, Jacob Hasselton, Gasper Stotler, George Lee, George Dansdell, Isaac Bonnett.

Page 213L [Blank]

Page 213R [Blank]

240   BEDFORD COUNTY QUARTER SESSIONS

Page 214L [Cover with doodles]

Page 214R   "Sessions Minutes Commencing January Sessions 1790."

Page 215L [Blank]

Page 215R   [January 1797]
At Bedford 26 January 1797 before James Riddle, George Woods, Hugh Barclay, James Martin, James Wells.

Constable	Township
Faithful Craton	Bedford Town
John Dibert	Bedford Township
James Kendal	Air
Jacob Emer	Bethel
Henry Whitstone	Colerain
Jonathan Cessna	Cumberland Valley
Christian Fritz	Brothers Valley
Thomas Spencer	Turkey Foot
Moses Frame	Quamahoning
John Lynch	Milford
John Burger	Elk Lick
David McVicker	Londonderry
Michael Ritchie	Providence
Michael Stall	Belfast
Jeremiah French	Hopewell
John Ullrick	Woodberry
Wm Gibson	
Thomas Carter	Dublin
John Zigler	Stoney Creek
Anthony Blackburn	St Clair

Grand Jury:
    Robert Spencer, foreman   Thomas Spencer (affirmed)
    Jacob Stevens   Jacob Moses (affirmed)
    William Kinworthy (affirmed)   William Clark
    James Gordon   Henry Wertz
    John Chrisman   James Taylor
    William Williamson   Henry Sides
    Thomas Kenton   David Wright
    James Alexander   William Boyd
    Jacob Countryman   George Kimmell
    John Ford   Eli Williams

Page 216L
Indictments returned.

1. Commonwealth v. Edward Stoy. Fornication. True Bill.

On motion Jonathan Henderson Esq. James Morrison admitted Attorney.

2. Commonwealth v. William Wilson and Baltzer Hess Overseers of Highways in Bedford Township. Neglect of Duty as Overseer. Defendants plead not guilty.

Commonwealth v. William Wilson and Baltzer Hess. Defendants in £20 each, Henry Whitstone in £20 and Nicholas Wilson in £20 for appearance of defendants next session to answer for Neglect of Duty.

Commonwealth v. Susanna Flick. James Spraig in £20 for appearance of James Spraig to next April session to testify.

Page 216R
Pennsylvania v. Simon Kenton and others. Misdemeanor. Ignoramus.

4. Pennsylvania v. George Masters. Larceny. True Bill. Defendant pleads not guilty. Testify for state: Joseph Buck, Jacob Smeeker, Henry Helm. Jury of John Harkleroad, Robert Adams, Robert Hemphill, William Vickroy, Lewis Ripley, John Nicum, Robert Miller, Peter [Hervine?], Marcus Meds___, Robert Allison, Agnis McDonnald, and Richard Evalt find defendant George Masters guilty. Judgment is that defendant restore to Joseph Buck the sum of £43.2.6 being the amount of money stolen and pay the like sum to the Commonwealth and that he undergo servitude of three years during which time he shall be confined and kept to hard labor.

Pennsylvania v. Edward Stoy. N° 1 this session. Fornication. Defendant pleads not guilty. Testify for prosecution: Margaret Bridges. Testify for defense: James Wells Esq. Jury of Samuel Way, John Harkleroad, Joseph Francis, William Beaty, Abraham Whetstone, Peter He___, Jacob Studebaker, Richard Ewalt, Robert Miller, John Kenton, Robert Hemphill, and Jacob Buse find defendant Edward Stoy guilty. Judgment that he pay fine of £10, that he pay Margaret Bridges £3 lying in expense, and two shillings per week from the time the child was born until it arrives at the age of two years, and the further sum of one shilling and six pence per week thence until the child arrives at the age of seven years, that he pay costs of prosecution and give security for performance of this judgment.

Page 217L
John Lafferty discharged by Proclamation.
5. Commonwealth v. Simon Kenton & others. Misdemeanor. True Bill.
6. Pennsylvania v. William Nicholas. Riot &c. True Bill. Defendant pleads guilty and submits to Court. Fined 6. and costs.

Page 217R
Pennsylvania v. Simon Kenton and others. N° 5 this session. Defendants plead guilty and submit to court. Sentence that they pay the fines annexed to their names and costs.

Simon Kenton	£7.10	George Sells	£1.10.0
Michael James Doyle	5	William Wilson	£15.0.0
Joseph Scullknot	£5.0.0	Hill Wilson	£0.5.0
Nicholas Wilson	£0.5.0	Jacob Reachard	£0.5.0
Conrod Haverstick	£1.10.0	Neil McMullen	£0.5.0
Andrew Sheets	£0.15.0	John Foster	£0.5.0
John Mackey	£0.5.0	Henry Beachley	£0.5.0
George Bostian	£0.5.0	John Brits	£1.10.0
John Utsler	£0.5.0	George Bowser	£0.5.0
Michael Samuels	£0.5.0	John Wisecarver	£0.5.0
Jacob Helm	£1.10.0	Ludwick Samuels	£0.5.0
Baltzer Hess	£1.10.0	Thomas Moore	£0.5.0
Martin Fritz	£0.5.0	Philip Wolf	not appearing

Jacob Nagle Esq......not appearing

Page 218L [Blank]

Page 218R [Loose paper bound in docket; see also 220L and 248R.]
Commonwealth v. Martin Toomy. Murder.
Testify for prosecution: Jacob Waltman, Henry Smith, And[w] [Cessler?], Pat[r] Haney, Anth[y] Smith, D[r] John Anderson, Bernard Exline, Peter Harker, William Cessna. Testify for defense: David Bell, Thomas Bradshaw, Mary Bradshaw, Rob[t] Bradshaw, Patrick Haney. Jury of William Griffith, James McKinney, Andrew Heath, Hugh Alexander, John Moore, Peter _en_ff, James Stewart, Charles Tigert, George Dansdill, Thomas Logan, Robert Ramsey, Joshua [Pearson?] find guilty of Murder in the first degree.

Page 219L [Not clear what this page is, nor whether it is in order.]
[unreadable crossed out] v.
~~George Smith~~ v.
[unreadable given name] ~~McFerren~~
Jurors: Frederick Kuntz, Charles Taggert, George Hull, Wendle Ott,

Isaac Cowell, John Cessna, Jacob Snyder, Joshua Pearson, James McKinney, Peter [Kenuff?], George Dantzell, James Nelson. [The names Nathan Clark and Michael Barndollar appear to the side.] May 1801 non-suit.

Page 219R
[Loose case paper from Toomy trial bound in docket.]
Scott Ad__ v. McCaslin. [Apparent jury of:] Jacob Snyder, George Dantzell, George Hull, Samuel B___, George Enslow Jr., Isaac Cowell, Nathan Hammon, William Griffith, Joseph Friend Sr., John Clark, Christopher Riley, Frederick Kuntz.

Auditors Dr John Anderson, William Proc__[cur off] and Andrew Work appointed for the ensuing year.

[Across bottom of page as for cover jacket when tri-folded] Commonwealth v. Toomy

Page 220L
[appears to be loose case paper from Toomy trial bound in docket.]
Commonwealth v. Martin Toomy for Murder.
Jury: John ____, William Griffith, James Stewart, John May, Samuel Bechtel, Charles Taggert, ~~Jacob Snyder~~, Geo Enslow Jr., Philip Coleman, James Nelson, Isaac Cowell, John Clark, John Cessna Jr.
Sentence for Martin Toomy passed 7th May that you be taken from hence to the Prison of Bedford County and from thence to the Place of Execution and there to be hung from the neck until you are dead.

Page 220R   [April 1795]
At Bedford 24 April 1795 before James Riddle, George Woods, Hugh Barclay.

Township	Constable	Supervisor of Roads	Overseer Poor
Bedford Town	John Williams		
Bedford Township	Peter Stifler	John Chrisman James Taylor	
Air	David John	Joshua Philips William Alexander	Benjamin Williams William Hunter
Bethel	Moses Graham	Joseph Graves Bernard Mann Jr.	Addis Linn Peter Smith
Colerain	Adam Exline	Jacob Bear John May	
Cumberland Valley	Brice Blair	Valentine Wyrick John Kan__	
Brothers Valley	Jacob Countryman	George Shenefield John Brubaker	Michael [Trayer?] Jacob Barnett
Turkey Foot	John Mitchell	Benjamin Innings Edward Kemp	John Jones Andrew Reems
Quamahoning	John Reed	Jacob [Loud?] Jacob Fronhiser	Christian Carver Jacob Smoker
Milford	Peter Fredline	John Lower Michael Tedrow	Henry Brooner Adam Creamer
Elk Lick	Jacob Houghstetler	Solomon Cloudfelty Joseph Lighly	
Londonderry	Joseph Boyer	Isaac Daniels Jacob Haun	Frederick Kepper Matthias Croy
Providence	Joseph McDonald	Michael Barndoller George Ensley	Peter Morgret Adam Kountz
Belfast	James Longstreath	John Strait Francis Welch	Obadiah Mellot John Mill___
Hopewell	Abraham Boolman	John Belt John Ronehart	George Nixon Adam Young
Woodbury	John Snyder	William Davis George Rhoads	William Dilts John Lower
Dublin	James Jameson	Michael Bear	George Wilds Robert Ramsey Sr.
Stoney Creek	Gudlip Reeman	Henry Becker Joseph Spiger	Christian Miller David Yoder
St Clair	Ro[bert Ada]ms	Elijah Adams James Williams	Jonathan Bo__ George Cofman

Page 221L [Blank]

Page 221R
Pennsylvania v. Overseers of Highways, Woodberry Township. William

Gilson Constable of Woodberry Township recognized in open Court in £20 to give evidence against the Supervisor of the High Way in Woodberry Township for Neglect of Duty.

John Lyon Esq. admitted as Attorney of Court of Common Pleas and Quarter Sessions on motion of James Hamilton Esq.

Republica v. Christian Stuble. Nathaniel Davis in £20, Jacob Hains in £20 for their appearance respectively next Court to give evidence against Christian Stuble.

Same v. Henry Mull. Lodwick Sharrah in £20 to appear next Court and give evidence against Henry Mull.

Same v. Same. Cornelius Martinus in £20 to give evidence against Henry Mull at next Court.

Page 222L
Pennsylvania v. Michael Miller. [no further information recorded.]

Commonwealth v. Henry Clapper and John Engle Overseers of Highways. Neglect of Duty. Henry Clapper in £20 to give evidence.

Pennsylvania v. Edward Stoy. John Webster in £50 for the performance of Sentence upon Edward Stoy last session for Fornication and Bastardy with Margaret Bridges.

Commonwealth v. Benj[n] Williams. Joseph Springer in £20 and John Garreson in £20 for appearance of Negro Peter at August session 1795 to give evidence against Benj[n] Williams for Assault & Battery upon Negro Peter.

Page 222R
Pennsylvania v. Elizabeth Whitehall (alias Mary Hoover). Joseph Briggs in £40 that he appear next Court to prosecute against the defendant for Felony. William Burd in £20 to give evidence in the above.

Page 223L [Blank]

Page 223R   [August 1795]
At Bedford 24 August 1795 before James Riddle, George Woods, and Hugh Barclay.

Township	Constable	Supervisor of Roads	Overseer Poor
Bedford Town	John Williams		
Bedford Township	Peter Stifler	John Chrisman James Taylor	
Air	David John	Joshua Philips William Alexander	Benjamin Williams William Hunter
Bethel	Moses Graham	Joseph Graves Bernard Mann Jr.	Addis Linn Peter Smith
Colerain	Adam Exline	Jacob Bear John May	
Cumberland Valley	Brice Blair	Valentine Wyrick John [Kemp?]	
Brothers Valley	Jacob Countryman	George Shenefield John Brubaker	Michael [Trayer?] Jacob Barnett
Turkey Foot	John Mitchell	Benjamin Innings Edward Kemp	John Jones Andrew Reems
Quamahoning	John Reed	Jacob Loud Jacob Fronhiser	Christian Carver Jacob Smoker
Milford	Peter Fredline	John Lower Michael Tedrow	Henry Brooner Adam Creamer
Elk Lick	Jacob Houghstetler	Solomon Cloudfelty Joseph Lighly	
Londonderry	Joseph Boyer	Isaac Daniels Jacob Haun	Frederick Kepper Matthias Cray
Providence	Joseph McDonald	Michael Barndoller George Ensley	Peter Morgret Adam Kountz
Belfast	James Longstreath	John Strait Francis Welch	Obadiah Mellot John Millbourn
Hopewell	Abraham Boolman	John Belt John Ronehart	George Nixon Adam Young
Woodbury	John Snyder	William Davis George Rhoads	William Dilts John Lower
Dublin	James Jameson	Michael Bear	George Wilds Robert Ramsey Sr.
Stoney Creek	Gudlip Reeman	Henry Becker Joseph Spiger	Christian Miller David Yoder
St Clair	Ro[bert Ada]ms	Elijah Adams James Williams	Jonathan Bo__ George Cofman

Page 224L   August 1795
Grand Jury:
   John Scott   John McGaughey
   Andrew Sheets   William McDermit
   Robert Spencer   David Field
   John Clarr   Thomas Norton
   John Brit   John Ewalt
   John Mortimore   Jacob Earnest
   Joseph Warford   Peter Fritline
   John [Brate?]   George Burger
   Jacob Wyant

Page 224R   August 1795
Pennsylvania v. John Graves. Moses Graham in £20 for his appearance this session to give evidence.

Pennsylvania v. Elizabeth Whitehall alias Mary Hoover. On motion of Commonwealth Prisoner to be sent to Fayette County for trial. Jo Briggs in £40 of Luzerne Town and David McVickar of Bedford Township Bedford County in £40 to prosecute. Duncan McVicar of same place in £40 that they all appear at the next Court of Quarter Sessions in Union Town for the County of Fayette to give testimony against Elizabeth Whitehall alias Mary Hoover.

1. Commonwealth v. Nicholas McGuire. Assault & Battery. Defendant pleads guilty and submits to Court. Fine one penny.

Page 225L
Pennsylvania v. Christian Struble. Nathaniel Davis in £20 for his appearance next session to give evidence.

Same v. Henry Mull. Cornelius Martinus in £20, Alexander Miller Esq. in £20, and Ludwick Sharrah in £20 for their appearance next session to give evidence.

2. Same v. Henry Mull. Larceny. True Bill.

3. Same v. Christian Stuble. Larceny. True Bill.

4. Same v. Henry Mull. Larceny. True Bill.

5. Same v. John Christman. Fornication.

Page 225R
6. Pennsylvania v. John Sells. Assault & Battery. August session 1795. Defendant pleads not guilty. Testify for prosecution: Wm Smith, Adam

Helm, George Reamer. Jury of Conrod Rush, Lewis Leiberger, Richard Baker, Paul Dust, Joshua Critchfield, John Fait, Bernard Bowers, Michael Rhine, Isaac Daniels, John Bridges, Joshua Robison, and Caleb Barnes say John Sells is not guilty.

7. Same v. Adam Hellam. Assault & Battery. Ignoramus.

Pennsylvania v. George Kinster. Committed for want of bail. Gest Vaughn in £100 for appearance of Lydia Vaughn next Court of Oyer & Terminer to prosecute and give evidence. George Kinster in £200 to appear and answer November session. Michael Murphy in £100 and Thomas Still in £100, Thomas ____ in £100 for appearance of George Kinster and that he be of good behavior.

8. Same v. William Smith. Assault. True Bill.
Defendant pleads not guilty. Afterwards he retracts his plea and submits to the Court. Fine thirty shillings and costs and defendant to give security himself in £100 and security in £250 to keep the peace towards Henry Hallem.

Page 226L
Pennsylvania v. William Smith. Wm Smith in £100 and C__ __ Webster in £50 that Wm Smith be of good behavior and keep the peace in particular toward Henry Hallem for one year.

Adam Buchannan in £20 for appearance of Hester Buchannan at next session to prosecute Richard Beatty.

9. Pennsylvania v. Richard Beatty. Fornication. True Bill.

Peter Roof of Colerain in £20 to attend present session and give testimony against Jos Lilley.

Peter Roof in £40 and Robert Boyd in £20 for appearance of Peter Roof next session to give evidence.

Page 226R August 1795
10. Pennsylvania v. Guest Vaughn. Assault.
Defendant pleads guilty and submits to Court. Judgment that he pay fine of five shillings. Security for good behavior 12 mo.

11. Pennsylvania v. Henry Clapper & John Engel Overseers of Woodberry Town. Neglect of Duty. Ignoramus.

12 Pennsylvania v. John Sells. Assault. True Bill.
Defendant pleads guilty and submits to Court. Testify for prosecution:

John Webster, Daniel Stoy. Judgment that John Sells pay fine of £3 and pay costs.

13 Commonwealth v. Jacob Cox. Assault & Battery. True Bill.

14. Commonwealth v. Daniel Stoy Esq. Assault. Ignoramus.

Page 227L   August 1795
Commonwealth v. Guest Vaughan. Guest Vaugh in £100 to be of good behavior especially to Th. Still.

Commonwealth v. John McGaughey. John McGaughey in £30 for his appearance November 1795 to answer.

Commonwealth v. Guest Vaughan. Guest Vaughan in £100 and Anthony Smith in £50 that Guest Vaughan be of good behavior for one year especially to Thomas Stills.

Commonwealth v. John Sells. John Sells in £100 and John Reamor on £50 that John Sells be of good behavior for one year and in particular to Dan__[page cut off] Stoy.

Page 227R
15. Commonwealth v. Samuel McCashlin. Presentment for Nuisance.

Commonwealth v. Joseph Lilly. W^m McDonald in £30, Robert Boyd in £30, James Boyd in £30, Isaac Childs in £30, Alisha Blodget in £30, Samuel Boyd in £30, Philip Kihl in £30, Robert Moore in £30 to appear next session to give evidence.

Commonwealth v. Joseph Lilley. Joseph Lilly in £40, David Jordan in £20 for appearance of Joseph Lilly to answer

Page 228L [Blank]

Page 228R   [November 1795]
At Bedford 16 November 1795 before James Riddle, George Woods, Hugh Barclay.

Township	Constable
Bedford Town	John Williams
Bedford Township	Peter Stifler
Air	David John
Bethel	Moses Graham
Colerain	Adam Axline
Cumberland Valley	Brice Blair
Londonderry	Joseph Boyer

BEDFORD COUNTY QUARTER SESSIONS

Township	Constable
Providence	Joseph McDonald
Belfast	James Longstreath
Hopewell	Abraham Boolman
Woodbury	John Snyder
Dublin	James Jameson
St Clair	Robert Adams

Page 229L November 1795
Grand Jury:

Alexander McGriger, foreman — John Stickman
Charles Rubey — Valentine Ripley
John Griffith — William Swager
Charles Dibert — Frederick Dibert
Peter Oyler — Laurence Oyler
John Croyle — Adam Hardbolt
John Coulter — David Quick
Jacob Herring — Henry Hallow
John Moore — John Ferguson

Page 229R
Commonwealth v. Michael Howard. Joseph McDonald Constable of Providence in £10 to give evidence.

On motion of Mr Smith, Richard L. Carmick Esq. admitted as Attorney of this Court.

1. Commonwealth v. George Kintser. Assault & Battery upon Lydia Vaughan. November session 1795. Defendant pleads not guilty. Jury of John Ritter, Joseph Truax, Jacob Hart, Joshua Pierson, Jacob Seylor, Edward Dayley, John Dickey, Christopher Reiley, Daniel Leiberger, Valentine Wert, Da__[cut off] Potts, and James Mortimore find George Kintser not guilty.

2. Commonwealth v. Same. Oyer & Terminer November 1795. Rape. Ignoramus.

Page 230L
3. Pennsylvania v. Joseph Lilley. Keeping a Disorderly House. Nov Session 1795. True Bill. Defendant pleads not guilty. Jury of Andrew Work, Joshua Pierson, Thomas Logan, Peter Weaverling, Joseph Bell, Nathan Hammond, John Wolf, William Drenning, John Clark, Adam Stiger, Jacob Hart, and John Ritter find defendant guilty. Defendant in

£100 that he be of good behavior until next April Term and then appear to answer what the Court shall decide.

On motion Mr Hamilton, George Armstrong Esq. admitted an Attorney of this Court.

4. Pennsylvania v. Abraham Cashman. Assault & Battery on Francis Gibbon. Submission by the defendant. Defendant fined five pounds and pay costs. Defendant in £100, Conrod Rush in £50 and George Enslow in £50 conditioned that Abraham Cashman be of good behavior for one year and that he appear at January Term to answer.

Page 230R
The Court appoints Hugh Barclay Esq., Thos Vickroy and Andrew Work as Auditors to settle the accounts of Commissioners and Treasurer for the ensuing year.

~~John Lafferty v. John Ritter.~~

Commonwealth v. Michael Howard. Tipling House. True Bill.

Commonwealth v. Abraham Brant. Attachment for Contempt returnable April 1796.

Page 231L [Blank]

Page 231R
[Loose paper. Docket entry for the case is on page 266R.]
Commonwealth v. Danl Barndoler. [Charge cut off.]
Witnesses for the prosecution: William Bagly, Jacob Crevinsgton Sr., John Murray. Witnesses for defense: Philip Fishburn, John Paxton, Philip Comfort, Catherine Comfort, Jacob Barndollar, James Martin Esq., John Richey, George Cashman, Henry Deal. Jury of Henry Deal, Henry Smith, Henry Lybarger, John England, David Pott, John Elder, William H____, John McDonald, Nicholas Boor, George Barnhardt, Fred^k Richert, and John Whip find Daniel Barndollar is guilty of taking the bee hive.

~~Warfard v. Reed~~. Inquisition set aside.

Penn^a v. Barndollar. ____ ____ in $120 for appearance of defendant next session.

Page 232L
Commonwealth v. Joseph McVicker. Bound in $100 for his appearance at next session to testify

Same v. L___ B___ bound in $100 for his appearance these sessions to testify.

David McVicker bound in $100 to appear at May session.

Patrick Hay__ bound in $50 to attend at this November session.

Penn[a] v. Rob[t] Moore. Assault & Battery. Robert Moore in $60 and Andrew Mann in $40. C. Stophel, John Biringer, & George Cashman in $40 each to give evidence.

Same v. George Beeman, Joseph Brown, and W[m] Crevingston for good behavior for six months particularly toward Martin Loy each in $60. John England in $60 security.

Same v. Andrew Mann Esq. Misdemeanor in Office. A. Mann in $100, James McKinney in $100 for appearance of A. Mann Esq. at May Court.

Page 232R   April 1796
At Bedford 25 April 1796 before ~~James Riddle~~, George Woods, Hugh Barclay, James Martin.

Township	Constable
Bedford Town	John Williams
Bedford Township	Peter Stifler
Air	David John
Bethel	Moses Graham
Colerain	Adam Axline
Cumberland Valley	Brice Blair
Brothers Valley	
Londonderry	Joseph Boyle
Providence	Joseph McDonald
Belfast	James Longstreath
Hopewell	Ab[m] Boolman
Woodbury	John Snyder
Dublin	James Jameson
St. Clair	Robert Adams

Page 233L   April 1796
Commonwealth v. Samuel Williams. Jacob Robb in £30 for appearance of Jane Robb August session 1796.

Commonwealth v. Samuel Williams. John Williams in £40 for appearance of Samuel Williams August session 1796.

Commonwealth v. [no name]. James Longstreth in $50 for his attendance during Court.

Same v. Moses Reed. Moses Graham in $60 for app^r this session.

Same v. Mackey. Thomas Beatte in [crossed out] for appearance of Tabth^a Beatte at next session.

Com^w v. Conrod Rush. Nol Proc.

Com^w v. Mackey. John Mackey in $10[cut off] for appearance to answer. Saml McCauslin in $100 bail.

Commonwealth v. George Smith. Defendant discharged on Proc to pay costs.

David John in $60 to ap^r this session to give testimony.

Page 233R
Grand Jury:

Isaac Bonnett	Samuel Livingston
Robert ___ son	John Rinehart
Conrod Atley	John Flook
~~David Springer~~	Jacob Shock
Abraham Buzzard	Michael Deberd
John Lyberger	Isaac Martin
Jacob Earnest	Thomas Bradshaw
Henry Stover	George Wilds
Jacob Snider	Thomas Celihan
	Asher Layton

Recg^s called forfeited.

Penn^a v. Joseph Lilley. The reco^g of Robert Moore called forft^d.

Same. v. Robt Moore. Re^{gs} of the deft and B Ferguson forft^d
Re^{gs} of Michael Blue forft^d.

Page 234L
Com^w v. Lilley. Jany session. Considered by the Court that the defendant pay fine of one cent and costs.

Same v. Moore, J. Lilly, Michael Blue, Peter Swartzholder, Christopher Cline. Defendants fined 7/6 and costs.

Page 234R   [April 1796]
Indictments to April Sessions 1796.

1. Commonwealth v. Empson McNight & Charles Sipes. Assault & Battery. Witnesses: Ge^o Dansdale, Dav^d Beagle, Dav^d Robbison, Martha Watson, John [Surious?], David Fields. Defendants submit to Court. Fined £3 each, one month imprisonment and security £200 for their good behavior for one year, and costs.

2. Same v. Same. Assault & Battery. Defendants submit a fine of 7/6 each to pay costs.

3. Same v. Thos Norton. Assault & Battery. True Bill.

4. Same v. George Free. Tipling House. True Bill.

5. Same v. Moses Reed, Luke Fetters, Joseph Graves, and Thos Wood. Setting up a Lot^y. True Bill.

6. Same v. Jacob Boreman, Wm Morton [Sr?], Mich^l George, Adam P___. Setting up a Lot^y. True Bill.

7. Same v. Benjamin Williams. Assault & Battery. Benjamin Williams in £100 and Robt Anderson in £50 for appearance of defendant at August session.

Page 235L
Commonwealth v. Cor^n [Durnagin?]. Kidnapping.

Page 235R   April 1796
Com^w v. _ _____. Thos Cromwell in $60 to appear next session to testify.

Same v. Boreman. James Longstreth in $60 for his appearance to testify.

Same v. Geo Free. David John in $60.

Same v. William. Joseph Springer in $60 and Negro Peter in $60 to give testimony.

Commonwealth v. Empson McKnight and Charles Sipes. William Lockart of Dublin Township in £200 for good behavior of the defendants for one year.

Com^w v. Anderson. Accr^d to Sup^r Court Cert^r allowed.

Com^w v. Thos Norton. Thos Norton in $60 Saml McCauslin in $60 to answer.

Commonwealth v. Robert M___. Robert Adams in $60 to give evidence.

Same v. James Hart, Charles Carral [Sewel?] in $60 to give ___.

Same v. John Crissman and James Taylor Sup^r of Bedford. John Liebarger, Conrod Atlee, Isaac Bonnett each in $60 to give evidence.

Page 236L [August 1796 & prior session] Commonwealth v. William Hartley. John Fluke, Henry Stover, and Abraham Buzzard each in $60 to give evidence.

Same v. George Humbert and Jacob Fore. Samuel Livingston and Jacob Shock each in $60 to give evidence.

Corn^{le} & Michael Barndoller defendants in $60 to appear to answer.

At Bedford fourth Monday of August 1796 before James Riddle, George Woods, James Martin, John Piper.

Grand Jury:
>Jacob Sailor, foreman   William Graham
>Joseph Hunt   John Johnston
>Nathaniel Hart   Jacob Chamberlin
>Thomas Leasure   Georg Claar
>John Williams   Valentine Werts
>William Wilson   John McCartney
>Nicholas Lyberger   John Moore
>Charles Ruby   Samuel Davidson
>James Ritchie   Jacob Helm
>Elijah Adams   [last name cut off]

Page 236R
Commonwealth v. James Anderson Jr. Habeas Corpus for the body of John Allen.

~~Commonwealth v. Peter Swartzwilder. Tipling House. Joseph McDonald in $40 to give evidence to the Grand Jury.~~

Commonwealth v. Moses Reed. Setting up a Lottery. Moses Graham in $60.

Commonwealth v. Jacob Boreman. Setting up a Lottery. Defendant pleads guilty. James Longstreth in $100 for the defendant's good behavior and appearance August session 1797.

Page 237L
~~Commonwealth v. William Donnigan. Kidnapping. Noli Prosequi.~~

William Randles admitted as an Attorney in this Court on motion of William Brown Esq.

Commonwealth v. Henry Ritter & Elizabeth Ritter. Assault & Battery. Jr. in £10 for appearance of the defendants.

~~Commonwealth v. Jacob Boreman.~~

Commonwealth v. Robert Means. Tipling House.
Robt Adams in $60 for his appearance November session [17]96 to give evidence.

Commonwealth v. John Fullman. Felony on the oath of John Graham. Henry ____ and Jacob Fullman each in $60 for the appearance of the defendant November session [17]96.

Commonwealth v. Joseph Lilly. Joseph Lilly in $60, Bernard Mann in $60 for appearance of defendant this session.

Page 237R
Commonwealth v. William Dornagan. Wm Griffith in $60 for his appearance next session to give evidence against the defendant. John Garretson in $60, Joseph Springer in $60, James Anderson Jr. in $60, and David Springer in $60 for their appearance to testify against the defendant.

Commonwealth v. Michael Howard. Tipling House. Thomas Arnolt in $40 to give evidence against the defendant.

~~Commonwealth v. Joseph Lilley. Forfeiture taken.~~

Commonwealth v. William Dunnigan. William Dunnagin in $400 and Ephrain William in $200 for the appearance of the defendant.

Commonwealth v. Joseph Springer. Assault & Battery. Defendant in $50 to appear. David Springer in $100 for the defendant's appearance November 1796.

The Order to viewers for a road from Trace's Mill being read the Court orders viewers to make report at November sessions of the courses.

Commonwealth v. James Anderson Jr. Assault & Battery. Defendant pleads guilty and submits to Court. Peter Dull in $60 to give evidence. Court orders a fine of three dollars and costs.

Page 238L
Chalkey Jones the Heir at Law of Abel James Surviving Trustee of Richard Hockley & Jeremiah Warder who together with the said Abel James were Trustees of Daniel Clark for the use of the Creditors of the said Daniel Clark v. Wm Smith D^r of Divinity. On the petition of

Chalkey James Heir at Law of Abel James – the Court grant the prayer of the petitioner and directs subpoena to the said Wm Smith to show cause at next Court if any he hath why the Deposition of Witnesses respecting the premises in said Bill & Petition __ Memorial should not be taken in Perpetuam rei Memoriam.

Commonwealth v. Joseph Springer. Assault & Battery. Wm Dunagin in $60 to appear November session 1796.

~~Commonwealth v. Buchannan. Assault.~~

Page 238R
Daniel Shoemaker in $30 for his attendance during this Court. Daniel Shoemaker Constable of Colerain Township.

Commonwealth v. John Frederick. Larceny. Defendant pleads not guilty. John Cessna, Jonathan Cessna and Jno Elder cash in $40 each to appear and give evidence for Commonwealth.

Commonwealth v. Joseph Springer. Defendant's recognizance forfeit. David Springer's recognizance forfeit.

Commonwealth v. John Slick. Thomas Jones prosecutor, Ephraim Adams witness, John [Lucas?] sworn.

Page 239L
Commonwealth v. Jno Slick. Assault & Battery on Thos Jones. Defendant pleads not guilty. Jury of Martin Stoler, Martin Mir__, Jesse Griffith, James Burns, Jesse Justice, Peter Foulk, James Smith, William Holloway, William Hunter, Isaac ____, Henry Champine, and Jacob Riprogle find defendant guilty. Judgment that defendant pay six dollars damages and costs. John Slick in $200, Thos Vickroy in $100 for John Slick's good behavior toward Thomas Jones and to appear next Court in January.

Commonwealth v. William Paxton. Michael Edward in $20 to give evidence on the part of the Commonwealth.

Commonwealth v. John Allison. Assault & Battery. Witnesses: Barndollar, Baker, Metchel, Gamble, R. Ewalt, D. Jourdon, D. Ryan. Defendant submits to Court protesting his innocence. Fine of 20 cents and costs.

Page 239R [1796]
Commonwealth v. John Fredricks. John Fredricks in £100, Jacob Easter

in £50 and Charles Wall in £50 for appearance of John Fredricks to answer for Larceny April session 1797.

Court of Common Pleas adjourned to Tuesday 20 December 1796.

Page 240L [1797?]
[Date cut off from top of page. Enough of year is visible to suggest this may be 1797.]

Valentine Ripley affirmed and to attend Grand Jury.

Constable	Township
Abednego Stevens	Air
John McIntire	St. Clair
George Wilds	Dublin
Abraham Teeter	Woodberry
George Adam Smouse	Colerain
Michael Rine	Cumberland Valley
John Stright	Belfast
John Newcomer	Hopewell
John Fisher	Bethel
John [Lydick?]	Londonderry
John Graham	Bedford
David Snider	Providence

Peter Stiffler is appointed Guardian of the Person and Estate of George Stiffler and Anthony Stiffler minor children of John Stiffler Dec[d].

Republica v. John Fredricks. Larceny.

Republica v. William Paxton. Defendant being called three times & disappeared. Recognizance forfeit. Joseph McDonalds recognizance forfeit.

Daniel Shoemaker recognized to attend during the present session.

Susanna Nemise being called & Disappeared her Recognizance forfeit.

Page 240R [Early 1797]
Pennsylvania v. John Fredricks. Larceny. Testified: John Cessna, John Elder, Jonathan Cessna, John Cutchel. For defendant: Charles Wall. Jury of Jacob Fawner, John Keisor, John Meese, Jn[o] Olinger, Ab[m] Martin, Conrod Snider, Jeremiah Joslin, Ab[m] Martin, John Leasure, Jacob Bechtel, John Stork, and John McCoy find defendant guilty. Court orders pay twenty one dollars to the Commonwealth and an equal

amount to the person from whom the goods were stolen and be in Confinement for two years.

Pleas adjourned to 22 May 1797.

Pennsylvania v. William Paxton. Joseph McDonald in $40 to appear next August session to give evidence.

Pennsylvania v. Peter Arnolt. Recognizance forfeit. Jacob Bonnet recognizance forfeit. Defendant bound in $200 and Jn° Devebaugh in $100 to appear next session.

Edward Taylor discharged by Proclamation there being no bill found against him.

Pennsylvania v. Thos Beatte. John Axline, John May, Patrick H____ [cut off], Daniel Shoemaker, Jacob Waltman, and Bernard Axline each in $100 to appear August 1797 to testify for Commonwealth.

Page 241L
Pennsylvania v. Tobias Painter, Mich. Denard, John Scott Esq., James Reiley, David Jourdon, James Spreague, Robt Spencer. The Court having heard testimony on both side, the defendant pleads guilty and submits to the Court. Fine twenty dollars.

Benjn Beetle discharged by Proclamation.

Pennsylvania v. James Spreague. Assault & Battery. Defendant submits. Fined four dollars and costs.

Pennsylvania v. Jacob Nigh. Commitment upon Suspicion of Stealing a Watch from Samuel Bener. April 97 the Court directs the prisoner be moved to Huntingdon.

Page 241R [Blank]

Page 242L [January 1798?]
At Orphans Court 22 January [1798?]. Wm Kerney eldest son of Wm Kerney late of Bedford County Yeoman and acknowledged himself to owe Grace Kerney widow of the said deceased, James Kerney, Margaret intermarried with John Levering, Grace intermarried with James M___, Eliza intermarried with Benjamin Hart and Mary intermarried with Daniel Levering children of the said William Kerney in the sum of £711.2.3 to be levied on Goods & Chattels & Lands & Temements for use of Grace Kerney widow, James, Margaret, Grace, Elizabeth & Mary.
———— Upon this condition that if the said William Kerney shall pay unto the widow the sum of eight pounds the 21st day of January 1799 and the

~~further sum of £8 the 21st day of January each and every year thereafter for her natural life. and also that the said W_m_ Kerney pay the said James, Margaret, Grace, Elizabeth and Mary each the sum of forty four pounds eight shilling and ten pence halfpenny the 1st day of January 1799 and immediately after the death of the widow the further sum of twenty two pounds four shillings and five pence one farthing to James, Margaret, Grace, Elizabeth and Mary then this recognizance to be void.~~
———— ~~Acknowledged this 21 January 1798 in open Court.~~

Page 242R   August 1797

Commonwealth v. William Paxton. Indictment for Assaulting & Beating Joseph McDonald Constable of Providence. Defendant submits to Court. Fined six cents and costs.

On motion Mr Nagle Roger Perry admitted Attorney of Court of Common Pleas and Quarter Sessions.

On proof of notice being served on the Ex^r of Wm Wilds deceased the Court appoint Jacob Wink & John Rankin Commissioners to take the Depositions of Witnesses concerning his Bill to be taken in Perpetium Rei Memorium.

Pennsylvania v. Peter Arnolt. Robert Spencer in $200 for his appearance to answer for Nuisance.

Pennsylvania v. Thomas Beetle. Larceny. True Bill. Defendant pleads not guilty. Testify for prosecution: John Axline, Patrick Heney, Barnard Axline, Daniel Shoemaker, John May. Jury of Ephraim Acres, Henry Sipes, George Rhoads, Jacob Sh__berger, Philip Knee, Joseph Shoup, Conrad Nicodemus, Joseph McFerren, Joseph Lilly, Benjamin Hull, John Hipple, and John Flickenger find Thomas Beetle guilty. Judgment that defendant pay 3 dollars 66 cents and costs and be confined in the House of Corrections for three years at hard labor.

Page 243L

Commonwealth v. Aquila Justice. Aquila Justice in $100 and John Crouse in $50 for good behavior of Aquila Justice for one year particularly towards Matthew Tracy.

Commonwealth v. Michael Barndollar in $1000 to produce the body of Negro Sal at next November session. Rule to take the deposition of Ephraim Blaine Esq. before Judge Barclay in presence of Negro Sal before next November Term to be read in evidence.

Commonwealth v. Philip Keel[Kreel?]. Philip Keel[Kreel?] in $60 and Conrod Rush in $60 for appearance of defendant next November session.

Forfeited Charles Williams
Forfeited John Williams
Appeared Elija Barton
Appeared George Enslow Jr
} each in $60 to give evidence at November session next.

Commonwealth v. George Echart. Larceny. True Bill.
Defendant pleads not guilty. Testify: J. Harcleroad, John England, John Deal, Martin Riley, Peter ____, Nicholas Kegg, George Croyle, Henry Kunts. Jury of Daniel S___man, Henry P_tt, Benjamin Ferguson, Robert Gibson, John Fleckinger, Charles Williams, Henry Sh__, George Sipes, Michael Stall, Robert Moore, Abraham Leedy, and John Stigert find defendant not guilty.

Page 243R
Commonwealth v. Matthew Tracy. Matthew Tracy in $100 and Martin Houser in $50 that Matthew Tracy be of good behavior and keep the peace particularly toward Aquila Justice for one year.

Court appoints George Buchannan Esq. Guardian of the person and estate of Mary Skelley a minor child of Hugh Skelley dec[d] killed in an action with the Indians on 16 July 1780.

Commonwealth v. Adam Barton. Assault.
Witnesses: Henry [Best?], James Williams, John Kniseley. Defendant pleads not guilty. Defendant retracts plea and submits to Court protesting his innocence. Fined two dollars and costs.

Page 244L   November Session 1797

George Gordon in $60 to give evidence. Abednego Stevens in $60 to give evidence.

Samuel Davidson appointed Guardian over the person and estate of W[m] Stewart a minor child of W[m] Stewart under the age of 14 years.

Adam Rheam in $60 to give evidence during this session. David Keef in $60 to give evidence.

Commonwealth v. Philip Keel. Assault.
Defendant pleads not guilty. Testify: Charles Williams, Jn[o] Williams, Elijah Barton, Ab[m] Cashman, James Boyd, George Enslow Jr. Jury of Jacob Bower, Ezekiel Cox, Laurence Bulger, Henry Peek, Benjamin

Stevens, John Ullery, Conrod Byerly, Christian Enslow, Henry Clapper, Jn⁰ [Stoutlier?], Fred^k Rice, and John Martin find defendant not guilty. John Ullery fined two dollars for non-attendance.

Commonwealth v. Thos Logan. Abednego Stevens in $60 to give evidence at next January session 1797.

Uriah Wink and George Dandsdill in $60 each to appear in January and be of good behavior.

Commonwealth v. John Friend Esq. Adam Ream in $60 to give evidence against John Friend Esq. for embezzling recognizance.

David Keiff, George Wilds, John Straight, Michael Rine, Ab^m Teetor fined 20/ each at November 1797.

John Fisher appointed Guardian over the person and estate of John Mincy a minor child of Danl Mincy dec^d.

Page 244R January Session 1798

Pennsylvania v. Mary Woodford. Bastardy Mary Woodford in £25. George Walman in £25 bail.

Same v. David Carson. Assault & Battery. Defendant in £20 and Adam Ream in £10.

Same v. Abel Barne and Eleanor Wilkey. Defendant in £20, E W in £20, Caleb Barns in £20 bail, Francis Wilkey in £10 bail.

~~Pennsylvania v. Mr Logan. Nuisance. Nolli Prosequi.~~

Pennsylvania v. Conrod Bower. Fornication. Mary Wolford in $100 to prosecute. George Waltman in $60 for the appearance of Mary Wolford April next.

Pennsylvania v. George Lucas. Forgery. Jacob Nagle in $100 and Isaac Bonnett in $100 to appear and give evidence against the defendant January 1798.

Page 245L
Pennsylvania v. George Lucas. Perjury. George Smith in $20 to give evidence.

James Gaff minor child of William Gaff dec^d chose James Agnew his guardian.

Pennsylvania v. John Friend Esq. Adam Ream in £20 to give evidence April 1798.

Pennsylvania v. George Lucas. Forgery. G. Lucas in $500 and Robt Spencer in $250. Forfeited.

Same v. Same. Ut supra.

Page 245R [Blank]

Page 246L [Penciled 245]   August Session 1798

Pennsylvania v. Elizabeth Flook. Fornication. Balsar Swartz in £100 to attend this session and give evidence.

Same v. Michael Halderbaum. Elizabeth Herman in $100 to appear and prosecute November 1798.

John Lyon admitted as Attorney.

Commonwealth v. Joseph Murray. John Ke__ in $60 to appear November 1798 to give evidence.

Same v. Thos Johnson. Fornication. Samuel Moss in $100 that Ephraim Moss attend November session next.

~~Same v. Jacob Po___. Assault & Battery.~~

Same v. Robert Gordon. Fornication. Robt Gordon in $300 Thos Johnson in $100 for appearance of Robt Gordon to answer at November session.

Page 246R
Commonwealth v. Frederick Dibert & Valentine Wertz. Neglect of Duty.

Commonwealth v. Abraham Buzzard & James Smith. Larceny.

Same v. James Bishop. Assault & Battery.
Testify: Andrew Mann, Esq., Wm Wallace, John Fisher, James McKinney. Defendant submits to Court. Fine of two dollars and costs.

Commonwealth v. Thomas Johnston. Fornication. Thomas Johnston in $200 and Thos Johnston Sr. in $100 for appearance of defendant November session to answer.

Same v. Jeremiah Hamilton. [Mary Reed] in $200 and Geo Danzell in $100 to appear and give evidence and for the daughter Mary's appearance to give evidence.

Commonwealth v. Cassandra James. Fornication. George James in $100 for appearance of defendant next session.

Page 247L
John Parron Guardian for his sister Poll aged 13 years – a negro girl – appointed by Court 28 August 1798.

An adjourned Court to be on 22nd of September next for having James ____ an em____ ____ & Henry Down.

William Reynolds, [crossed out], [cross out] ~~Taylor~~, Thos Vickroy and Hugh Barclay appointed to settle the Public debts of the Commissioners.

Pennsylvania v. Abraham Buzzard and James Smith. Larceny. Testify: Jacob ~~Hoover~~, Peter Barndollar, Jacob Barndollar, Mich. Barndollar. Jury of Valentine Easter, Abraham Troxel, Christian Wike, John Blair, Henry Williams, Bernard Exline, Jacob B[ishop?], Willm Vancleve, John Dodson, James Longstreth, Godfrey [Huff?], and Nicholas McGuire find defendant not guilty.

Commonwealth v. James Agnew. Nuisance.
James Agnew in $100 to attend next session and answer.

Page 247R
Commonwealth v. Adam Fox [Fore?]. Jacob Eddleman swore the peace against defendant and was bound in $200 to appear next session and give evidence. Fox to give security in $200 and surety in $100 for his appearance.

The Court appoint William Griffith guardian for negro Bett daughter of Negro Hagard.

Anthony Naugle and Robert Spencer freeholders to settle the accounts of Supervisors.

Commonwealth v. Geo. Fore. Henry Kunts in $60, Peter Kunts in $60 and Danl Smith in $60 for appearance to give evidence and prosecute.

Pennsylvania v. Thos Thornhill. Jacob U__ and John B___ in $100 to appear next session and give evidence against defendant.

John Garretson v. George Wisecarver. Common Pleas. Testify: Jess Griffith, Henry Swage, John Blair, John Slick, Wm Griffith, Jno Wisegarver. Jury of Jacob Boreman, John Johnston, Isaac Martin, Nathan Wright, Edwd Huston, Uriah Wink, Simon Kinton, Nicholas [Bow?], John Sliger, Henry Whitstone, Henry Bruner and Christopher [Mier?] find for Plaintiff. Damages 15/0 and costs.

Page 248L
Commonwealth v. Mich. Haward. Court directs the defendant to give

security in $400 and bail in equal amount and to be of good behavior particularly toward John Hartzel.

Commonwealth v. Francis Moans. Francis Moans in $200 and Amos Evan in $100 for appearance of defendant November session and be of good behavior.

Commonwealth v. Thos Thornhill. Thos Thornhill in $200 and George Smith in $100 for appearance of Thos Thornhill next session and to be of good behavior.

Commonwealth v. Peter Arnold. Presentment for Nuisance. Peter Arnold in $100 and Robert Gibson in $60 for appearance of Peter Arnold next session.

Page 248R [August 1798]
[The following is in the hand of the court clerk and on docket paper. A loose paper from the case is bound in the docket at pages 218R, 220L.]
Commonwealth v. Martin Toomy. Murder. Defendant pleads not guilty. Testify: Dr J. Anderson, Barnard Axline, Jacob Waltman, Henry Smith, Andrew Kepley, Pat^k Heney, Peter Harker, Anthony Smith, Charles Gordon, William Cessna. Jury of John Whip, George Hartin, Jacob Bowman, Isaac Fic___, Elisha Gr__[cut off], Henry Markley, Isaac Martin, Pe__[cut off] Hoover, John Johnston, Wm Davis, Thomas Stevens and Robert Orbison find guilty of murder in the first degree.

30 August 1798 George Funk appointed Guardian of Elizabeth Mean under 14 and chosen by Rachel and their Guardian.

The Court order that the Jail Keeper be allowed 12½ cents per day for every cri[minial] confined in the jail and 7 cents for every Debtor.

Page 249L
Commonwealth v. John Stiger. [cut off] in $100 to give evidence April next. John Stiger in $100 and Joseph Warford in $60 for appearance of defendant April [17]99.

Same v. Thornhill. Evan Chaney in 100 [no currency symbol for many amounts on this page], Humphrey Picket in 100, and Amos Evans in 100.

Penn^a v. Rob. Gordon. Charles Gordon in 200 for appearance of Cassandra James at April session to prosecute.

Same v. Same. Robt Gordon in 200 to answer at April. Jno Gordon in 100 bail.

Same v. Henry Miller, John McNutt, Pat Thomas & George Ainsley. $60 each to appear April [17]99.

Same v. Francis Gibbs. Francis Gibbs in $80, [blank] in $40, [blank] in $40 for appearance of F[.] Gibbs April [17]99 and that he keep the peace towards Sarah Gibbs for one year.

Same v. Thos Thornhill. Thos Norton and George Smith each in $200 to prosecute April term next.

John McDonald chose Geo[.] Wilds
Abm & John Myer —— Sam Beach__
Christina —— D^o ——

Page 249R
Petition of inhabitants of Woodberry Township requesting Court to appoint auditors to settle accounts of the Supervisors for two years past at April Term next – To remove the action Buck_ v. Fluck.

On the 25th February came into an adjourned Court Derry Ryan and not having proved the ___ of Notices on his Creditors to the satisfaction of the Court he is remanded until 23rd April 1799. Jane Ryan bail for his appearance.

Jacob Saylor one of the Guardians of the children of Thos McGaughey dec^d asks to be dismissed from his guardianship. The Court grants and appoints William Ward Esq. in his place.

Page 250L
Anthony Smith appointed Guardian over the person and estate of George Oster under the age of 21 years by his own request.

Page 250R
Pennsylvania v. George Enslow. Assault & Battery. Patrick Thomas, John McNutt, Henry Miller and Sarah Gibbs each in $60 for their appearance at August sessions and also to prosecute against Francis Gibbs.

Same v. F. Gibbs. Francis Gibbs in $80 and Caleb Thompson in $40 for appearance of F. G. at August session and surety of the peace.

Same v. John Stiger. Assault & Battery. In $60 to answer at August session. Also Elener Stiger, Sarah Stilwell and Ann McKinney in $60 for their appearance at August session to give evidence.

Same v. Thornhill. Enos Rogers, Evan Cherry, Humphrey [Burket?] and Wm Wright each in $60 for their appearance at August session to give evidence.

Same v. Rob. Gordon. George James in $200 for appearance of Cassandra James at August session to prosecute.

Same v. Same. Rob. Gordon in $300 to appear at August to answer. John Stackman in $150 for the appearance of R. Gordon.

Same v. Jane [James?] Cowel. Jane [James?] Cowel in $60. George Barton in $80 for appearance of Jane [James?] Cowel next session to answer.

Page 251L

Penn^a v. Dan. Miller Jr. D. Miller Jr. in $100 to appear and answer. Dan. Miller in $100 for appearance of D. Miller Jr.

Same v. Same. John Perdu and ____ Low_ in $60 to give evidence.

Same v. James Wilson. James Wilson in $100 and William Wilson in $100 to keep the peace particularly toward John Richey Esq.

Page 251R

David Stiffler v. Valentine Ripley. Witnesses: Jn° Swan, Geo. Harbaugh, Barbara Harbaugh and Wm Griffith. Jury of Martin Loy, Jacob Studebaker, James Parron, Jacob Fore, David Fields, Wm Small, Henry Deal, Vendle Ott, David Potts, Joseph Hunt, Jacob Boreman and Robert Gibson. The plaintiff suffered a nonsuit.

The Court allows 20 cents per day to the Jailor of this County for each Debtor and Criminal in confinement until August session 1799.

Penn^a v. Negro Bob. Habeas Corpus. Samuel Silley, Hugh Barclay and Robert Spencer bound jointly in $200 to produce the Body of Negro Bob ["Patterson" is interlined] next Court to be held August next and that they will be held answerable for the wages of said negro to his master in case the said negro shall be remanded to his master.

Page 252L [Blank]

Page 252R [Blank]

Page 253L [penciled 252]   August Session 1799

The Court assess fine of sixty seven cents upon Addis Linn for disorderly behavior in open Court.

[Following two cases grouped together.]
Commonwealth v. John Stiger.
Same v. Jane Cornell otherwise called Jane Dean. Assault & Battery.
Witnesses: Jane Cornell, Adam Stiger, Ann McKinney, Jane Stiger, Nancy McKinney, Jane Stilwell, Jane Warford, John Stiger, Andrew Mann Esq., Elizabeth Smith. Jury of Jacob McCain, William Vancleve, Jacob Hendershot, Joshua Pearson, Peter Barnhardt, Robert Gibson, Richard Baker, Daniel Clark, Adam Croyle, Matthew McFerren, Henry Whetstone, and Joseph Powel find defendants guilty. Court directs fine upon John Stiger of eight dollars and he pay costs. Court directs fine upon Jane Cornell also Jane Dean of eight dollars and costs.

[Following two cases grouped together.]
Same v. Geo. Ensley alias Ansley.
Same v. Henry Miller, Jno McNutt, Pat^r Thomas, George Ensley.
Witnesses: Francis Gibbs, James Martin Esq., Jeremiah Joslin, George Ensley. Jury of Robert Orbison, Cornelius Devore, Valentine Oster, Edward Daily, Jacob Hendershot, Valentine Wertz, Henry Whetstone, Jonathan Bowen, Michael Holderbaum, Joseph Kelly, Jacob Stevens, and John Elder find defendants not guilty.

Page 253R
Same v. John Cessna Jr. Fornication. Arthur Ray in $100 for appearance of Mary Williams November session to pros[ecute].

Same v. Same. Jonathan Cessna in $200 for his appearance November session to answer for Fornication.

Commonwealth v. Francis Gibbs. Assault & Battery.
Witnesses: Henry Miller, George Ensley, John McNutt, Pat^r Thomas, Sarah Gibbs, Jeremiah Joslin, James Martin, John Dickey Esq. Jury of Jacob Hendershot, Joshua Pearson, Peter Barnhardt, Robert Gibson, Richard Baker, Daniel Clark, Adam Croyle, Robert Hemphill, Benjamin Stevens, John Elder, Jacob Stevens, and Matthew Mc__[cut off] find defendant not guilty.

Same v. George Oster. Henry Smith in $100 to appear November and prosecute.

Pennsylvania v. James Wilson. Assault & Battery.
Wm Wilson in $60 for appearance of James Wilson November 1799.

Same v. James Wilson. Ut Supra.

Page 254L
Same v. James Wilson, William Wilson, and Mich. Wilson. John

Ritchey Esq. in $200 for appearance of George Ritchey, Gideon Ritchey, and John Ritchey Jr. at November session to give evidence.

Commonwealth v. Thomas Thornhill. Misdemeanor. Jury of Valentin Oster, Adam Croyle, Joseph Powell, Valentin Wertz, Matthew McFerran, Joshua Pearson, William Vancleve, Daniel Clark, Robert Gibson, Jacob Stevens, Richard Baker, and Jacob Hendershot find defendant not guilty.

The Court assess a fine of six dollars on each of the following for non-attendance as jurors: Isaac Bonnett, Andrew Sheetz.

Page 254R
James Black v. John Colepenny. Witnesses: Jn° Black, Jn° Webster, Jn° Warshabaugh, Wm Faith, Peter Glasner. Jury of Daniel Hardman, Daniel Clark, Valentine Oster, Valentine Wertz, Peter Troutman, Isaac Fickes, Joseph Kelly, Michael Hailderbaum, Robert Gibson, Adam Croyle, Richard Baker, and Wm Vancleve. Plaintiff being called did not answer and became nonsuit.

Commonwealth v. Martin Riley Esq. Witnesses: Matthew Taylor, Thos Vickray. Jury of Joseph Kelly. Adam Croyle, Valentine Wertz, Jonathan Cessna, Robert Gibson, Jacob McClane, Daniel Clark, William Vancleve Jr., Michael Holderbaum, John Elder, Richard Baker, and Peter Troutman find Martin Riley guilty.

Page 255L
The Court assesses a fine of six dollars against the following for non-attendance as juror: Frederick Hill, James Stewart, Wm Wilson, James Longstreath, Frederick Debert, Peter Smith, Andrew Sheets, Robert Moore, Richard Elder, Henry Smith.

[Loose paper bound with docket page]

Peter Smith of Bethel }	Nov 1799
Peter Smith of D° }	
Richd Elder }	
Richd Elder }	Nov 1799 of Hopewell
Richd Elder }	
Henry Smith of Colerain	Nov 1799
Isaac Bonnet of Bedford	Augt 1799
Andrew Sheets D°	D°

Mr Morrison wishes a certified copy of James Walkers Will and the Executors Letters Testamentary.

Page 255R
Commonwealth v. George Oster. Novr Sepr 1799. Testify: Henry Smith, Jacob [surname blank], Henry V__man, John Jones, Samuel Henderson, Geo. Wolf. Jury of Peter Foulk, Jacob Smith, Robert Akers, John Brit, W^m __zer, Simon Kenton, Charles Gordon, Daniel Dannels, Joseph Dodson, Christopher Nagle, Conrod Cox, and Ephraim Akers find defendant guilty. Fine four dollars and costs.

Commonwealth v. John White. The Court assess a fine of two dollars and costs of prosecution.

Commonwealth v. Abraham Buzzard. Indictment for Assault & Battery. John Paxton in $60 to prosecute at April. Abraham Buzzard in $60 and Edward Conner in $60.

Commonwealth v. John Cessna. Adultery. Jonathan Cessna in $200 for the appearance of the defendant at January session 1800.

Same v. Same. Arthur Ray $100 for the appearance at January to prosecute.

Same v. Jn° Hendrickson. Defendant discharged. Having appeared, nothing alleged against him.

Page 256L
Commonwealth v. Thomas McConnell. Indictment for Larceny. Defendant pleads guilty and submits to Court protesting his innocence. The Court directs the prisoner to pay the value of the goods stolen to the owner to the value of three dollars; pay the like sum to the Commonwealth; undergo a servitude of one year three months at hard labor and pay the costs of prosecution. Prisoner to be conveyed from this place to the Work House in Philadelphia and there to work his servitude.

[Following two cases grouped together.]
Same v. James Martin.
Same v. Patrick Haggerty. Peter Lamhart and Thomas Norton in $50 to give evidence at January 1800.

Commonwealth v. William Henry. Indictment for Assault & Battery. Defendant pleads guilty and submits to Court and protests his innocence. The Court assesses a fine of 6 dollars and costs and that he be bound over for one year for his good behavior and appear in the Court to abide the Sentence of said Court. William Henry in $100.

Same v. Peter Arnolt. Nuisance. Peter Arnolt in $200 to answer April next. John Moore [does not say why John Moore's name appears].

Page 256R
Ephraim Wallace v. John Keiser. [Testify:?] Geo O___, James Longstreath. Jury of John Elingier, Nicholas Boor, Noah Barton, Conrod Cox, Ephraim Akers, Peter Houlk, Daniel Daniels, Andrew Sheets, Jacob Smith, John Dodson, Robt Akers, and Frederick Hill do find for Plaintiff Twelve Pounds and 17^s.

Commonwealth v. James Wilson. Testify: Gideon Richey, George Richey, Wm Wilson, Thomas Flanagan, Henry Sides, Jacob Criviston, Hugh Barclay, Hugh Ensfield, John Piper Esq., Peter Morgart. Jury of Henry Smith, Peter Smith, Christopher Nagle, William Frazer, Elijah Barton, Michael Dibert, George Gordon, Lewis Hershiser, Joseph Dodson, Martin Longstreath, James Longstreath, and John Britt say the defendant is not guilty.

Benjn Burd Esq v. James Sprague Adm^r of George [Rufe?]. Testify: Duncan McVicker. Jury of Jacob Smith, Andrew Sheets, Conrod Cox, Daniel Daniels, John Elengier, Noah Barton, Peter Foulk, Nicholas Boor, John Dodson, Robert Akers, Ephraim Akers, and Frederick Hill say they find for the defendant.

Page 257L
Commonwealth v. John Cessna. Jonathan Cessna in $300 for John Cessna's appearance at April session 1800 to answer for Fornication.

Same v. Same. Arthur Ray in $100 for appearance of Mary Williams Prosecutrix at next April session.

Page 257R
Cash for a Certified copy of a rule of Ct – 3 [cut off].

Page 258L   April Term 1800

On motion of Saml Riddle Esq. John Shippen Esq. admitted as Attorney of this Court.

Henry Roudenbush	Constable	Greenfield Twp
John Fore	Constable	Providence Twp
Lewis Cheney	Constable	Hopewell Twp
John Straight	D^o	Belfast Twp
Laurence Bulger	D^o	Air Twp
John Fore	D^o	Providence Twp
Michael Young	D^o	Londonderry
Joshua Pearson	D^o	Bedford

Page 258R [penciled 259]
At Bedford 28 April 1800 before James Martin, John Dickey, John Piper and John Scott.

Constable	Township
David Keefer	Bedford Borough
William Griffith	Bedford Township
John Hancock	St. Clair
Jeremiah Joslin	Providence
Adam Ream	Colerain
James McKenney	Bethel
John McFadden	Belfast
Thomas Stevens	Air
Michael Bare	Dublin
Lewis Chaney	Hopewell
Michael Rowdebush	Woodberry
Christian Meese	Cumberland Valley
Wm Troutman	Londonderry
Nicholas McGuire	Green Field

Grand Jury:
  John Moore
  Christley Moyer
  David Quick
  Ephraim Adams
  Rinehart Wolf
  Thomas Ray
  George Hardinger
  Nicholas Boor
  Henry Williams
  Charles Beighel
  Joshua Wright
  Jonas Robbison
  William Rose
  Jesse Griffith
  James Taylor
  Allen Rose
  Henry Bruner
  Michael _ins
  Peter Arnold
  Valentine [Wirick?]
  John Elder
  Amos Evans

James Phletcher, Daniel McConnale, Joseph Johnston. By consent defendants recognizances forfeited and respited until next session.

Page 259L
[Large table below; abstracted on following two pages.]

Township	Constable	Supervisors	Overseers	Freeholders	Appraisers
Bedford Twp	Joshua Pierson	Edward Dailey James Anderson	Nicholas Wilson Henry Cuntz	Wm Griffith James Williams John Christman Wm Wilson	William Wilson William Griffith
Bethel	John Mann	Moses Graham Adis Linn	Benjamin Truax Michael Miller	Wm Clark Thos Bowen Sam^l_ay Alex^r McGregor	Valentin Oster Jacob Moses
St Clair	Samuel Way	James Gordon Robert Adams	John Bowser Isaac Fiekes		
Londonderry	Nicholas Libarger	Philip Waggoner Joseph ____	Jacob Ehenberger John F____	Andrew Emerick Joseph Boyer Cornelius Devore	
Dublin	Michael Young	Jacob Shack Matthias Ambrosure	George Dansdill Michael Young	John Noble David Fields	Robert Ramsey Wm Justice
Cumberland Val	Nicholas Boor	John McCoy George Hardinger		Jn° Mc__aine Sam^l___ton Jacob Myers Wm Kay	
Hopewell	Lewis Chaney	W^m McElvaine John Lane	Matthias Long Evan Griffith	Henry Markly Edwd Cowan Jacob____ Jn° Helsinger	Martin Houser Jacob Houser

Docket 2: 1771–1801

Township	Constable	Supervisors	Overseers	Freeholders	Appraisers
Woodberry	Michael Rowebush	Conrod Nicodemis John Snider	Michael Hay Philip Knee	James Crawford Richd Shirly George Lingefeth	
Greenfield	Henry Rowdebush	John Dodson Henry Bigle		Reynolds Morton John Morton Jac Boreman Michael Stall	Obadiah Mellot Henry Bates
Belfast	John Straight	John Blackwood Adam Painter	Henry Laverin Francis Welch	Elijah Barton Joseph ——— Ja^s Mortimore Ab^r Martin	Fredk Coots Benjn Martin
Providence	John Fore	John Moore Peter Morgert	Wm Cornel Edward Dansals	Jno ——— Jacob Bor ——— Vendel Ott	
Air	Laurence Bulger	Fred^k Bor ——— Charles Tygert	Abedno Stevens Saml Bechel		
Colerain	Jacob Adams	Edward Rose William Resler			

Page 259R
Commonwealth v. William Hartley Jr. Joshua Wright in $50 to give evidence.

Same v. John Parks. Ephraim Adams in $50 to give evidence.

Same v. Fred^k Rothrock. John Moore in $50 to give evidence.

Same v. Simon Kinton. Defendant in $200 and John Kinton in $100 for appearance of defendant next Court of Quarter Sessions.

Same v. John Cessna Jr. Arthur Rhay in $200 and John Kinton in $100 for appearance of defendant next Court of Quarter Sessions.

Same v. John Cessna Jr. Jonathan Cessna in $200 for the appearance of defendant next session to answer.

Same v. Simon Kinton. Lawrence Lambers in $100 for the appearance of Rachel Hand next session to prosecute.

Same v. Ab^m Buzzard. Ab^m Buzzard in $100 to answer. Anth^y Smith in $50 for appearance of defendant.

Page 260L [April 1800 & immediately prior]
Penn^a v. John Smith. John Smith in $200 and William Kenworthy in $100 that the defendant be of good behavior particularly toward Peter Mock and appear at next session to show cause why this recognizance should not be continued.

April Sessions 1800

The Overseers of the Poor of Dublin Township v. The Overseers of the Poor of Hopewell Township. Appeal from order of the justices of the peace to remove the pauper herewith mentioned. Court appoint the Monday of next session for hearing the parties upon twenty days notice to the appealers. At September session 1800 on motion and argument the appeal was quashed.

Page 260R [Blank]

Page 261L [penciled 260]   [September 1800]
At Bedford first Monday of September 1800 before James Riddle and associate Justices.

Grand Jury:
  William Patterson
  Jacob Baer
  Joshua Critchfield
  Joseph Powell
  Peter [Knuffs?]
  Jacob Link
  Cornelius Devore
  Fredereck Hem
  Abraham Martin Esq.
  Samuel Way
  Andrew Mann Esq.
  Jacob Richard
  James Gordon
  Abednego Stevens
  John Zant
  Casper Creamer
  John Knisely
  William McCulloch
  Joshua Wright
  James Mortimore

List of Licensed Tavern Keepers
  John Head
  George Wilds
  Benjamin Burd
  Samuel Longstreath
  John Graham
  John Park
  Christopher Enslow
  William Ward
  James Taylor
  Jacob Has__on
  George Ice
  Isaac Bonnett
  Jane Ryan
  Joshua Wright
  John Knisely
  George Ritchie
  James Jamison
  Henry Deal
  Jacob McClean
  Robert Spencer
  James Parsons
  Henry Miller
  William McCulloch
  William Vickery
  Casper Stotler
  George Dandsdill
  David Field
  John Noble
  Jacob Fore

Page 261R   [September 1800]
  Daniel Coyle
  Robert Moore
  William Hartly
  John Miller
  Valentine Wertz
  Samuel Selly

On motion Mr Shippen, Joseph Weigley admitted as Attorney of this Court and the Court of Common Pleas.

Commonwealth v. Joseph McVicker Constable of ___ Township. Joseph McVicker in $40 for his appearance the present session to testify for state.

Commonwealth v. Conrod Appleman. Tipling House. Ignoramus.

Commonwealth v. Peter Roof. Larceny. True Bill. Defendant in $200 for appearance to answer next Term. Henry Whitstone in $100 for appearance of Peter Roof next session to answer.

Commonwealth v. Daniel Shoemaker, Jacob Adams and Adam Shoemaker. $60 each to appear next session and testify against Peter Roof for Larceny.

Page 262L
Commonwealth v. Abraham Buzzard. Assault & Battery. Witness for state: John Paxton, John Davis. Jury of James McKinney, Michael Barndollar, Benjamin Stevens, George Enslow Jr., Patrick Hagerty, Joel Hancock, Daniel Shoemaker, Henry Miller, John Williams, Robert Hemphill, John Jenkins, and ____ Shearer who say Abraham Buzzard is guilty. Fine one dollar.

Same v. Simon Kenton. Fornication. Testify for state: Rachel Hand, Rachel Adams. Testify for defense: Martha Marshell, James Heydon. Jury of Daniel Stutzman, Hugh Hamilton, Joel Hancock, John Jenkins, Michael Barndollar, Daniel Coyle, Jacob Bishop, Daniel Shoemaker, Christian Nagle, Henry Miller, John Helm, and John Dodson who find Simon Kenton guilty. Fine £10 and costs. Also to pay Rachel Hand fifty dollars lying in expense.

Page 262R
Commonwealth v. M____ Allen. Attachment awarded against M____ Allen.

Same v. John Cessna Jr. Fornication. Witnesses for state: Mary William. Jury of Michael Barndollar, Patrick Haggerty, Christian Nagle, Samuel Livingston, Daniel Shoemaker, John Jenkins, Benjamin Stephens, John Helm who find John Cessna Jr. guilty. Fine £10 and costs. Judgment that John Cessna Jr. pay to Mary Williams ten dollars for lying in expenses and one half dollar per week from the birth of the child until it arrive at the age of two years and from thence to pay the sum of two shillings and six pence per week until the child arrive at the age of seven years, each of the said payments due quarterly. Also that he do indemnify the Township of Cumberland from the maintenance of said child and that he appear at the expiration of the said seven years to abide further order of the Court for further maintenance.

Page 263L September 1800
Agents for ensuing elections.

Londonderry District	Captain Richard Baker, Captain John Ken__er
Cumberland Valley	John Coulter, John Cessna
Bedford District	Martin Riley, Anthony Nawgle
Hopewell District	Amos Evans, William Young
Woodberry	Henry Markly, William Young
McConnelstown District	John Davis, Benjamin Burd
Londonderry District	James McKinney, Moses Graham

Page 263R [Blank]

Page 264L [November 1800]
At Bedford fourth Monday of November 1800 before James Riddle and his associate Judges.

Grand Jury:
    Amos Evans
    Patrick Hayny
    John Black
    William Davis
    John Snider
    Michael Murphy
    George Leeman
    John Britt
    George Bowser
    John McCartney
    Solomon Adams
    John Ling
    Abraham Buzzard
    Martin Loy
    Robert Gorden
    Peter Oyler
    Andrew Sloboum
    John Meese
    William Scovil

List of Licensed Tavern Keepers:
    Joseph Flickinger
    David Beckwith
    Charles Sewell
    Thomas Norton
    John Snider

On motion Mr Shippen, William Wallace admitted Attorney of this Court and the Court of Common Pleas.

Page 264R
Republic v. Peter Roof. Larceny. Jury of George Smith, John Proctor, Michael Holderbaum, Christopher Riley, Daniel Miller, Daniel Cyphers, William Vickroy, Conrod Smith, George Henry, Conrod Haverstock, John Algire, and Matthias Smith say defendant is not guilty.

Pennsylvania v. Adam Shoemaker. Adam Shoemaker in $100 for Tipling House and Daniel Shoemaker in $100 for appearance of Adam. Daniel Shoemaker in $50 and Peter Harcher in $40 to give evidence at February session next. Witnesses: Adam Shoemaker, Daniel Shoemaker, John Fore, Jacob Shoemaker, Peter Harcher, Peter Keller, Mary Smouse.

Pennsylvania v. William Herd. Indictment for Larceny. True Bill. Saml Selby in $50 to testify.

Pennsylvania v. John Snider. Indictment for Tipling House.

Page 265L November 1800

Pennsylvania v. Lewis Fluck. Tipling House. Recognizance before Mr Reiley Esq. & recognizance filed to appear next February Court.

Pennsylvania v. Jacob Hesselton. Tipling House. True Bill.

Pennsylvania v. James Anderson and Edward Daily Supervisors of the High Ways. Neglect of Duty.

Same v. Conrod Nickdemess and John Snider Supervisors of Highways. Neglect of Duty.

Same v. John Park. Tipling House. True Bill.

Page 265R November 1800

Pennsylvania v. Jacob Fore. Tipling House. True Bill.

Commonwealth v. Peter Arnold. Nuisance. Ignoramus.

Same v. Benj. Burd. Tipling House. Ignoramus.

Same v. George Lee. Tipling House. Ignoramus.

Same v. John Knicely. et Supra. Ignoramus.

Same v. Joshua Wright. et Supra. Ignoramus.

Page 266L [February 1801]
At Bedford February 1801 before James Martin, John Dickey, John Piper and John Scott.

Grand Jury:
- Christopher Reiley
- Henry Williams
- Lewis Fluck
- Abraham Shoup
- Jacob Mealy
- Elijah Adams
- Michael May
- John Wallick
- Joseph Walter
- William Drenning
- James Gordon
- James Taylor
- Andrew Smith
- John Reiland
- Jacob Fore
- John Boyce
- Henry Horn
- Henry Coontz
- John Dibert
- Gasper Creamer
- Michael Sill
- Andrew Sheetz

Licensed Tavern Keepers:
- William Davis
- Henry Betz
- Henry Horn
- Lewis Flook

Pennsylvania v. Thomas Norton. Tipling House. True Bill.
Patrick Hagerty in $50 to attend this session.

Same v. John McIntyre, William Shepard and Mary May. Assault & Battery. True Bill.

Same v. Thomas Shaw. Tipling House. True Bill.

Same v. Jacob Riegar. Assault & Battery. True Bill.

Same v. Robt Moore. Assault & Battery.
Robt Moore in $60. Andrew Mann Esq. in $40. Christian Stophel, John Berringer and George Cashman each in $40 to give evidence.

Page 266R
Pennsylvania v. Andrew Mann Esq. Misdemeanor in Office.
Andrew Mann in $100 and James McKinney in $100 for appearance of defendant at May session next.

Same v. Daniel Barndollar. Larceny. Witnesses for prosecution: William Bagley, Joseph Creviston Jr., John Murray. Testify for defendant: Philip Fishburn, John Paxton, Philip Cumfort, Catherine Cumfort, Jacob Barndollar, James Martin Esq., John Richey Esq., George Cashman, Henry Deal. Jury of Henry Deal, Henry Smith, Henry Lyberger, John England, David Potts, John Elder, William Hazlett, John McDonald, Nicholas Boore, George P. Barnhart, Frederick Reegart, and John Whip who say Daniel Barndollar is guilty of stealing the bee hive.

Pennsylvania v. Daniel Barndollar. Larceny. John Paxton in $120 for appearance of Daniel Barndollar next May session.

Pennsylvania v. Henry Walen. Larceny. Defendant pleads guilty and prays a small fine. Judgment of the Court is that defendant return the property to the owner if not already done or pay the value thereof, pay the like sum to the Commonwealth, undergo a servitude of fifteen months in the Penitentiary House in Philadelphia, and pay costs.

Same v. William Herd. Two Indictments for Larceny. Defendant pleads guilty. Witnesses: Samuel Selby, George Selby, Judgment that the defendant restore the property to the owner if not already done or pay the value thereof, pay a like sum to the Commonwealth, undergo a servitude in the Common Jail of Bedford County for three months, and pay costs.

Page 267L February 1801
Pennsylvania v. Elizabeth Snelbecker. Constable of St. Claire Township returns Elizabeth Snelbecker for Fornication. Joseph McVicker in $100 for his appearance next May session to testify for Commonwealth.

David McVicker in $100 for his appearance next May 1801 to testify on behalf of the Commonwealth against James Anderson and Edward Daily Supervisors.

Pennsylvania v. Geo Beamon, Joseph Brown, Joseph Walker, Wm Crevingston. Misdemeanor. Ignoramus. Discharged by Proclamation. Geo Beamon, Joseph Brown and Wm Crevingston in $60 for their good behavior particularly toward Martin Loy. John England in $60 Security.

Same v. William Bagley. Assault & Battery. Ignoramus.

Same v. Susanna Fox. Fornication. Ignoramus.

Same v. William Bagley. Tipling House. Ignoramus.

Same v. [cut off]__ncis Dicks. Tipling House. Ignoramus.

Page 267R February 1801 [and May 1801]

Pennsylvania v. Adam Shoemaker. Tipling House. Ignoramus.

May Session 1801.
At Bedford first Monday 1801 before James Riddle and Justices.

Pennsylvania v. Elizabeth Snelbecker. Fornication. True Bill. Joseph McVicker in $50 for his appearance next session to give evidence.

Pennsylvania v. Robert Moore. Assault & Battery. True Bill.
Testify for state: Christian Stophel. John Biringer. For defense: John
Weaverling, Jacob Weaverling. Jury of Alexander McGregor, Jonathan
Hammond, George Ensloe Jr., Frederick Kuntz, Wendle Ott, John Clark,
James McKinney, Andrew Heath, Philip Coleman, Peter [Kinuff?],
Charles Tagert, and James Nelson who find Robert Moore not guilty.

William Brestler fined five shillings for Intoxication and Disorderly
Conduct before open Court.

Page 268L   May 1801
Pennsylvania v. George Kimmell. Assault & Battery.
Testify for state: Henry [Basse?], Jacob McVicker, Jacob Wyant. For
defense: Jacob Miller, Valentine Wyrick, Andrew Mann. Defendant
submits to Court and prays for a small fine. Fine one cent and costs.

Pennsylvania v. Robert Moore. Assault & Battery. True Bill.

Pennsylvania v. John Oakes. Assault & Battery. True Bill.

Pennsylvania v. Benjamin Ferguson. Larceny. Ignoramus

Pennsylvania v. Peter Arnold. Nuisance. True Bill.

Pennsylvania v. Peter Arnold. Nuisance. True Bill.

Page 268R
Cover with large letters reading "Sessions Minutes" with "August
Term" [no year] in typical handwriting.

Page 269L [Blank]

Page 269R   [January, April 1795]
Licensed Tavern Keepers January Session 1795

George Dansdill	John Bridges
Joseph Buck	Valentine Werth
Robert Spencer	George Wilds
Jacob Shock	James Black

Licensed Tavern Keepers April Session 1795

William Ward	Marcus Medscur
Ephraim Wallis	George Humburgh
Joseph Fleckinger	James Taylor
Daniel Bower	Daniel Moor
Henry Shaver	Jacob Four
Derry Ryan	Joseph Lily
Michael Barndollar	George [Wymer?]

Page 270L [August 1795]
Licensed Tavern Keepers August Session 1795
    George Ice   Wm Davis
    George Anderson   John Miller
    Cornelius Martin   Casper Stodler Jr.
    W^m McDermot   George Brimer
    David Jordan   George Dansdell
    George Burker   George Enslow
    Lewis Flick   James Jameson
    Benjn Burd Esq.   Jacob Zigler
    Michael Lowry   Wm Small
    Isaac Bonnett   Joseph Lilly
    John Kimmel   James Taylor
    Derry Ryan   Robt Spencer
    Valentine Wertz   Wm Ward
    George Wilds   Michael Barndollar

Page 270R [November 1795]
Tavern Keepers recommended November Session 1795
    John Fletcher   Bethel Township
    Duncan McVicker Bedford Township
    Enoch Skinner   Dublin Township
    David Beckwith   Providence Township

Page 271L [Blank]

Page 271R
[Aitkins?] v. ~~Robt Galbreath~~. Rule to show cause at November Term why an attachment should not ___ against him for not paying the monies recovered by him George Campbell Esq. Plaintiffs Agents. November Term 96 continued to April Term.

Page 272L
George Kimmell v. Peter Sweitz. N° 10 August Term 1795.
Sworn: Jacob Countryman, Simon Hay, ___ Boyer, John Kimmell, Cornelius Martinus. Jury of Adam Reem, Jese Griffith, John Snider, Wm Hunter, Abraham Ripley, David Kuntz, John Foster, Jacob Steven, Wm Holloway, Jacob Riprogle, John Slouther, and James Bur_[cut off] find for the non suit.

James Black v. Jacob Chamberlin. N° 27 Jan Term 1796.
Sworn: James Puc, Ab^m Faith, James Martin Esq. Jury of James Smith, Lewis Flook, Henry Champine, John Conoway, Peter Foulk, Martin Miren, Nicholas McGuire, Isaac Fickus, William Hay, Anthony Sheets,

Anthony Nawgel, and John Snider find for the Plaintiff one hundred and thirty dollars and six cents.

Page 272R
Adam Miller v. Matthias Zimmerman. August Term 1797.
Testify: George Burkher, Ebraham Cable, James Sprague, Mary Miller. Jury of Nichol__ [cut off] Oster, Bernard Axline, Conrod Nicodemis, John Axline, George ____ [cut off], Ephraim Acres, Henry Werner, Joseph McPharen, John Hipple, Abraham Clevenger, Joseph Lilley, and Jacob Shneb__ [cut off] do say that they find for the [nothing further].

Page 273L
Ephraim Wallace As^{ee} of Peter Swartzwalder v. James Martin and Abraham Martin. No 34 and 35 August 1796. Jury of Fred^k Reichart, Thos Norton, Benjamin Pittman, John Algiers, Philip Croyle, John S___, John Utzler, Robt Ramsay, Francis ____, John Meser, Simon Hay, Benjamin Stevens say that they find for the Plaintiff.

Page 273R [February 1799]
25 February 1799 Philip Wolf came into Court and made it appear to the satisfaction of the Court that a bond bearing date 05 March 1781 for five pounds due to George Woods late of Bedford was Discharged and Paid to the said G. Woods, having heard the testimony of Wm Scovel, Robt Spencer and Phebe Wolf.

25 February. Came into Court Phebe Wolf and asked the Court to appoint Hugh Barclay Esq. Guardian over the Person and Estate of her son Alexander Woods and Thomas Vickroy Guardian of the Person and Estate of her daughter Hetty Barclay Woods both under the age of fourteen years.

Page 274L [bound upside down]   [May 1801]

Recognizances taken in open Court.

John Rowser, William Griffith, and James Gordon bound in $100 each for their attendance next Court to testify against Mary May and others.

Pennsylvania v. John McIntyre, William Shepherd, and Mary May. William Shepherd and Mary May in $200 each for their appearance next session to answer. [struck out] and Nathan Hammond in $200 each for their appearances May 1801.

Frederick Clingerman, John Bumgardner, Christian Stophel and Michael Blue in $100 each for their attendance next session to testify against Robert Moore.

Recognizances before Justices of the Peace.

Commonwealth v. Joseph McDonald. Defendant in $400 to keep the peace. John Shafer in 200 his security.

Commonwealth v. Theophilus Shafer. Defendant in $400 to keep the peace. Stephen Garlick in 200 security.

Terms & Definitions

&c. Archaic form of *et cetera* ("and other things").

Capias. Warrant for arrest often issued on failure to appear in court.

Certiorari. An order from a higher court to a lower court directing the lower court to deliver a case record.

Et al. Latin phrase *et alii* meaning "and others."

Ex parte. Done for the benefit of one party without notice to the other party.

Gaol. Jail.

jur.~ This term will be seen when perusing the original dockets. Where seen, it is an abbreviation indicating that an oath was sworn as a juror. This abbreviation should not be confused with abbreviations for junior, often seen in these records as jun, jun^r, or j^r. To prevent any confusion, these abstracts do not include abbreviations for an oath sworn while they do include notations for junior. This definition is included for those who follow up with research in the original record.

Ignoramus. The grand jury did not find cause for trial and therefore did not return an indictment. The case did not go to trial.

Lying in. Childbirth. Usually used to refer to compensation for expenses of childbirth. When a date is present, that date is likely the birth date of the child.

Misprison of Treason. Seditious or rebellious conduct against the government. Appears in Docket 2 during the American Revolution.

Nolle Prosequi, sometimes seen in these records with variant spellings such as "Noleprosequiti." Formal notice that the prosecution has abandoned the action against the defendant and will not prosecute.

Non Cul. A plea of not guilty.

P. *Per* when seen in context such as *3 shillings P week*.

[Ad] perpetuam rei memoriam. For the perpetual remembrance of the thing. Seen in docket 2 without the word *ad*.

Pounds/shillings/pence. Monetary currency. 2/6 is two shillings and six pence. 20/ is 20 shillings. £1.5.0 is one pound, five shillings, and zero pence.

Presentment. A Grand Jury, without an indictment request from a prosecutor, returns a formal accusation that a crime has been committed.

Profer [proffer]. To put before the Grand Jury for acceptance (ask an indictment).

Recognizance. Bond or surety taken to ensure the appearance of a defendant or witness in court. The phrases "John Smith in £10 for appearance of Fred Jones" or "John Smith tent [sometimes seen *ten't*] £10 for appearance of Fred Jones" mean that John Smith put up ten pounds as recognizance to ensure the appearance of Fred Jones at trial. Often Fred Jones will be the defendant but frequently recognizances ensure the testimony of witnesses. The words *ten't* and *tent* are seen in the original record and have been omitted from these abstracts.

Traverse. Formal denial of allegation.

True Bill. The grand jury found cause for trial and returned an indictment against the defendant.

Ut supra. Latin phrase meaning "as above."

Index

Names in the abstracts retain the spelling seen in the dockets. Since spelling was phonetic during this time period, consider spelling variants when researching specific individuals. Phonetic equivalents may use different first letters for the surname, such as with the Urie surname, found in these records as both Urie and Oury. The modern Pencil/Pensyl surname appears in these dockets as Wensyel.

Names can be difficult to transcribe with ink smudges, bleed though, fading, and sloppy handwriting. If the clerk's sloppy letter *a* looks like an *o*, then the name appears in the these abstracts with an *o*. Thus, sloppy handwriting and deterioration of the original produce still more spelling variants. Proper abstracting practice transcribes the name as written, not subject to any interpretation. So, for example, these abstracts contain the surnames Cessnaa, Cissna, and Cissnay, all variants of the modern Cessna surname. The index attempts to group well known phonetic variants for local family surnames under a single surname entry, but no attempt at such a convenience can be exhaustive. The Cessna spelling variants appear in the index under the surname entry **Cessna (Cessnaa, Cissna, Cissnay)**.

Underscores denote portions of the original that cannot be read and this index retains any underscores. Allow for the possibility that a portion (or perhaps all) of a name could not be read.

As there is only one instance in these dockets where a surname is provided for a slave, such individuals are indexed with unknown surname "___." Where the dockets identify an individual as "negro" the index includes the notation "[Negro]" after the given name.

___
    ___, 251, 254
    __derick, 182
    Bett [Negro], 264
    Bob [Negro], 267
    Christina, 266
    Daniel, 229
    David, 219
    Francis, 285
    Frederick, 177
    George, 113, 285
    Hagard [Negro], 264
    Hannah [Negro], 224
    Henry, 12, 256
    Isaac, 257
    Jacob, 216, 270, 274
    James, 264
    Jn°, 275
    John, 106, 119, 125, 167, 215, 243, 265
    Joseph, 274, 275
    Peter, 261
    Peter [Negro], 226, 245, 254
    Philip, 140
    Rachel, 265
    Sal [Negro], 260

Thomas, 248
Ulrich, 113
William, 107, 108, 119, 149, 190, 234
___ail
  John, 119
___annard
  John, 189
___ay
  Sam¹, 274
___burgh
  John, 121
___crow
  George, 168
___en_ff
  Peter, 242
___ger
  Matthias, 180
___ides
  Henry, 164
___ind
  Jeremiah, 193
___ins
  Michael, 272
___iston
  Andrew, 167
___key
  Benson, 176
___lack
  ___, 196
___ner
  Samuel, 164
___olye
  Charles, 119
___or
  John, 167
___oras
  Peter, 231
___rimly
  John, 177
___son
  Robert, 253
___tchfield
  Nathaniel, 188
___ther
  Thomas, 174
___ton
  Robert, 170
  Sam¹, 274
___tor
  John, 202
___tz
  ___, 118
___y
  Thomas, 43
___zer
  W^m, 270

—A—

A___
  Henry, 215
Abbot (Abbet, Abbit)
  Benjamin, 104, 113, 119, 132
  Elizabeth, 132, 134
Able
  Samuel, 143
Abraham (Abrahams, Abarahms)
  B___, 189
  Barzel (Bezil), 190, 193
  Enoch, 55, 62
  Henry, 36, 47, 49, 53, 56, 57, 58, 59, 62, 66, 94, 97, 104, 112, 118, 176, 190, 193
  Reuben (Ruben), 189, 190, 193
Abram (Abrams)
  Barzel (Barzil), 191, 194, 195
  Henry, 104, 171, 177, 190, 191, 192, 195
  Reuben (Reubin), 191, 192, 194, 195
  Thomas, 128
Acres. *See* Akers
Ad___
  Scott, 243
Adam (Adams)
  An___, 191
  Elijah, 34, 205, 224, 244, 246, 255, 281
  Elijah, Jr., 159
  Ephraim, 257, 272, 276
  Jacob, 42, 91, 275, 278
  Joseph, 214
  Rachel, 278
  Robert (Rob¹), 68, 157, 162, 181, 182, 183, 193, 198, 223, 226, 228, 229, 241, 244, 246, 250, 252, 254, 256, 274
  Robert [Jr.], 183
  Robert, Big., 198
  Solomon, 139, 145, 223, 229, 279

INDEX

Addison
    John, 158
Agnew
    James, 212, 262, 264
Ainsley
    George, 266
Aitkins
    ___, 284
Akers (Aker). *See also* Eaker
    Abiah (Abia), 149, 159, 202
    Ephraim, 260, 270, 271, 285
    Robert (Robt), 270, 271
    William, 153
Albright
    Casper, 140
    John, 126, 127, 128, 155
Alexander
    Alex^r, 209, 220
    Hugh, 184, 242
    Jacob, 18, 55
    James, 240
    John, 92
    Joseph, 121
    William (Willm, W^m), 92, 121, 139, 166, 198, 209, 212, 219, 244, 246
    William, Jr., 202
Algiers (Algire)
    John, 279, 285
Allehouser
    Frederick, 136
Allen
    Andrew, 28, 43, 44, 46, 54
    John, 146, 181, 255
    M___, 278
Allison
    John, 257
    Robert, 241
Am___
    John, 216
Amberson
    Matthias, 56
Ambrose (Ambroser, Ambrozer, Ambrosure)
    Frederick (Fred^k), 29, 34, 66, 97, 101, 105, 125
Ambrosure
    Matthias, 274
Americk. *See also* Emerick
    Andrew, 155

Ames
    Nathaniel, 208
Ammor___
    John, 216
Amorine (Amrine)
    Abraham, 171, 173
    Frederick, 171, 173
    George, 114, 116, 117, 118, 177
    Henry, 107, 117, 118, 186, 188
    Henry, Jr., 185, 186, 188
    Henry, the elder, 186
Anderson
    ___, 118, 254
    __is, 118
    Daniel, 143, 152, 197
    George, 226, 284
    J., D^r, 265
    Jacob, 190
    James, 8, 11, 12, 14, 25, 30, 34, 41, 51, 63, 66, 90, 98, 104, 110, 125, 126, 136, 145, 168, 173, 187, 195, 196, 221, 223, 224, 228, 237, 274, 280
    James, Jr., 146, 166, 167, 195, 255, 256
    James, Sr., 202
    Jno, 151
    John, 88, 89, 151, 156, 175, 180, 212, 220, 221
    John, Dr., 200, 242, 243
    Richard, 96
    Robert (Robt), 200, 216, 221, 254
    Samuel (Saml), 17, 19, 22, 32, 36, 38, 39, 45, 46, 69, 97, 105, 108, 111, 118, 176, 178, 181, 182, 194
    Thomas (Thos), 50, 58, 59, 79, 94, 104, 108, 117, 118, 124, 153, 160, 170, 174, 175, 176, 192, 196, 197, 200, 202, 223, 224, 237
    William (W^m), 123, 129, 136
Angle. *See also* Engle, Ingle
    Clement, 104, 113
Ankeny (Ankney)
    Christian, 219
    George, 235
    Peter, 188
Ansley. *See also* Ensley
    Geo., 268

Anthony, 258
   Christian, 103, 113, 149, 181
   Peter, 166
Appleman
   Conrod, 239, 277
Armit
   Samuel, 49
Armstrong
   George, 251
   Henry, 64, 99, 114, 140, 178, 179, 195
   John, 125, 136, 235
Arndt
   ____, 224
   Jacob, 224
Arnold (Arnolt)
   Peter, 259, 260, 265, 270, 272, 280, 283
   Thomas, 256
Arter
   Matthew, 131
Ash
   Adam, 103
   Henry, 168
   John, 10
Ashbaugh
   John, 195
Ashman
   George, 80, 123, 130
   Jacob, 119
Assher
   Anthony, 141
Atlee (Atley)
   Conrod, 253, 255
Augustine (Augistine)
   Peter, 120, 202, 236
Auld
   Doc^t, 227, 228
Axline. *See also* Exline
   Adam, 249, 252
   Bernard (Barnard), 260, 265, 285
   John, 260, 285

—B—

B___
   Barbara, 185
   John, 264
   Jonathan, 167
   L___, 252
   Peter, 104
   Samuel, 243
   Thomas, 140
B__gh
   Philp, 140
B__man
   Jacob, 23
B__res
   Henry, 218
B__z
   Jacob, 234
Baer
   Jacob, 277
Bagley (Bagly, Beeghley, Beghley, Beighley, Bieghley, Bigehley, Bighley, Bughly)
   Michael, 104, 120, 122, 139, 140, 149, 158, 188
   William, 251, 281, 282
Baker
   ____, 257
   __est, 182
   Arnest (Arnet, Arnst), 53, 119, 184
   Ernest (Earnest, Earnist), 59, 63, 98, 104, 108, 114, 115, 116, 123, 166, 169, 170, 176, 179, 202, 230, 232
   Henry, 143, 215
   Jacob, 167, 199, 210
   Peter, 162, 214
   Richard, 91, 248, 268, 269, 279
   Valentine, 128
   William (W^m), 137, 170, 214, 231
Bale
   John, 29, 30, 31, 33
Balla (Ballah). *See also* Bella
   James, 139, 150, 220
Ballam
   Adam, 143
Baltzer
   Mary, 13
Bam
   Adam, 202
Baman
   William, 65
Banfield
   Thomas, 25
Bar
   Michael, 272
Barcidol
   Joseph, 140

Barclay
  Hetty, 285
  Hugh, 82, 86, 87, 88, 123, 124, 125, 129, 132, 133, 136, 139, 142, 144, 147, 149, 153, 155, 157, 158, 161, 184, 189, 190, 191, 192, 197, 199, 201, 204, 208, 213, 215, 219, 226, 240, 243, 245, 249, 251, 252, 264, 267, 271, 285
Barger
  John, 136
Bark__
  Peter, 126
Barker (Barkher)
  George, 175
  Valentine, 127
Barkey
  Jacob, 104
Barndollar (Barndoler, Barndoller)
  ____, 251, 257
  Daniel (Dan¹), 251, 281, 282
  Jacob, 251, 264, 281
  Mich., 264
  Michael, 137, 166, 174, 175, 197, 202, 220, 230, 237, 238, 243, 244, 246, 255, 260, 278, 283, 284
  Peter, 264
Barndt
  Peter, 238
Barne (Barnes). *See also* Barns
  Abel, 262
  Caleb, 248
Barnett (Barnet, Barnets)
  ____, 65
  Jacob, 244, 246
  James, 34, 66, 101, 113, 125
  Peter, 174, 197, 237, 239
Barney
  Thomas, 48
Barnhardt (Barnhart)
  George, 251
  George P., 281
  Jacob, 168, 172, 201, 204, 227
  Peter, 268
Barns. *See also* Barne
  Caleb, 262
Barrel
  Samuel, 17

Barrett
  Samuel, 9
Barrick
  Samuel, 69
  William, 55
Barton
  Adam, 261
  Elijah (Elija), 261, 271, 275
  Elisha, 202
  George, 124, 139, 153, 159, 267
  Noah, 271
Basse
  Henry, 283
Bastion (Bostian)
  George, 230, 242
Bates
  David, 118
  Henry, 275
Bateson
  Hannah, 136
Bauman
  John, 222
Bays
  Thomas, 19, 22, 27
Bea_ley
  Frederick, 156
Beach__
  Sam, 266
Beachley
  Henry, 242
Beagle. *See* Beegle
Bealer (Bealor). *See also* Beeler
  Christian, 11, 16
  Christopher, 16
  Joseph, 15, 23, 25, 26
Beam
  Henry, 140
Beamon. *See also* Beeman
  Geo., 282
Bean
  Ludwic, 143
Beans
  John, 10, 13, 25
Bear
  Jacob, 219, 244, 246
  Michael, 244, 246
Beard
  William, 40, 42
Beatty (Beatte, Beaty)
  Edward, 112, 113

James, 54, 207, 225
Richard, 248
Tabth[a], 253
Thomas, 253
William, 136, 149, 158, 241
Bechel
    Sam[l], 275
Bechtel
    Jacob, 258
    Samuel, 212, 243
Becker
    Henry, 244, 246
Beckwith
    David, 220, 279, 284
Bee__l. *See also* Beegle
    Charles, 204
Beechey
    Abraham, 140
Beeckley
    Henry, 230
Beeghley. *See* Bagley,
Beegle (Beagle, Beighel, Bigle)
    Charles, 272
    Dav[d], 254
    Gavin, 126, 128
    Henry, 275
Beeler. *See also* Bealer
    George, 223
Beeman. *See also* Beamon
    Chrisley, 99
    Christopher, 64
    George, 252
    William, 100
Beetle
    Benj[n], 259
    Thomas, 260
Beghley (Beighley). *See* Bagley
Beighel. *See* Beegle
Bell
    David, 117, 242
    James, 172
    John, 35
    Joseph, 104, 111, 167, 195, 250
    Philip, 15
    Robert, 14, 24
    Theopolis, 151
    William, 107
Bella. *See also* Balla
    James, 42, 45, 46, 49, 50, 53

Bellows
    James, 34
Belt
    John, 244, 246
Belyen. *See* Bilyew
Bener
    Samuel, 259
Benford
    James, 19, 23
Bennett
    Joseph, 23
Berger
    John, 188
Berkey
    ____, 121
    Abraham, 125
    Jacob, 120
Berkshire
    Dickey, 184
Berringer (Biringer)
    John, 252, 281, 283
Best (Betz)
    Henry, 261, 281
Beyer
    Joseph, 155
Beyman
    George, 238
Biddle (Bittle)
    John, 119, 125, 195
Bieghley (Bigehley, Bighley). *See* Bagley
Bigg__
    He__, 220
Bigham
    Hugh, 28
Bigle. *See* Beegle
Bilew (Bilyew, Bilyu)
    John, 58, 59, 63, 94, 95, 98
    Uriah, 119
Billow
    James, 180, 188
Bird. *See also* Burd
    James, 69
Biringer. *See* Berringer
Bishop
    __my, 162
    George, 166, 202, 209, 219
    Jacob, 264, 278
    James, 263

Jonathan, 22
Bittinger
  Henry, 125
Black
  James, 38, 55, 120, 127, 139, 140, 148, 149, 150, 167, 173, 174, 176, 202, 205, 221, 222, 269, 283, 284
  Janet (Jennet, Jennett), 203, 205
  Jn°, 269
  Job, 190
  John, 155, 162, 203, 204, 205, 206, 279
  Paul, 193
  William, 68
Blackburn
  Anthony, 158, 223, 226, 240
  Thomas, 68, 120, 144, 158, 160, 172, 195
Blackwell
  Nathaniel, 138
Blackwood
  John, 275
Blain (Blaine)
  Ephraim, 260
Blair
  Brice, 112, 114, 115, 116, 179, 181, 244, 246, 249, 252
  Brice, Jr., 181
  Henry, 203
  John, 131, 264
  Nancy, 203
  Sarah, 203
  Thomas (Thos), 98, 121, 130, 131, 132, 136, 178, 203, 206, 220, 232, 233
Blocher
  Jacob, 239
Blodget (Bludget). *See also* Budget
  Alisha, 201, 249
Blough
  Jacob, 219
Blue
  Barnabas, 230
  Bernard, 153
  Michael, 236, 253, 285
Bo___
  Daniel, 239
  Jonathan, 244, 246
Bocher
  Peter, 44, 46, 51

Bodder
  Nicholas, 214
Bogart
  Margaret, 189
Bogs
  And^w, 69
Bole
  A____, 188
Bonjour (Bonjoir)
  Andrew, 12, 20
Bonnel
  John, 179
Bonner
  John, 177
Bonnet (Bonnett)
  ____, 118
  David, 92
  Isaac, 88, 220, 229, 238, 239, 253, 255, 262, 269, 277, 284
  J., 227
  Jacob, 87, 89, 90, 91, 173, 229, 259
  Jn°, 180
  John, 104, 109, 110, 111, 115, 118, 154, 173, 174, 175, 176, 177, 178, 180, 192, 196, 205, 209, 213, 237
Boolman
  Abraham (Ab^m), 244, 246, 250, 252
Boor (Boore)
  Jacob, 157
  Nicholas, 251, 271, 272, 274, 281
Bor___
  Fred^k, 275
  Jacob, 275
Borden
  James, 13
Boreland. *See* Borland
Boreman (Boerman, Boorman, Boremand). *See also* Bowman
  ____, 254
  Jac., 275
  Jacob, 166, 214, 217, 221, 254, 255, 256, 264, 267
Borland (Boreland)
  Andrew, 149, 150, 157, 158
  Saml, 104
Borndrager
  Andrew, 139

Bostian. *See* Bastion
Bough
    Peter, 218
Bow
    Nicholas, 264
Bowen
    Jonathan, 268
    Thos, 274
Bower (Bowers)
    Adam, 206, 207, 212, 233
    Andrew, 210
    Barnet, 218
    Bernard, 218, 248
    Conrod, 262
    Daniel, 233, 234, 283
    George, 236
    Jacob, 261
    John, 211, 215
    Margaret, 215
    Peter, 234
Bowler
    Jacob, 104
Bowman. *See also* Boreman
    Jacob, 265
Bowser
    George, 228, 231, 242, 279
    John, 53, 215, 274
    Michael, 107
Boyce
    John, 65, 100, 163, 170, 281
Boyd
    Andrew, 121
    James, 249, 261
    John, 182, 184, 185, 187, 189
    Robert, 157, 185, 191, 248, 249
    Samuel, 249
    William (Willm, W^m), 119, 124, 131, 137, 138, 139, 141, 146, 155, 181, 182, 184, 189, 190, 240
    William, Jr., 124, 137, 142
Boyer
    ____, 284
    George, 124
    John, 114
    Joseph, 159, 244, 246, 249, 274
Boyle
    Charles, 34, 35, 39, 69, 120
    Joseph, 252
Boys
    John, 164, 231

Brackenridge
    Hugh Montgomery, 192
    Thomas, 123, 183
Bradshaw
    David, 117, 147
    Mary, 242
    Robert (Robt), 9, 10, 20, 23, 29, 30, 31, 33, 56, 59, 62, 95, 98, 182, 188, 189, 190, 191, 242
    Robert, Jr., 180
    Thomas, 67, 68, 116, 159, 170, 209, 242, 253
Brady
    John, 232
    Morris, 16
Brandon
    Catherine, 210, 211, 214
Brannan
    David, 164
Brant
    Abraham, 251
Brate
    John, 247
Brayler
    Emanuel, 227
Breathead (Brathead). *See also* Brothead
    Edward, 180
    John, 177, 180
Breight
    Philip, 173
Brenner
    George, 119
    Susanna, 172
Brent
    George, 9, 17
Brestler
    William, 283
Breton
    George, 23
Brewer
    John, 227
Bridges (Briges)
    James, 238
    John, 55, 175, 181, 182, 205, 218, 223, 227, 238, 248, 283
    Margaret, 223, 227, 241, 245
Briggs
    Jo., 247
    Joseph, 245

Brimer
  George, 284
Brindle
  Joseph, 214
Britt (Brit, Brits, Britz)
  John, 222, 231, 242, 247, 270, 271, 279
Broen
  Henry, 112
Bromfield
  William, 61, 96
Broombach
  Jacob, 217
Brooner
  Henry, 244, 246
Brothead. *See also* Breathead
  John, 158
Brouch
  George, 153
Browler
  Michael, 234
Brown
  Benjamin (Banjamin), 130, 131, 134, 138, 141, 234, 235
  Daniel, 130, 131, 134, 138, 141
  David, 27, 206
  Henry, 112, 113, 180, 200, 209, 221, 222
  Hugh, 51
  Jacob, 117
  James, 182, 189
  Joseph, 252, 282
  Joshua, 130, 131, 134, 138, 141
  Richard, 12, 15, 16, 22, 24, 28, 37, 40, 42, 43, 47, 50
  William, 255
  William M., 157
Browner
  George, 44, 46, 47, 49
Brownfield
  Empson, 14
Brubaker
  John, 244, 246
Bruner (Brunner)
  George, 140, 181
  Henry, 140, 216, 219, 264, 272
  Jacob, 171
  Stephen, 168, 169, 171, 202, 216
  Susana (Susanna), 169, 171

Bryan
  George, 78
Bryner
  George, 237
Buchan__
  George, 127
Buchanan (Buchannan, Buchannon)
  ____, 257
  George, 115, 128, 193, 261
  Hester, 248
Bucher
  Peter, 181
Buck
  David, 189
  John, 186
  Jonathan, 121
  Joseph, 218, 220, 238, 241, 283
  Thomas (Th^o), 56, 58, 84, 94, 120, 155, 157, 161, 162, 170, 179, 185, 190, 208, 209, 220
Buck__
  ____, 266
Buckley
  Henry, 203
Budget. *See also* Blodget
  Alisha, 200
Bugh
  Peter, 214
Bughly. *See* Bagley
Bulger
  Laurence, 261, 271, 275
Bullman
  Abraham, 136
Buman
  William, 59
Bumgardner
  John, 285
Bur__
  Andrew, 149
  James, 284
Burd. *See also* Bird
  ____, 118
  Benjamin (Benjmin, Benj., Benjn), 14, 37, 84, 86, 87, 119, 157, 158, 161, 166, 174, 175, 193, 194, 195, 221, 222, 225, 239, 271, 277, 279, 280, 284
  Elizabeth, 118
  James, 205

John, 14, 16, 23, 24, 28, 31, 34, 36,
  40, 41, 66, 67, 69, 187, 188, 195
Thomas, 28, 190
William, 245
Burg (Burge)
  John, 21, 186
Burger (Burker, Burkher)
  George, 174, 175, 238, 247, 284,
    285
  John, 159, 219, 223, 226, 240
Burget (Burgat). *See also* Burket,
  Burger
  George, 65, 195
Burk
  John, 19, 20
  Thomas, 136, 166
Burke
  George, 153
Burker. *See* Burger
Burket (Burkhart). *See also* Burget,
  Burger
  Catherine, 225
  George, 100, 117, 136, 186
  Humphrey, 267
  Israel, 158, 235
Burkham
  Charles, 69
Burns
  James, 239, 257
Burntrager
  Christian, 219
Burress
  Henry, 218
Burse
  Jacob, 239
Burtnet
  Adam, 155
Burton
  Joshua, 181
Buse
  Jacob, 241
Bush
  Henry, 150, 222
  Jacob, Jr., 188
  Peter, 213, 215
  Thomas (Thos), 59, 184, 187
Buterbaugh (Butterbaugh)
  Jacob, 87, 173, 222

Buzzard
  Abraham (Ab^m), 216, 253, 255,
    263, 264, 270, 276, 278, 279
Byerley (Byerly)
  Conrod, 262
  Michael, 34

—C—

C__
  Ann, 120
  Isaac, 156
  John, 125, 195
  Richard, 118
C___n
  John, 178
C__vin
  John, 176
Ca__
  James, 25
Cable
  Abraham, 80, 83, 92, 104, 105, 106,
    125, 129, 132, 135, 139, 142,
    144, 157, 158, 161, 162, 164,
    176, 178
  Abraham, Jr., 234
  Ebraham, 285
  Jacob, 45, 46, 55, 62, 66, 97, 210
  Martin, 157
Cadawallader (Cadwalader)
  Jacob, 173
  John, 157
Cagg. *See* Kegg
Cahil
  Edwd, 69
Cairns. *See* Karns, Kerns
  Michael, 14
Caldwell (Calwell)
  Charles, 29, 30, 31, 39
  David, 111, 120, 122, 126
  Joseph, 14
  Matthew, 139, 145, 146
  Robert, 36, 41
  William, 23
Callihan. *See* Celihan
Camp
  Edward, 125
Campbell (Campbel, Campble)
  Elizabeth, 36
  George, 192, 284
  John, 8, 14, 22, 69, 131

INDEX 299

Terrence, 128, 170
Thomas, 12, 15, 19, 21, 23
Canber
   John, 188
Cannan (Canan)
   Henry, 130, 135
   John, 132
Cannon
   John, 81
Cap
   Peter, 123
Car___
   John, 120
Cardue
   George, 232
Carlisle
   David, 114, 115, 155, 182
   William, 152, 155
Carmack (Carmick)
   Richard L., 227, 228, 250
Carmichael. *See also* Charmichael
   ___mes, 120
   James, 26, 80, 108, 111, 113, 176
   John, 120
   Samuel, 104
Carnachan
   James, 15, 17
   John, 16
Carnivan
   John, 182, 183
Carpenter
   Matthias, 127
Carr. *See also* Karr, Kerr
   Samuel, 193
Carroll (Carral)
   Charles, 254
   Joseph, 38
Carson
   David, 262
   James, 119
Carswell
   James, 180
Carter
   Rachel, 160, 162, 175, 176
   Thomas, 186, 220, 223, 226, 240
   William (Will[m]), 126, 144, 162, 167, 168, 169
Carvel
   James, 27
Carver
   Christian, 244, 246
   John, 150
Casebeer
   John, 177
Casebold
   John, 13
Cashman
   Abraham (Ab[m]), 251, 261
   Abram, 213
   George, 251, 252, 281
   Mary, 156, 157
Casnor
   Jacob, 30
Casteel
   Shadrick (Shadwick, Shederick), 41, 98, 179, 180, 181, 184, 188, 194
Cav___
   James, 15
Cavel
   James, 15
Cavener (Cavnor)
   Edward, 237
   Jacob, 31
Celihan
   Thomas, 253
Cellars (Cellers)
   Joseph, 56, 58, 59, 94, 124
Cells. *See also* Cills, Sells, Sills
   George, 97
Cerly
   Matthias, 177
Cessler
   And[w], 242
Cessna (Cessnaa, Cisna, Cissna, Cissnay)
   Charles (Cha[s]), 8, 20, 23, 26, 27, 34, 43, 46, 47, 51, 103, 108, 110
   Elizabeth (Elisabeth), 210, 211, 215
   Evan, 29, 30, 31, 39
   John, 13, 17, 18, 19, 23, 26, 28, 32, 36, 43, 47, 64, 79, 80, 81, 84, 89, 103, 105, 107, 111, 115, 116, 118, 123, 125, 129, 132, 133, 136, 137, 139, 142, 144, 146, 149, 155, 162, 166, 169, 179, 181, 183, 188, 193, 195, 210, 211, 215, 216, 218, 243, 257, 258, 270, 271, 279

John, Jr., 124, 207, 209, 213, 215,
    217, 243, 268, 276, 278
Jonathan, 43, 53, 55, 60, 61, 64, 67,
    95, 96, 99, 139, 150, 158, 166,
    209, 213, 219, 223, 226, 240,
    257, 258, 268, 269, 270, 271,
    276
Stephen, 60, 96
William, 91, 242, 265
Ch__ington
    John, 162
Chamberlain (Chamberlin)
    Jacob, 127, 230, 255, 284
Chambers
    James, 52
Champine
    Henry, 257, 284
Chance
    Samuel, 203, 236
Chaney (Chany, Cheany, Cheney, Cheny)
    Benjamin, 194
    Edward (Edwd), 194, 209, 220
    Evan, 265
    Gilbert, 188
    Lewis, 271, 272, 274
    Nathan, 216, 227, 228
    Nathaniel, 236
    Thomas, 22, 27
Chapman
    Henry, 151, 152, 155, 156
    Henry, Jr., 151, 152, 156
    John, 151, 152, 156
    John, Jr., 156
    Nathaniel, 151, 152
Charier
    Giles, 16
Charmichael. *See also* Carmichael
Cheany (Cheney, Cheny). *See* Chaney
Check (Cheeck)
    John, 100, 101
Cherry (Cherrys)
    Benjamin, 140, 159, 193
    Evan, 267
    Raloh, 25
Chiffinton
    John, 58
    Thomas, 58

Chilcot (Chilcott, Chilcotte)
    Benjamin, 130, 134, 138, 139, 141
    Humphrey (Umprey), 130, 134,
        136, 138, 139, 141
    John, 130, 134, 138, 139, 141
    Robison (Robeson), 65, 101, 130,
        134, 138, 139, 141
Childs
    Isaac, 249
Chrisman (Christman). *See also* Crisman
    John, 98, 198, 230, 232, 240, 244,
        246, 247, 274
Christ
    Nicholas, 10, 13
Christy
    William, 23
Chuck
    John, 65, 66
Cills. *See also* Cells, Sells, Sills
    Dorothy, 103
    George, 62, 103
Cizer
    Lewis, 216
Claar (Clarr)
    Georg, 255
    John, 247
Clagage (Claggage). *See* Clugage
Clapper
    Henry, 220, 245, 248, 262
Clark (Clarke)
    Daniel, 256, 268, 269
    James, 68
    Job, 189, 191, 194
    John, 167, 214, 223, 243, 250, 283
    Nathan, 243
    Stephen, 223
    Walter, 22, 46, 49, 50, 53
    William (W^m), 66, 88, 240, 274
    William, Jr., 68
Claudfelty. *See* Cloudfelty
Clem
    Martha, 105
    Samuel, 11, 13
Clevenger
    Abraham, 150, 167, 208, 213, 285
    William (W^m), 207
Cline. *See also* Kline
    Christopher, 253
    Henry, 124

Jacob, 147, 156, 174
Nicholas (Nicklas), 110, 111, 112
Clingerman
  Frederick, 285
Clink
  John, 127, 128, 135, 140, 150
Cloudfelty (Claudfelty)
  Solomon, 219, 244, 246
Clugage (Cluggage)
  ___, 118
  Francis, 66, 111, 127, 128, 188
  Gavin (Gaven), 26, 35, 39, 65, 101
  George, 113, 123
  James, 39, 40, 113, 176, 188
  Ja^s, 69
  Robert (Robt), 8, 9, 12, 15, 26, 30, 35, 39, 41, 77, 78, 81, 129, 188, 194
Co__
  Valentine, 162
Co__nning
  John, 170
Coal
  Margaret, 127
Coats
  Jonathan, 53, 54
Cocher
  Philip, 234
Cochran
  John, 228, 239
Coffman. *See also* Cuffman
Coffman (Cofman)
  Ann, 21
  George, 155, 244, 246
Cogan
  Nicholas, 233
Coil. *See also* Coyle
  James, 180, 183
Colbert
  William (Willm, W^m), 163
Cole
  Broad, 44
Coleburn
  Robert, 158, 225, 227
Colegate. *See* Colgate
Coleman (Colemane, Colmane)
  George, 125, 133, 203, 214, 215
  Jacob, 18
  Mackem, 55

Philip, 136, 145, 162, 209, 213, 215, 217, 243, 283
Colepenny (Colpenny). *See also* Corpenny
  John, 142, 167, 216, 238, 239, 269
Colgate (Colegate)
  Asaph Moore, 130, 131, 134, 138, 139, 141
Collay
  Joseph, 119
Collins
  Benjamin, 15
  Henry, 224
  Luke (Looke), 27, 69
  Moses, 224
  Rachel, 224
Colpenny. *See* Colepenny
Colvin
  William, 33
Comb (Combes, Combs, Coomb, Coombs)
  Edward, 12, 17, 29, 32, 33, 46
  John, 17
  Joseph, 29, 32, 33
Comfort (Cumfort)
  Catherine, 251, 281
  Philip, 251, 281
Comp
  Richard, 118
Compton
  William, 66
Conner (Connor)
  Edward (Edwd), 142, 144, 146, 152, 155, 236, 270
  James, 235
  John, 14
  Mary, 112, 114, 116
  Patrick, 116
Conway (Conoway)
  John, 284
  Thomas, 184
Cook
  Thomas, 16
Coomb (Coombs). *See* Comb
Coontz (Coons, Coots, Counts, Countz, Cuntz). *See also* Koontz
  Christina, 135
  Cristine, 132
  Fred^k, 275
  Henry, 274, 281

L___, 142
Lorentz, 36
Michael, 142
Nicholas, 119
Peter, 232
Peter, Jr., 232
Philip, 192
Samuel, 232
Susanna, 211
Copenhoven (Copenhover, Covanhoven, Covenhoven)
Balser (Baltzer, Balzer), 129, 136, 141
John, 239
Joseph, 216, 238
Cor___
Isaac, 156
Cormming
John, 48
Corn
Ebenezer, 10
George, 10, 33
Solomon, 10
Cornelius
John, 127, 128
Joseph, 181
William, 130, 134, 138
Cornell (Cornel)
Christopher, 207
Jane, 268
W^m, 275
Corpenny. See also Colepenny
John, 159
Cotswell
Charles, 38
Cotton
William, 130, 134, 138
Coulter
John, 218, 250, 279
Thomas (Thos), 9, 15, 17, 33, 45, 54, 69, 77, 78, 82, 85, 123, 124, 125, 127, 129, 132, 133, 136, 139, 142, 149, 155, 157, 158, 161, 162, 166, 181, 185, 188, 215, 225, 226
Countryman
Jacob, 202, 240, 244, 246, 284

Counts (Countz). See Coontz, Koontz
Covalt
Abraham, 29, 32, 33, 56, 108, 111
Bethuel (Betheul, Bethul, Bithul), 83, 119, 142, 147, 149, 151, 155, 162, 166, 170
Covanhoven (Covenhoven). See Copenhoven
Covar
Peter, 216
Covel
William, 21
Cover
Nicholas, 233
Cow
Valentine, 206, 220
Cowan
Edward (Edwd), 149, 274
William (W^m), Jr., 145
Cowel (Cowell)
Christian, 209, 219
Christopher, 162, 202
Isaac, 139, 243
James, 267
Jane, 267
Cox
Conrod, 270, 271
Ezekiel (Ezekial), 202, 209, 219, 261
Jacob, 249
Joseph, 27
Michael, 18
Coyle (Coyl). See also Coil
Brian (Bryan), 30, 31
Christian, 178
Daniel, 239, 277, 278
James, 80, 83, 104, 113, 132, 139
John, 83, 123
Samuel, 174, 175, 237
Cra__
John, 140
Cra_m_
John, 135
Craig
James, 69
Samuel, 22, 27
Craton
Faithful, 240

Cravens (Cravins)
  John, 133, 137, 138, 152, 153, 154, 155, 190, 191, 192
Crawford
  Ann, 51
  James, 275
  William, 14, 15, 77
Cray
  Matthias, 246
Creamer. *See also* Kreamer
  Adam, 244, 246
  Casper, 277
  Gasper, 281
Creechlow. *See* Critchlow
Creighton (Creaton, Creton)
  Faithful, 213, 219, 223, 226, 230, 232
  Henry, 19, 22, 27
  John, 23, 37, 41, 43
Crevingston (Creviston). *See* Crivingstone
Crise
  Adam, 124, 143
  Frederick, 153, 154, 156
Crisman (Crissman). *See also* Chrisman
  John, 45, 46, 63, 255
  William, 91
Criswell
  Walter, 122
Critchfield. *See also* __tchfield
  Joshua, 248, 277
  Nath[l], 150
Critchlow (Creechlow)
  William, 38, 56
Crivingstone (Crivistone, Criviston, Crevingston, Creviston). *See also* Grivingston, Livingston
  Jacob, 192, 271
  Jacob, Sr., 251
  Joseph, Jr., 281
  Nicholas, 153, 154, 179, 189
  W[m], 252, 282
Croil. *See* Croyal
Croll
  John, 150, 159, 167
Cromwell
  Tho[s], 254

Crosby
  James, 218
Crosier
  Thomas, 47
Crossan (Crosan, Crossen, Crossin)
  Edward, 119
  James, 133
  John, 208
  Samuel (Sam[l]), 142, 144, 146
  Samuel, Jr., 83, 143, 152, 155
  Thomas, 36, 48, 84, 104, 105, 113, 129, 132, 142, 146, 147, 188
Croy
  Matthias, 220, 244
Croyle (Croyal, Croil). *See also* Croll
  Adam, 68, 139, 140, 157, 164, 202, 220, 268, 269
  Charles, 220
  Daniel, 150
  George, 141, 150, 157, 200, 231, 261
  James, 104
  John, 250
  Philip, 285
  Thomas, 8, 9, 25, 32, 107
Cryder
  Michael, 20, 31, 32, 36, 38, 39, 41, 45, 46, 97, 111, 113, 129, 180, 188
Cuffman. *See also* Coffman
  Jacob, 234, 236
Culbertson
  James, 14, 15, 51, 52, 55
  Robert, 8, 14, 15, 19, 21, 32, 34, 37, 46, 52, 53, 59, 113, 137, 180, 189, 198, 236
Cumfort. *See* Comfort
Cummins
  John, 118
  Joseph, 184
Cunningham
  James, 18, 29, 32, 34, 35, 36, 41
  John, 18, 32
Curry
  James, 64, 99, 100
  John, 64, 99, 100
Curtz. *See also* Kurtz
  Jacob, 215

John, 156, 174
Cutchel
  John, 258
Cyphers
  Daniel, 279
Cysor
  Jacob, 235

—D—

D___
  Jeremaih, 140
Da___
  Andrew, 14
Dady
  John, 156, 159, 162
Dagay
  Jacob, 176, 177
Daily (Dailey, Dayley)
  Edward, 250, 268, 274, 280, 282
  James, 12
Dalton
  James, 12, 14, 37, 171, 229, 232
  Thomas, 52
Dan__, 249
Dandsdell (Dandsdill). See Dansdell
Daniel (Daniels, Dannels). See also Dansals
  Daniel, 91, 270, 271
  Edward, 149, 220, 222
  Isaac, 244, 246, 248
  Samuel, 35, 39, 46, 49, 50, 53, 188
Danilap. See also Dunlap
  John, 183
Dansals. See also Daniel
  Edward, 275
Dansdell (Dandsdell, Dandsdill, Dansdale, Dansdill, Dantzdell, Danzell, Dantzell)
  Geo., 254, 263
  George, 144, 159, 209, 238, 239, 242, 243, 274, 277, 283, 284
Dart
  John, 104, 113, 180
Daul__
  Matthiu, 126
Davebaugh (Davibaugh). See also Defebaugh, Dieffebaugh
  ___, 183

Adam, 225, 233
Casper, 38, 40, 43, 106, 114, 115, 116, 176, 183
Daniel, 206
Jacob, 147, 167, 225, 233
James, 200
John, 120, 161, 174, 175, 196, 205, 223, 231, 233
David
  Catherine, 164, 175
  E___, 175
  Eliezer (Elazir), 110, 118, 170
  Katherine the younger, 118
  Thomas, 115
Davidson (Davison)
  Hugh, 82, 104, 113, 125, 178, 180, 188
  Samuel (Saml), 29, 32, 44, 45, 54, 78, 79, 82, 83, 106, 113, 117, 122, 139, 142, 180, 228, 229, 255, 261
Davies
  John, 175
  Joseph, 184
  Joshua, 183
  William, 184
Davis
  B., 183
  Bartholomew (Bartholomus), 39, 40, 114, 115, 120, 183
  Eliezer, 179
  James, 120
  John, 88, 93, 140, 141, 175, 212, 239, 278, 279
  Joshua, 57, 58, 94, 184, 188, 193
  Lydia, 11
  Margaret, 120
  Nathaniel, 22, 245, 247
  Samuel, 20, 119, 121, 131
  Thomas (Thos), 17, 18, 69, 186, 188, 198
  William (W^m), 90, 239, 244, 246, 265, 279, 281, 284
Davison. See Davidson
Dayley. See Daily
Deakins
  John, 218
Deal
  Henry, 251, 267, 277, 281
  John, 261
  Philip, 137, 139

INDEX 305

Dean. *See also* Deen
  Alexander, 129, 197
  James, 49, 50, 53
  Jane, 268
  Jarnet, 46
  John, 197
  Matthew, 80
  Susanna, 189
Deatch
  Mathias, 29
Death
  Duskey, 25
  John, 18
  Tuskin, 34
Debert (Deberd). *See also* Dibert
  Charles, 206
  Frederick, 269
  Michael, 253
Deck
  Henry, 239
Decker
  John, 16
Dedier (Dedior). *See* Didier
Deen. *See also* Dean
  William, 21
Defebaugh (Devebaugh, Devenbaugh). *See also* Davebaugh, Dieffebaugh
  Casper, 53
  George, 225
  John, 239
Delap (Delapt)
  Richard, 55, 65, 66, 67, 101, 102, 114, 118
Delong
  Aaron, 10, 11, 16
  Francis, 10
  Solomon, 10
  Zachariah, 10, 11
Denard
  Mich., 259
Devebaugh (Devenbaugh). *See* Defebaugh
Devee
  Henry, 175, 179
Devole (Devol, Dibol)
  Elizabeth, 109, 112, 114, 116
  John, 109, 112, 114

Devore (Devoure)
  Cornelius, 84, 86, 89, 150, 157, 158, 161, 166, 176, 180, 218, 222, 225, 268, 274, 277
  Jacob, 218, 221, 222, 225
  Luke, 150, 173
  Shafit, 125
Dewalt
  Michael, 84
Dibert (Diepert, Dipert, Divart, Diver, Divert Divirt). *See also* Debert
  __ael, 179
  Charles, 172, 250
  Frederick (Frederic), 133, 144, 164, 198, 200, 223, 250, 263
  John, 31, 144, 149, 153, 156, 157, 164, 181, 185, 193, 219, 223, 226, 228, 240, 281
  Michael, 31, 33, 34, 35, 36, 112, 120, 144, 157, 181, 185, 200, 207, 228, 271
Dick__
  John, 125
Dicken (Dickens)
  Amos, 90, 139
Dickey
  John, 88, 122, 125, 162, 174, 175, 196, 197, 237, 238, 239, 250, 268, 272, 280
Dicks
  __ncis, 282
Dickson
  William, 45, 46
Didier (Dedier, Dedior)
  Henry, 16, 60, 64, 66, 67, 96, 99
  Peter, 175, 221, 238, 239
Dieffebaugh (Diffebaugh). *See also* Davebaugh, Defebaugh
  Casper, 104
  Daniel, 170
  John, 170
Dilts
  William, 124, 244, 246
Dipert. *See* Dibert
Dishong
  Baltzer, 121
  Morris, 124, 140, 198
Dively
  Martin, 219

Divert (Divart, Diver, Divirt). *See*
   Dibert
Diviney
   William, 119
Diving
   Andrew, 103
Dixon
   Andrew, 87, 209
   William, 34, 35, 37, 41, 55
Doc
   William, 191
Dodrige
   John, 9, 10
Dodson
   John, 264, 271, 275, 278
   Joseph, 270, 271
Dollinger. *See also* Drolinger
   Philip, 213
Dolton
   James, 102, 103
   Margaret, 103
Donaldson (Donnaldson)
   Aaron, 206
   Mary, 135
   Moses (Mosis), 113, 130, 131, 132, 135, 182
Donnald
   Aaron, 200
Donnigan
   William, 255
Donohow
   Joseph, 113
Donough
   John, 39, 40
Dornagan
   William, 256
Dough__
   John, 127
Dougherty (Doughtery)
   Andrew, 208
   Benjamin, 31
   Bernard (Barnard), 8, 17, 26, 29, 32, 33, 34, 39, 41, 45, 49, 51, 53, 55, 62, 68, 71, 75, 77, 78, 79, 80, 81, 82, 83, 97, 102, 111, 117, 120, 123, 125, 129, 132, 136, 139, 142, 144, 147, 155, 176, 179, 185, 186, 188, 191, 193, 197
   Jno, 175
   John, 137
   Robert, 208, 210, 214, 215
Doughman
   John, 128
Douglass
   Joseph, 234
Down
   Henry, 264
Downy
   Thomas, 134
Doyle
   James, 229
   Michael James, 242
Drake
   Benjamin, 122
   Oliver, 51, 188
Drenning (Drennan, Drennen, Drennin)
   Samuel (Saml), 8, 9, 12, 17, 20, 28, 31, 36, 47, 54, 67, 69, 185
   William, 147, 149, 156, 157, 159, 216, 250, 281
Drolinger (Drollinger). *See also* Dollinger
   Mrs., 215
   Philip, 211, 214, 215
Dubbs
   Frederick, 162, 209, 213, 216, 217
Dugle
   Joseph, 234
Dull
   Peter, 256
Dunlap (Dunlop). *See also* Dannilap
   James, 12, 14, 18, 19, 62, 97, 98, 104, 108, 113, 115, 180, 188
   Richard, 53, 59, 98, 100, 101, 115
   Robert, 95
Dunnigan (Dunagin, Durnagin)
   Cor^n, 254
   William (W^m), 256, 257
Durst
   Casper, 108
Dust
   Paul, 248
Duval
   Elizabeth, 109
   John, 109
Dwire
   Isaac, 158

Shaphat, 209
William, 55
Dyer
   William, 57, 58, 59, 94

—E—

E___
   Christian, 224
   David, 94
Eacre. *See* Eaker
Eage
   Catherine, 144, 145
   David, 144, 145
   Frederick, 144
Eaker (Eacre). *See also* Acres, Akers
   Joseph, 11, 17
Earnest
   George, 157, 214, 215
   Jacob, 225, 231, 247, 253
Eastep
   Robert, 18
Easter
   George, 202
   Jacob, 164, 257
   Valentine, 139, 150, 182, 216, 264
Eberly
   Henry, 139
Eby
   George, 133
Eccles (Ecles, Eceles, Eckles)
   William, 40, 43, 51, 67, 68
Echart
   George, 261
Eddleman
   Jacob, 264
Eddy (Ody)
   David, 114
   Gavin, 108, 109, 112, 114
   Gavin, Jr., 109, 112, 114, 116
Edington
   Charity, 108
   Philip, 106
Edmonton
   Thomas, 105
Edward (Edwards)
   ___, 121
   John, 120
   Michael, 257
   William, 65, 101

Ehenberger
   Jacob, 274
Eine
   Joseph, 69
Eire
   George, 23
Elde
   John, 200
Elder
   George, 64, 65, 100, 106, 107, 124, 137, 177, 184, 185, 192, 193, 194
   Ignatius (Ignatious), 160, 174, 197
   James, 212, 213, 215
   Jno, 257
   John, 104, 119, 123, 125, 149, 158, 166, 212, 213, 214, 215, 218, 251, 258, 268, 269, 272, 281
   Richard (Rich^d), 269
   William, 177, 178
Elderton
   James, 183
Elinger (Elengier, Elingier)
   John, 158, 271
Elliot (Eliott, Elliott, Elloit, Ellot)
   Barbara, 67
   Benjamin (Benj^a, Benjn), 26, 40, 69, 82, 83, 118, 169, 175, 179, 181, 191
   Elinor, 36
   John, 124, 176
   Robert, 37, 41, 45, 46, 48, 52, 55, 56, 66, 97, 182, 192
   William, 27, 31, 32, 36, 38, 40, 41, 43, 62, 69, 98, 194
Elon
   Henry, 55
Elvey
   Thomas, 10
Emer_
   Jacob, 240
Emerick. *See also* Americk
   Andrew, 209, 274
Emment
   Wendal, 209, 219
Engel (Engle). *See also* Angle, Ingle
   Clements, 125
   John, 220, 245, 248
   Michael, 219

England. *See also* Ingland
   James, 64, 99, 147, 164
   John, 114, 115, 116, 149, 176, 179,
      251, 252, 261, 281
Ensfield
   Hugh, 271
Ensley (Ensle, Ensly). *See also*
   Ansley
   George (Geo.), 28, 126, 144, 157,
      176, 177, 187, 188, 193, 200,
      201, 207, 244, 246, 268
   George, Jr., 177, 221, 239
   John, 174
Enslow (Ensloe)
   Christian, 262
   Christopher, 239, 277
   George, 28, 103, 104, 108, 118,
      144, 157, 176, 177, 180, 197,
      251, 266, 284
   George (Geo.), Jr., 144, 243, 261,
      278, 283
   Henry, 181
   John, 29
Erich
   John, 221
Ernstberger
   Paul, 44, 46, 51
Errat
   Catherine, 185, 186
Erwin (Ervin). *See also* Irwin
   David, 58, 59, 61, 65, 66, 67, 68,
      100, 101, 115, 116, 118, 175,
      179
   Joseph, 15, 17, 69
Espy
   David, 9, 38, 47, 79, 80, 81, 82, 83,
      84, 85, 86, 87, 124, 129, 132,
      136, 139, 149, 157, 175, 191,
      197, 225, 229, 230, 237
Estingus (Estungus)
   James, 16
Evalt. *See also* Ewalt
   John, 9, 25, 104
   Richard, 241
Evans (Evan)
   Amos, 88, 265, 272, 279
   David, 143, 198
   E___, 120
   Edward, 113, 215
   Rachel, 215

Everly
   Henry, 160, 162, 202, 236
   Peter, 180
Everts (Evarts)
   Jacob, 218, 221
Ewalt. *See also* Evalt
   John, 104, 180, 185, 193, 204, 247
   John, Jr., 133
   R., 257
   Richard, 241
Exline. *See also* Axline
   Adam, 244, 246
   Bernard, 242, 264

—F—

F___
   John, 274
Fait
   John, 248
Faith
   Abraham (Ab^m), 125, 141, 168,
      210, 284
   John, 171, 173
   W^m, 269
Falker
   George, 129
Fanagan
   Thomas, 90
Farin. *See also* Ferran
   William, 108
Faris
   Thomas, 114, 117
Farmer
   William, 119, 126
Fawner
   Jacob, 258
Feather
   George, 54
   Jacob, 53, 157, 205
   Michael, 18, 31, 119
   Michael, Jr., 192
Fee
   John, 121, 125, 128, 129, 176, 178,
      194
   John, Jr., 121, 122
   John, Sr., 121, 122, 126
Ferguson. *See also* Forgeson,
   Furguson
   Benjamin, 208, 215, 261, 283
   Christopher, 166

Elizabeth, 105, 106
Henry, 180
Hugh, 12, 28
John, 24, 59, 139, 159, 167, 202, 250
Thomas, 107
Ferran. *See also* Farin
Joseph M., 175
Ferrel (Ferrol)
   James, 147
   William, 146
Ferrence
   Nicholas, 205, 206, 207
Fetter (Fetters)
   Luke, 206, 254
   Michael, 193
Fic___
   Isaac, 265
Fickes (Fickus, Fiekes, Fike)
   Isaac, 90, 269, 274, 284
   John, 209
Fidler
   Timothy, 149
Field (Fields)
   David, 220, 239, 247, 254, 267, 274, 277
Fifer. *See also* Pfeifer
   Martin, 161
Fillebaugh
   Valentine, 140
Filson (Philson)
   Robert, 126, 127, 128, 197, 205
Fink
   Michael, 121, 122
Fishburn
   Philip, 251, 281
Fisher
   Henry, 203
   Jacob, 8, 45, 46, 49, 50, 53, 104, 162, 166, 210
   John, 12, 17, 21, 45, 46, 48, 121, 139, 164, 258, 262, 263
   Jonathan, 27
   Peter, 162
   Philip, 186
Fiske
   John, 144
Fittrees
   John, 111

Fitzsimmons
   Nicholas, 54
Flanagan
   Thomas, 271
Fleckinger
   John, 261
   Joseph, 283
Fleeharty (Fleehart, Fleetharty, Flegherty, Fleharty, Freeharty, Friehart)
   John, 9, 10, 24, 26, 28, 29, 34, 45, 46, 49, 50, 53, 106, 108, 114, 116, 150, 153, 158, 159, 160
   John, Sr., 153
   Joshua, 189
   Sarah, 159, 160
Fleming
   James, 56
Fletcher (Phletcher)
   Archibald, 104
   Jacob, 90
   James, 11, 15, 17, 23, 29, 36, 45, 46, 47, 96, 104, 157, 205, 272
   James, Jr., 137
   Ja^s, 69
   John, 91, 214, 215, 221, 233, 239, 284
Flick
   Adam, 219
   Jacob, 143
   Lewis, 284
   Susanna (Susannah, Sussanah), 221, 224, 241
Flickenger (Flickinger)
   John, 260
   Joseph, 279
Fluck (Flook, Fluick, Fluke). *See also* Foulk
   ___, 266
   Elizabeth, 263
   John, 253, 255
   Lewis, 238, 239, 280, 281, 284
Fochs. *See also* Fox
   George, 168
Foley
   James, 22, 27, 37, 69, 111, 182
Foor. *See* Fore
Ford
   Barnard, 158, 166
   Barnet, 214

David, 231
John, 240
Simon, 231
Fore (Four)
  Adam, 264
  Geo., 264
  Jacob, 239, 255, 267, 277, 280, 281, 283
  John, 271, 275, 280
Forgeson (Forgisson). *See also* Ferguson, Furguson
  Hugh, 23
  John, 22
Forney
  Joseph, 202
Foster
  John, 230, 242, 284
  Lewis, 149
  Mary__, 205
Foulk (Foulke). *See also* Fluck
  George D., 90
  Peter, 257, 270, 271, 284
Foust
  Henry, 236
Fouzer
  John, 213
Fox. *See also* Fochs
  Adam, 264
  Jacob, 113, 153, 180, 188
  Michael, 202
  Peter, 214
  Susanna, 282
Frame
  Moses, 219, 223, 224, 226, 227, 240
Francis
  James, 129
  Joseph, 241
Franklin
  Jonah, 134
  Joseph, 178
  Josiah, 130, 131, 134, 138, 141
Fraser (Frazer)
  Jean, 30
  John, 9, 12, 15, 18, 22, 25, 26, 28, 71, 75, 77
  Joseph, 162
  Margaret, 8
  William (W^m), 136, 137, 160, 185, 195, 271

Frederick
  John, 257
Frederigill (Fredrigal, Fredrigill, Fredrigle)
  Nancy, 152
  Sarah, 152, 165
  William, 13, 26, 43
Fredline (Fridline, Fritline)
  Frederick, 184
  Ludwick, 184, 188
  Peter, 244, 246, 247
Fredricks
  John, 257, 258
Free
  George (Geo.), 254
French
  James, 103, 193, 231, 232
  Jeremiah, 209, 213, 216, 217, 220, 223, 226, 240
  Lot, 123
Friehart. *See* Fleeharty
Friend
  Andrew, 189, 191, 194, 195
  Andrew, Jr., 193
  Charles, 190, 193, 195
  Jeremiah, 190, 195
  John, 17, 20, 22, 27, 37, 86, 113, 114, 115, 116, 119, 125, 129, 139, 150, 158, 159, 176, 179, 180, 183, 188, 226, 262
  John, Sr., 26
  Joseph, 12, 17, 55, 104, 119, 125, 139, 150, 158, 209
  Joseph, Sr., 243
  Nichel, 155
  Nicholas, 155, 156, 159, 162
Friggs
  Robert, 17
Fritline. *See* Fredline
Fritz
  Christian, 143, 219, 223, 226, 240
  Martin, 170, 229, 242
Froman
  Paul, 16
Fronhiser (Frownheiser)
  Jacob, 220, 244, 246
Fry
  Abraham, 214
  John, 157

INDEX 311

Fryer
　Michael, Sr., 219
Fullman
　Jacob, 256
　John, 256
Fulton
　Hugh, 151
　John, 15
Funk (Funck)
　George, 8, 30, 41, 54, 63, 66, 68, 81, 98, 101, 102, 106, 114, 124, 139, 142, 154, 162, 166, 169, 170, 183, 208, 228, 265
Furguson. *See also* Ferguson, Forgeson
　John, 150
Furray
　John, 219

—G—

G__
　Abraham, 104
　Tom, 14
　William, 66
G__ing
　John, 139
Ga__
　William, 101
Gadd (Gad)
　Ignatius, 130, 136, 141
　William, 131
Gaff
　James, 262
　John, 190
　William, 32, 122, 129, 139, 150, 158, 176, 177, 180, 188, 204, 211, 212, 262
Galacher. *See* Gallacher
Galbrath (Galbraith, Galbreath)
　___t, 120
　James, 35, 39, 40, 113, 119, 125, 188
　John, 120
　Mr., 30, 195
　Richard, 129
　Robert (Robt), 8, 78, 79, 93, 94, 123, 125, 132, 141, 192, 284
Gallacher (Galacher)
　John, 37, 40, 42

Galloway
　James, 34, 45, 46, 55, 62
　John, 69
Gamble
　___, 257
Gandy
　Mary, 164
Gardner
　John, 203, 210
　William (W^m), 150, 159, 161, 210
Garner
　Joseph, 206
　William, 161
Garretson (Garreson, Garrison)
　Israel, 59
　John, 225, 226, 245, 256, 264
　Mary, 65, 100
Geery
　Gillian, 165, 166
Gelliland (Gillelan, Gilliland)
　Philip, 25, 110, 150, 154
Gelmor. *See* Gilmore
George
　Mich^l, 254
　Paul, 169
George III, 75, 76, 78
Gibbon (Gibbons)
　Francis, 251
　Morris, 110
Gibbs (Gib)
　F., 266
　Francis, 157, 158, 160, 170, 223, 266, 268
　Sarah, 266, 268
Gibson
　David, 15
　Ja__, 177
　James, 18, 104, 176, 202, 204, 210
　John, 139, 149, 159, 162
　Robert, 120, 135, 136, 138, 161, 181, 184, 212, 261, 265, 267, 268, 269
　William (W^m), 123, 136, 139, 146, 240
Gilliland. *See* Gelliland
Gilmore (Gelmor, Gilmor)
　___, 176
　James, 37, 50, 119, 144, 145, 146, 147, 148, 162, 178, 196, 237
　John, 147

Margaret, 144
Gilson
　William, 245
Ginklesberger
　Albright (Albrigh), 209, 213, 216, 217
Gisl
　Thos., 16
Gist
　Thomas, 12, 77
Glassner (Glasner, Glessner)
　Henry, 188
　Jacob, 97, 139, 149, 158, 209, 210
　Peter, 269
Glen (Glenn)
　Archibald, 113
　John, 104
Goble
　Henry, 162
　John, 116
　Stephen, 179
Good
　Abraham, 122, 210
　Jacob, 140, 166, 180, 200
　John, 158
Goosehorn
　George, 117
Gordan (Gorden, Gordon)
　Charles, 126, 127, 135, 137, 138, 265, 270
　George, 261, 271
　James, 123, 124, 207, 240, 274, 277, 281, 285
　Jn°, 265
　Moses, 110
　R., 267
　Robert (Rob., Robt), 263, 265, 267, 279
Gousa
　Jacob, 236
Gr__
　Elisha, 265
Grady
　Elisha, 144, 203
Graham
　George, 146, 225
　James, 12, 28, 29, 32, 33, 37, 41, 42, 45, 46, 48, 49, 50, 53, 181, 182

John, 13, 114, 123, 137, 145, 146, 175, 178, 184, 194, 239, 256, 258, 277
Milly, 146
Moses, 166, 172, 199, 202, 204, 206, 211, 214, 244, 246, 247, 249, 252, 253, 255, 274, 279
William, 255
Graves
　John, 247
　Joseph, 244, 246, 254
　Samuel (Saml), 34, 114, 119, 139, 170, 181
Gray (Grey)
　Absalom (Absolom), 55, 113, 119
　Edward, 109, 110, 112
　Robert, 180
Greathouse
　William, 116, 181
Green
　Richard, 119, 139
Grier
　David, 9
Griffith (Griffiths)
　David, 143, 146, 178, 182
　Ebenezer, 86, 127, 128, 132, 135, 143
　Evan, 274
　Jesse (Jess, Jese), 257, 264, 272, 284
　John, 119, 135, 250
　M^r, 224
　Rachel, 178, 182
　William (W^m), 166, 170, 209, 225, 226, 242, 243, 256, 264, 267, 272, 274, 285
Grindle
　Jacob, 221
Grivingston (Grivingstone). *See also* Crivingstone, Livingston
　Nicholas (Nickolas), 176, 179
Gro__
　George, 220
Groner
　John, 237
Grove (Groves)
　Geo. Michael, 172
　Mary, 205
Gudgel
　Andrew, 18

INDEX

Guilford
  John, 56
Gulick
  John, 158
Gundy
  Joseph, 150, 202
Guthrey (Gultrie)
  Hugh, 17, 22
  William, 24, 127

—H—

H___
  William, 251
H__genbug
  Louisa, 221
Ha__m_s_
  Lovey, 189
Hagan (Haggan, Haggans)
  John, 114, 115, 116, 166
Hagar
  Jacob, 128
Hagerty (Haggerty)
  Patrick, 270, 278, 281
Haines (Hain, Hains)
  Abraham, 57
  Jacob, 210, 220
  John, 80, 111, 119, 125, 218, 222, 225
Halderbaum (Hailderbaum)
  Michael, 263, 269
Hale
  James, 119
Haley
  Matthew, 16
Hall
  Elizabeth, 152, 164, 165
  Elizabeth May, 20
  Henry, 37
  Jacob, 111
  Samuel (Saml), 104, 105, 162, 216
  Samuel, Jr., 216
  Sarah, 37, 105
  Thomas, 104, 113
  William (Willi^m, W^m), 210, 211, 213, 215
Hallem
  Henry, 248
Hallow
  Henry, 250

Hamburgh
  George, 237
Hamet
  Edward, 119
Hamill. *See also* Hammel
  Robert, 166
  Samuel, 199
Hamilton
  Hance, 101
  Hans, 28, 65, 66, 67, 68, 101, 102, 103
  Hugh, 278
  James, 245
  Jeremiah, 263
  John, 106, 114, 136, 178, 184
  Jonathan, 153
  Mr., 195, 206, 251
  Robert, 131, 164, 165, 168, 172
  Thomas, 153
  William, 51, 52
Hamlin
  John, 155
Hammel. *See also* Hamilll
  Robert, 122
  Samuel, 172
Hammer
  Tobias, 91
Hammon (Hammond)
  Jonathan, 283
  Michael, 157
  Nathan, 16, 172, 202, 243, 250, 285
Hance. *See also* Hantz
  Peter, 22, 27
Hancock
  Joel, 278
  John, 272
Hand
  Rachel, 276, 278
Haney (Hayny, Heney)
  Patrick (Pat^k, Pat^r), 120, 151, 164, 166, 170, 194, 202, 204, 205, 242, 260, 265, 279
Hanger (Hangin)
  John, 122, 123, 124
  Philip, 123
Hanna (Hannah)
  Jane, 27
  Robert, 8, 9, 11, 12, 15, 24, 26, 27, 77
  Thomas, 26

Hannan
  James, 125
Hantz. *See also* Hance
  Peter, 21
Harbaugh
  Barbara, 267
  Geo., 267
Harcher
  Peter, 280
Harcleroad (Harkleroad)
  J., 261
  John, 172, 199, 241
Hardbolt
  Adam, 250
Hardin. *See also* Hartin
  Ignatius, 163, 164, 170
  Isaac, 127
  John, 163, 170
Hardinger
  George, 89, 272, 274
Hardistie
  Thomas, 34
Hardman
  Daniel, 269
Hardy
  James, 161, 162, 163
  Rachael, 162
  Rachel, 163, 170
Harford
  James, 232
Hargor
  John, 124
Harker
  Peter, 242, 265
Harkleroad. *See* Harcleroad
Harmon
  Philip, 216
Harnet
  Edward, 139, 189
Harradar
  Henry, 216
Harred (Harrod)
  John, 29, 113
  William, 24
Harris
  John, 140, 182
Harrison
  Saml, 69
Hart
  Benjamin, 259

Eliza/Elizabeth (Kerney), 259, 260
Jacob, 88, 149, 166, 250
James, 207, 211, 215, 254
John, 162, 207, 215
Nathaniel, 147, 168, 255
William, 17, 29, 32, 33, 45, 46, 115, 189, 209
Hartford
  John, 183
  Patrick, 43, 44, 47, 66, 111, 177, 183
Hartin. *See* Hardin
  George, 265
Hartley (Hartly)
  William (Willm, W^m), 133, 134, 136, 137, 150, 153, 161, 163, 175, 200, 202, 220, 230, 231, 232, 233, 237, 238, 239, 255, 277
  William, Jr., 276
Hartsock (Hartstock)
  Peter, 46, 55
Hartzel (Hartzell)
  ____, 225
  Conrad (Conrod), 156, 162, 232, 233
  Edward, 125
  Henry, 158
  Jacob, 83, 86, 119, 125, 142, 149, 155, 157, 158, 162, 164, 166, 173, 188, 228, 235
  John, 225, 233, 265
Has
  George, 28
Has__on
  Jacob, 277
Hasselton (Hesselton)
  Jacob, 239, 280
Hatch
  Elisabeth (Elizabeth), 61, 96
  John, 61, 64, 96, 99
  Mrs., 64
Hatfield
  Adam, 15
Haugar (Hauger, Haugen, Haugher)
  John, 126, 127, 128
  Philip, 127
Haun
  Jacob, 244, 246

Haverstock (Haverstack, Haverstick, Haverstook)
    Conrad (Conrod), 159, 172, 221, 229, 242, 279
Haward
    Mich., 264
Hay (Hays, Hey). *See also* Hoy
    Daniel, 42, 103, 119
    Francis, 150, 166, 214, 220
    Margaret, 21
    Mary, 36, 102, 114
    Michael, 124, 275
    Nicholas, 100
    Simon, 209, 284, 285
    Thomas (Th°), 8, 12, 22, 23, 28, 29, 36, 38, 40, 41, 42, 43, 45, 46, 49, 50, 52, 53, 62, 81, 102, 115, 136, 143, 175, 177, 215
    William, 284
Hay__
    Andrew, 216
    Patrick, 252
Hayle
    Christ__, 162
Hayrader
    Andrew, 217
    John, 217
Hazlett
    William, 281
He__
    Peter, 241
Head
    Bigger, 202
    Edward, 52, 53, 56
    John, 239, 277
Heath
    Andrew, 242, 283
Heckman (Hickman)
    Ezekiel, 10, 13, 14, 15, 21
Heffer
    Jacob, 143
Heiple (Heible). *See also* Hipple
    Christian, 126, 158
Hellam (Hellem, Hellum)
    Adam, 158, 248
    Jacob, 122, 128, 232
Heller
    Henry, 151
    Martin, 151

Helm. *See also* Hem
    Adam, 248
    Frederick (Frederic), 18, 34, 115, 179, 193
    Henry, 241
    Jacob, 120, 127, 179, 206, 242, 255
    John, 127, 278
Helsel
    John, 147, 148
    Tobias, 210
Helsinger
    Jn°, 274
Hem. *See also* Helm
    Fredereck, 277
Hemminger
    John, 235
Hemphill (Hempill)
    Adley, 67
    Robert, 147, 204, 241, 268, 278
Hendershot
    Barbaara, 162
    Jacob, 34, 108, 162, 178, 189, 268, 269
Henderson
    Edward, 36, 43
    Jonathan, 214, 241
    Samuel, 270
Hendricks
    Andrew, 20
    James, 106
    John, 22, 27, 221, 222
Hendrickson
    James, 181, 182
    Jn°, 270
    John, 108, 209
Henry
    George, 92, 279
    James, 34, 41, 46, 47, 51, 66, 114
    John, 36, 38, 40, 41
    Richard, 38
    Robert, 32, 40
    William (W^m), 143, 153, 161, 200, 201, 228, 232, 270
Henton
    William, 41
Herd
    William, 280, 282
Herman
    Elizabeth, 263

Herring
  Jacob, 250
Herron (Heron)
  Jacob, 204, 216
Hersch (Hersh)
  Jacob, 55, 106, 108
Hershiser
  Lewis, 172, 271
Hervine
  Peter, 241
Hess (Hesse)
  Baltzer (Balzer), 133, 150, 167,
    168, 219, 228, 237, 241, 242
  Henry, 151, 220
  Sarah, 156
Hesselton. *See* Hasselton
Hessler
  Lewis, 226
Hey. *See* Hay
Heydon
  James, 87, 164, 278
Hickman. *See* Heckman
Higgins
  Edward, 42, 43, 44, 67
  Fergus, 126
  Joseph, Jr., 222
  Joseph, Sr., 222
Hight. *See* Hite
Hilderbrand (Hildebrand)
  Michael, 148
  Peter, 11
Hile
  Walter, 113
Hill
  Caleb, 210, 212
  Frederick, 154, 221, 225, 227, 231,
    269, 271
  Jacob, 234
  John, 156
Hillock
  Rebecca, 152
Himmel
  John, 215
Hinish
  George, 233, 236
Hinkson
  John, 11, 14
Hipple (Hiple). *See also* Heiple
  Christian, 202
  Henry, 93

John, 210, 260, 285
Hite (Hight)
  Conrad, 160, 161
  John, 9, 111
Hoch. *See also* Houk
  Simon, 147
Hockley
  Richard, 256
Hoerhill (Hoeshill)
  Justinius (Justinus), 68, 102
Hoff
  Sarah, 156
Hoffman
  Jacob, 208, 210, 214
Hoge
  Daniel, 14
Hogland
  Henry, 16
Hoil. *See* Hoyle
Hoker
  Casper, 122
Holderbaum
  Michael, 268, 269, 279
Holiday (Holliday)
  William, 38, 56, 182, 187
  William, Jr., 123, 176
  William, Sr., 123
Hollar (Holler)
  Henry, 214
  Valentine, 231
Holley
  Henry, 59
Holloway
  William (W^m), 257, 284
Holtz
  Jacob, 178, 189, 203
  John, 203
Hoof
  Jacob, 233, 234
Hook
  Michael, 225
Hoover
  Casper, 139
  Henry, 121, 212
  Jacob, 60, 61, 62, 63, 66, 96, 97,
    99, 104, 111, 172, 264
  John, 64, 147, 156, 162, 164, 174,
    215
  Mary, 245, 247
  Pe__, 265

Hopkearn
 Conrod, 159
Hopkins
 John, 86, 140, 142, 199, 201, 204, 206, 208
Hoplitz
 Adrian, 161
Hopper
 Robert, 129
Hoppinger
 Conrad, 162
Horn
 Henry, 281
Hornler
 Andrew, 139
Horsal
 Justinius, 134
Horse
 George, 45, 48, 110, 166
 John, 155, 156, 159, 162
 William, 205
Hos
 Stophel, 23
Hosler. *See also* Houser
 John, 10, 13, 16
Hostatler (Houghstatler, Houghstaller, Houghstetler)
 Christian, 119
 Jacob, 219, 244, 246
 John, 202, 209
Hougland
 Richard, 77, 78
Houk. *See also* Hock
 Michael, 222
Houlk
 Peter, 271
Houser. *See also* Hosler
 Elisabeth, 10
 Henry, 123
 Jacob, 274
 John, 10
 Martin, 202, 204, 261, 274
How
 James, 20
Howard
 George, 51
 Michael, 250, 251, 256
 William, 16, 19, 21
Howe
 John, 99

Hoy. *See also* Hay
 Daniel, 139
Hoyle (Hoil, Hoyl)
 Adam, 234, 236
 Jacob, 234
 Walter, 29, 125
Hudson
 George, 119, 125, 188
Huff. *See also* Hupp
 Godfrey, 147, 264
 Jacob, 235
 John, 8, 10, 13, 20, 69
 Michael, 9, 10, 12, 18, 29, 41, 60, 63, 96, 99
Huffnagle
 Michael, 118
Hughes (Hughy)
 James, 14, 32
Hull
 Benjamin, 260
 George, 242, 243
Humberg (Humburger, Humbugh, Humburgh)
 Frederick, 113, 141
 George, 238, 283
Humbert
 George, 255
 John, 162
Humble
 Peter, 30
Hunt
 Ann, 163
 Joseph, 237, 255, 267
 Ralph, 186
 Thomas, 92
 William, 14, 66
Hunter
 Alexander, 158
 James, 126
 John, 90
 William (W^m), 180, 188, 198, 209, 244, 246, 257, 284
Hupp. *See also* Huff
 John, 18
Husband (Husbands)
 Herman (Harman, Harmon, Hermon), 47, 49, 56, 103, 113, 129, 133, 167, 172, 180, 199
 James, 216

Husk
  Nathaniel, 16
Huston
  Edwd, 264
  Jesse, 122, 124
  John, 122
  Robert, 122, 127, 159
Hynes
  John, 209

—I—

Iaam (Iams). *See also* Sams
  Adam, 12, 17
  George, 137
Ice
  George, 277, 284
Iler
  Nicholas, 106, 107, 108, 109
  Philip, 150
Imfelt
  Michael, 143, 192
Imler (Imbler, Imlir)
  George, 104, 123, 140, 147, 148, 188, 198, 200, 223, 224, 231
  John, 133
Ingland. *See also* England
  Rachel, 217
Ingle. *See also* Angle, Engle
  Clement (Clemant, Clemens), 140, 150, 181, 182
  Michael, 214
Inglebright
  John, 203
Inglesburger
  Jacob, 220
Innings
  Benjamin, 244, 246
Ireland
  Hance, 21, 22, 24
Iron (Irons)
  Michael, 230, 231
Irwin. *See also* Erwin
  ___, 118
  David, 42, 43, 114, 179, 183
  Joseph, 12
  Lawrence, 11
Isor (Izor)
  Philip, 121, 143, 150, 159
Iwales
  Mary, 105

William Martin, 105

—J—

Ja__t
  Nathaniel, 116
Jack
  Samuel, 55
  William (W^m), 165, 168, 169, 170, 237
Jackson
  George, 19, 120, 179, 188
Jacobus
  John, 121, 124
James
  Abel, 256, 257
  Cassandra, 263, 265
  Chalkey, 257
  George, 127, 137, 138, 227, 263
  James II, 76
  James III, 76
  James VIII, 76
Jameson (Jamison)
  James, 126, 143, 159, 173, 174, 175, 202, 237, 238, 239, 244, 246, 250, 252, 277, 284
  Thomas, 11, 14, 69
Jarrard (Jarrot)
  Nathaniel, 57, 125
Jeffery
  John, 122
Jenkins
  Evan, 18, 28, 108
  John, 121, 278
Jennings
  Benjamin, 181
  Sarah, 190
Jenton
  John, 187
John
  David, 126, 151, 152, 244, 246, 249, 252, 253, 254
  Jacob, 113
  Mary, 151
  Robert, 28
Johns (Johnes)
  Joseph, 119, 216
Johnson
  Christopher, 56
  George, 205
  James, 13, 113

INDEX 319

John, 17, 23, 168, 169, 176, 200
Joshua, 90
Richard, 178
Thomas (Thos), 28, 31, 45, 46, 54, 97, 104, 193, 263
William, 133
Johnston (Johnstone)
  George, 136
  James, 106, 113
  John, 168, 183, 184, 185, 186, 187, 201, 255, 264, 265
  Joseph, 46, 180, 188, 272
  Richard, 192
  Thomas, 36, 47, 54, 66, 116, 193, 195, 263
  Thos, Sr., 263
Jolley (Jolly)
  Benjamin (Banjamin), 22, 30, 31, 37, 41, 63, 98
Jones
  Amos, 139, 185
  Chalkey, 256
  David, 55, 61, 79, 82, 104, 111, 120, 129, 132, 139, 142, 143, 144, 149, 158, 161, 164, 166, 176, 183, 188, 195
  Ignatius, 15, 18
  Isaac, 143, 144
  John, 15, 113, 133, 180, 216, 225, 244, 246, 270
  Joseph, 10, 15, 19, 20
  Thomas (Thos), 15, 24, 34, 43, 69, 257
  William, 110, 111, 118, 129, 183, 196, 202, 209
Jordan (Jourdon)
  D., 257
  David, 202, 204, 205, 221, 223, 239, 249, 259, 284
Joslin
  Jeremiah, 258, 268, 272
Judah
  Matthias, 105
Justice
  Aquila, 260, 261
  Grace, 105, 140, 141, 189
  Jesse, 257
  William (W^m), 180, 274

—K—

K____
  John, 149
  Thomas, 125
  William, 124
K___ns
  Fred^k, 206
K__niger
  George, 214
Kagg. *See* Kegg
Kaman
  Patrick, 40
Kan__
  John, 244
Karns. *See also* Cairns
  Leonard, 107
Karr
  James, 20
  Janet (Jannet, Jennet), 20, 23
Katz
  Jacob, 238, 239
Kaufman (Kauffman)
  George, 160, 163
Kay, 98
  W^m, 274
Ke___
  George, 212
  John, 263
Kean
  Morris, 58
Kebble (Keble, Kepple)
  Abraham, 9, 18, 20, 24, 25
  Philip, 119
Kebler
  Jacob, 122
Keck. *See* Kegg
Keef (Keiff)
  David, 261, 262
Keefer (Keeffer, Kefer, Keffer, Keifer, Kiffer)
  Adam, 44, 46, 51, 119, 140, 145, 146, 147, 148, 149, 233, 234
  David, 206, 272
  Jacob, 140, 148, 149, 180, 202
  Jacob, Jr., 148
Keel (Keil, Kihl)
  Philip, 249, 261
Keeler
  Elizabeth, 65

Keg_y
  John, 159
Kegg (Kagg, Keg)
  Nicholas, 65, 98, 231, 232, 261
  William (W^m), 231, 232
Keifer. *See* Keefer
Keiff. *See* Keef
Keil. *See* Keel
Keiser (Keisor). *See also* Kiser
  John, 258, 271
Keller
  Elizabeth, 100
  Francis, 10
  George, 12, 40, 53, 56, 167, 172, 199, 202, 204
  Henry, 151
  Jacob, 10
  John, 43, 44
  Martin, 151
  Peter, 280
Kellerman
  George, 221
Kelly
  John, 23
  Joseph, 9, 15, 18, 20, 34, 45, 46, 49, 50, 53, 55, 111, 113, 119, 123, 125, 176, 180, 185, 268, 269
  Matthew, 34, 37, 128
  Moses, 124
  Thomas, 109, 124
Kemble. *See* Kimble
Kemp
  Edward, 149, 219, 244, 246
  John, 246
Ken__er
  John, 279
Kendal
  James, 223, 226, 240
  John, 219
Kenerin (Kencerin, Kinerin, Knerin)
  Henry, 177
  Justis Henry (Justius Henry), 177, 178, 182
Kennard
  John, 137, 138, 141
Kennedy
  Thomas, 152, 170
  William, 102, 187

Kenny
  Robert, 90
  William, 104
Kenton. *See also* Kinton
  John, 114, 228, 241
  Simon, 187, 213, 215, 217, 228, 241, 242, 270, 278
  Thomas, 8, 9, 12, 14, 19, 24, 104, 137, 185, 188, 207, 209, 240
Kenworthy (Kinworthy)
  William, 240, 276
Kepley
  Andrew, 265
Kepper
  Frederick, 244, 246
Kerney
  Elizabeth (Eliza), 259, 260
  Grace, 259, 260
  James, 259, 260
  Margaret, 259, 260
  Mary, 259, 260
  William (W^m), 28, 30, 31, 108, 140, 150, 259, 260
Kerns. *See* Cairns, Karns
Kerr (Ker)
  James, 145
  Samuel (Saml), 32, 164
  William, 123
Kershner
  David, 216
Ketcham (Ketchim)
  Philip, 130, 131, 132, 134
Ki_ley
  W^m, 129
Kihl. *See* Keel
Kilgore
  David, 11, 17
Kilpatrick (Killpatrick)
  John, 111, 141, 235
Kimber
  Richard, 64, 100
Kimberlin (Kimberline)
  Abraham, 37, 38
  Jacob, 50
  John, 38, 41, 51
  Sarah, 50, 51
Kimble (Kemble, Kimbel)
  Abraham, 202
  George, 29, 120, 140
  Jacob, 168, 202, 204

Michael, 157
Philip, 29, 30, 31, 33
Kimmel (Kimel, Kimmell, Khemal, Khemel)
David, 216, 220
George, 34, 124, 168, 222, 224, 234, 240, 283, 284
John, 175, 205, 214, 215, 237, 238, 239, 284
John, Doctor (Doct^r), 227, 233
Philip, 150, 214, 219
Philip, Jr., 124
Kincaid (Kinkead)
Ann (Anne), 65, 100
James, 15, 65, 100
John, 65, 100
Kinder
Adam, 237, 238
King
Christopher, 157
John, 185
Philip, 86, 149, 159, 235
Kinner
Ann, 177
Kinster (Kintser)
George, 248, 250
Kinton (Kiton). *See also* Kenton
James, 36
John, 89, 230, 276
Simon, 172, 230, 264, 276
Thomas, 21, 22, 27, 33, 45, 46, 48, 55
Kinuff
Peter, 283
Kinworthy. *See* Kenworthy
Kirby
William, 176
Kirkpatrick
John, 112
Kirts
John, 8, 11
Kiser. *See also* Keiser
Christian, 209
Kissinger (Kisinginger, Kessinger, Kis^{gn})
George, 217, 222
Jacob, 221
Kline. *See also* Cline
Leonard, 153

Klink
John, 132
Knagey (Knagy). *See also* Nagle, Naugle
Christian, 180, 202, 204
Knause
Jacob, Jr., 56
Knee
Philip, 139, 260, 275
Knerin. *See* Kenerin
Knight. *See also* Night
Elizabeth, 120
Nicholas, 225, 229, 230, 231
Philip, 160
Kniper (Knipper)
Godfrey, 53
John, 202
Knisely (Knicely, Kniesly, Kniseley)
John, 239, 261, 277, 280
Knox
Thomas, 121, 122
Knuffs (Kenuff)
Peter, 243, 277
Koontz (Koon, Kountz, Kunts, Kuntz). *See also* Coontz
Adam, 221, 244, 246
Catherine, 37
David, 284
Frederick, 242, 243, 283
Henry, 261, 264
Lawrence, 31
Lorentz, 37, 38
Michael, 233
Peter, 264
Kooser
John, 202
Kowel. *See also* Cowel
Christian, 158
Kreamer (Krimer). *See also* Creamer
Adam, 149
Margaret, 22
Kreel
Philip, 261
Kurtz. *See also* Curtz
Jacob, 215

Lafferty
  James, 159, 160, 161, 162, 203
  John, 120, 137, 159, 193, 242, 251
  William, 226, 232, 233
Laird
  Jacob, 119, 121, 178, 179, 180, 183
Laman. *See also* Leeman
  Benidict, 113
Lambers
  Lawrence, 276
Lambert
  Jacob, 153, 154, 155, 156
  John, 202
Lamhart
  Peter, 270
Lamp__
  John, 87
Lane
  Ebenezer, 69
  John, 274
Langdale
  Elizabeth, 203
Lant
  Valentine, 113
Lashey
  John, 158
Laton. *See* Layton
Latta (Lata)
  John, 37, 41, 45, 120
  William, 22, 28, 32, 52, 69
Laughlan
  William, 120
Laverin
  Henry, 275
Lavoyer
  Daniel, 20
Layton (Laton, Leaton)
  Asher, 103, 227, 253
  James, 190
  Obadiah, 106, 176
  Obiah, 103
  Samuel, 103, 177, 180
  Sarah, 190
Laz__
  Thomas, 133
Lazar (Lazare, Lazer, Lazier). *See also* Leaser, Leasure, Levear
  John, 218
  Thomas, 125, 176
Le__ket
  William, 227
Leader
  Henry, 236
Leap
  Peter, 209
Leaser (Leazer). *See also* Lazar, Levear
  Abraham, 11, 17
  George, 69
Leasure. *See also* Lazar, Levear
  John, 258
  Thomas, 119, 120, 255
Lee
  George, 239, 280
Leech (Liech)
  Nicholas, 110, 111, 113
  Stephen, 53, 55
Leedy
  Abraham, 261
Leeman. *See also* Laman
  George, 279
Leiberger. *See* Lybarger
Leman
  Benedict, 104, 166
Lemmon (Lemon)
  Archibald, 141
  J__m, 162
  Thomas, 176
  W., 52
  William, 52
Leonard
  Enoch, 217
  Patrick, 179, 181, 183, 193
Levear. *See also* Lazar, Lesure
  John, 162
Levering
  Daniel, 259
  John, 259
  Margaret (Kerney), 259, 260
  Mary (Kerney), 259, 260
Lewis
  ___, 39
  David, 55
  Joshua, 104, 126
Lewiston
  Andrew, 149

Libarger (Liberger). *See* Lybarger
Lickey
   Benson, 111
Liddle. *See* Little
Lieberger. *See* Lybarger
Liech. *See* Leech
Lighly
   Joseph, 244, 246
Lighterberger
   George, 19
Lilley (Lille, Lilly, Lily)
   ___, 253
   J., 253
   Jos., 248
   Joseph, 137, 214, 230, 238, 249, 250, 253, 256, 260, 283, 284, 285
Ling
   Anthony, 204, 225
   John, 279
Lingenfelter (Lingefeth)
   Abraham, 123
   George, 92, 275
Link
   Jacob, 277
Linn. *See also* Lynn
   ___, 17
   Adam, 119
   Addis (Adis), 158, 244, 246, 267, 274
   Andrew, 23, 25
   Benjamin, 10, 11
   Hugh, 165, 166
   John, 228
   Mary, 10, 11
   William, 10, 11, 15
Lint
   Conrod, 209
Little (Liddle, Lyttle)
   Absolom, 20, 25
   James, 14, 17, 19, 21, 22, 31, 32, 33, 34, 35, 36, 38, 39, 45, 46, 52, 53, 66, 97, 101, 108, 109, 111, 112, 113
   John, 83, 125, 132
Littleton. *See also* Luking
   John Burd, 40, 42, 43
Livengood (Livingood)
   Christian, 172
   Peter, 167, 180

Livingston (Livingstone, Liviston). *See also* Crivingston, Grivingston
   Andrew, 159
   Christian, 204
   Henry, 111, 113, 118, 143, 152, 153, 154, 155, 196
   John, 136, 189
   Nicholas, 114, 115, 116
   Samuel, 253, 255, 278
Lloyd
   Henry, 39, 180, 188
Loan
   Benjamin, 47, 136
Lochberger
   Jonathan, 190
Lochery (Lochrey, Lochry)
   Archibald, 14, 16, 25
   Jeremiah, 11
   William, 8, 9, 11, 12, 15, 77
Lockhart (Lockart)
   Silas, 123
   William, 254
Logan
   David, 136
   Hugh, 123, 189, 190, 191, 193
   James, 141
   M^r, 262
   Thomas (Thos), 90, 242, 250, 262
Loge
   John, 123
Logue
   Hugh, 194
Long
   Christian, 49, 67, 68
   Frederick, 224
   Matthias, 274
   Richard, 17, 22, 32, 34, 36, 37, 39
   William, 130, 134, 138, 181, 188
Longnecher
   Michael, 129
Longstr_
   Martin, 177
Longstreath (Longstradth, Longstraith, Longstrath, Longstreck, Longstretch, Longstreth, Longstrolik)
   James, 239, 244, 246, 250, 252, 253, 254, 255, 264, 269, 271
   Jno, 137

John, 137
Martin, 14, 28, 57, 61, 78, 93, 94,
    110, 114, 176, 177, 201, 271
Mary, 184
Philip, 141
Samuel, 277
Loud
    Jacob, 244, 246
Loude
    Daniel, 29
Loughlin
    Rob[t], 69
Lower
    John, 244, 246
Lowrey (Lowry)
    Abraham, 29, 30, 31, 32, 33, 104
    Alex[r] Scott, 237
    David, 104, 125
    John, 239
    Michael, 284
Loy
    Martin, 124, 138, 140, 148, 203,
        216, 237, 252, 267, 279
Loyd
    Henry, 113
Lucas
    G., 263
    George, 200, 262, 263
Luck
    Nicholas, 186, 191
    Yost, 180
Luckey
    B___, 120
Luking. *See also* Littleton
    John Burd, 41
Lupton
    Benjamin, 236
Luter
    Martin, 203
Lutz (Ludz)
    Andrew, 114, 115, 116
Lybarger (Lebarger, Leiberger,
    Libarger, Liberger, Liebarger,
    Lyberger, Lyenburger)
    Daniel, 250
    George, 119, 125, 176
    Henry, 127, 216, 251, 281
    John, 253, 255
    Lewis, 248

Nicholas, 119, 125, 127, 140, 176,
    209, 224, 255, 274
Nichols, 126
Lydick
    John, 167, 258
Lyler
    John, 159
Lynch
    John, 223, 226, 240
Lynd
    Will[m], 69
Lynn. *See also* Linn
    Addis, 209, 219
Lyon
    John, 245, 263
    Samuel (Sam[l]), 16, 69
    Thomas, 25
Lyttle. *See* Little

—M—

M___
    George, 81
M___
    Christopher, 150
    Grace (Kerney), 259, 260
    James, 259
    John, 220
    Peter, 196
    Robert, 254
    William, 216
Machanel. *See* Mackerel
Mackane. *See also* Mackerel,
    McCain
    Benjamin, 130
    John, 130
Mackerel (Machanel, Mackeral).
    See also Mackane
    Benjamin, 134, 138
    John, 130, 134, 138
Mackey (Mackay). *See also*
    McKay
    ___, 253
    John, 151, 230, 242, 253
Magaw
    Robert, 8, 22
Magill
    Charles (Chas.), 30, 39, 41
    Charles, Jr., 30
Mallen (Mallon). *See also* Mellott
    John, 9, 15

Mallot (Malott, Mallott). *See* Mellott
Mann (Man)
  A., 252
  Andrew (And^r), 12, 18, 28, 37, 41, 45, 48, 85, 91, 104, 155, 214, 221, 222, 230, 231, 252, 263, 268, 277, 281, 283
  Bernard, 256
  Bernard, Jr., 244, 246
  D., 93
  David, 91, 92, 93
  Jacob, 36, 47, 48, 180
  John, 274
Mardes
  George, 227
Markle
  Christopher, 209, 213, 216, 217
Markley (Markly)
  Henry, 89, 265, 274, 279
  Jacob, 108, 159
  John, 113, 119
  Joseph, 167, 172
Marshall (Marshell)
  John, 21
  Martha, 278
Marshdollar
  John, 237
Marstaller
  Frederick, 118, 202, 204
Martin (Marton)
  Abraham (Ab^m, Ab^r), 89, 170, 174, 175, 197, 236, 258, 275, 277, 285
  Benjamin (Benjn), 59, 68, 84, 133, 157, 158, 160, 207, 212, 220, 239, 275
  Cornelius, 284
  George, 148
  Isaac, 227, 253, 264, 265
  Jacob, 214
  James, 22, 53, 57, 58, 59, 61, 62, 78, 79, 81, 82, 85, 91, 93, 94, 97, 101, 104, 108, 111, 113, 115, 122, 126, 128, 129, 131, 132, 133, 136, 139, 142, 143, 144, 147, 149, 153, 155, 166, 170, 176, 178, 180, 182, 183, 185, 188, 195, 199, 201, 206, 208, 213, 217, 219, 221, 230, 240, 251, 252, 255, 268, 270, 272, 280, 281, 284, 285
  Jesse, 23
  John, 230, 235, 262
  Judge, 236
  Paul, 193
  Samuel, 204
  William, 103
Martinus
  Cornelius, 203, 209, 213, 215, 217, 239, 245, 247, 284
Mason
  Isaac, 21
  John, 170
Masters
  George, 148, 241
  John, 150, 159
  Samuel, 216
Masterson
  John, 22
  Thomas, 27
Mattock
  Frederick, 234
Mauer. *See also* Moor, Moore, Mourer
  Andrew, 188
  Michael, 224
Mauk (Maugh)
  Peter, 214, 215
Maulay. *See* McAulay
May
  Daniel, 43, 204
  George, 121, 209, 213, 216, 217
  John, 90, 212, 219, 233, 243, 244, 246, 260
  John A., 223
  John Andrew, 106, 129, 136, 137, 153, 162, 198, 207
  Mary, 281, 285
  Michael, 162, 206, 233, 281
Mc___
  David, 196
  Matthew, 268
  Samuel, 58
  Thomas, 196
Mc___aine
  Jno, 274
Mc___eary
  Jane, 158
Mc___ll
  William, 179

McAllister
  Matthew (Mathew), 32, 41, 43, 48
McAshlan. *See* McCashlan
McAulay (McAuley, McAullay,
  Maulay). *See also* McCauley
  ___, 118
  Cornelius (Cor.), 41, 43, 47, 49, 52,
    58, 59, 65, 68, 79, 80, 82, 94,
    101, 102, 114, 115, 129, 143,
    152, 191, 192, 196, 197
McC___
  Thomas, 119, 125
McCain. *See also* Mackane,
  Mackerel
  Jacob, 239, 268
McCall. *See also* McCauley
  Rebecca, 161
  William, 24, 27, 31, 37, 43, 66, 179
McCanan (McCannan, McCannon)
  James, 207, 210
  Sarah, 207, 210
McCanna
  Felix, 192
McCartney
  John, 255, 279
  Joseph, 206
McCarty (McCardie)
  Daniel, 97, 203, 227, 228, 232, 235
McCashlan (McAshlan,
  McCahshlan, McCahslan,
  McCashlan, McCashland,
  McCashlin, McCaslin). *See also*
  McCausland
  ___, 243
  James, 8, 30, 224, 225
  John, 194, 195
  Margaret, 42
  Robert, 203, 205, 206
  Samuel (Sam., Sam[l]), 29, 30, 31,
    33, 35, 36, 41, 42, 43, 45, 46,
    49, 50, 53, 61, 96, 98, 102, 103,
    118, 129, 140, 141, 145, 146,
    147, 151, 158, 174, 176, 178,
    181, 182, 185, 187, 192, 193,
    194, 195, 196, 197, 198, 203,
    205, 206, 225, 230, 232, 237,
    249
  Samuel, Jr., 63
  Samuel, Sr., 66

McCaughen. *See also* McGaghan
  Patrick, 21
McCauley (McCaulay, McCally).
  See also McAulay, McCall
  Cornelius, 176
  William (W[m]), 220, 232, 233
McCausland (McCauslin). *See also*
  McCashlan
  James, 21
  Samuel (Sam[l]), 145, 146, 253, 254
McClane
  Jacob, 269
McClay (McClea). *See also*
  McLean
  James, 25
  Moses, 23
McClean. *See* McLean
McClellan (McLellan)
  Benjamin, 24, 29
  John, 18, 20, 22, 27, 34, 176, 177
McClemens (McClimans,
  McLemans)
  John, 123, 206, 230, 231
  William, 143
McClure
  John, 56
McComb (McCombe, McCoomb)
  Allen, 121, 123, 139, 187
  William (W[m]), 12, 19, 28, 52, 54,
    103
McCon___
  Daniel, 177
McConnell (McConnale,
  McConnel)
  ___, 32, 118
  Alexander, 120, 121, 129, 183
  Andrew, 202, 220
  Daniel, 27, 28, 31, 41, 56, 57, 58,
    59, 61, 62, 94, 98, 133, 176,
    183, 196, 197, 212, 272
  Robert (Rob[t]), 202, 220, 237
  Thomas, 270
  William, 9, 10, 12, 13, 15, 17, 18,
    20, 22, 24, 77
  Zachariah, 27
McConner (McConnor)
  James, 206
  Rob[t], 69
  Sarah, 205

McCormick
  Alexander, 57, 104, 180
McCoy
  James, 164
  John, 258, 274
McCrory (McCrorey)
  David, 29, 40
McCullough (McCoullogh, McCoullough, McCullock, McCulloch, McCullouch)
  Drusilla, 193, 195
  George, 10, 11, 126, 152
  William (W^m), 239, 277
McCune
  James, 176
McCurdy
  Daniel, 62, 113, 176, 177
McDaniel
  Duncan, 121
  James, 111, 178
  Ja^s, 178
  Joseph, 175, 179
  W^m, 214
McDermott (McDermit, McDermitt, McDermod, McDermot)
  William (W^m), 173, 175, 218, 220, 239, 247, 284
McDonald (McDonals, McDonnald)
  Agnis, 241
  D____, 196
  Duncan, 121, 123, 176
  James, 105, 106, 108, 113, 114, 116, 117, 181
  John, 38, 147, 251, 266, 281
  Joseph, 126, 128, 131, 189, 244, 246, 250, 252, 255, 258, 259, 260, 286
  William (W^m), 8, 205, 249
McDowell
  George, 14
McElvaine. *See* McIlwain
McFadden
  John, 272
McFarran (McFarren, McFerran, McFerren, McPharen, McPharran)
  ____, 242
  Andrew, 130, 131, 135

Duncan, 155
Joseph, 131, 135, 143, 159, 175, 222, 260, 285
Matthew, 268, 269
McGaffin
  Benjamin, 188
McGaghan (McGaghon, McGahagan). *See also* McCaughen
  John, 161, 170
  Patrick, 10, 11
McGaughey (McGaughy)
  ____, 118, 196
  Arthur, 83, 84, 109, 110, 121, 122, 124, 128, 147, 149, 174, 237, 238
  John, 109, 110, 137, 161, 166, 170, 174, 175, 228, 237, 238, 239, 247, 249
  Thomas (Thos), 83, 84, 121, 128, 156, 161, 174, 175, 196, 197, 214, 266
McGeary
  William, 24
McGibbon
  Thomas, 137
McGill
  Charles, 28
  Will. (W^m), 189, 190
McGinnis
  Matthew, 217
McGregor (McGreger, McGriger, McGrygar)
  Alexander (Alex^r), 164, 250, 274, 283
McGuffay
  Benjamin, 113
McGugan
  Daniel, 16
McGuiness
  James, 105
McGuire
  Bartholomus, 116
  Daniel, 105
  Nicholas, 247, 264, 272, 284
  Patrick, 104, 108
McHenry
  Charles, 121
McIlwain (McElvaine)
  William (W^m), 122, 274

McIntire (McIntyre)
   John, 258, 281, 285
   Robert, 143
   William, 186
McIntosh
   Daniel, 151
   Donald, 151
McKay. *See also* Mackey
   Eneas, 23
   James, 14
McKee
   Alexander, 77
   James, 188
   Samuel, 14
McKeehan
   David, 206
McKenna
   James, 215
McKenney (McKenny). *See* McKinney
McKenzie (McKinze, McKinzey)
   Gabriel, 53
   James, 23
   Robert, 103
   William, 21, 177
McKerney
   Michael, 121
McKewn
   John, 189, 190
McKinley (McKinly)
   James, 24
   John, 18, 30, 31, 34, 36, 184
McKinney (McKenney, McKenny, McKiney, McKinny)
   Ann, 266, 268
   James, 42, 48, 149, 158, 190, 191, 242, 243, 252, 263, 272, 278, 279, 281, 283
   John, 18, 28, 42, 48, 189, 193
   Joseph, 42, 110
   Nancy, 268
   Robert, 42
   Sarah, 187
McKnight (McNight)
   Empson, 254
McLean (McClean, McKlean). *See also* McClay
   Alexander, 23
   Archibald, 79
   Azariah, 202, 220
   David, 123, 165, 170
   Jacob, 174, 175, 196, 202, 205, 212, 214, 222, 229, 238, 277
   John, 217, 219
   William (W^m), 130, 131, 134, 138, 141
McLellan. *See* McClellan
McLevey (McLevy)
   William, 57, 180
McMean
   ___, 24
McMichael
   Daniel, 58, 59, 94, 145, 146
McMoultrie
   William, 120
McMu___
   James, 149
McMullen (McMullan, McMullin)
   James, 33, 37, 42, 123
   Neal, 229
   Neil, 164, 242
   Patrick, 42
   Peter, 106, 107, 108, 122, 129
McMuthrie
   William, 122
McNaman
   John, 111
McNamar
   Morris, 116
McNaullay
   John, 54
McNeal (McNeill)
   Hector, 116, 192, 207, 208, 232
McNutt
   Jno, 268
   John, 266, 268
McQuity
   Samuel, 94
McSurley
   Elizabeth, 225
McVicker (McVicar, McVickar)
   David, 220, 223, 226, 240, 247, 252, 282
   Duncan, 150, 159, 173, 175, 220, 225, 237, 247, 271, 284
   Jacob, 283
   Joseph, 251, 282
McWhinney
   Bryce, 123

INDEX 329

Mea__
 Christopher, 139
Mealy
 Jacob, 281
Mean
 Elizabeth, 265
 John, 265
 Rachel, 265
Means
 Christopher, 204
 Daniel, 126
 Robert, 221, 222, 256
Mease. *See also* Meese
 Christian, 219
 Christopher, 166, 199, 205
Meds___. *See also* Metzger
 Marcus, 241
Meek (Meeks)
 Jacob, 23
 Joshua, 15, 69
 Lewis, 190
Meese. *See also* Mease
 Christian, 237, 272
 John, 258, 279
Megill
 Charles, 51
Melan (Mellan, Mellen, Millan)
 Felix, 64, 65, 128, 138, 161, 166, 172, 199
Mellott (Mellot, Melott, Mallot, Mallott, Malott). *See also* Mallen
 John, 12, 13, 18, 19, 36, 45, 46, 47, 48, 57, 59, 61, 62, 78, 93, 94, 97, 101, 202, 207, 208, 225
 Obadiah, 167, 244, 246, 275
Meloch
 John, 139
Menzies
 Thomas, 32, 34, 36, 65, 66, 97, 100, 101
Merkley
 Jacob, 119
Mes__ly
 Frederick, 81
Meser
 John, 285
Metzger (Medscur, Metsgar, Metzgar). *See also* Meds__
 Marcus, 174, 175, 238, 283

Meyers
 George, 18
Mier. *See also* Myer, Myers
 Christopher, 264
Mifflin
 Thomas, 85, 87
Milburn
 John, 159
Miles
 George (Ge°), 177, 178
Miley
 Abraham, 17, 20, 23, 26, 33, 34, 42, 45, 54, 59, 60, 61, 62, 63, 64, 65, 66, 67, 81, 82, 92, 95, 96, 97, 98, 99, 100, 101, 104, 114, 115, 116, 125, 127, 128, 131, 139, 147, 176, 177, 180, 182, 185, 202, 211
 Abraham, Jr., 180, 202, 209, 215, 216, 218, 219
 Henry, 218
Milikin. *See* Milligan
Mill
 John, 203
Mill___
 John, 244
Millan. *See* Melan
Millbourn
 John, 246
Miller
 Abraham, 29, 235
 Adam, 85, 189, 192, 224, 285
 Alexander, 42, 43, 44, 247
 Christian, 17, 209, 244, 246
 Christopher, 8, 12, 13, 20, 59, 63, 64, 98, 99, 210
 D. Jr., 267
 Dan., Jr., 267
 Daniel (Dan.), 267, 279
 Felix, 58, 59, 94, 100, 119, 124, 159
 Gasper, 58
 Henry, 209, 213, 216, 217, 239, 266, 268, 277, 278
 Jacob, 40, 64, 99, 178, 179, 191, 283
 John, 9, 12, 18, 23, 28, 31, 34, 41, 54, 69, 119, 140, 165, 166, 167, 175, 203, 234, 235, 237, 238, 239, 277, 284
 John, Jr., 236

Mary, 171, 285
Michael, 245, 274
Nicholas, 235
Oliver, 11, 12, 13, 14, 69
Peter, 153, 167, 199
Robert, 241
Samuel, 15, 17
Thomas, 58
Yost, 204
Millick
John, 125
Milligan (Milliken, Millikin)
George, 8, 9, 12, 25, 32, 57, 58, 94, 98, 110, 114, 185
James, 25, 29, 34, 36, 43, 47, 49
Milton
John, 168
Mincy
Danl, 262
John, 262
Mir__
Martin, 257
Miren
Martin, 284
Mires
James, 25
Mitchell (Metchel)
___, 257
Hugh, 105, 106, 111
James, 48, 158, 167, 190, 191, 194, 199, 202, 204, 209, 213, 215, 217
John, 36, 39, 45, 50, 51, 108, 125, 126, 127, 128, 172, 194, 199, 216, 244, 246
Thomas, 189, 190, 194
Moans
Francis, 265
Mock
Peter, 276
Money
Bernard (Barnard), 12, 110, 111, 113
Jacob, 12, 18, 19
Montgomery
James, 23
Samuel, 127, 128
Thomas, 111
William, 38
Moon
Zebulon, 124

Mooney
Jacob, 97, 113
Moor. *See also* Mauer, Moore, Mour
Daniel, 218, 283
Moore. *See also* Mauer, Moor, Mour
___, 253
Charles, 175
Davis, 133
Francis, 79
James Francis, 51
John, 8, 9, 11, 14, 15, 23, 24, 52, 56, 61, 64, 67, 69, 86, 95, 99, 104, 124, 130, 133, 134, 138, 167, 188, 190, 242, 250, 255, 270, 272, 275, 276
Levi, 104
Robert (Robt), 9, 17, 23, 26, 28, 29, 31, 34, 53, 59, 96, 113, 180, 182, 188, 223, 231, 239, 249, 252, 253, 261, 269, 277, 281, 283, 285
Samuel (Saml), 9, 10, 20, 28, 37, 52, 54, 56, 57, 58, 59, 69, 94, 97, 103, 115
Thomas, 93, 230, 242
Zebuland, 21
Moorehead (Morehead)
Samuel, 25
Thomas (Thos), 106, 107, 108, 111
Moran
Edward, 180
Morgan
John, 62, 67, 68, 98, 125, 181, 188
Thomas, 130, 134, 138
Morgart (Morgert, Morgret)
Peter, 164, 167, 174, 175, 197, 207, 220, 229, 237, 238, 244, 246, 271, 275
Morningstar
Daniel, 44, 46, 47, 49, 50
Jacob, 44, 46, 47, 49, 50, 180
Morr___
Francis, 224
Morris
William, 125
Morrison (Morison)
Abraham, 223
Duncan, 136, 221
James, 241

INDEX

Joseph, 9, 10, 18, 19, 20, 28, 54, 56, 59, 62, 64, 100, 113, 126, 139, 159, 163, 176, 177, 178, 179, 180, 182, 188, 198
Joseph S., 92
M^r, 269
Morrow
  William, 106
Mortimer (Mortimor, Mortimore)
  James, 120, 133, 150, 168, 178, 250, 277
  James, Jr., 232
  Ja^s, 275
  John, 18, 19, 23, 32, 36, 38, 40, 41, 108, 168, 176, 179, 232, 247
  John, Jr., 214
Morton
  James, 104
  John, 275
  Reynolds, 275
  Richard, 14, 48
  Robert, 16, 19
  William (W^m), 48, 122, 124, 140, 150, 209, 213, 216, 217, 254
Moses
  Jacob, 240, 274
Moss
  Christina, 168
  Ephraim, 263
  Euphemia, 168
  Joseph, 168
  Loruhanna, 192
  Mary, 168
  N___, 168
  Samuel, 142, 168, 169, 192, 263
Mountain
  Joseph, 181, 182, 190
  Martha, 106
Mour (Mourer, Mowrer). *See also* Mauer, Moor, Moore
  Michael, 204, 216, 227, 235
Moyer
  Christley, 272
Mull
  Henry, 245, 247
Mullen
  Patrick, 43
Murphy (Murphey)
  Alexander, 126, 128, 131
  Hannah, 181
  Henderson, 41, 59, 63, 98

Michael, 215, 248, 279
Thomas, 36
William, 102
Murray (Murry)
  John, 251, 281
  Joseph, 220, 263
  Mary, 208, 211
Musser
  John, 209
Myer. *See also* Mier, Myers
  Abm., 266
  Christina, 266
  John, 266
  John Baltzer, 13, 18
Myers. *See also* Mier, Myer
  Cornelius, 203
  Frederic, 14
  Henry, 205
  Jacob, 136, 274
  James, 15
  Mary, 11
  Matthias, 177, 193

—N—

Na___
  Leonard, 123
Nagle (Nagel). *See also* Knagey, Naugle
  Anthony, 83, 114, 115, 116, 118, 124, 147, 170, 173, 175, 176, 182, 192, 196, 197, 229
  Christian, 278
  Christopher, 270, 271
  Frederick (Fredrick), 17, 30, 41, 42, 44, 48
  Jacob, 161, 206, 207, 225, 231, 242, 262
  M^r, 260
Nanzant
  George, 130, 134, 138
Naugle (Nawgel, Nawgle). *See also* Knagey, Nagle
  Anthony, 162, 174, 197, 236, 237, 238, 264, 279, 285
  Frederick, 8
Nave (Neave)
  Jacob, 140, 202
Neal (Neill). *See also* O'Neal
  William, 171, 172, 173

Neff (Niff)
    Henry, 119, 125, 127
    John, 127, 128
Neill. *See* Neal
Neimer (Nemier)
    John, 159
    William, 109, 112, 115, 120
Nelon
    Isaac, 191
Nelson
    Abraham, 108, 119
    Frederick, 106
    James, 183, 243, 283
    William, 113, 125, 127, 128
Nemise
    Susanna, 258
Newcomer
    John, 258
Nicholas (Nichols, Nickles)
    John, 15, 16, 18, 20, 22, 24, 219
    William, 242
Nicholson
    William, 167, 193, 194, 195
Nick___. *See also* Nycum
    John, 167
Nicodemus (Nickdemess, Nicodemis)
    Conrad (Conrod), 260, 275, 280, 285
Nicum. *See* Nycum
Nigh
    Jacob, 259
Night. *See also* Knight
    Mary, 120
Nixon
    George, 66, 116, 135, 159, 167, 214, 244, 246
    Rebecca, 163
    William (W^m), 161, 162, 200, 202, 229
Noble
    David, 181, 182, 185
    John, 93, 239, 274, 277
Noffsinger (Noseaker)
    John, 167, 209, 213, 216, 217
Noland
    Pierce, 44, 46, 51
    William, 44, 46, 47, 49, 51
North
    Elizabeth, 163

Norton
    James, 132
    Thomas (Thos), 126, 131, 132, 133, 135, 137, 138, 147, 150, 162, 170, 189, 223, 234, 247, 254, 266, 270, 279, 281, 285
Nycum (Nicum, Nickham, Nickum, Nucham). *See also* Nick___
    John, 155, 169, 170, 204, 241
    William (W^m), 231, 233

—O—

O___
    Geo., 271
Oakes
    John, 283
Oats
    Philip, 171
Oburn
    Joseph, 113
Ody. *See* Eddy
Ogden
    Albert, 164, 165
    Ezekiel (Ezekial), 164, 165
    John, 136
Ogle
    Alexander, 89
    Thomas, 15
Oldfather
    Frederick, 104, 202, 204
Olinger
    Jno, 258
    John, 209, 219
O'Neal. *See also* Neal
    Peter, 226
    Timothy, 183
Orbison
    John, 178
    Robert, 205, 265, 268
Organ
    David, 116, 117, 192
Orlton
    Hugh, 119, 129, 130, 131, 132, 134, 138, 139, 141, 181
Orr
    William, 190
Orrenton
    Hugh, 120

Oster
  George, 266, 268, 270
  Jacob, 213
  Nichol__, 285
  Valentine (Valentin), 268, 269, 274
Oswalt (Oswald)
  Michael, 126, 127, 128, 142, 144, 147, 149
Ott
  Nicholas, 162, 172, 173
  Philip (Phillip), 170, 171, 172, 173, 200
  Wendle (Vendel, Vendle, Wendal), 120, 242, 267, 275, 283
Oury (Oulery, Ullery). *See also* Urie
  Daniel, 52, 149
  John, 262
  Wendal, 20
Overhholtz
  Abraham, 123
Oyler
  Joseph, 216
  Laurence, 250
  Peter, 223, 250, 279

—P—

P__
  Adam, 254
  Benj^m, 145
  J__, 221
P_tt
  Henry, 261
Pa____
  Godfrey, 206
Pa__on
  Thomas, 14
Pact
  Michael, 173
Pain
  Margary, 21
Painter
  Adam, 275
  Godfrey, 124
  Tobias, 259
Palm
  Adam, 166
Palmer
  Daniel, 184

Panter
  Godfrey, 143
Parish
  Joseph, 130, 134, 138
Park (Parks)
  John, 239, 276, 277, 280
  Samuel, 207
Parker
  Saml, 207
  William (Willm), 8, 9, 10, 14, 20, 23, 25, 26, 27, 28, 34, 42, 48, 57, 59, 61, 62, 69, 78, 93, 94, 96, 97, 101
Parkison
  John, 118, 182
Paron (Parone, Parran, Parron). *See* Perrin
Parsons
  James, 239, 277
Patterson
  Bob [Negro], 267
  Francis, 18, 32
  J__, 114
  James, 34, 45, 46, 49, 54, 55, 63, 98, 115, 116, 119, 125, 126, 135, 139, 150, 158, 181, 182, 193
  William (Willm, W^m), 83, 86, 120, 125, 136, 144, 147, 149, 155, 158, 164, 166, 189, 190, 191, 210, 277
Patton
  Benj^m, 15
  James, 183
  John, 121
  Matthew, 188
Paul
  Black, 193
Paxton
  Elizabeth, 142
  James, 45
  John, 136, 137, 139, 153, 161, 176, 185, 197, 251, 270, 278, 281, 282
  John, Jr., 137
  John, Sr., 230
  Samuel, 12, 46, 57, 58, 94, 161, 170, 180
  Thomas, 18, 22, 24, 28, 46, 52, 53, 61, 78, 104, 111, 120, 123, 141, 183, 185, 188

William (W^m), 93, 94, 159, 172,
    199, 202, 204, 211, 221, 222,
    233, 236, 257, 258, 259, 260
Pears
    Isaac, 25
Pearson (Peirson, Person, Persons,
    Pierson)
    Hermon, 206
    Joshua, 90, 228, 242, 243, 250, 268,
       269, 271, 274
Peck
    Benjamin (Benjmin), 165
    George, 17
    John, 122, 123, 221, 233
    Peter, 207
Peek
    Henry, 261
Pencil/Pensyl. *See* Wensyl
Pendergrast (Pendergrass)
    Garrett (Garret), 11, 14, 15, 21, 69
Pendleton
    Philip, 8
Penn
    John, 71, 75
Pennel (Pannel, Pennal)
    Thomas, 112, 116, 179, 181
Penrod. *See also* Pernod
    David, 158, 171, 172, 175, 218, 238
    Elizer, 172
    Emanuel (Emmanuel), 172, 199
    Israel, 126
    John, 55, 56, 103, 113, 119, 125,
       146, 149, 168, 180, 181
    John, Jr., 140
    Solomon, 122
Pentecost (Penecost, Penetecost)
    Dorsey (Dorset), 15, 16, 26, 27, 77
Peobles
    Alexander, 21
Perdew (Perdu, Purdew, Purdue)
    John, 267
    L___, 128
    Laban, 127
    William, 113
Pernod. *See also* Penrod
    John, 47, 49
Perrin (Perrine, Paron, Parone,
    Parran, Parron, Purron)
    George, 125
    James, 45, 267

John, 17, 46, 67, 68, 125, 202, 264
Joshua, 227
Nicholas, 180, 188
Poll, 264
Perry
    Roger, 260
    Willm, 69
Peter (Peters)
    John, 9, 10, 18, 31, 37, 41, 50, 60,
       63, 96, 99, 176, 177
    John, Doctor (Doct^r), 66, 108, 112,
       117
Peterson
    William, 132
Pettyjohn
    William, 25
Pfeifer. *See also* Fifer
    Martin, 232
Phibs
    Richard, 52
Philip (Philips)
    Evan, 34, 45, 46, 55, 62
    John, 237
    Joshua, 244, 246
    William, 46, 49, 50, 53, 129, 227,
       228
Phillipy
    Frances, 159
Philson. *See* Filson
Picket
    Hethcock (Hethcote), 65, 101
    Humphrey, 265
Pinkerton
    Richard, 112, 116, 141, 221
    Richard, Jr., 221
    William, 235
Pinslay (Pinsley). *See also* Pursley
    John, 41, 47
Piper
    James, 15, 24, 26, 27, 32, 35, 39
    Jo__, 52
    John, 32, 36, 39, 77, 78, 81, 82, 86,
       88, 92, 163, 167, 170, 255, 271,
       272, 280
    John, Col., 96
    William, 163, 170
Pittinger
    Henry, 119
Pittman (Pitman)
    ____, 48

Benjamin, 204, 285
Richard, 122
William (W^m), 61, 66, 97, 110, 124, 138
Plummer
   John, 41
   Samuel, 143
Po___
   Jacob, 263
Po_t
   Michael, 156
Poel
   Michael, 159
Poit
   Michael, 173
Pollack (Pollock)
   James, 11, 14, 15, 20, 25, 26, 27
Pollard
   Jonathan, 236
Pomroy
   John, 14
Poorman
   Jacob, 140, 150, 167, 169, 170, 212
   Jacob Jr., 159, 172, 199, 200
Port
   Michael, 138
Porter
   James, 216
   William, Jr., 122
Potts (Pott)
   Da__, 250
   David, 161, 226, 251, 267, 281
   Jonathan, 144
Powell (Powel, Pawel)
   John, 17
   Joseph, 268, 269, 277
   Mr., 23
   William, 14, 19, 22, 27
Prather (Prether)
   Thomas, 171, 197
Presser
   Catherine, 10
   Henry, 10, 11
Price
   Andrew, 45
   James, 16
   Merryman, 130, 134, 138
   Samuel, 139, 211, 212
   William, 16, 130, 131, 134, 138, 141

Priestly
   Jonathan, 129
Prigmore (Prigmor)
   Jonathan, 121, 122
   Joseph, 113, 180
Proc___
   William, 243
Proctor (Procter)
   John, 21, 24, 34, 279
   William (Willm, W^m), 8, 9, 12, 18, 20, 25, 39, 41, 45, 56, 62, 77, 78, 81, 84, 86, 97, 114, 115, 116, 123, 125, 129, 132, 133, 136, 139, 142, 144, 149, 153, 162, 164, 166, 169, 185, 187, 188, 195, 226
   William (Willm, W^m), Jr., 9, 15, 49
Prosser (Prossor)
   Charles, 130, 134, 138
Province
   John Willm, 69
Puc
   James, 284
Puchy
   Abraham, 150
Purdew (Purdue). *See* Perdew
Pursel
   Benjamin, 119
Pursley. *See also* Pinsley
   Benjamin, 56
   John, 37, 45, 47
Putnam
   John, 207

—Q—

Query (Quainy, Querry)
   Alexander, 28, 52, 53
   Charles, 18, 62
Quick
   David, 250, 272
Quin
   Patrick, 43, 60, 63, 66, 67, 96, 99, 102

—R—

R___
   Frederick, 120
R___d
   Michael, 204

R_gar. *See also* Reighard
  Henry, 147
Ralston
  David, 113, 188
Raman
  Godfrey, 209
Rambo
  Moses, 119, 210, 219
Ramsey (Ramsay)
  John, 23, 26, 37, 39, 40, 104, 113, 119, 125, 180, 189, 190, 191
  Martha, 96
  Robert (Robt), 39, 40, 119, 125, 150, 159, 167, 242, 274, 285
  Robert, Sr., 244, 246
  William (W^m), 134
Randles
  William, 255
Rankin
  Hugh, 30, 31
  John, 87, 111, 260
Rassler. *See* Ressler
Ray. *See also* Rhea, Wray
  Arthur, 268, 270, 271
  Thomas, 139, 166, 272
Read. *See* Reed
Ream (Reem, Reems)
  Adam, 262, 272, 284
  Andrew, 202, 244, 246
Reamer
  George, 248
Reardon
  Margaret, 47
  Thomas, 16
Reasnor (Resner, Resnor, Riasnor)
  Peter, 9, 10, 12, 13
Reddock
  John, 11
Reed (Read, Reid)
  ___, 251
  Ann, 23
  Gideon, 118
  John, 62, 104, 113, 123, 133, 149, 158, 180, 181, 202, 244, 246
  Levi (Levy), 163, 164
  M___, 163
  Mary, 263
  Moses, 12, 13, 14, 17, 18, 28, 46, 51, 80, 103, 108, 114, 133, 176, 185, 188, 195, 253, 254, 255

Reem (Reems). *See* Ream
Reeman
  Gudlip, 244, 246
Reeves
  James, 54
  John, 111
  Thomas, 111
Reid. *See* Reed
Reiff
  George, 104
Reighard (Reachard, Reegart, Reichart, Reicher, Reickart, Reiger, Reighart, Reigher, Reikard, Richert, Rickard, Riegar, Rigar). *See also* R_gar
  Frederick (Frederic, Fred^k), 12, 34, 68, 108, 158, 194, 225, 229, 251, 281, 285
  Henry, 136, 161, 230
  Jacob, 172, 229, 242, 281
Reiland. *See* Ryland
Reiley (Riley, Reily)
  Christopher, 89, 228, 231, 243, 250, 279, 281
  Cornelius, 122
  David, 89
  James, 259
  Martin, 87, 89, 121, 129, 202, 204, 208, 229, 261, 269, 279
  M^r, 280
  Peter, 120, 122
Replogle (Reppleogle, Riprogle)
  Eve, 145
  Jacob, 257, 284
Resner (Resnor). *See* Reasnor
Ressler (Rassler, Resler)
  William, 227, 275
Reyer (Reyers)
  Daniel, 24, 29
Reynard (Rinard, Rynard). *See also* Rinehart
  David, 8, 29, 30
  Henry, 236
  John, 209, 220
Reynolds (Reynold)
  Francis, 48, 105, 108, 236
  George, 104, 119, 125, 188, 195
  John, 14, 105
  William, 264

Rhea (Rhay). *See also* Ray, Wray
  Arthur, 227, 276
  Samuel, 113
  Thomas, 104, 150, 158
Rheam
  Adam, 261
Rhine. *See* Rine
Rhinehart. *See* Rinehart
Rhoades (Rhoad, Rhoade, Rhoads, Rhode, Roads, Rodes)
  __il, 179
  Daniel, 184, 194
  Gabriel, 9, 31, 40, 69, 120, 140, 155, 176, 188, 200
  George, 220, 244, 246, 260
  Henry, 9, 10, 12, 21, 24, 34, 37, 47, 49, 51, 61, 79, 93, 96
  Hen^y, Senr, 69
  Jacob, 9, 10, 124, 125, 127, 128, 140, 155
  John, 34, 69, 108, 119, 158
  Joseph, 46, 49, 50, 53, 119
  Rebecca, 127
  Sarah, 42
Riasnor. *See* Reasnor
Rice
  Aaron, 46, 49, 50, 51, 53
  Andrew, 46
  Frederick (Fred^k), 113, 180, 209, 262
  John, 52
  William, 180
Richard (Richert, Rickard)
  Frederick, 229
  Jacob, 277
Richardson
  Richard, 60
Richey (Richie, Richy). *See* Ritchey
Rickerts
  Chaen, 180
Rickets
  Jeremiah, 104
  Ruleph, 224
Riddle (Riddel)
  James, 157, 219, 222, 226, 240, 243, 245, 249, 252, 255, 276, 279, 282
  John, 159
  Robert, 123

Samuel (Saml), 167, 271
William, 12, 14, 57, 58, 59, 94
Riggle
  John, 123
Right. *See also* Wright
  Elizabeth, 177
Riley. *See* Reiley
Rinard. *See* Reynard
Rine (Rein, Rhine, Rines, Ryne)
  Jacob, 37, 49, 66
  Michael, 218, 248, 258, 262
Rinehart (Rhinehart, Rhinhart, Ronehart, Rynhart). *See also* Reynard
  Daniel, 154
  David, 31, 33, 40, 43, 56
  John, 194, 244, 246, 253
  Philip, 164, 200, 214, 215
Ripley
  Abraham, 284
  Lewis, 241
  Valentine, 124, 216, 250, 258, 267
Rippy
  Elijah, 41, 43
Rise
  George, 175
Ritchey (Ritchie, Ritchy, Richey, Richy)
  Abraham, 9, 10
  Adam, 230, 231
  George, 239, 269, 271, 277
  Gideon (Geddian, Gedeon, Gedion, Giddion, Gigeon, Guideon), 20, 25, 26, 29, 34, 35, 37, 41, 59, 63, 65, 66, 81, 98, 100, 101, 117, 176, 177, 178, 182, 269, 271
  Jacob, 204
  James, 255
  John, 87, 119, 124, 128, 140, 149, 178, 226, 229, 251, 267, 269, 281
  John, Jr., 269
  Michael, 220, 222, 223, 226, 230, 240
  William, 10
Ritter
  Elizabeth, 256
  Henry, 256
  John, 250, 251

Roads. *See* Rhoades
Robb
  Jacob, 252
  Jane, 252
Robenot
  Stephen, 19
Robertson
  William, 15
Robeson
  Thomas, 89
Robinson
  Hugh, 112, 183
  Hugh, Jr., 183
  James, 132, 209
  Jonas, 213, 216, 217
Robison (Robbison)
  Dav^d, 254
  Hugh, 111, 127, 128, 157, 159, 160
  James, 135
  Jonas, 272
  Joshua, 248
Rockwell
  Nathaniel, 130, 134
Roderock. *See* Rothrock
Rodes. *See* Rhoades
Rogers
  Enos, 267
  Philip, 14
Rohrer
  Frederick, 212
Roof (Rufe). *See also* Ruff
  George, 271
  Michael, 205
  Nicholas, 158, 194
  Peter, 248, 278, 279
Root
  David, 154, 155
Rose
  Allen, 8, 9, 12, 14, 17, 18, 19, 24, 28, 46, 139, 214, 215, 272
  Edward, 8, 9, 17, 18, 19, 26, 54, 59, 63, 98, 113, 166, 193, 202, 226, 275
  William, 17, 272
Ross. *See also* Russ
  Andrew, 8
  James, 168
  Joseph, 11, 13
Rothrock (Roderock)
  Frederick (Fred^k), 239, 276

Roudenbush (Rowdebush, Rowebush)
  Henry, 271, 275
  Michael, 272, 275
Rough
  George, 140
Rowler
  Jacob, 104
Rowser
  John, 285
Royal (Royle)
  Thomas, 203, 226
Royce
  Aaron, 56
  Andrew, 55
  John, 51
Royer
  Daniel, 29, 30, 31, 52, 53, 56, 104, 113, 143, 164, 165, 166, 167, 168, 169, 170, 180, 188
  Esther, 168
  Samuel, 167, 168, 169, 170
Ruby (Rubey)
  Charles, 32, 37, 52, 54, 56, 61, 62, 66, 97, 98, 103, 106, 107, 108, 129, 175, 179, 192, 194, 250, 255
  Eleanor, 120
Ruch
  John, 233
Ruff. *See also* Roof
  Matthias, 159
  Michael, 116, 159, 188
  Nicholas, 111, 200
  Peter, 145
Rumick
  George, 182
Rush
  Conrad (Conrod), 158, 163, 207, 216, 227, 237, 238, 239, 248, 251, 253, 261
  Daniel (Danl), 163, 164
  Elizabeth, 190, 191, 194
  Henry, 13, 45, 48, 104, 120, 162, 169, 198
  Henry, Sr., 110
  Jacob, 18, 19, 34, 45, 48, 69, 126, 144, 146, 168, 169, 170, 204
  Jacob, Jr., 28, 110
  Jacob, Sr., 28

John, 30, 31, 33, 35, 103, 130, 178, 220, 230, 236
Margaret, 107
Peter, 119, 146, 164, 202
Thomas, 195
William, 113, 190, 191
Rushin
   John, 131
Russ. *See also* Ross
   Adam, 220
Russell (Russel)
   John, 64, 99
Rutledge (Rutlidge)
   Isaac, 221
   Jesse, 171
Ryan
   D.__, 257
   Derry, 128, 130, 136, 141, 174, 175, 200, 206, 213, 220, 222, 237, 238, 239, 266, 283, 284
   Jane, 239, 266, 277
   John, 43
   Timothy, 32, 34, 37, 41, 43, 49, 51, 52, 53, 56, 60, 63, 66, 68, 96, 98, 102, 103, 108, 128, 130, 135, 187, 195
Ryland (Reiland)
   John, 167, 281
Rynard. *See* Reynard

—S—

S__
   James, 106
   John, 285
   Peter, 155
S__field
   Nathaniel, 167, 176
S__man
   Daniel, 261
S_ade
   Elizabeth, 127
Sa__age
   Mary, 191
Sahlor (Sailor). *See* Saylor
Salts
   Henry, 42
Saltzgiver (Saltzgaver)
   Jacob, 172, 230
Sample
   David, 8

Samuel, 14
Sampson
   John, 24
Sams (Saam, Sam). *See also* Iaam
   Adam, 8, 9, 20, 31, 32, 43
Samuel (Samuels)
   Adam, 52
   Conrad, 31, 33, 40, 52, 190
   Ludwic (Ludwick), 150, 186, 229, 232, 242
   Michael, 232, 242
Sapington
   Joseph, 37
Sapp (Sap)
   Frederick, 140
   John, 214
Sartorius (Satorious, Satorius, Satorus)
   William, 112, 117, 153, 154, 174, 179
Saunders (Sanders)
   Benjamin, 46, 55, 104
Saylor (Sahlor, Sailor, Seylor, Syler)
   __, 197
   __cob, 182
   Catherine, 207
   Jacob, 28, 32, 43, 51, 53, 61, 62, 80, 97, 98, 111, 117, 123, 125, 129, 162, 176, 178, 180, 204, 216, 223, 250, 255, 266
   John, 140, 150, 164, 175, 202
Schell
   Peter, 93
Schitlor
   Henry, 29
Scofil. *See* Scovel
Scott
   David, 32, 52
   John, 85, 88, 247, 259, 272, 280
   Robert, 19, 61, 79, 104
Scovel (Scovell, Scofil, Scovil, Scovill)
   Mary, 153
   William (W^m), 42, 47, 62, 65, 67, 68, 98, 101, 103, 147, 153, 162, 195, 215, 223, 230, 279, 285
Scullknot (Scullnot)
   Joseph, 229, 242

Seel
  John, 235
Seeman
  Peter, 170
Sel__
  Samuel, 239
Selby
  George, 282
  Samuel (Sam¹), 207, 280, 282
Sell (Sells). *See also* Cells, Cills, Sills
  George, 9, 12, 242
  John, 173, 247, 248, 249
  Ludwick (Ludwic, Ludwig), 38, 41, 104, 130
  Michael, 9, 12, 33, 56
  Solomon, 104
Selly
  Samuel, 277
Seltzer
  Lewis, 69
Serjant
  Jonathan, 60, 63, 67, 98
Sewell (Sewel)
  Charles, 254, 279
Sh__
  Henry, 261
Sh___man
  Isaac, 227
Sh__berger
  Jacob, 260
Shack (Shacks). *See* Shock
Shadacer
  Valentine, 8
Shader
  Simon, 168
Shadwick
  Casteel, 62
Shaffer (Shafer)
  Adam, 125
  Henry, 161
  Theophilus, 286
Shaler
  James, 195
Shannon
  Samuel, 11, 13, 25
Shark
  Jacob, 220
Sharpe
  Barkin, 46

Sharrah (Shara, Sharra, Sharran, Sharrow). *See also* Shearer
  Jacob, 113, 119, 130, 131, 134, 138, 141
  John, 134
  Ludwick (Lodwick), 245, 247
Shaver
  George, 181
  Henry, 159, 168, 169, 170, 174, 283
  John, 110, 113, 114, 115, 116, 120, 170, 202, 207
  Mary, 105
  Peter, 81
  Simon, 150, 169, 173, 200
Shaw
  Thomas, 281
Shearer (Sherrar). *See also* Sharrah
  Jacob, 131
  John, 10
  William, 10, 15
Shee
  Richard, 42, 43, 44
Sheets (Sheetz)
  Andrew, 200, 230, 242, 247, 269, 271, 281
  Anthony, 284
  Tilman, 158
Shekley
  Peter, 209
Shelby
  David, 126
  Evan, 29, 104
Shelly
  Evan, 34
Shenafeld (Shenefelt, Shenefield, Shinefeldt, Shinefelt)
  George, 188, 214, 215, 244, 246
Shenywolf (Shonewolf)
  Joseph, 25, 31
Shepherd (Shepard, Sheppard, Shepeard)
  John, 69
  Solomon, 11, 15, 17
  William, 281, 285
Shields
  James, 150, 159, 167, 209, 220
Shillcoat
  Benjamin, 131
  Humphrey, 131
  John, 131

Robison, 131
Shilling
    Jacob, 25
Shingledecker
    George, 61, 96
Shippen
    John, 271
    M^r, 277, 279
Shirley (Shirly)
    Richard (Rich^d), 91, 275
    William, 17, 21, 32, 69, 104, 119, 124, 126
Shneb__
    Jacob, 285
Sho__
    John, 113
Shoaf (Shoef, Shofe). *See also* Shoup
    John, 180, 202, 204
    Sebastian (Shebastian), 58
Shock (Shack, Shacks, Shocks)
    George, 39
    Jacob, 159, 167, 238, 253, 255, 274, 283
Shoemaker
    Adam, 278, 280, 282
    Anthony, 93
    Daniel, 257, 258, 260, 278, 280
    Jacob, 280
Shonewolf. *See* Shenywolf
Shopell
    Philip, 168
Shores
    Thomas, 11
Short
    Peter, 203
    W^m, 222
Shoup (Shoupe, Shope, Shoub). *See also* Shoaf
    Abraham, 281
    Bastian, 55
    George, 64, 100
    Jacob, 58
    Joseph, 149, 158, 260
    Sebastian, 140, 149, 202
Shute
    Philip, 23, 25
Sicles
    Henry, 88

Sides
    Henry, 133, 141, 209, 213, 215, 217, 225, 240, 271
Silley
    Samuel, 267
Sills (Sill). *See also* Cells, Cills, Sells
    Dorothy, 103
    George (Geo.), 102, 180, 186, 192, 205, 228
    John, 200, 232, 235
    Ludwick (Ludwic), 113, 118, 120, 126, 197
    Michael, 104, 113, 120, 123, 124, 157, 180, 185, 188, 225, 230, 281
    Solomon, 119
Silver, 35, 40
    Richard, 91
Simmons
    Cornelius (Cor^s), 185, 193
Simon
    John, 14
Simonton
    William, 111
Simpson
    Hugh, 110, 117, 118, 180, 181, 185, 190
    Margaret, 117, 118
    Thomas, 18
Sinclair
    John, 13
    Samuel, 25
Sinker
    John, 18
Sinnett
    Jacob, 27
Sipes
    Charles, 28, 254
    George, 261
    Henry, 260
Siple
    James, 69
Skelley (Skelly)
    Hugh, 65, 100, 104, 119, 124, 261
    Mary, 261
Skin___
    Reuben, 149
Skinner
    Enoch, 238, 239, 284

John, 139, 175, 238
Joseph, 190
Reuben (Reubin, Ruben), 125, 129, 181
Samuel (Sam¹), 8, 11, 25, 62, 98, 106, 114, 115, 161, 176, 184, 191, 192
William, 132
Sl____
   Andrew, 227
Slaughter
   Henry, 20
Slegart. *See also* Sliger, Stigers
   David, 146
Slei____
   David, 162
Slick
   Jn°, 257
   John, 257, 264
Slicker
   Lawrence, 48
Sliger. *See also* Slegart, Stigers
   David, 223, 226
   John, 264
Sloan
   William, 28, 34, 36, 45, 46, 56
Sloboum
   Andrew, 279
Slouther
   John, 284
Small
   William (Wᵐ), 223, 267, 284
Smart
   William, 55
Smeeker
   Jacob, 241
Smiley (Smily)
   Robert, 21, 38, 68, 160, 172, 173, 209
Smith
   ____, 59
   Adam, 136
   Andrew, 239, 281
   Anthony (Anthʸ), 127, 128, 137, 150, 164, 205, 230, 233, 242, 249, 265, 266, 276
   Benjamin (Benjᵐ, Benjⁿ), 162, 206, 207
   Catherine, 169, 171, 173
   Conrod, 216, 279
   Daniel (Danˡ), 206, 264
   Daniel Lindle, 234
   Devereaux, 69
   Elizabeth, 268
   Emanuel (Emmanuel), 106, 109, 177, 186
   George (Geo.), 87, 97, 123, 161, 242, 253, 262, 265, 266, 279
   Henry, 147, 206, 226, 242, 251, 265, 268, 269, 270, 271, 281
   Jacob, 108, 158, 160, 167, 175, 270, 271
   James, 14, 18, 22, 23, 25, 26, 141, 231, 234, 257, 263, 264, 284
   John, 103, 125, 127, 173, 276
   Matthias, 279
   Mr., 60, 119, 167, 195, 250
   Peter, 9, 10, 18, 19, 36, 40, 47, 53, 97, 106, 107, 108, 110, 120, 149, 150, 155, 156, 159, 160, 162, 166, 169, 170, 186, 244, 246, 269, 271
   Philip, 158, 171, 174
   Rebecca, 175
   Richard, 200, 223
   Robert, 57
   Samuel, 167
   Thomas, 33, 77, 78, 92, 134, 143, 144, 145, 153, 166, 172, 188, 199, 204, 206, 208, 213, 215, 225, 229
   W., 161
   William (Wᵐ), 114, 247, 248, 257
   William, Dr., 57
   Wᵐ, Dʳ Div., 256
   Zachariah, 109
Smithson
   Daniel, 10, 13, 18
Smoker
   Jacob, 124, 139, 150, 244, 246
Smouse
   David, 232
   George, 162
   George Adam, 258
   John, 162
   Mary, 280
Snelbecker
   Elizabeth, 282
Snider
   Christian, 92
   Conrod, 258
   David, 258

Jacob, 253
James, 12
John, 221, 275, 279, 280, 284, 285
Joseph, 221
Snyder
   Adam, 202
   Jacob, 238, 239, 243
   John, 139, 150, 159, 167, 202, 222, 244, 246, 250, 252
   Margaret, 171, 173
Sommerville
   James, 129
Sook. *See also* Zook
   John, 209
Sophia
   Electoress of Hanover, 76
Souders
   John, 153, 154
South
   Francis, 159
Sparks
   Degory, 28, 30
   Joseph, 168, 170, 189, 230
   Joseph, Jr., 167
   Solomon, 159
   William, 23, 25
Spear (Spears)
   Henry, 10, 11, 15, 16, 69
Specher. *See* Spicker
Spencer (Spenser, Sponsor)
   Ann, 193, 195
   James, 30, 31, 33, 35, 62, 104, 113, 117, 176, 181, 219
   John, 121
   Rebecca, 113
   Robert (Rob[t]), 161, 239, 240, 247, 259, 260, 263, 264, 267, 277, 283, 284, 285
   Thomas, 216, 219, 223, 226, 240
Spicker (Spiker, Specher)
   Christian, 34, 36, 45, 46, 55, 56, 124, 139, 150
   John, 140
   Samuel, 140
Spiger
   Joseph, 244, 246
Sprague (Spraig, Spraige, Sprauge, Spreague)
   James, 217, 222, 224, 241, 259, 271, 285

Springer
   David, 253, 256, 257
   Jacob, 147
   Joseph, 220, 245, 254, 256, 257
   Michael, 11
Spurgeon
   Ezekiel (Ezekial), 166
   James, 17
   John, 9, 10, 23, 181
   William, 17, 23
Squires
   George, 106
   Rebecca, 106
St. Clair
   Arthur, 9, 11, 18, 41, 45, 49, 71, 75, 77, 78
   Daniel, 147
   Mr., 26
Stackman. *See also* Stegman, Stickman
   John, 267
Stafford
   Thomas, 119
Stall
   Adam, 234
   Henry, 219
   Michael, 146, 170, 220, 223, 226, 240, 261, 275
Stam
   Adam, 35, 36, 41
Standley
   Elizabeth, 187
Stanley
   John, 67, 102
Statler (Stattler). *See also* Stotler
   Casper, 66, 174, 175
   Gasper, 204
Steckleather
   George, 196
Steel
   Andrew, 25, 31, 32, 40, 48
Steffer
   Peter, 149
Stegman. *See also* Stackman, Stickman
   Henry, 51
Stegner
   Adam, 46
   Henry, 44

Stephens (Stephen). *See also*
Stevens
  Abendnego, 89
  Benjamin, 195, 198, 278
  Giles (Gilles), 65, 66, 101, 115, 183
  Richard, 28
  Thomas, 29
Stephenson (Stevenson)
  Jacob, 239
  John, 15, 26, 27
  Thomas, 51
Stevens (Steven). *See also*
Stephens
  Abednego (Abadnigo, Adidnego, Abedn°), 131, 166, 202, 212, 219, 258, 261, 262, 275, 277
  Benjamin (Benj^m, Benjn), 24, 126, 128, 137, 139, 145, 146, 150, 158, 165, 262, 268, 278, 285
  David, 130, 131, 134, 138
  Davis, 141
  Giles, 35, 39, 131, 134, 136, 138, 141, 178, 180, 183
  Jacob, 240, 268, 269, 284
  James, 109
  John, 141
  Samuel (Saml), 145
  Thomas, 24, 265, 272
  William, 130, 131, 134, 138, 139, 141
Stevenson. *See* Stephenson
Steward
  John, 226
Stewart
  Charles, 25
  David, 129, 133
  James, 115, 242, 243, 269
  John, 203
  Robert, 125
  W^m, 261
Stickman. *See also* Stackman, Stegman
  John, 250
Stiffler (Stifler, Stiffner)
  David, 267
  George, 258
  Jacob, 229, 232
  John, 258
  Peter, 31, 40, 56, 146, 172, 221, 228, 229, 233, 244, 246, 249, 252, 258

Stigers (Stiger, Stigert). *See also*
Slegart, Sliger
  Adam, 162, 202, 209, 219, 250, 268
  Elener, 266
  Jane, 268
  John, 261, 265, 266, 268
Still (Stills)
  Thomas (Th.), 248, 249
Stillwell (Stilwell)
  Elias, 77, 78
  Jane, 268
  Jeremiah, 41, 48
  John, 89, 113, 139
  Obadiah, 12, 13, 32, 33, 46
  Obadiah, Jr., 29
  Sarah, 266
Stine
  Benjamin, 223
Stinson
  John, 69
Stockberger
  Elizabeth, 54
Stocks
  Robert, 47
Stockw__
  William, 103
Stodler. *See* Stotler
Stoker
  Basil, 10, 11
Stoler
  Martin (Marton), 202, 257
Stoner
  Christian, 149
  Christopher, 210
  Philip, 34, 35, 37, 41, 45, 141
Stophel. *See also* Styphel
  C, 252
  Christian, 281, 283, 285
Storey (Story)
  Thomas, 59, 61, 63, 66, 67, 95, 98, 101
Stork
  John, 258
Stotler (Stodler, Stoutlier). *See also*
Statler
  Casper, 122, 169, 171, 197, 237, 238, 239, 277
  Casper, Jr., 284
  Gasper, 239
  Jn°, 262

Stover
    Henry, 214, 253, 255
Stoy (Stoys)
    Daniel, 46, 66, 87, 108, 143, 151, 192, 224, 227, 235, 249
    David, 205
    Edward, 223, 224, 227, 241, 245
    Henry, 78
Straight (Strait, Stright)
    John, 167, 209, 220, 244, 246, 258, 262, 271, 275
Strain
    Joseph, 238
Strawbill
    Philip, 167
Strawn
    Isiah, 149
Struble (Stuble)
    Christian, 245, 247
Stuart
    Charles, 37, 38
    James, 116
Studebaker (Studdybaker, Studdybecker, Studybaker)
    Jacob, 149, 159, 200, 231, 241, 267
Study
    Christian, 146, 150, 158, 209
Stuff
    Michael, 207
Stull
    Adam, 214
Stutzman
    Daniel, 278
Styphel. *See also* Stophel
    William, 69
Sullivan
    Honor, 30
Summerville
    George, 61
Surious
    John, 254
Swager (Swage, Swager)
    Henry, 141, 264
    William, 206, 216, 250
Swales
    Mary, 105
    William Martin, 105
Swan
    Jn°, 267

Swar___
    Frederic, 149
Swartz (Swarts)
    Balsar, 263
    Frederick, 136
    George, 168, 170, 233
Swartzell (Swartzill)
    Matthias, 159, 162
    Sally, 159
    Sarah, 162
Swartzwelder (Swartswilder, Swartzwalder, Swartzwilder, Swarzwilder)
    Danl, 221
    Peter, 124, 140, 147, 150, 151, 159, 200, 211, 212, 213, 214, 216, 217, 221, 222, 253, 255, 285
    Philip, 208
Sweitz
    Peter, 284
Swigart
    George, 117
    John, 117
    Leonard, 116
Swink
    C___, 167
    Casper, 202
Switcher
    George, 234
Switzer
    Peter, 202
Swope (Swop)
    Lawrence, 26
    Peter, 145, 146
Sykes
    Charles, 14

—T—

T___
    John, 167
Taggert (Tagert, Tigert, Tygert)
    Charles, 185, 212, 242, 243, 275, 283
Tantlinger
    Catherine, 152, 157
Tarwater
    Jacob, 108
Tate (Tait)
    Benjamin, 23

John, 82, 122, 123, 124, 126, 131,
    140, 141, 143, 145, 146, 147,
    148, 176, 193, 197, 200, 201
Thomas, 147
Taylor
    ___, 264
    Edward, 131, 132, 135, 136, 142,
        147, 150, 176, 179, 189, 259
    Jacob, 134
    James, 132, 200, 201, 207, 220,
        229, 239, 240, 244, 246, 255,
        272, 277, 281, 283, 284
    Jane, 131, 134, 135, 147, 150
    Matthew, 68, 144, 269
Teagarden
    Abraham, 15, 18
    William, 18, 19
Tedrow (Tidrow)
    George, 168, 235
    Michael, 209, 244, 246
    Michael, Jr., 213, 216, 217
Teeter (Teetor, Teitor, Tieters)
    Abraham (Ab^m), 141, 258, 262
    John, 56, 159
Theobold
    Prior, 16
Thi__mel
    Jacob, 119
Thomas
    Alexander, 224
    Henry, 18, 131
    Patrick (Pat., Pat^r), 266, 268
Thompson (Thomson)
    Caleb, 266
    Edward, 17
    George, 185
    Isaac, 123
    James, 167
    John, 115, 183
    Margaret, 115
    Mary, 205
    Robert, 69
    Samuel (Saml), 22, 24, 35, 37, 39,
        40, 49, 55, 104, 116, 129, 151,
        152, 156, 193
Thorlton. *See also* Thornton
    John, 36, 38, 41
Thornhill
    ___, 265, 267
    Thomas (Thos), 264, 265, 266, 269

Thornton. *See also* Thorlton
    Thos, 69
Ti__
    William, 146
Tidrow. *See* Tedrow
Tissue
    William (Willm), 159, 167
Titus
    Nathaniel, 136
    Peter, 20, 23
Todd (Tod)
    Andrew, 81, 111
    John, 57, 58, 59, 61, 62, 64, 67, 94,
        95, 96, 98, 99, 102, 186, 187
    Samuel, 49, 61, 62, 98
    William (Willm, W^m), 49, 51, 80,
        136, 174, 175, 185, 188, 196,
        197, 200, 229, 238, 239
Tomlinson
    Jno, 218
    John, 218, 221, 222, 225
Tool
    Edward, 151
Toomy
    ___, 243
    Martin, 242, 243, 265
Torrence
    Ellinor, 108
Touchman
    Frederick, 104
Tracy
    Matthew, 260, 261
Travers
    William, 180
Trayer (Tryer)
    Michael, 188, 244, 246
Trench
    James, 103, 115
Trimble
    James, 136, 151
    John, 151
    William (W^m), 151, 152
Troop
    William (Willm), 11, 69
Troutman
    Peter, 269
    W^m, 272
Troxel
    Abraham, 264

INDEX 347

Truax (Trueaxe)
   Benjamin (Benjn), 17, 36, 46, 47,
      97, 104, 120, 274
   Jacob, 14
   Joseph, 250
   Samuel, 97, 220, 227
Tryer. *See* Trayer
Tucker
   Jacob, 10
   William, 186
Turner
   W^m, 118
Tygert. *See* Taggert
Tyshee
   William, 61, 79

—U—

U__
   Jacob, 264
Uirke
   Christopher, 221, 222
Ullerick (Ulbrick, Ullrick)
   John, 220, 223, 226, 240
Ulster
   John, 214
Uncel (Unsel)
   Frederick, 44, 46, 47, 49, 51
Urie (Uries, Ury). *See also* Oury
   Peter, 146
   Robert, 184
   Thomas, 49, 52, 54, 56, 79
   Wendal, 10, 69
Utsler (Utslar, Utzler)
   John, 231, 242, 285
   Martin, 233

—V—

V__
   William, 132
V__ht
   William (W^m), 135
V__man
   Henry, 270
Van Maitire (Vanmater, Vanvaiter, Vanvater)
   Benjamin, 108, 110
   Jacob, 16
Vance
   David, 24
   Robert, 22, 27

Vancleve
   William (Willm, W^m), 264, 268, 269
   William, Jr., 269
Vaughn (Vaughan)
   Gest (Guest), 248, 249
   Jesse, 214
   Lydia, 248, 250
Vertress
   Frederick, 44, 46, 51
Vickery (Vickray, Vickroy, Vicroy)
   Thomas (Thos), 61, 84, 135, 136,
      206, 251, 257, 264, 269, 285
   William (W^m), 239, 241, 277, 279
Vought
   William, 119

—W—

W__field
   Benjamin, 182
W__man
   Adam, 202
Wadsworth (Watsworth)
   Robert, 124, 184
Wafeld
   Garret, 145
Wagerline (Wagerlin, Wegerline)
   Philip, 97, 133, 164, 193
Waggoner
   Christopher, 93
   John, 220
   Philip, 274
Waldeck (Waldecker)
   Ludwick, 165, 170
   Mary, 165, 167, 170
Walen
   Henry, 282
Walker
   David, 189, 190, 191
   James, 269
   John, 12, 26, 57, 58, 94, 104, 113,
      121, 180, 188
   Joseph, 282
Walkinghoff
   Reinhart, 18, 19
Wall
   Charles, 119, 258
Wallace. *See also* Wallis
   ____, 118, 196

Ephraim, 107, 121, 122, 123, 144,
    150, 154, 158, 159, 167, 171,
    175, 179, 198, 220, 238, 271,
    285
James, 108
Samuel, 163, 169
William (W^m), 263, 279
Wallack (Wallick, Wallock)
    John, 281
    Michael, 56, 136
Waller. *See also* Walter
    Conrad, 14
Wallis. *See also* Wallace
    Abraham, 176
    Ephraim, 283
Walt
    John, 55
Walter. *See also* Waller
    Conrad, 25
    John, 55
    Joseph, 207, 281
Waltman (Walman)
    George, 219, 222, 262
    Jacob, 242, 265
Ward
    John, 11, 171, 172, 173
    William (W^m), 81, 85, 129, 135,
        139, 144, 162, 174, 196, 197,
        226, 229, 237, 239, 266, 277,
        283, 284
Warder
    Jeremiah, 256
Ware
    William, 46
Warford (Warfard). *See* Wolford
Warren
    Edward, 140, 141, 151
Warshabaugh (Washabaugh,
    Washbaugh, Washenbaugh)
    Henry, 55, 104, 184
    Jno, 269
Wasson
    Robert, 104
Watson
    Martha, 254
    Moses, 31, 34, 52
    Thomas, 19, 125
    William, 118

Watsworth. *See* Wadsworth
Waugh
    Alexander, 215
Way
    Jacob, 232
    Samuel, 241, 274, 277
Wayman
    John, 62
Wean
    John, 177
Weaverling
    Jacob, 283
    John, 283
    Peter, 222, 250
Webster
    C____, 248
    Jno, 269
    John, 168, 169, 174, 175, 238, 245
    John B., 174
Wegerline. *See* Wagerline
Weigley
    Joseph, 277
Weimer (Weymer, Wimer,
    Wymer)
    Abagail, 237
    Frederick, 25, 56, 103, 113, 159,
        189, 190, 191, 210
    George, 210, 219, 231, 234, 283
    John, 120, 125, 209, 213, 215, 217
    John, Jr., 209
Welch
    Francis, 90, 209, 220, 244, 246, 275
Welfair
    Godfrey, 140
Wells
    Benjamin, 16, 27
    George, 9, 12
    James, 12, 13, 15, 18, 79, 86, 87,
        93, 123, 124, 129, 132, 139,
        142, 149, 153, 161, 164, 170,
        213, 214, 215, 217, 219, 222,
        227, 240, 241
    James, Jr., 22, 24
    John, 197
    Richard (Rich^d), 9, 12, 14, 15, 23,
        25, 26, 29, 69
    Samuel, 15
Wendmiller
    Conrad, 69

Wensyel (Wenzel)
  John, 37, 46, 47, 49
Werford. *See* Wolford
Werner
  Henry, 285
Wertz (Wert, Werth, Werts, Wirt (Wirts, Wirth, Wirtz)
  George, 194, 207
  Henry, 57, 60, 63, 66, 68, 88, 94, 96, 99, 102, 104, 106, 107, 110, 111, 116, 139, 145, 148, 153, 162, 166, 170, 174, 175, 191, 192, 196, 225, 229, 230, 237, 240
  Peter, 158, 174, 175, 196, 237
  Valentine (Valentin), 238, 239, 250, 255, 263, 268, 269, 277, 283, 284
Weston
  Thomas, 22, 27, 187, 188, 191
  William (W^m), 187, 188, 191
Wheeler (Whealler)
  Delilah, 44
  Samuel, 130, 131, 134, 138, 139, 141
Whetstone. *See also* Whitestone
  Abraham, 153, 241
  Christian, 119, 148
  Henry, 137, 222, 268
  Matthias, 126
  Michael, 31, 46, 58
Whip
  John, 251, 265, 281
Whipkey
  James, 103
  John, 103
White
  Andrew, 28, 30, 31, 55
  Aquilla (Aquila), 37, 38, 43, 44, 46, 47, 49, 50
  Christian, 173
  John, 167, 172, 199, 270
Whitehall
  Elizabeth, 245, 247
Whitesides
  Peter, 58, 60, 63, 67, 68, 94, 95, 98, 102
Whitestone (Whitstone). *See also* Whetstone
  Abraham, 172

Henry, 164, 178, 223, 226, 240, 241, 264, 278
Michael, 46
Wi___
  Henry, 124
Wiand (Wians). *See also* Wyant
  Jacob, 164, 238
Wickerham
  Adam, 16
Wike
  Christian, 264
Wilds (Wild)
  George (Geo.), 150, 159, 174, 175, 202, 223, 238, 239, 244, 246, 253, 258, 262, 266, 277, 283, 284
  William (W^m), 167, 199, 260
Wiley
  Jacob, 193
Wilker
  Paul, 202
Wilkey
  Eleanor, 262
  Francis, 262
Wilkins
  John, 51, 52
  Thomas, 32
  William, 202, 204
William
  ___, 254
  Benjamin, 126
  Ephrain, 256
  Mary, 278
  William, 123
Williams
  ___, 216
  Anna, 205, 207, 210
  Benjamin (Benjn), 128, 158, 166, 202, 209, 211, 214, 219, 220, 244, 245, 246, 254
  Charles, 261
  Eli, 240
  Elizabeth, 123
  Enoch, 55, 97, 104, 219
  Ephraim, 123
  Evan, 16
  George, 225, 233
  Henry, 119, 125, 127, 128, 139, 205, 226, 264, 272, 281
  Isaac, 10, 11

James, 44, 55, 57, 123, 141, 202,
204, 244, 246, 261, 274
Jn°, 261
John, 10, 120, 127, 128, 203, 225,
244, 246, 249, 252, 255, 261,
278
Joseph, 91
Margaret, 189
Mary, 268, 271, 278
Mordecai (Moredecai), 202, 204,
208
Samuel, 252
Thomas, 57, 58, 59, 94
William, 126, 127, 128, 159, 161
Williamson
John, 226
William, 240
Wills
James, 83, 97, 157
John, 97
Wilson (Willson)
___, 118
Charles, 189, 190, 191
George, 8, 9, 12, 15, 77, 120, 125,
194
Hill, 189, 190, 191, 229, 242
James, 8, 49, 165, 167, 170, 178,
183, 210, 267, 268, 271
John, 19, 32, 69, 97, 125
Joseph, 12, 13
Mich., 268
Mr., 22
Nicholas, 56, 211, 215, 229, 241,
242, 274
Thomas (Thos), 80, 83, 104, 132,
209
William (W^m), 62, 66, 97, 116, 123,
126, 150, 153, 160, 161, 169,
179, 207, 215, 219, 229, 230,
236, 237, 241, 242, 255, 267,
268, 269, 271, 274
Wilt
James, 158
John, 59, 62, 63, 66, 80, 81, 95, 97,
98, 113, 115, 176, 192
Wimer. *See* Weimer
Windmiller. *See* Wendmiller
Winger (Wingerd)
Jacob, 97, 209

Wink
Jacob, 84, 86, 153, 155, 158, 166,
188, 198, 209, 221, 260
Uriah, 264
Winkfield
Benjamin, 111
Winton
Thomas, 185, 187
William, 62, 66, 97, 185, 186
Wirick (Wyrick)
Valentine (Valentin), 184, 189, 190,
191, 202, 204, 211, 214, 215,
244, 246, 272, 283
Wirt (Wirts, Wirth, Wirtz). *See*
Wertz
Wise
Henry, 129
William, 45
Wisegarver (Wiscarver,
Wisegarber)
George, 12, 14, 31, 40, 56, 61, 62,
66, 68, 97, 108, 112, 114, 115,
120, 140, 143, 155, 189, 190,
191, 193, 205, 264
Jn°, 264
John, 232, 242
Witherspoon
Jas., 42
Wolf (Wolfe)
George (Geo.), 41, 53, 270
John, 200, 250
Leonard, 198
Phebe, 107, 285
Philip, 147, 193, 207, 232, 285
Reinhart (Reynart, Reynhart,
Rheynhart, Rhinehart, Rinehart,
Rynhart), 12, 43, 54, 113, 146,
179, 189, 191, 212, 272
Renard (Reynard, Reynarde,
Reynhard, Rinard), 8, 9, 21, 25,
190
Richard, 162
Wolford (Walford, Warford,
Warfard, Werford)
___, 251
Andrew, 171, 173
Elazer, 221
Frederick, 171, 173
Henry, 42, 46, 48
James, 181, 182
Jane, 268

John, 214, 215
Joseph, 133, 149, 209, 213, 215, 217, 247, 265
Joshua, 17
Mary, 262
Wood (Woods)
Alexander, 285
G., 285
George, 9, 12, 15, 18, 20, 25, 26, 33, 39, 41, 44, 45, 54, 66, 77, 78, 82, 84, 85, 87, 101, 161, 162, 164, 166, 170, 173, 179, 189, 199, 201, 204, 206, 208, 213, 215, 217, 219, 222, 225, 226, 240, 243, 245, 249, 252, 255, 285
George, Jr., 88
Henry, 204, 206, 225
Hetty Barclay, 285
Jane, 30
Jean, 8
John, 14, 147, 173, 195, 204
Samuel, 170
Thomas (Thos), 20, 32, 36, 47, 48, 58, 67, 68, 94, 102, 103, 113, 137, 180, 188, 254
William, 82, 124
Woodford
Mary, 262
Woodside (Woodsides)
Jonathan, 227, 235
Work
Andrew, 205, 243, 250, 251
Workman
William, 125
Worley
Achor, 45, 46, 55
Ezekiel (Ezekial), 26, 29, 34, 159, 160, 162, 177
Worrel
Isaac, 104
Wray. *See also* Ray, Rhea
Arthur, 204, 216
Thomas, 216
Wright. *See also* Right
Adam, 57, 58, 59, 94

David, 202, 240
Joshua, 220, 239, 272, 276, 277, 280
Nathan, 93, 215, 219, 264
Robert, 203
Samuel, 167, 202
William (W^m), 21, 267
Wyant. *See also* Wiand
Jacob, 247, 283
Wymer. *See* Weimer

—Y—

Yerryhouse
John, 18, 19
Yoder
David, 244, 246
Jacob, 119
Young
Adam, 10, 28, 114, 115, 116, 186, 202, 231, 244, 246
Andrew, 202, 220
John, 60, 61, 63, 64, 66, 67, 95, 98, 99, 101, 105, 106, 111, 112, 113, 116, 117, 176
Ludwick, 205
Michael, 271, 274
Nathan, 12
William, 279

—Z—

Z____
Elizabeth, 185
Mary, 185
Zant
John, 277
Zigler
Jacob, 284
John, 202, 209, 220, 223, 226, 240
Zimmerman (Zimerman)
Matthias, 222, 224, 285
Michael, 167, 209, 224, 227, 235
Sarah, 224
Zook. *See also* Sook
Yost, 167

www.ingramcontent.com/pod-product-compliance
Lightning Source LLC
Chambersburg PA
CBHW070227230426
43664CB00014B/2234